UNANSWERED
QUESTIONS

What the September Eleventh Families Asked and the 9/11 Commission Ignored

RAY McGINNIS

Praise for Ray McGinnis'
Unanswered Questions: What the September Eleventh
Families Asked and the 9/11 Commission Ignored

"Gaze at an intriguing portrait. Contemplate the unanswered questions of September Eleventh, the victims' family members posing them with rising urgency, and the US government stonewalling their search for answers. What is going on here? Ray McGinnis is an artist. He allows the members of the Family Steering Committee for the 9/11 Independent Commission to speak for themselves. They do so eloquently, raising a host of queries challenging the public story. The government's devastating non-response provokes still deeper questions. Can a government investigate itself for a crime that has given it the rationale for a permanent war on others? What has been going on here for almost two decades?

Take a deep breath. Read and absorb this brilliant narrative, seen through the courage of those who turned suffering into demands for every scrap of evidence to be found in the sanitized crime scene and the more-accessible public domain. See the post-September-Eleventh world we live in through their enlightening questions."

~ James W. Douglass, author of *JFK and the Unspeakable*

"For the many people who choose to look away from the events of 9/11, perhaps for fear of what they might find, this book presents a powerful challenge. Ray McGinnis elegantly weaves together the heartbreaking experiences of those who lost loved ones on 9/11 with the dismally inaccurate and incomplete official investigations that have plagued our understanding of what happened that day. Truth, however, 'is the daughter of time, not of authority,' and *Unanswered Questions* will undoubtedly serve as a powerful contribution to both the establishment of an accurate historical record and political accountability."

~ Piers Robinson, Academic, Member of the "Working Group on Propaganda and the 9/11 Global 'War on Terror,'" lead author of *Pockets of Resistance: British News Media, War and Theory in the 2003 Invasion of Iraq*

"Just like the assassinations of President John F. Kennedy, Robert Kennedy, Martin Luther King, and the attack on the USS Liberty, the destruction of the World Trade Center ... is another cover-up. Congratulations to Ray McGinnis for asking the hard, unanswered questions. We cannot let the government get away with its implausible and unbelievable explanation."

~ Paul Craig Roberts, former Assistant Secretary of the Treasury for Economic Policy in the Reagan White House and Associate Editor of the *Wall Street Journal;* author of *The Neoconservative Threat to World Order*

"Those who lost loved ones on September 11 deserve our support. For if we really care about peace and justice, we must take a closer look at the tragic events of 11 September 2001, which led to countless wars and mass surveillance. As Ray McGinnis explores in his book, these families' unanswered questions are a good place to begin."

~ Daniele Ganser, author of *NATO's Secret Armies: Operation Gladio and Terrorism in Western Europe*, historian and co-founder of the Swiss Institute for Peace and Energy Research

"McGinnis offers a uniquely humane perspective on 9/11, presenting superb new research on the official but unanswered questions of families who lost loved ones."

~ David Ray Griffin, author of *The Christian Gospel for Americans*

"*Unanswered Questions* is an important book on the relentless efforts of victim family members to get truth and justice for their loved ones. Many important questions remain unanswered. This is unacceptable 20 years on. The cover up continues today. I will never stop seeking justice for my brother. Some of the evidence highlighted in this book will form part of my legal action in the UK to reopen my brother's Inquest."

~ Matt Campbell, 9/11 family member whose brother Geoff died while attending a conference on the 106th floor of the North Tower.

"The dissident families of 9/11 victims have, through their intelligence, courage, and persistence, opened a portal to a kind of parallel political universe. It is a universe full of deceit and corruption, but it is real and we had better become familiar with it. We owe a debt of gratitude to Ray McGinnis for telling the story of these brave people and keeping the portal open."

~ Graeme MacQueen, author of *The 2001 Anthrax Deception*

"As the events of September 11, 2001 continue to haunt the world, Ray McGinnis explores key questions the families of September Eleventh victims formulated while seeking a fact-driven investigation about this stunning introduction to the 21st century. It was these families who forced an investigation upon the strangely reluctant Bush-Cheney administration. In a comfortable, engaging style, he responds to many of their questions by immersing the reader in a fascinating background of largely unreported big-picture facts. Startling realities come to light. I believe that this deeply researched and carefully referenced book offers a unique and invaluable insight into 9/11. It is an original and illuminating read for novices and experts alike."

~ Elizabeth Woodworth, coauthor of *9/11 Unmasked*

"Finally, the 9/11 book I have been waiting for. Unsensational, fact-based, and devastating to the official story. It's easier to show what didn't happen than what did, which is why the families' questions were so important and should still be asked of the still-living witnesses and possible conspirators. Bravo to Ray for organizing this complicated story so cogently."

~ **Lisa Pease, author of** *A Lie Too Big To Fail: The Real History of the Assassination of Robert F. Kennedy*

"In this compelling book, Ray McGinnis reviews the heartfelt questions of 9/11 victims' family members in light of the failed government investigations and the work of steadfast independent investigators. The result is an invaluable framework for understanding the crimes of September 11 and the crucial need for truth."

~ **Kevin Ryan, September Eleventh whistleblower formerly with Underwriters Laboratories, author of** *Another Nineteen: Investigating Legitimate 9 /11 Suspects,* **and editor of the** *Journal for 9/11 Studies.*

"It is impossible to overemphasize the importance of this book. The massacres of September 11, 2001, the foundational event of recent times, claimed thousands of victims whose relatives still cry out for truth and justice. Ray McGinnis brilliantly documents those murders and the decades of agonizing efforts of the victims' families to seek justice and truth from the American government. Their search had been met with lies and dissimulation piled upon dissimulation to protect the guilty. Reading *Unanswered Questions* will roil you to the depths of your soul. McGinnis powerfully unfurls layer upon layer of fact, the government fiction, in a timeline that brings us to the twentieth anniversary of these atrocities. While reading it, one cannot help but think of the innocent victims of that terrible day and their suffering families; and the innocent throughout the world who have been murdered by the US government in the name of September 11. The "War on Terror" has been waged by a government that refuses to tell the truth about who the terrorists were on September 11, 2001."

~ Ed Curtin, author of *Seeking Truth in a Country of Lies*, was born and raised in the Bronx. His son-in-law, who worked on the 100th floor of the South Tower, escaped the death that claimed the lives of 176 of his co-workers. And Curtin knew well his father's friend, Timothy O'Sullivan, who worked on the 39th floor of the North Tower and died on September 11.

"The events of September 11th, 2001, were a tragedy the world could never have imagined…. However, since the event, nothing has brought that day back to the forefront of my mind like reading this book. Aptly titled 'UNANSWERED QUESTIONS: What the September Eleventh Families Asked and the 9/11 Commission Ignored,' it has been written over time, and thoroughly researched. What makes it such compelling and heartrending reading, is that throughout are the testimonies of the survivors, and those who lost friends and family. We discover the people behind the statistics…. The tragic catalogue of inconsistencies in the timeline of events reported in the media, though often buried beneath the headlines, are exposed…. Only 9% of [the 9/11 families] questions were satisfactorily addressed… This is simply not good enough! This book is not only a voice for those who have been left behind, but also an accurately researched account for those who believe the cover-up will be exposed, and the truth revealed, one day."

~ The Columbia Review of Books & Film

UNANSWERED
QUESTIONS

RAY McGINNIS

Vancouver, BC, Canada: NorthernStar Publications, [2021] | Includes bibliographical references and index.

LCSH: September 11 Terrorist Attacks, 2001. | Terrorism victims' families – United States. | National Commission on Terrorist Attacks upon the United States. 9/11 Commission Report. | Terrorism-United States-Prevention. | Intelligence service - United States - Evaluation. | National Security - United States. | War on Terrorism, 2001-2009. | BISAC: HISTORY/United States/21st Century. | POLITICAL SCIENCE/Civic & Citizenship.

ISBNs: 978-1-77374-081-2 (Hardcover); 978-1-77374-080-5 (Paperback); 978-1-77374-082-9 (eBook)

Classification: LCC:HV6432.7 .M34 2021 | DDC:973.931-dc23

Cover Design & Interior formatting by Edge of Water Designs, edgeofwater.com

Permissions
The author has made every effort to trace the ownership of all copyrighted materials in this work and believes that all necessary permissions have been secured. If any errors or omissions have inadvertently been made, proper corrections will gladly be made in the future. Thanks are due to the following author and publisher for permission to use the material included: Excerpts from *Wake-Up Call: The Political Education of a 9/11 Widow* by Kristen Breitweiser, copyright © 2006. Reprinted by permission of Grand Central Publishing, an imprint of Hachette Book Group, Inc.

Dedicated to:

The Family Steering Committee for the 9/11 Independent Commission, as well as all others who lost colleagues and loved ones on September Eleventh and asked questions to make their nation safe.

"Here is the American bargain. Each of us, as individual citizens, take a portion of our liberties and our lives and pass them to those we elect or appoint as our guardians. And their task is to hold our liberties and our lives in their hands, secure. That is an appropriate bargain. But on September 11th that bargain was not kept. Our government, all governments, somehow failed in their duty that day. We need to know why."

~ 9/11 Commissioner Jim Thompson

"[The Commission] is to examine and report on the facts and causes relating to the September 11th terrorist attacks" and "make a full and complete accounting of the circumstances surrounding the attacks."

~ President George W. Bush, November 15, 2002

"How did the FBI know exactly where to go only a 'few hours' after the attacks? How would the FBI know to visit a store in Bangor, Maine, only *hours* after the attacks? ... How did they know which neighborhoods, which flight schools and which restaurants to investigate so soon in the case? ... How are complete biographies of the terrorists, and their accomplices, created in such short time? Did our intelligence agencies already have open files on these men? Were they already investigating them? Could the attacks of September 11th been prevented?"

~ Kristen Breitweiser, wife of Ronald Breitweiser, 39
Testimony before the House Permanent Select Committee
on Intelligence and the Senate Select Committee
on Intelligence, September 18, 2002

"For eighteen months our families have been denied the truth that a thorough investigation would reveal. As a family member I am frustrated, to have suffered the loss of a son and yet be required to spend time away from my family and fight for the establishment of a commission that should have been in place on the day of (that) tragic event."

~ Mary Fetchet, mother of Bradley James Fetchet, 24,
National Commission on Terrorist Attacks
Upon the United States, March 31, 2003

"The ability of the 9/11 families to come together, educate themselves about national security and national politics, and raise their voices to demand action, is in the best tradition of grassroots democracy in this country."

~ Thomas Kean and Lee Hamilton, 9/11 Commission Co Chairmen
Without Precedent: The Inside Story of the 911 Commission

TABLE OF CONTENTS

PART FOUR: ACCEPTANCE AND DISSENT

FOREWORD

September Eleventh, for many people, is history. But not so for those who lost loved ones on that fateful day. Each September Eleventh, 9/11 family members stand at podiums and read the names of loved ones who died in the attacks. Yet few of us are aware that 9/11 families pressed for an independent investigation into the attacks against the objections of the Bush White House. Few are aware 9/11 families presented hundreds of questions to the 9/11 Commission to aid the investigation.

Like many people recovering from tragedy, they want closure. That closure would require at least a credible account of what happened. Sadly, their questions have largely not been answered. With all its resources for research and investigation, the American government designated $3 million, and eventually spent only $14 million, to, as President Bush stated, "uncover every detail and learn every lesson of September the Eleventh." In comparison, over $80 million was spent in the 1990s investigating Bill and Hillary Clinton regarding the death of deputy White House counsel Vince Foster, the Whitewater scandal, and the Bill Clinton-Monica Lewinsky sex scandal. Principally, the 9/11 Commission blamed the attacks on "a failure of imagination." Either the government does not know much about what happened, or it declines to tell.

Some people will object to this characterization, saying that the government has provided an account: *The 9/11 Commission Report*. Granted. But it contains so many inconsistencies and is often so vague that those with serious questions remain frustrated and upset. Indeed, what they are told only raises new questions. Too often, 9/11 families are told that the information they seek is classified, even when it is hard to believe that there are good reasons for withholding it.

Ray McGinnis has written a book that takes the concerns of those whose loved ones died in that awful atrocity with utmost seriousness.

He does what he can, starting with some of the questions the 9/11 families asked the 9/11 Commission to investigate, and searches for answers. Since the 9/11 families are not the only people who are curious about these matters, the answers he offers in this book are of much broader interest.

Obviously, there are many questions that he cannot answer, but what is surprising is how much reliable information he has found. The government and the press have not done a good job of keeping the mourners informed—or the general public. Simply to learn what can be known may help toward at least a partial closure.

For others, the primary focus of concern is less a matter of closure and more to prevent a repeat. No one can question that our vaunted security system failed utterly to protect us on that infamous day. Surprisingly, none of those who were actors in this debacle have been punished, or even reprimanded. They have kept their jobs, and even been promoted. Why is this? Does it mean that human beings had no responsibility for the failure? Does the fault lie entirely in the system?

In that case, all the more, we citizens need to be assured that the system has been radically improved. All of us want this assurance. But when we inquire, we are told that nothing is to be gained by blaming people.

Citizen inquiry into the government's account is characterized as speculation, even as our government instructs us: "If you see something, say something." Or we are confronted with silence, sometimes justified as the protection of state secrets.

Perhaps the many branches of government involved in this failure have engaged in a thorough self-examination and have adjusted their practices and policies to ensure that they will not fail again. Perhaps the failure of interdepartmental communications has also been fully examined. But if so, we need more than casual assurance that we have no need to worry. We received that verbal assurance before the 9/11 event.

If they would tell us where the system broke down, we would be assured that they knew what to fix. Surely, they could tell us a bit about this without risking the nation's security. Vague assurances of the kind we have received—basically just asking us to trust them—provide no closure for those who most deeply care.

The live proceedings of the Watergate conspiracy and the Iran-Contra Affair were broadcast daily. In contrast, the 9/11 Commission proceedings only achieved mainstream coverage with the appearances of Richard A. Clarke and Condoleezza Rice. Otherwise, the proceedings of the 9/11 Commission were mostly a footnote buried beneath the headlines.

After the 9/11 Commission concluded, the Chairman, Thomas Kean, and Vice Chairman, Lee Hamilton, said it was "set up to fail." The *Los Angeles Times* called Kean and Hamilton's book, *Without Precedent: The Inside Story of the 9/11 Commission*, "A devastating account of how the Bush administration blocked the 9/11 Commission at virtually every step."

McGinnis' book is inherently critical of our government. He agrees that the needs of those whose questions he is writing about have not been taken seriously. He tells the story of their repeated frustrations and disappointments.

Speaking simply for myself, I say that people who go to great lengths to keep others ignorant appear to have something to hide. I feel certain that those who have experienced refusal of real information for so long must sometimes share this suspicion.

But McGinnis notes that the questioners are a varied group. There is no consensus among them. He leaves the question of why things have happened as they have for readers to decide for themselves. He just tells us what happened.

May that information bring some bit of closure to those who need it! In any case, all who read this book will be reliably and richly informed. And as a bonus they will find it quite wonderfully readable.

John B. Cobb Jr.

John B. Cobb Jr. is an American theologian, philosopher, and environmentalist. He is author of more than fifty books. After the release of *The 9/11 Commission Report*, Cobb was a signatory to an October 2004 petition by one hundred prominent Americans across the political spectrum—and over fifty 9/11 family members—asking for a deeper investigation into the attacks on September Eleventh.

INTRODUCTION

*"I was always hopeful that we would get a report
that would answer my questions."*
~ Mindy Kleinberg, wife of Alan Kleinberg, 39

On September 11, 2001, the media reported that four planes were hijacked in American air space. The first of these, American Airlines Flight 11, flew into the North Tower of the World Trade Center at 8:46 a.m. Eastern Standard Time (EST). Seventeen minutes later, United Airlines Flight 175 crashed into the South Tower. The third, American Airlines Flight 77, flew into the west side of the Pentagon at 9:37 a.m. Finally, United Airlines Flight 93 crashed shortly after 10:00 a.m. in rural Pennsylvania after passengers and crew attempted to retake the plane.

After 56 minutes of fire concentrated around the crash site, the South Tower suddenly collapsed within ten seconds at 9:59 a.m., killing those still inside the building—including emergency personnel and first responders. Black smoke billowed from the North Tower for a total of 102 minutes before it, too, suffered a complete structural failure at 10:28 a.m. Firefighters were astonished. The Twin Towers were the fifth- and sixth-tallest buildings in the world at the time of their destruction.

The other buildings in the World Trade Center were damaged in the collapse of the Towers. One of them, World Trade Center Building 7, suffered a sudden collapse at 5:20 that evening. A massive pile left at Ground Zero included 200,000 tons of steel, debris from offices, and the victims' remains. In all, nearly 3,000 lives were lost that day.

As early as 9:30 a.m. EST, before all the planes had reached their targets, there were reports that Osama bin Laden was responsible for the attacks. Other commentators that day suggested Saddam Hussein, in Iraq, was responsible, while still others mentioned Iran.

Everyone who was old enough to go to kindergarten remembers where they were on September Eleventh. These attacks have profoundly shaped the world we live in. We've come to understand ourselves as living in a post-9/11 world.

Those most directly affected by the events of that day were the families of the September Eleventh victims. This includes first responders whose coworkers died when the towers fell.

In the aftermath, the families of the September Eleventh victims began to emerge from their shock, even as the grief of that day was seared into their beings. They started to meet, offer support, cry, and speak about their losses. They began to deal with the grisly details of identifying their loved ones' remains. Some family members just wanted to try to put their shattered lives back together and heal. Some became depressed and took medication. Some wanted to ask their government questions.

Asking questions after a murder is a natural human instinct. Whenever someone's life is taken violently, most of society understands that a basic social contract has been violated. This understanding is reflected in the Biblical commandment, "Thou Shalt Not Kill."

This understanding is also reflected in the fictional stories we create and share. Agatha Christie's sixty-six crime novels have resulted in over two billion sales. The genius of her crime novels lies in her accessible plots:[1] a murder is committed; a number of persons are identified as suspects who are possibly responsible for the murder(s); the suspects conceal secrets that must be revealed in order for the case to be solved; the detective pursues the case by asking questions, exploring possible scenarios and devising a strategy to discover how the crime was committed by following where the evidence leads.

In Sir Arthur Conan Doyle's *Sherlock Holmes* detective stories, Holmes uses his intuition to follow hunches. The detective seeks to discover what clues and evidence the perpetrators of the crime left behind.

But in the case of 9/11, why ask questions? Wasn't it obvious what happened?

Kristen Breitweiser, author of *Wake-Up Call: The Political Education of a 9/11 Widow*, lost her husband Ron in the 9/11 attacks. He died in the South Tower. She stated, "In watching our loved ones die on television over and over again, we knew what our pain was: It was understandable, explainable, and definable. And we knew why we felt our pain: Our husbands had been brutally murdered."[2]

At first, the US government promised answers. Secretary of State Colin Powell assured the public he'd produce a white paper with conclusive evidence proving that Osama bin Laden was responsible for the attacks. He told MSNBC News, "we are hard at work bringing all the information together, intelligence information, law enforcement information. And I think in the near future we will be able to put out a paper, a document that will describe quite clearly the evidence that we have linking him to this attack."[3]

But that was soon contradicted. The White House Press Secretary Ari Fleischer told reporters "I think there was just a misinterpretation of the exact words the secretary used ... I'm not aware of anybody who said white paper, and the secretary didn't say anything about a white paper yesterday."[4] Less than a month later, on October 8, Seymour Hersh of *The New Yorker* reported that when senior CIA and US intelligence officials were asked about the evidence of bin Laden's guilt they conceded, "one day we'll know, but at the moment we don't know."[5]

As reporters questioned the credibility of the allegation that Osama bin Laden was responsible for the attacks on September Eleventh, Press Secretary Ari Fleischer told the media that the American people needed to "trust us" and "watch what they say, watch what they do."[6] There was no need for the government to produce evidence; surely, their assertions after the attacks were enough. Every patriotic American knew this. Why would America start a war in Afghanistan if they weren't certain they knew who was responsible?

Yet, Kristen Breitweiser discovered "the facts that lay behind our husbands' murders were different. The facts were not so understandable, definable, or explainable. We didn't know why our nation had been so vulnerable on the morning of the attacks. Why jets were not scrambled on time to intercept the four hijacked airliners. Why evacuation protocols in the Twin Towers were not followed." She wondered how hijackers could board flights with Mace and box cutters, both prohibited weapons. Why weren't terrorists thwarted when they had been under surveillance?[7]

The families of the September Eleventh victims drew up their own list of questions that they wanted their government to answer. They established an organization called the "Family Steering Committee for the Independent 9/11 Commission" (also referred to in this book as "Family Steering Committee," and "FSC"). Together, they began a campaign to press for an investigation into what happened on September Eleventh. They wanted America to learn from its failure to keep the country defended.

The founding members of the Family Steering Committee (FSC) included Kristen Breitweiser, Patty Casazza, Mindy Kleinberg, and Lorie Van Auken. All four women were from New Jersey and lost their husbands in the collapse of the World Trade Center Towers, earning them the title of "The Jersey Girls" or "The Jersey Widows" in the press. The other original members of the FSC included:

- Carol Ashley, mother of 25-year-old Janice Ashley, who died in the North Tower
- Beverly Eckert, wife of Sean Rooney, who died in the South Tower
- Mary Fetchet, mother of 24-year-old Bradley Fetchet, who died in the South Tower
- Monica Gabrielle, wife of Richard Gabrielle, who died in the South Tower
- Bill Harvey, husband of Sara Manley Harvey, who died in the North Tower

- Carie Lemack, daughter of Judy Larocque, who died on American Airlines Flight 11 when it crashed into the North Tower
- Sally Regenhard, mother of 28-year-old Christian Michael Otto Regenhard, a probationary firefighter who died in the rescue efforts at the World Trade Center
- Robin Wiener, sister of Jeffery Wiener, who died in the North Tower

In their search for answers, the members of the FSC researched published articles related to the events of September Eleventh. They printed articles and put them into binders. Reading various news stories, they noticed inconsistencies with the timeline of events reported in the media.

For instance, spokespersons for the Federal Aviation Administration (FAA) stated that the first call to send out fighter jets to intercept the hijacked planes (a process in the military that is known as "scrambling") was at 8:34 a.m. Yet, the North American Aerospace Defense Command (NORAD) reported that the decision to scramble took place at least six minutes later. However, American Airlines told the 9/11 Commission the airline didn't initiate a request to scramble fighter jets until after 8:45 a.m.

All three agencies should have had a documented time for the order. So why the discrepancy? FSC members noted it was standard protocol for jets to take off to intercept hijacked planes within eight minutes of notification. If the FAA's notification to scramble at 8:34 a.m. was accurate, the FSC argued that the hijacked planes should have been intercepted before they crashed into the World Trade Center.

Having a coherent timeline for what happened on the morning of 9/11 was one of many challenges in the investigation of what happened, and an obstacle to learning lessons from the event. The Family Steering Committee wanted to learn the facts, not theories or government spin.

According to their website, "In the fall of 2001 … FSC members began the first of many trips to Washington DC to demand that Congress create legislation for an independent investigation into the September 11th terrorist attacks."[8] They lobbied politicians, and faxed and phoned members of the House of Representatives, United States Senate, and the White House. In time, the Family Steering Committee secured the backing of Senators and Congressional Representatives.

Finally, they achieved results. On November 27, 2002, President George W. Bush signed a bill creating the *National Commission on Terrorist Attacks Upon the United States*, commonly referred to as the 9/11 Commission. Bush said he wanted the 9/11 Commission to "make a full and complete accounting of the circumstances surrounding the attacks."

The 9/11 Commission consisted of ten members, plus staff. The members were:

- Thomas Kean, Chairman
- Lee Hamilton, Vice Chairman
- Richard Ben-Veniste
- Max Cleland (resigned in 2003)
- Fred Fielding
- Jamie Gorelick
- Slade Gorton
- Bob Kerrey (replacing Cleland in 2003)
- John Lehman
- Tim Roemer
- James Thompson

The Commission staff were overseen by Executive Director Philip Zelikow, who was chosen by the Chairman and Vice Chairman.

The Family Steering Committee presented to these Commission members questions that they wanted explored. The questions were received by lawmakers and commissioners as credible, relevant, and timely.

Prior to the first hearings, many family members learned that dereliction of duty was a punishable offense.[9] On September Eleventh, routine military response to intercepting hijacked planes failed on four occasions. The most well-defended building in the country, the Pentagon, was not defended. Were there personnel who vacated their post or were incapable? Were there personnel whose actions or omissions while on duty rose to the level of criminally negligent behavior?

The Family Steering Committee were not the only ones with questions. Stephen Push represented the organization "Families of September 11." His wife, Lisa Raines, died on American Airlines Flight 77 when it hit the Pentagon. He told the commissioners "9/11 was foreseeable. And it could have been prevented. … I'm not advocating conspiracy theories. I don't believe that anyone in the government had specific knowledge of what would happen on 9/11." However, Push contended, "I think this commission should point fingers. I'm not suggesting that you find scapegoats, but there were people, people in responsible positions who failed us … We ask these questions for all Americans. For all the people who may be the next victims of terrorism. For future generations. … good luck in your search for the truth." [10]

Like Stephen Push, most family members who lost loved ones on September Eleventh did not rush to judgment. But they did recall that when the Challenger Space Shuttle crashed, killing seven crew members, a report was issued within four months. But after September Eleventh, the government stonewalled and only agreed to authorize an investigation after fourteen months.

Family Steering Committee members were in daily communication by phone and email during the 20-month life of the 9/11 Commission. Two commission staff were designated to liaise with FSC members. During its investigation, and in the fight to have the *Report*'s recommendations implemented by lawmakers, the Family Steering Committee issued forty-nine formal statements to the 9/11 Commission. Most Family Steering Committee members also personally testified before the 9/11 Commission.

Instead of being alienated from politics, the 9/11 families engaged their political system. Their concerns were championed by lawmakers on Capitol Hill. They sought to ask the toughest questions and hold their government to account. Most of all, they wanted to make America safe again.

When the 9/11 Commission released their final report in July 2004, many family members who had lost loved ones kept an open mind. Family Steering Committee member Mindy Kleinberg, whose husband Alan died in the North Tower, stated, "I was always hopeful that we would get a report that answered my questions." [11]

However, after *The 9/11 Commission Report* was released, the Family Steering Committee found 70% of their questions remained unanswered. Only 9% of their questions were satisfactorily addressed. A final 21% of their questions were given incomplete answers.

Many family members felt the investigation into the attacks was not conducted in a manner that properly connected the dots. Lorie Van Auken stated that it only raised more questions. She told radio show host Peter B. Collins: "We always said if there are conspiracy theories out there then it is the government's fault because they did not ever really explain, or show, or want us to know what happened."[12]

Given what the media was reporting in the fall of 2001, the families wondered why those in charge weren't worried about the nation remaining vulnerable to more terrorist attacks. The questions the 9/11 families asked are the starting point for any responsible questioning of what happened that day.

Yet, the mainstream media has given scant exposure to the families' questions. Over the years, when 9/11 families' questions are restated by members of the general public, they are ridiculed by the press and receive *ad hominem* attacks.

Consequently, there is no agreed-upon standard of language to use when seeking to hold those in positions of authority accountable. Historian Timothy Snyder has raised concerns about the obstacles to agreeing on basic facts when discussing government accountability.

He writes, "to abandon facts is to abandon freedom. If nothing is true, then no one can criticize power, because there is no basis upon which to do so. If nothing is true, then all is spectacle." [13]

America began as a nation of pilgrims and pioneers. They were fearful, as reflected in the Declaration of Independence, that King George III of England had a secret "design to reduce them under absolute Despotism," and plotted "the establishment of an absolute Tyranny over these States."[14] The United States was founded in reaction to the Founders' certainty that those elected to public office were capable of plots and conspiracies.

Consequently, the United States Constitution's Article 2 Section 4 states, "The President, Vice President and all civil Officers of the United States, shall be removed from Office on Impeachment for, and Conviction of Treason, Bribery, or other high Crimes and Misdemeanors." [15] The Founders warned against the blanket dismissal of charges of conspiracy and for citizens to stay alert.

Suspicion of government complicity can range from the ludicrous to the justifiable; however, suspicion of government conspiracy must be supported by evidence. In a time of crisis, it's natural to want to trust statements made by a nation's leaders.

Yet, statements by government officials are not to be regarded as infallible and in need of no further probing. When President Bush told Americans there were weapons of mass destruction in Iraq, most accepted the claim.[16] When President Clinton told the nation, "I did not have sexual relations with that woman, Miss Lewinsky," many wanted to believe him.[17] When President Nixon told the nation he was speaking to them with absolute "candor" that he knew nothing about the Watergate break-in, many wanted to trust him.[18] But when glaring contradictions occur, it's important to take notice. Just because something is the story of record, doesn't mean that it is true. Or that it's false.

The Warren Commission was launched seven days after President John F. Kennedy was assassinated; as Deputy Attorney General Nicholas

Katzenbach advised, "The public must be satisfied that Oswald was the assassin; that he did not have confederates who are still at large." [19] *The Warren Report* was issued ten months after the assassination, in which it was determined Oswald was the lone gunman.[20] In 1976, JFK's murder was reinvestigated, and it was concluded that there was a "probable conspiracy." [21] President Gerald Ford later recalled that he and others at the Warren Commission "were very, very careful when we wrote our final report not to say flatly that Lee Harvey Oswald acted alone and was not part of a conspiracy."[22]

The attack on Pearl Harbor was investigated numerous times.[23] In 1975, the Senate investigated abuses by the CIA.[24] After the Iran-Contra Affair, a dozen officials were either indicted or convicted.[25] Watergate, the Savings and Loan Scandal, the Challenger Space Shuttle, and the Bill Clinton-Monica Lewinsky affair were each investigated promptly.

In her testimony before the 9/11 Commission on March 31, 2003, Mary Fetchet said, "As a family member I am frustrated, to have suffered the loss of a son and yet be required to spend time away from my family and fight for the establishment of a commission that should have been in place on the day of (this) tragic event. ... It is now 18 months later."[26]

Senators John McCain and Joseph Lieberman introduced a bill before the US Senate on December 20, 2001, to investigate what happened on the day of the attacks. McCain told fellow senators, "as we did after Pearl Harbor and the Kennedy assassination, we need a blue-ribbon team of distinguished Americans from all walks of life to thoroughly investigate all evidence surrounding the attacks, including how prepared we were and how well we responded to this unprecedented assault."[27]

Senator Lieberman said, "Like many of my constituents, I too want to know how September 11 happened, why it happened, and what corrective measures can be taken to prevent it from ever occurring again. The American people deserve answers to these very legitimate questions about how the terrorists succeeded in achieving their brutal objectives, and in so doing, forever changing the way in which we Americans lead our lives. The overriding purpose of the inquiry must be a learning exercise, to understand what happened without preconceptions about its ultimate finding." [28] In late November 2002, President George W. Bush finally signed legislation to establish the 9/11 Commission.

Since the 9/11 Commission issued its *Commission Report*, many 9/11 families have championed its recommendations. This includes participation in the board of the National 9/11 Memorial & Museum, which subscribes to its conclusions. Other 9/11 families have expressed dissatisfaction with the investigation.

Lorie Van Auken, speaking to a conference in Toronto on the tenth anniversary of the attacks, said "The old questions still linger and new ones have arisen. A real investigation into 9/11 has never been done. This is incredible, considering the direction we have taken as a country."

Van Auken pointed out that the 9/11 story of record is the basis for American foreign policy. Wars in Afghanistan and Iraq were launched. The PATRIOT Act and the War on Terror have changed American society. She emphasized that "the proper place for the 9/11 proceedings would be a courtroom with subpoena power, rules for swearing in witnesses, and established protocols for handling questioning, cross examination and evidence. And ultimately, one would hope, real accountability for the actions that led to the deaths of so many."[29]

It is not unreasonable for the families of 9/11 victims to want answers. It is not unreasonable for the general public to want answers. And the first steps in getting those answers are to examine the facts we have and ask questions from an open mindset. However, these simple steps can appear monumental if we cannot engage in an informed discussion. That is what this book seeks to achieve: inviting readers to examine their assumptions about the story of record by reflecting on the experience of the Family Steering Committee's quest for a complete accounting of what took place.

In the intervening years, there have been critiques and allegations from commentators, authors, and dissenting groups regarding the government's official story of what happened on the day of the attacks. However, this book confines itself to questions the Family Steering Committee raised with the 9/11 Commission.

The first section of this book chronicles the September Eleventh families' journey from grief to advocacy, including the information and news stories they were exposed to as they prepared questions for the 9/11 Commission to investigate. The second section explores some of the FSC's formal statements to the 9/11 Commission. The third section covers a sample of the questions the FSC never received answers to. A final section of chapters chronicles what has unfolded since the *Report* was published, including the common stances of acceptance and dissent that various families have adopted since.

PART ONE: FROM GRIEF TO ADVOCACY

~1~

Calamity

"Now it was literally a living hell! The feeling of death hung in the air."
~ Janette MacKinlay, resident, Apartment 4C, 110 Liberty Street,
New York

On the cusp of war in Afghanistan, news stories featured people who lost their lives on September Eleventh. The *Staten Island Advance* published a story about a firefighter who lost his life. Their headline read, "Arthur Barry, 35, firefighter, traveled through North America."

Barry was described as someone who loved his freedom and expressed it by going on road trips. In 2000, Barry had taken a 10,000-mile motorcycle trip from Manhattan to Fairbanks, Alaska. He was a member of the Fire Department of New York (FDNY) in Lower Manhattan.

Though Barry "was on vacation that day," he happened to have taken "the Staten Island Ferry into the city just to drop off a heavy-duty machine at his firehouse near the South Street Seaport." Barry arrived "after the company had responded to the attack" on the North Tower. Arthur Barry "found a friend, Firefighter Eric Olsen, and the two of them walked to the scene of the disaster." The article numbered Arthur Barry as officially remaining "among the missing." The last time he was seen alive he was entering the North Tower.[30]

Another firefighter, who was off-duty on the morning of September Eleventh, was Paul Keating. The headline confirming his death at the World Trade Center read, "Paul Keating, 38, Firefighter, Was Known for His Jokes."

Keating had joined the FDNY in 1995. His father said, "He was really in love with the job. His conversation was all about it." The only hesitation Keating had was the funerals; earlier in 2001, four of his firefighter comrades had died battling fires.

On the morning of September Eleventh, Paul Keating was startled out of his sleep when he heard the first plane crash into the North Tower. He told his sister on the phone that "he could see debris and glass flying around." In his apartment, "the windows are blown out and the rooms are full of dust." Keating's apartment was just steps away from the World Trade Center. Speaking to his sister, Keating said, "I'm going to the World Trade Center to help my brothers." And that was the last she heard from him.[31]

A friend of both Paul Keating and Arthur Barry was Janette MacKinlay. She was one of the many displaced in Lower Manhattan who had to put their lives back together. Those who lived close to the World Trade Center were alive—but they had lived through hell.

Janette MacKinlay lived at 110 Liberty Street, one hundred feet from Four World Trade Center (WTC4). She had moved to Manhattan from Oakland, California, in 1997. She was in the World Trade Center complex every single day visiting the "little city" with its coffee shops, retail stores, cafes, banks, and "the little old lady selling roses and batteries for 'one daaaalar'." [32]

An artist, Janette often visited the Lower Manhattan Cultural Arts Commission at WTC6, and organized arts and culture events at the Palm Court at the World Financial Center by the Hudson River. She was looking forward to attending a dance performance with friends at the WTC Plaza the night of September Eleventh.

Janette says of that morning, "I remember I was in the kitchen. I had flowers in my hand and the building [South Tower] started coming down. Our windows blew in. The debris ... cloud burst into our window at fifty miles per hour."

She and her partner, Jim Leece, retreated to the lobby of their building and saw that the "killer cloud" had blocked the sun: it was virtually night outside. In addition to being pitch-black, the debris cloud advanced down Cedar Street at a frightening speed, "hurling concrete dust and flying steel beams."

Janette and Jim went back upstairs to get towels to cover their faces so they could breathe. She recalls, "I wondered how long it would take to die from inhaling that smoke and dust." [33] She remembers walking down Cedar Street, where each step produced a cloud of dust. Everyone looked like a snowman because they were covered in the dust. They encountered some police officers, who told them to go inside the TGI Fridays on Broadway in the Financial District, because "we were told the second tower was expected to come down and to avoid shattering glass we would have to go into the basement."

A while after the dust had settled from the North Tower's collapse, Janette and Jim returned to their building at 110 Liberty Street. They stared at the World Trade Center. Janette recalls, "Now it was literally a living hell! The feeling of death hung in the air." [34]

Janette and Jim's Liberty Street fourth floor apartment was uninhabitable. They were displaced for the foreseeable future. At first, Janette and Jim stayed with their friend, Ira, at his studio at 29th Street and 11th Avenue. They went to Brooklyn's Red Cross Disaster Relief Center and appreciated the first-rate meals provided. Janette was amazed at the flower arrangements at the buffet tables. "A typical buffet breakfast included an assortment of sweet rolls, muffins, bagels, cereal, oatmeal, fresh fruit salad, scrambled eggs, bacon, sausage, pancakes, and waffles. Lunch and dinner were just as lavish." The tables for displaced persons whose homes were impacted by the World Trade Center debris cloud "had tablecloths, a fresh floral arrangement, and a box of Kleenex."

The Red Cross put Janette and Jim in the Empire Hotel. But Jim's reaction to the debris cloud was worsening. On October 2, Jim left for Raleigh, North Carolina, for medical care. Janette returned to Oakland, California, on October 16, 2001.[35]

First responders were also deeply affected by the attacks. Christopher Gioia, a Chief at the Franklin Square & Munson Fire Department on Long Island, lost his good friend and colleague Thomas Hetzel, 33. Gioia had attended Hetzel's wedding some years before the attack. Hetzel joined the Franklin Square & Munson Fire Department and was volunteering at the age of eighteen with their Hook & Ladder Company. He served with Franklin Square for fifteen years.

Hetzel grew up loving big red trucks and his vibrant German-American family. As a child, he and his siblings used their feet to make homemade sauerkraut. He played German music and danced the polka at German heritage festivals. The day he died, he was wearing his silver German eagle necklace.

On the morning of September Eleventh, Hetzel was called to duty with his fire station on the Upper East Side of Manhattan, and headed into the North Tower. Diana Hetzel told the *New York Daily News* that she learned her husband was in the North Tower working an elevator to ferry first responders up and down from the 24th floor. Fellow firefighter Lou Cacchioli described being with Tommy Hetzel. Boarding the elevator to ferry more firefighters up from the lobby, the elevator doors closed. It was then that they heard an explosion, which knocked out the lights and stalled the elevator.[36]

Firefighter Thomas Turilli remembers when he was in the North Tower lobby he gave his "radio to ... Louie Cacchioli ... The [elevator] door closed, they went up ... and all of a sudden you just heard ... bombs going off, like boom, boom, boom, like seven or eight ..."[37]

At this point, Tommy Hetzel pried open the elevator doors.

Luckily, they were not between floors, and many were able to get out on the 24th floor and take the stairs. But Hetzel was still inside the North Tower when it collapsed. His body was found in the lobby of the North Tower.

All the trucks from Long Island's Franklin Square & Munson Fire Department carry a picture of Tommy Hetzel. His coworkers at the fire station recalled with emotion that their nickname for him, "Hollywood," was because Hetzel often arrived wearing sunglasses and a tank-top. In Garden City on Long Island, a block of Kilburn Road is named Thomas J. Hetzel Road in his honor.

Others had family members die. FSC member Lorie Van Auken, of East Brunswick, New Jersey, lost her husband, Kenneth Van Auken. He worked on the 105th floor of the North Tower: the first of the two towers to be hit, although the second to collapse. Van Auken remembers, "He left a message that began with 'I love you' and went on to let me know that he had felt the building get 'hit by something.' Ken didn't know if he would 'get out' … essentially he was calling to say goodbye. I knew that my husband had survived the initial strike, but that's all I knew … While I sat in utter shock from what I was watching on television, I continued to hope for a glimpse of Ken, somewhere in the chaos of people running and jumping from the buildings … Suddenly, Ken's building exploded into dust and I watched as people tried to run away from the gigantic wall of smoke and debris that seemed to follow them down the street. Really? Steel-framed skyscrapers could disintegrate just like that?"[38]

Bill Harvey, another FSC member, married Sara Manley on August 11, 2001. Bill and Sara had been married at a wedding chapel in Chapel Hill, North Carolina. The magenta-colored napkins at the reception had matched the roses carried by the flower girls, part of the flair that reflected Sara's attention to beauty and detail. After their wedding, they went on a honeymoon in Italy.

In her workplace Sara was a specialist in telecommunications companies, deciding which stocks were the best to purchase for different portfolios. She had held her position since 1993, and was known as someone who made a positive difference every time she walked into a room. Before her death, Sara volunteered to help with the Fabretto Children's Foundation, an organization that aided those in need in rural Nicaragua.[39]

Sara was vice president and senior financial securities analyst with Fred Alger Management on the 93rd floor of the North Tower. As with the other occupants of the North Tower who were above the 91st floor, Sara had no means of escape—drywall had collapsed in the stairwells, plugging the way to the floors below.

For those who lost loved ones, grief was expressed in many ways. Carie Lemack, also a FSC member, reflected how she and her sister had their own journeys coming to terms with the loss of their mother, Judy Larocque, who was a passenger on American Airlines Flight 11 when it slammed into the North Tower. "For my sister and me, some differences were harder than others. She could not bear to sort through Mom's clothing and found it difficult to consider the thought of wearing any of them, even though they had often "shared outfits" the way close mothers and daughters can. I, on the other hand, felt closer to my mom by putting on her t-shirts and sweaters. … I was less able to bear and appreciate the well-meaning attention of the people who descended on our house after Mom's murder. My sister took great comfort in their interest and support."[40]

Carie Lemack wrote about a particular challenge she faced in a paper she published titled "The Journey to September 12th: A 9/11 Victim's Experiences with the Press, the President, and Congress." In it she wrote, "On 11 September, the whole world watched my mother being murdered on television. Millions have seen that footage time and time again since then. I have not. In fact, inadvertently viewing her murder is now one of my greatest fears. For my sister and me, and for others who lost loved ones on 11 September 2001, this is part of our new reality. My mom, Judy Larocque, was a passenger on American Airlines Flight 11. It is not something one expects, after losing a parent, to have to be constantly vigilant that someone might show her final moments on television, but this is one of the bizarre aftermaths that still plagues me."[41]

As a newly-widowed mother, with a toddler to raise on her own, FSC member Kristen Breitweiser was traumatized from the events of September Eleventh. Her whole world had fallen apart. She remembers the night of September Eleventh and what she did before she went to sleep. She went into the bathroom and put toothpaste on her husband's toothbrush to exemplify her conviction that he was going to return. She recalls looking into the mirror while she put the toothpaste on his brush and saying aloud "Okay, Sweets, your toothbrush is waiting. You have to come home now so you can brush your teeth."

Later she told a police officer about what she'd done and realized that she'd marred her husband's fresh DNA when she put "the toothpaste on his toothbrush." When the officer gave her an uncomprehending glance, his reaction didn't matter to Breitweiser, as it helped her hold onto hope. She left the toothbrush out on the counter for months hoping Ron might somehow be found alive.[42]

Due to what happened on September Eleventh, Americans collectively went through trauma as a nation. For people like Kristen Breitweiser the trauma was horrendous, macabre, and unreal. The dimensions of the atrocity were incomparable. She and the other family members felt they were left on their own.[43]

Even for people far away from the collapsing Twin Towers, the trauma was overwhelming. Psychologist Marti Hopper in Boulder, Colorado, recalls her own reaction to the events of 9/11. "The horrors of 9/11 were televised all over the world and they were televised live. We witnessed the deaths of almost three thousand of our fellow Americans ... this had a very severe and traumatic impact on a large majority of the population. I, myself, cried for weeks after September eleventh."[44]

Carie Lemack recalls the media circus that followed the attacks as they chased after what she refers to as "the crying family members."

"At the airport, at our homes, even at memorial services, cameras and microphones were thrust in our faces to record our every cracked voice and tear."[45]

Out of the grieving thousands left behind on September Eleventh, a small group of families emerged to demand answers. Patty Casazza was one of those, and she later assisted in founding the Family Steering Committee. Before September Eleventh, she had been married to John F. Casazza, and they lived together in Colts Neck, New Jersey.

John worked for Cantor Fitzgerald on the 104th floor of the North Tower. She was able to speak with him when he phoned her from his office. She recalls, "I was actually doing laundry when I got a call from my husband. He had thought that a bomb had gone off in his building. By the time he'd called me he checked all the avenues and said 'the floors are already filling up with the thick black smoke and I don't think we're going to make it.' He said 'I love you, tell John that I love him,' our son."

On September Eleventh, when John Casazza died, Patty had to adjust to becoming a widow and single mother. She often found it difficult to sleep, and as a way to make sense of her personal tragedy, she'd go to the computer to search out information to answer her questions. Patty recalls that after September Eleventh, "my family didn't want me asking any questions. They told me that I should just be grieving and healing. But part of my healing process was finding out exactly what happened."[46]

The families of the September Eleventh victims had barely a week to absorb the shock and adjust to their feelings of grief when Congress passed a $15 billion federal aid package for the US airline industry on September 21, 2001. Congress also established a government fund to compensate those related to the victims of the attacks, although the details would be determined later.[47] Kristen Breitweiser recalls that during the debate on September 21, 2001, one of the members of Congress recognized that if the 9/11 families were given nothing while the airlines were given a bailout, there would be a political firestorm.[48]

The airline aid package passed by Congress was a sign that political pressure would be needed if the families of the September Eleventh victims were to have any impact in Washington DC.

In his book, *Rubble: How 9/11 Families Rebuilt Their Lives And Inspired America*, author Bob Kemper writes that one of the challenges the families faced was how to organize. There were examples of other "victims'" groups in contemporary politics who'd had some success in making political change. There was Mothers Against Drunk Driving (MADD), or the more recent Oklahoma City bombing in 1995. But many of these groups were for more answerable crimes, where the perpetrators could be tried and convicted.

In the end, the victims' group that provided the most useful template was formed by the victims' families of the bombing of Pan Am Flight 103 over Lockerbie, Scotland, in 1988.[49] There were 259 passengers and crew who died on board the flight and eleven others on the ground when the plane crashed. Libya accepted responsibility for the bombing of the plane in 2003.[50] The families who lost loved ones on the Pan Am flight had to exert immense political pressure to get the United States government to look into the incident, since it involved a foreign protagonist.

FSC member Carie Lemack recalls that several weeks after the attacks she picked up the phone and contacted George Williams, the president of the largest Pan Am family organization. Williams had lost his son, Geordie, in the terrorist attack on the Pan Am flight. The Pan Am families had lobbied the US government to change the laws that prevented victims from suing foreign nations or individuals from foreign nations who were responsible for acts of terrorism. The Pan Am families also lobbied the United Nations to impose sanctions on Libya, valued at the time in excess of $23 billion.

Lemack remembers an excellent piece of advice George Williams gave her. The FBI was going to be meeting soon with September Eleventh families. He told her, "bring a sign-up sheet, at the FBI briefing, bring some paper and pens, because that's the only time you can get names." If September Eleventh families were going to connect, it wasn't going to be through contacting government or relief organizations, because they wouldn't give out other families' contact information.

So, at the FBI briefing with the September Eleventh families, Carie and her sister brought a sign-up sheet. They persuaded the agents to let them make an announcement and they took their first steps toward creating a family victims' organization: an initial group called "Families of September 11," before the creation of the FSC.[51]

Lemack purchased a copy of Ernest Wittenberg's book, *How To Win in Washington: Very Practical Advice About Lobbying, the Grassroots, and the Media*. In the book it stated that "The Bill of Rights gives you the *right* to lobby the government; it doesn't come with instructions." For families saddled with grief, few had time to educate themselves on the intricacies of advocacy and lobbying. They needed some legal assistance to help with that.[52]

Unlike with the founding of other advocacy groups, the events of September Eleventh were not on a small scale. Around 3,000 people were murdered. They left behind children, siblings, and parents, as well as uncles, aunts, cousins, nieces, and nephews. There were some tens of thousands of people directly affected by the attacks. It may be no surprise that, despite having a common experience of grief and loss, the family members didn't all think the same way, vote the same way, or have the same priorities for responding to the awful devastation of living in "a post-9/11 world."

Consequently, numerous organizations formed where September Eleventh family members could direct their energies. Some of these included:

- 9/11 Families for a Secure America
- 9/11 Families to Bankrupt Terrorism
- Coalition of 9/11 Families
- Families of September 11
- Fix the Fund

- Give Your Voice
- LMDC Families Advisory Council
- September 11th Advocates
- September 11th Families for Peaceful Tomorrows
- Skyscraper Safety Campaign
- Tuesday's Children
- Voices of September 11th
- World Trade Center Families for Proper Burial
- World Trade Center United Family Group

Each of these organizations had their own focus. For instance, one of the primary goals of the "Skyscraper Safety Campaign" was to have a "Federal Comprehensive Investigation" with subpoena power to scrutinize the collapse of the World Trade Center, including design, construction, evacuation procedures, and firefighting techniques.[53]

The Skyscraper Safety Campaign was founded by soon-to-be FSC member Sally Regenhard. Her son, Christian, was 28 when he died in the towers' collapse. A former US Marine, he had graduated from the Fire Academy in July 2001. He was still under "probation" with the FDNY when he died, starting a career in his firefighter father's footsteps. At his memorial service on October 26, 2001, in lieu of flowers, the family requested that donations be made to "The Christian Michael Otto Regenhard Fund for Justice, Humanity and the Environment," reflecting the values Christian cherished.

In his short 28 years, Christian Regenhard had traveled to 22 countries, "rock-climbing, scuba diving, running marathons, traveling and disappointing a parade of women." He studied art, tried writing at San Francisco State University, and earned a dozen medals as a US Marine.[54]

In December of 2001, Sally Regenhard turned her grief into action by founding the Skyscraper Safety Campaign alongside Monica Gabrielle who had lost her husband, Richard.

Because each organization had a different focus, some families became involved with more than one. In addition to joining the eventual Family Steering Committee, Beverly Eckert co-founded "Voices of September 11th" (along with Mary Fetchet), and around May 2002, Beverly joined a group called "September 11th Families for Peaceful Tomorrows." The group fashioned its name after Martin Luther King Jr.'s quote, "wars are poor chisels for carving out peaceful tomorrows."[55]

Families joining this organization were opposed to marshaling a war effort in Afghanistan, and later Iraq, in response to the death of their loved ones on September Eleventh. Along with others in Peaceful Tomorrows, Beverly Eckert now gave some of her energy to protesting the drumbeat to wage war in Iraq.[56]

The co-founder of Peaceful Tomorrows, Rita Lasar, lost her brother Abraham Zelmanowitz, who worked in the North Tower of the World Trade Center. He perished while waiting for firefighters to help a wheelchair-bound co-worker escape the building. Three days later, President George W. Bush cited Zelmanowitz's courage in a speech at the National Cathedral.

But his sister, Rita, began to fear that her brother's sacrifice would be used as justification for recklessness abroad. On September 17, she sent a letter to the *New York Times* to express her concern. She wrote, "It is in my brother's name and mine that I pray that we, this country that has been so deeply hurt, not do something that will unleash forces we will not have the power to call back."[57]

The letter attracted widespread attention. Dozens of spouses, children, and siblings of victims of the attack called or wrote to her to share their concerns.

In January 2002, Rita traveled to Afghanistan with three other 9/11 family members to protest the US/NATO bombing of civilians as part of a delegation organized by Global Exchange. While in Afghanistan, they witnessed some of the outcomes of American military action. These September Eleventh family members were deeply concerned that killing many thousands of Afghan civilians would not make America safer. Instead, they contended that these casualties would increase terrorist recruitment.

As the US deployed forces across the Middle East in the name of a "war on terror," Rita chose another path. "I will stay behind just as my dear brother did," she promised audiences. "I will stay behind and ask America not to do something we can't take back."

The September 11th Families for Peaceful Tomorrows organization came into being soon after that. In the organization's own words, its initiators shared "a belief that the violence that took their loved ones' lives could spin out of control, and fear could be manipulated by politicians and the media to justify foreign and domestic policies that would increase violence while decreasing US citizens' rights and liberties over the years to come."[58]

In addition to the families of September Eleventh victims, there were other groups that formed who were colleagues of firefighters, police, and paramedics who died as first responders. One of these was the "FealGood Foundation."

John Feal was working at Ground Zero and the Pile. On September 16, 2001, a steel beam crushed one of his feet. The beam weighed over 7,900 pounds. He had respiratory problems from breathing the air at Ground Zero that he had been told was safe to breathe. In March 2018, John Feal would tell a New Zealand reporter, "I can block it out, everything I saw and did, but if I shut my eyes, the smell just overwhelms me, it brings me to places I don't like going. Certain things trigger it. I stay away from them."[59]

When he was injured, Feal made several attempts to get assistance for medical bills that were piling up. Being denied health coverage by government authorities at every turn, John Feal started his group so that other first responders suffering from injuries and illnesses could lobby for aid. He worked with others to help first responders fill out the proper forms to get health benefits and navigate the bureaucracy.

Over the years, his foundation has helped the 83,000 first responders who contracted illnesses after coming to work on Ground Zero. He laments that the first responders have to "beg, crawl and plead" members of Congress to pass legislation to provide needed assistance. Feal remarks, "these are people who come out and say, 'Never forget 9/11,' but who put up roadblocks and obstacles to pass legislation for sick and injured '9/11 heroes.'"[60]

For the families of the September Eleventh victims, there were a wide variety of challenges. Kristen Breitweiser remembers she couldn't confirm her husband was legally dead, since there was no body, without completing lots of forms. In order to get his death certificate verified, the company where Kristen's husband worked, Fiduciary Trust, had to sign an affidavit verifying that her husband, Ron, was last seen at work at the World Trade Center on the morning of September 11, 2001. Kristen also had to sign an affidavit testifying that the last time she saw Ron Breitweiser was when he left their home in Middle Township, New Jersey, to head to work in the North Tower. She felt the situation was preposterous that she'd need to prove her husband was killed at the World Trade Center. "Who would want to lie about something like that?"[61]

Another reminder for the families of their murdered loved ones was the work being done at Staten Island's landfill site, which would now live up to its region's gruesome-sounding name: Fresh Kills. On September 12, at 2 a.m., truckloads of rubble began to arrive. Workers manually searched the pile of rubble using rakes and shovels. They found fingers, hands, feet, skulls, and other body parts. There were photographs, wedding bands, jewelry, and loose change that amounted to $76,318.47. Sifting machines separated recyclables from the mound of debris.[62] Kristen Breitweiser received Ron's wedding ring, while a friend received her husband's body back with only his toes and fingers missing.[63]

During the week of Christmas 2001, Congress passed legislation for the "September 11th Victim Compensation Fund (VCF)." The victims' relatives learned they could only sue terrorists as designated by their government. And if they tried to sue any individual, agency, or corporation, they'd be exempt from receiving any compensation.

Congress put a cap on airline liability to not exceed the existing limits of their insurance policies (approximately $1.5 billion per plane). The relatives objected, saying it penalized people who had other death benefits.

Kristen Breitweiser observed that the government had it backward. Longstanding public policy advocated people getting pension plans and acquiring life insurance policies. But deductions in the VCF were a disincentive to established retirement planning.[64] Lorie Van Auken noted that "The proper place for the 9/11 proceedings would be in a courtroom with subpoena power, rules for swearing in witnesses and established protocols for handling questioning, cross examination and evidence." But the terms of the VCF closed that avenue to the families.[65]

Another confounding aspect to the terms of the Victim Compensation Fund was that families of September Eleventh victims could lose their payout claims if they decided to sue alleged Saudi funders of terrorism related to the attacks.[66] By December 2003, when the deadline for submitting a claim for the VCF arrived, ninety-seven percent of the 2,973 families eligible to apply for compensation through the fund had done so.

~ 2 ~

The Search For Answers

"We are going to get to the bottom of this and we are going to make sure someone is held responsible so that nobody else ever has to walk in our shoes."
~ Kristen Breitweiser, wife of Ronald Breitweiser, 39

While most families accepted the compensation the government apportioned them, seventy families decided not to apply for the fund. Instead, they opted to sue a range of government agencies and private companies.

Among these was Beverly Eckert of Stamford, Connecticut. Her husband, Sean Rooney, had died in the South Tower. He worked on the 98th floor and had climbed up to the 105th floor, hoping to gain access to the roof. But the doors to the roof were locked; Sean Rooney and others remained trapped in the tower. Rooney was not able to be rescued by helicopter, as happened to evacuees from the World Trade Center bombing in 1993.

Beverly Eckert told the press, "my lawsuit requires all testimony be given under oath and fully uses powers to compel evidence."[67] She later joined the Family Steering Committee.

Another person who pursued a lawsuit against the government was Ellen Mariani. Her husband, Louis Neil Mariani, had worked at the Blue Ribbon Dairy Farm in Bedford, Massachusetts, before retiring in his late 50s. Neil died when United Airlines Flight 175 was flown into the South Tower of the World Trade Center.

Neil and Ellen had been married for 13 years. They were on their way to the wedding of her daughter, Gina, in California. Neil had decided at the last minute to attend, and so was on a separate flight scheduled to arrive in California three minutes after Ellen's flight.[68]

Few families pursued a legal remedy like Beverly Eckert and Ellen Mariani. This was because the bill passed in Congress made it clear that the families of the 9/11 victims wouldn't be able to have a day in a US court if they took the compensation package. There would be no formal legal proceedings where they would be able to see witnesses testify, and have a court hold people accountable under penalty of perjury for lying on the stand. There would be no 'discovery': a pre-trial procedure in a lawsuit where each party obtains evidence from others through requests for further information, requests for production of documents, requests for admissions, and depositions.

With the door shut to legal avenues, many families began to focus now on advocating for a Blue-Ribbon panel, independent of the White House, to investigate what really happened on September Eleventh. These families wanted to get to the bottom of what went wrong. Why had America's military defenses failed so utterly to protect its citizens?

FSC member Patty Casazza was among a group of 9/11 families asking questions. She and others began to lobby for an investigation into the events of September Eleventh. However, they met many objections from the Bush Administration.

President Bush was opposed to establishing a special commission to probe into the events of September Eleventh. He preferred any investigation be "confined to Congress." The president wanted any discussions about the events of September Eleventh to occur in closed-door meetings of congressional intelligence committees. Bush was concerned that leaked information from an investigation would encourage the terrorists.[69]

FSC member Carie Lemack remembers reading the *Washington Post* headline: "Bush Seeks To Restrict Hill Probes Of Sept. 11." The article on page A4 of the paper began, "President Bush asked House and Senate leaders yesterday to allow only two congressional committees to investigate the government's response to the events of Sept. 11, officials said."[70] Lemack was outraged. She had an instant reaction: "As I read this article in the 30 January 2002 edition of the *Washington Post*, I became both infuriated and invigorated."[71]

Kristen Breitweiser recalled the reason she, Patty Casazza, Mindy Kleinberg, and Lorie Van Auken banded together in New Jersey to press for an inquiry into the events of September Eleventh. She noted that "In addition to the look of shock, we also shared another look that few family members had at this point in time. It was a look that said, 'We are going to get to the bottom of this and we are going to make sure someone is held responsible so that nobody else *ever* has to walk in our shoes."[72]

The White House had been less-than-cooperative in giving a green light to have an investigative body look into the events of September Eleventh. Despite a few public statements in favour of an investigation, the White House seemed to be stonewalling. According to many of the families seeking an investigation, "Dick Cheney ... had been the principal attack dog on the independent commission with an extreme and vitriolic assault."[73]

On January 24, 2002, a phone call from Vice President Cheney to the Senate majority leader Tom Daschle was overheard by a *Newsweek* reporter. It was a warning from the vice president that an investigation into 9/11 would be a "very dangerous and time—consuming diversion for those of us who are on the front lines of our response today."[74]

Some families wondered why the vice president and the president wanted to thwart any investigation into the attacks. The opposition families encountered also included Republican senators and congressional representatives. It baffled Breitweiser that almost all the Republicans FSC members met with were against efforts to learn from the failures to defend America on September Eleventh.[75]

Frustrated with the stonewalling of an investigation, in April 2002 a number of family members began planning for several days of meetings with members of Congress in mid-June. Four of them were the widows from New Jersey. Reporters dubbed them the "Jersey Girls." They arranged to leave their children with babysitters for several days. Then the four Jersey widows met over the next two days, individually, with over a dozen members of Congress.

Kristen Breitweiser told Indiana Congressman Tim Roemer, "It's not about politics. It's about doing the right thing. It's about the safety of the nation." When the four widows met in the office of Arizona Senator John McCain, Breitweiser said "just give me a list of the people who are giving you problems and we'll knock on doors."[76]

At the end of the second day of meetings, busloads of relatives, friends, and allies of the families of the September Eleventh victims held a rally in Washington on June 11, 2002.

One of the speakers was widow Ellen Mariani from Derby, New Hampshire. Wearing a shirt with dozens of American flag pendants and a large photo of her deceased husband, Neil Mariani, Ellen said, "I want a real investigation. I don't want lip service. I'm angry, and I'm not going away."[77]

"Jersey Girl" Mindy Kleinberg, whose husband Alan died in the North Tower of the World Trade Center, also spoke at the rally. She told those gathered on the lawn on the sunny Washington day, "No stone must remain unturned. We are asking you, America, to stand behind us. I want to be able to look into the eyes of my children, and tell them the evil is over there, that they are safe and that their country is secure. Nine months have passed and I still cannot do that. I do not have answers."[78]

The families were encouraged to see Connecticut Senator Joe Lieberman in attendance at the rally. He became an important voice on Capitol Hill advocating for an inquiry. And although the Bush administration as a whole proved adversarial, specific Republican members of both Congress and Senate stood behind the victims' families in their attempts to be heard.

The actual idea to go to Washington DC, knock on doors of lawmakers, and have a rally came from the family support group of Pan Am Flight 103, which was bombed over Lockerbie, Scotland. Bob Monetti had lost his twenty-year-old son, Richard, on the flight.[79] Monetti told them, "You're not getting any answers. It's time for a rally."

Patty Casazza remembers her reaction to Bob Monetti's proposal: "We had no idea what we were doing, but we didn't think we couldn't do it."[80]

The June rally connected members of various September Eleventh family groups. It was a catalyst for the formal formation of the Family Steering Committee. While individual members of what would become the FSC had been lobbying separately for an inquiry, now they were acting collectively to lobby for politicians to get to the bottom of what had led to the attacks.

For many family members who had lived ordinary lives, coming under the media spotlight for their political actions and to offer opinions on topics such as the Afghanistan War was a steep learning curve. Over the winter of 2001, Carie Lemack had a number of interviews with various media outlets, including the *New York Times*, MSNBC, and CNN. She recalls, "As an average citizen, I had never been on national television before."

While Lemack hoped she could get the support of the general public behind the cause of the families' search for truth, there were practical details she now had to consider. "Would there be beauticians to help with my hair and makeup? What should I wear? At that early hour, would I have a chance to get breakfast at the studio, or should

I wake up even earlier to find some food?"[81]

Although they didn't yet have an independent investigation separate from the government, a governmental organization had been announced in February of 2002, titled "The Joint Inquiry into Intelligence Community Activities Before and After the Terrorist Attacks of September 11, 2001." However, the Joint Inquiry had only been authorized to look into *intelligence* failures on September Eleventh. Co-chair Senator Bob Graham stated that the Joint Inquiry would not play "the blame game about what went wrong from an intelligence perspective."[82]

Kristen Breitweiser was asked to testify in front of the Joint Inquiry on September 18, 2002. In her testimony, Breitweiser gave a personal account of her last phone call to her husband Ron, who died in the South Tower. She told those assembled, "My three-year old daughter's most enduring memory of her father will be placing flowers on his empty grave. My most enduring memory of my husband, Ronald Breitweiser, will be his final words to me: 'Sweets, I'm fine, I don't want you to worry, I love you.' Ron uttered those words while he was watching men and women jump to their deaths from the top of Tower One. Four minutes later, the tower was hit by United Flight 175. I never spoke to my husband, Ron, again."[83]

After that, she launched into a catalogue of failures that were widely reported in the US media. These included details about the ineptness and negligence of NORAD, the CIA, the FBI, the airlines, the Port Authority, the City of New York, the FAA, Secret Service, the US military, and those in senior positions of leadership.

Citing a *New York Times* article about how agents descended on flight schools within hours of the attacks, she asked, "How did the FBI know exactly where to go only a few hours after the attacks? How did they know which neighborhoods, which flight schools and which restaurants to investigate so soon in the case? ... How are complete biographies of the terrorists, and their accomplices, created in such short time? Did our intelligence agencies already have open files on these men? Were they already investigating them? Could the attacks of September 11th been prevented?"[84]

Breitweiser cited Condoleezza Rice, National Security Advisor for the United States, in her June 28, 2001, statement that "it is highly likely that a significant al Qaeda attack is in the near future, within several weeks." She also referenced the statement from Richard Clarke, the National Coordinator for Security, Infrastructure Protection, and Counter-terrorism for the United States. He had said on July 5, 2001, "something really spectacular is going to happen here and it's going to happen soon."

The impact of Kristen Breitweiser's testimony before the Joint Intelligence Committee was extremely damning for the government. Her remarks were well-documented. She connected the dots in a cogent and powerful speech to the members of the Congressional committee in a public hearing.[85]

Within days, the White House dropped its opposition to creating an open investigation. A number of media commentators and political veterans on Capitol Hill were surprised that President Bush had an about-face. But after the damaging public testimony before the Joint Intelligence Committee, *Newsweek* suggested that the president had little choice since they were faced with "a coalition of angry family members of 9-11 victims." One staff member with the White House said, "There was a freight train coming down the tracks." Yet Bush insisted that in the interests of national security the White House wouldn't release any documents that would reveal what the president knew and when he knew it.[86]

Stephen Push, representing 1,500 family members of 9/11 victims through his organization "Families of September 11," voiced his concern that the White House announcement was "carefully crafted to make it look like a general endorsement but it actually says that the commission would look at everything except the intelligence failures."[87]

On September 24, 2002, the United States Senate voted 90-8 in favor of establishing an inquiry into the attacks.[88] However, on October 10, Bush retracted his support for creating an inquiry.[89] Once again, the families of the victims had to lobby for an investigation. This time, they were successful.

In late November, Congress approved legislation and formally created the "National Commission on Terrorist Attacks Upon the United States," commonly known as the "9/11 Commission." The description of the Commission's mandate was to "examine and report on the facts and causes relating to the September 11th terrorist attacks" and "make a full and complete accounting of the circumstances surrounding the attacks." Bush signed the Congressional bill into law November 27, 2002.[90]

On November 29, 2002, former Secretary of State Henry Kissinger was appointed to head the 9/11 Commission. Instead of asking the 9/11 Commission to find out what mistakes were made within the US government, Bush stressed the value of the 9/11 Commission's work would be to find out about the "tactics and motives of the enemy."

In an opinion piece, the *New York Times* wondered "if the choice of Mr. Kissinger is not a clever maneuver by the White House to contain an investigation it long opposed." The *Times* felt that a "final reckoning" was "overdue" in having the Bush Administration explain how all the federal agencies, including military, intelligence, federal aviation, border security, and others, left America inexplicably vulnerable to attack.[91]

Kissinger's involvement was protested because he had long been suspected of pivotally supporting the coup in Chile on September 11, 1973, when General Augusto Pinochet overthrew President Salvador Allende.[92] Congressional and Senate investigations in 1975 into the activities of the FBI and the CIA had found that the CIA had been complicit in the overthrow of Allende.[93]

The *Chicago Tribune* wrote "the president who appointed him originally opposed this whole undertaking." Kissinger is "known more for keeping secrets from the American people than for telling the truth" and asking him "to deliver a critique that may ruin friends and associates is asking a great deal."[94]

The BBC also remarked on Kissinger's shady past. Due to past involvements and political intrigue, in 2002 it was challenging for Kissinger to travel outside America. Judges in Argentina, Chile, France, and Spain wanted Kissinger to appear before them in court to answer questions related to war crimes in Central America, Chile, Bangladesh, Cambodia, East Timor, Laos, and Vietnam.[95]

The *Los Angeles Times* published an editorial with the headline "Kissinger Wrong for the Job." They noted Bush had said that the investigation should "follow all the facts wherever they lead." Kissinger promised to go "wherever the facts lead us and to ignore foreign policy considerations." The paper cautioned that the rhetoric from the president and Kissinger was appealing. But given Kissinger's penchant for secrecy, the 9/11 Commission needed to do its "work in the open, not in secret."[96]

A number of members of the families of September Eleventh victims arranged a meeting with Henry Kissinger. In his book, *The Commission: The Uncensored History of the 9/11 Investigation*, Philip Shenon describes the scene that took place. The dozen designated family members arrived at Manhattan's 350 Park Avenue. They cleared security, but were checked a second time upon arrival on the twenty-sixth floor outside the offices of Kissinger Associates.

As the meeting began over coffee, Kissinger was pressured to reveal his client list by the victims' relations.[97] The federal ethics law required Kissinger and the other members appointed to the 9/11 Commission to reveal their business clients to ensure that there was no conflict of interest.[98]

While Kissinger was pouring the coffee, one of the Jersey widows, Lorie Van Auken, inquired if he had "any clients named bin Laden?" Kissinger spilled coffee across the table, spurned the question, and nearly fell off the sofa where he'd been seated. Several of the 9/11 widows rushed over to steady him and clean up the spilled coffee.

Kissinger explained that he had a "fake eye," which affected his depth perception. He soon brought the meeting to a close.[99]

The next morning, Kissinger faxed the White House his letter of resignation, explaining it would not be possible to release his client list as it would damage the "consulting firm I have built and own."[100]

On December 14, 2002, it was announced that the new Chairman of the 9/11 Commission would be the former Republican governor of New Jersey, Thomas Kean.[101] Congressman Lee Hamilton was named Vice Chairman.

When the 9/11 Commission first met, they faced budgetary constraints. It was reported on January 20, 2003, that the 9/11 Commission would be given a $3 million budget to do its work. In contrast, the investigation to find out if President Bill Clinton was having an affair with Monica Lewinsky cost over $50 million.[102]

The 9/11 Commission requested additional funding, but was turned down by Bush in March 2003, shortly before the 9/11 Commission's first public hearings.[103] The *New York Times* wrote that the White House, having failed to steer the investigation under the secretive leadership of Henry Kissinger, was now employing "budgetary starvation as a tactic to hobble any politically fearless inquiry." In its opinion piece of March 31, 2003, the paper offered that America demanded "an unflinching 9/11 search." However, shortchanging the Commission and preventing it from getting to the bottom of what happened would only risk domestic safety. 9/11 Commission member Tim Roemer, warned, "facing the facts won't kill us. Not getting them might."[104]

The 9/11 Commission had its first public hearing in New York City on March 31, 2003. In his opening comments, Chairman Thomas Kean said "The American people want answers to so many questions around 9/11." Kean talked about fanatics, and the questions surrounding what those defending the USA might have been aware of so that they could "somehow have averted this tragedy." Was there intelligence that pointed to the attack?

Kean added, "Our purpose is to find out why things happened, and what we can do to prevent this ever happening again. We will be following paths and we will follow those individual paths wherever they lead. We may end up holding individual agencies, people and procedures to account. But our fundamental purpose will not be to point fingers."[105]

Many of the 9/11 families sat in shocked silence. They thought that the primary purpose of the 9/11 Commission would be to find out who fell down on the job and make sure they weren't holding the same position the next time America faced an attack.

Vice Chairman Lee Hamilton spoke next, and his statements echoed the purpose the Commission imagined for itself. Hamilton said, "Our primary task is to answer one essential question: What can we do to prevent another 9/11?" The focus was not about the mistakes of the past, but about what could prevent a future attack.[106]

In response to the statements of Chairmen Kean and Hamilton, Stephen Push of Families of September 11 stated, "I'm not advocating conspiracy theories. I don't believe that anyone in the government had specific knowledge of what would happen on 9/11." Yet, Push said, "I think this commission should point fingers. I'm not suggesting that you find scapegoats, but there were people, people in responsible positions who failed us."

Push's wife, Lisa Raines, died on American Airlines Flight 77, which crashed into the Pentagon. He told the commissioners "9/11 was foreseeable. And it could have been prevented. We ask these questions for all Americans. For all the people who may be the next victims of terrorism. For future generations ... good luck in your search for the truth."[107]

Beverly Eckert hoped that the 9/11 Commission would do their job. She said in an interview "I'm not a conspiracy theorist." But, she was shaken by a "sinister" 90-page report, "Rebuilding America's Defenses," by neo-conservative think-tank "The Project for a New American Century (PNAC)." In the report, published in 2000, PNAC proposed the need for a new "Pearl Harbor event to happen, before the American public would be mobilized in supporting some of their agenda." The report urged that the United States needed to "preserve American military preeminence" by greatly increasing military spending. However, in the post-Cold War era this could not be speedily achieved "absent some catastrophic and catalyzing event – like a new Pearl Harbor."

Even more concerning, in Eckert's opinion, was that the authors of the report included Vice President Dick Cheney, Secretary of Defense Donald Rumsfeld, Deputy Secretary of Defense Paul Wolfowitz, and the Undersecretary of State for Arms Control and International Security Affairs, John Bolton. Eckert felt it important that authors of the report "be called by the Commission and asked to explain their line of thinking and their expectations, given the suggestion that this would be a good thing."[108]

But not all was disconcerting. For many families, the remarks of 9/11 Commissioner Jim Thompson at the opening hearing were a hopeful sign that the investigation would yield answers. He said, "Here is the American bargain. Each of us, as individual citizens, take a portion of our liberties and our lives and pass them to those we elect or appoint as our guardians. And their task is to hold our liberties and our lives in their hands, secure. That is an appropriate bargain. But on September 11th that bargain was not kept. Our government, all governments, somehow failed in their duty that day. We need to know why."[109]

FSC members also anticipated that the 9/11 Commission would be able to verify President Bush's claim that Osama bin Laden was not only the prime suspect, but guilty as charged. FSC member Kristen Breitweiser noted "Bin Laden had murdered 3,000 victims, four of whom were our husbands."[110]

~ 3 ~

The Complete 9/11 Timeline

"We will make no distinction between the terrorists who
committed these acts and those who harbor them"
~ President George W. Bush

As part of their healing process following the attacks, members of the Family Steering Committee began to read articles in the news to make sense of the events of September Eleventh.

Lorie Van Auken recalls, "I spent pretty much all my time reading and researching at the beginning, because it was really hard to find things. ... You know, my kids were upstairs and I was in the basement where my computer was researching, so people would call me up that they were hungry and things like that ... But at night, especially after everybody was in bed, I would go downstairs. I couldn't sleep, so I was very busy researching and I was on the phone with different people and emailing different people. ... it was a rough time. But a lot of hours. Pretty much all my free hours."[111]

Mindy Kleinberg notes that "one article led to a question that begat another question that begat another question. And when you couldn't thread them together and you couldn't come to an answer that made sense … we started to catalogue our questions." [112] The FSC members printed articles they read in the media and put them into binders according to topic.

While they were reading articles related to the attacks, FSC members discovered independent investigator Paul Thompson and his website. He detailed over 5,000 articles and news stories from mainstream media sources that were related to the events of September Eleventh in an exhaustive chronology. FSC members found his website invaluable in making decisions about which questions to ask the 9/11 Commission.

Mindy Kleinberg recalls "it was all our binders … laid out beautifully online. It had the ability to connect the dots."

Lorie Van Auken recalls her reaction to discovering Paul Thompson's timeline and the over 5,000 mainstream news articles he'd assembled. "We started to see his research, that was, for me a meeting of the minds. Because it was like, oh my God! This is what I was looking at."[113] Van Auken notes Thompson "would put a time up there and then he would back it up with mainstream media sources so you could understand why there were discrepancies in the timeline" between statements made by NORAD, the FAA, the White House, and others.

Patty Casazza said "Having lost loved ones on 9/11, we had the passion and drive to research and follow through with our quest for answers, but until we stumbled across Paul Thompson's exquisitely detailed and well sourced timeline on the Internet much of the information that we found out about the events surrounding 9/11 were out of context or unverifiable. Paul's timeline gave us a much-needed measure of clarity when our lives were filled with ambiguities."[114]

Paul Thompson began researching the attacks in May 2002, after CBS leaked a story about the August 2001 President's Daily Brief "Bin Laden Determined To Strike." He reflects, "you could have one story that comes out on the front page and another story … on page B12. I found that many times the story that comes out on B12 is more important than what comes out on the front page. … As a casual observer of the news I'd never noticed any of this stuff. And if you start to put all those rather obscure stories together, you end up with an almost completely different narrative. For just about any area relating to 9/11 the story is quite different if you dig deeper into the news."[115]

Thompson said that the events of September Eleventh are "a scandal of tremendous proportions. It makes Watergate look small. There's a strange lack of interest of people both on the left and on the right. Nobody seems to want to uncover the truth and just follow leads, wherever they may go. 'Cause I think it goes to a lot of really damaging places. We can't have these wars and reorganize our way of life based on a false understanding of what 9/11 was."[116] Thompson's Internet timeline was later published in book format as *The Terror Timeline: Year by Year, Day by Day, Minute by Minute: A Comprehensive Chronicle of the Road to 9/11 — and America's Response.*

Lorie Van Auken recalls how the Family Steering Committee decided which questions to submit to the 9/11 Commission. "We all wrote questions and we submitted them. We would just write them and we passed them around. We ... would edit it and clarify it to make the question clearer, to make sure that everybody knew what the person meant."[117]

After the Family Steering Committee had carefully worded each of their questions, they'd hand them to the commissioners, in advance of scheduled testimony, and hope they'd be asked of the intended witnesses in front of the Commission. They did this at formal meetings, such as the one on May 15, 2003, in Madison, New Jersey, with Chairman Kean, Deputy Director Chris Kojm, and Family Liaison Manager of the New York Office, Emily Walker, and additional Family Liaison 9/11 Commission staff person Ellie Hartz. At that meeting the eight FSC members in attendance, along with Stephen Push, asked that the 9/11 Commission investigate "Why was General Mahmoud of Pakistan meeting with Senator Bob Graham and Rep. Porter Goss, the chairmen of the Senate and House Intelligence committees, on the morning of September 11 and what were they talking about?" At that meeting with 9/11 Commission staff FSC members also asked: "Who were the Pentagon officials who advised on September 10th not to fly the next day due to security concerns? Who gave them the warning and where did that individual get the information? Why wasn't the same warning given to the American public?"[118]

FSC members were in daily communication with the commissioners. Handing in person the questions in advance of upcoming hearings ensured commissioners couldn't say later they never got the questions. But in the vast majority of cases, the 9/11 commissioners asked questions that were poorly-formed, and instead of formal inquiry, they infused their questions with friendliness and camaraderie with the witnesses. Consequently, FSC members would make additional attempts, during breaks in the hearings, to get other commissioners to ask questions. These were often prompted by evasive witness testimony the families knew to be sketchy or simply false.

In the rush to war in Afghanistan, FSC members became more aware of the media questioning the certainty of the White House's claim that Osama bin Laden was responsible for the attacks on September Eleventh.

The families read a *Washington Post* story from January 2002 about a diary entry the president wrote on September 11, 2001. "That night, he dictated: 'The Pearl Harbor of the 21st century took place today. We think it's Osama bin Laden.'"[119] The linkage of the attacks on September Eleventh with Iraq were key in President Bush's letter to the US. Congress on March 18, 2003, regarding the *Authorization for Use of Force Against Iraq Resolution of 2002*. The president informed the Speaker of the house that it was imperative to go to war with Iraq "to take the necessary actions against international terrorists and terrorist organizations, including those nations, organizations, or persons who planned, authorized, committed, or aided the terrorist attacks that occurred on September 11, 2001."[120]

Even as early as 8:30 p.m. on September 11, 2001, the president was direct with his statement, "we will make no distinction between the terrorists who committed these acts and those who harbor them". The next day, on September 12, President Bush publicly commented, "The deliberate and deadly attacks which were carried out yesterday against our country were more than acts of terror, they were acts of war."

Bush's speech writer David Frum later commented, "Within 48 hours, [Bush] had made the two key decisions that have defined the war on terror. First, this is a war, not a crime. And second, this war is not going to be limited to just the authors of the 9/11 attack but to anyone who assisted them and helped them and made their work possible, including states. And that is a dramatic, dramatic event. And that defines everything."[121]

The families read a *New York Post* story by Robert Novak on September 13, 2001, about the hijacking of the four planes. The article noted, "Security and airline officials agree privately that the simultaneous hijacking of four jetliners was an inside job probably indicating complicity beyond malfeasance. ... In the rage and mourning following Tuesday's disaster, few officials wanted to dwell on how a 10-year hiatus of airline hijackings in the country could be followed by four in one hour."[122]

The *Washington Post* reported that on September 17, 2001, President Bush signed a two and a half page "top secret" document. It detailed the administration's plan to invade Afghanistan and change its regime. According to administration officials interviewed about the document, it also gave the Pentagon its orders to begin plans to invade Iraq.[123] The BBC ran a story on September 18, 2001, that reported "the US was planning military action against Osama Bin Laden and the Taleban" by "mid-July" of 2001.[124]

On September 23, Secretary of State Colin Powell appeared on *Meet the Press*. He was asked, "Will you release publicly a white paper, which links him [Osama bin Laden] and his organization to this attack, to put people at ease?" Powell responded by saying that the administration was busy gathering all its intelligence and law enforcement information and putting it into one document. Said Powell, "in the near future, we will be able to put out a paper, a document, that will describe quite clearly the evidence that we have linking him to this attack."[125]

However, by the next day the White House was reneging on pressure from nations in the Middle East and some NATO allies to produce proof of Osama bin Laden's guilt. White House Press Secretary, Ari Fleischer, explained to an astonished press gallery it would not be possible to release any paper proving bin Laden's guilt because the evidence was classified and releasing it would compromise US intelligence agencies and national security.

One reporter directly asked the press secretary whether there was "any plan to present public evidence so that the average citizen, not just Americans, but people all over the world can understand the case against bin Laden?" Fleischer dodged the question by saying, "In a democracy it's always important to provide the maximum amount of information possible. But I think the American people also understand that there are going to be times when that information cannot immediately be forthcoming."

Other reporters complained it was problematic for the White House's answer to Americans, and other nations around the world, to be, "That's classified. Trust us."[126]

Part of the controversy concerning the certainty of Osama bin Laden's guilt arose from statements bin Laden made after the attacks denying any involvement. A *Reuters* headline from September 13 read "Taliban Says Bin Laden Denies Role in Attacks." In it, Taliban ambassador to Pakistan Mullah Abdul Salam Zaeef stated "We asked from him, (and) he told (us) we don't have any hand in this action."[127]

Taliban officials insisted it would not be possible for bin Laden to orchestrate the attacks given the "complete restrictions on communications" because of bin Laden's status as a "guest" in Afghanistan.[128] Bin Laden also released a statement that was broadcast on Al Jazeera, saying "The US government has consistently blamed me for being behind every occasion its enemies attack it. I would like to assure the world that I did not plan the recent attacks, which seems to have been planned by people for personal reasons. I have been living in the Islamic emirate of Afghanistan and following its leaders' rules. The current leader does not allow me to exercise such operations." The story was picked up in the *Wall Street Journal*, CNN, and the Associated Press.[129]

President Bush was asked if he trusted bin Laden's insistence that he had no part in the attacks. Bush said, "No question he is the prime suspect. No question about that."[130] And Vice President Dick Cheney, in an interview on *Meet the Press*, said he had "no doubt that (bin Laden) and his organization played a significant role" in the 9/11 attacks.[131]

On October 7, 2001, America invaded Afghanistan in an effort to hunt down Osama bin Laden and capture him dead or alive. The invasion was called Operation Enduring Freedom.[132] After the bombing began, the Taliban offered to arrange for Osama bin Laden to be handed over to an international tribunal.

FSC members read a *Guardian* story where the Taliban's deputy prime minister Haji Abdul Kabir stated that the Taliban would require evidence that bin Laden was behind the September Eleventh terrorist attacks in the US. Kabir added: "we would be ready to hand him over to a third country." But President Bush said in response, "There's no need to discuss innocence or guilt. We know he's guilty."[133]

In early October, an agreement was reached among the leading Pakistani parties with the Taliban. A deal was in place for bin Laden to be extradited to Pakistan and "stand trial for the September 11 attacks." The 9/11 families learned the deal was such that he would be held under house arrest in Peshawar. Apparently both bin Laden and the Taliban leader, Mullah Omar, approved of the arrangement. In Pakistan, Osama bin Laden would go before an international tribunal, "which would decide whether to try him or hand him over to America."[134]

However, an official speaking for the US administration told the *Daily Mirror* "casting our objectives too narrowly" risked "a premature collapse of the international effort if by some lucky chance Mr. bin Laden was captured." President Bush rejected any involvement of an international court to weigh the evidence of bin Laden's guilt.

The effort to capture bin Laden, however, seemed frustrated with inexplicable obstacles. Between November 2001 and January 2002 there were multiple puzzling news stories about an airlift near Kunduz to evacuate Pakistanis. Many were fighting alongside the Taliban. Disturbingly, many in the airlift were members of al Qaeda.

FSC members read in *The New Yorker* of a secret airlift in late November 2001. Journalist Seymour Hersh's best numbers came from intelligence agents in India, who estimated the airlift exceeded 5,000 fighters. Defense Secretary Donald Rumsfeld declined to comment even when pressed. Hersh, responding to the government's professed ignorance about the air lift, commented on Pentagon talking points. "All this talk about 'I don't know, nobody has come forward to me.' We control the air space. We saw everything that moved. No plane could fly from Konduz to Pakistan without getting shot down unless we let it happen, and we let it happen. And I think there's just no other way to explain it."[135]

On October 4, 2001, the British government released a document from the Prime Minister's Office with the title, *Responsibility for the Terrorist Atrocities in the United States.* FSC members read the BBC story with interest. The British document expressed certainty that "Osama Bin Laden and al-Qaeda, the terrorist network which he heads, planned and carried out the atrocities on 11 September 2001."[136] Buried in the assertion was a note that qualified the claims. The disclaimer noted that the document did "not purport to provide a prosecutable case against Osama Bin Laden in a court of law."[137]

The BBC made note of this disclaimer from the Office of the Prime Minister on October 5. In their report, "The Investigation and the Evidence," the BBC stated that "US and British officials have indicated that they are unable to reveal all the evidence for security reasons." In their sub-heading, "Strength of the Evidence," the lead sentence began, "There is no direct evidence in the public domain linking Osama Bin Laden to the 11 September attacks. At best the evidence is circumstantial."[138]

On December 13, 2001, the Pentagon released a video of Osama bin Laden that was said to have been made around November 9. The US military had discovered the video near the end of November in a private home in Jalalabad, Afghanistan. In the tape, bin Laden was boasting about having planned the attacks on September Eleventh. NPR reported that the US military was certain this proved that bin Laden was responsible for the attacks.[139]

However, *The Guardian* ran a news story with the headline "US Urged to Detail Origin of Tape," about responses from leaders in Muslim nations and their "growing doubt … about the authenticity of the film." FSC members read the article, which detailed the convenience of a video being "handed to the Pentagon by an unnamed person or group" from a private home, which just so happened to contain a confession by Osama bin Laden to being responsible for the attacks on September Eleventh. The article summarized, "for many the explanation is too convenient."

In the article the editor of *Computer Video* magazine, Bob Crabtree, was interviewed. Crabtree said that unless one knew more about the source of the video, it was futile to state with any certainty that the video was authentic and unaltered. Crabtree concluded, "The US seems simply to have asked the world to trust them that it is genuine."[140]

FSC members learned there were problems with bin Laden's appearance in the video. He had also appeared in a video on November 3 and another shortly after November 16. In these, bin Laden appeared frail, gaunt, and pale, his beard white. Dr. Sanjay Gupta spoke on CNN on January 21, 2002, commenting that bin Laden looked like he might have a "chronic illness."[141] So why would bin

Laden appear so healthy in a video taken on November 9?

Concurrently, there were reports in the news that bin Laden was dead. In late December 2001, the *Telegraph* cited Bush Administration officials who claimed "the al-Qa'eda leader was already dead."[142] On December 26, 2001, FOX News carried a story first reported in the *Pakistan Observer* that "Usama bin Laden has died a peaceful death due to an untreated lung complication." The report cited a Taliban leader, who alleged to have been at bin Laden's funeral. According to the source, bin Laden was suffering from a serious lung complication and had succumbed to the disease in mid-December, in the vicinity of the Tora Bora mountains.[143]

Meanwhile, Pakistan president Musharraf told CNN in January 2002 he thought bin Laden was "dead because the suspected terrorist has been unable to get treatment for his kidney disease. I think now, frankly, he is dead for the reason he is a ... kidney patient." Apparently, he had taken two dialysis machines with him into Afghanistan.[144]

On January 28, 2002, longtime CBS News anchor Dan Rather reported that Osama bin Laden had been in a Pakistani Military hospital in Rawalpindi under the jurisdiction of the Pakistani Armed Forces on September 10, 2001. He received a kidney dialysis treatment and was released on September Eleventh. Days later, Pakistan backed the war on terror.[145]

In his State of the Union speech on January 29, 2002, President Bush turned his attention from Afghanistan back to Iraq. He described Iraq as part of an "axis of evil," and made no mention of bin Laden. Iraq, Iran, and North Korea were harboring terrorists, and Saddam Hussein was the "true threat."[146]

By March 2002, there was a shift away from bin Laden to target Saddam Hussein. The 9/11 families read the remarks of Charles Heyman, editor of *Jane's World Armies*, who told the *Christian Science Monitor* "There appears to be a real disconnect" between the US military's conquest of Afghanistan and "the earlier rhetoric of President Bush, which had focused on getting bin Laden."[147]

In March 2002, President Bush said "I don't know where [bin Laden] is … You know, I just don't spend that much time on him … to be honest with you. … I'll repeat what I said. I truly am not that concerned about him." [148] Six months after the attacks, President Bush wasn't interested in finding the person he had named "the prime suspect"—or verifying if he was still alive.[149]

FSC members read an interview on CNN in April 2002 of General Richard Myers, who was in charge of NORAD on September Eleventh. The general was asked about the progress in capturing Osama bin Laden, and whether the US was any closer to finding him. General Myers replied, "Well the goal has never been to get bin Laden. Interesting, I just read a piece by some analysts that said you may not want to go after the top people in these organizations. You may have more effect by going after the middlemen, because they're harder to replace." [150]

These, and other, news stories in Paul Thompson's *Complete 911 Timeline* only left members of the Family Steering Committee with more and more questions.

PART TWO: FAMILY STEERING COMMITTEE STATEMENTS TO THE 9/11 COMMISSION

~ 4 ~

Family Steering Committee Report Card for the 9/11 Commission, September 2003

"This is supposed to be an investigation of September 11. This is not supposed to be a sales pitch for the Iraq War!"
~ Lorie Van Auken, wife of Kenneth W. Van Auken, 47

After Thomas Kean was appointed chairman of the 9/11 Commission, he met with Family Steering Committee members in January of 2003. Kean cleared his schedule for over four hours. Kristen Breitweiser experienced Kean as approachable, genuinely interested in their concerns, and "genial and open." Kean "told us that he was committed to working together and wanted to turn over every rock in carrying out his investigation."[151]

In comparison, Vice Chairman Lee Hamilton had a reputation as lacking "the taste for partisan fights." By default, Hamilton always "assumed the best about people." He was a close personal friend of both Secretary of Defense Donald Rumsfeld and Vice President Dick Cheney. Hamilton knew them as "Don and Dick" and "trusted both men to always tell the truth."

Additionally, Lee Hamilton was known as someone who never

saw the signs of a scandal, even if it slapped him in the face. In his book, *The Commission*, Philip Shenon wrote that Lee Hamilton "was not considered much of an investigator in Congress, at least when it came to ferreting out evidence of scandal." Hamilton had said of himself, "I don't go for the jugular."[152]

Hamilton was not someone who pursued allegations against anyone vigorously. Looking back on the Iran-Contra Affair in 1987, Hamilton said, "I had the word of the national security adviser … Colonel North, eyeball to eyeball, man to man, person to person. On the other hand, I had newspaper reports—unconfirmed—but nobody would come forward." [153] When evidence of the affair proved true, Hamilton himself acknowledged that he had been "gullible."

In February 2003, FSC members met with Lee Hamilton. They stressed the need for the 9/11 Commission to be transparent and hold the government accountable. Kristen Breitweiser remembers a list of demands the 9/11 families put forward to ensure a proper investigation of the attacks. These included open, public hearings, witnesses to be required to take an oath before testifying, the commissioners to ask hard-hitting questions, and "to subpoena early and often … We wanted answers to our thousands of questions."[154]

The families felt the public hearings for the Joint Inquiry had been effective, setting the bar for an accountable method of conducting an investigation. However, Hamilton questioned what merit there was in having open, public hearings. He wasn't interested in keeping the public informed about the 9/11 Commission's progress. Also present with the FSC members was Bob McIlvaine, a member of September 11th Families for Peaceful Tomorrows. McIlvaine said he was alarmed at Hamilton's attitude.[155]

The 9/11 Commission was hobbled from the beginning. Even the chairmen, Kean and Hamilton, reflect that "The story of how the 9/11 Commission was created and began its work is one of false starts."[156] They recall that in February 2003, the Commission still didn't have a phone number. This hampered communication between 9/11

Commissioners, Commission staff, 9/11 family members, and the press. Because the Commission office was in a CIA-related building, most of the Commission staff didn't have access to their offices for months until they had received their security clearances. In addition, the Commission went for some time without a fax machine, a web site, office supplies, even a coffee maker.[157]

In February 2003, Congress gave the 9/11 Commission $3 million to investigate the attacks. But with 80 staff to pay, the Commission would go broke by August 2003. It would take at least $14 million for the Commission to do its work, half of which would go to pay for Commission staff salaries. The rest would pay for travel, equipment, and supplies.[158]

When the Commission began their first public hearings, Mary Fetchet testified, "We deserve answers to a long list of questions we have … I am frustrated to have suffered the loss of a son and yet be required to spend time away from my family and fight for the establishment of a commission that should have been in place on the day of [the] tragic events."[159]

As the Commission's public hearing schedule lagged and commissioners spent their precious time flattering witnesses, Kristen Breitweiser began to think that Lee Hamilton viewed public hearings as "very dangerous."[160]

Kean and Hamilton told the other commissioners they had no plans to issue subpoenas. This mystified several members of the Commission and stunned Commission staff. With a mandate to finish its work by late May 2004, if the Commission faced obstacles to obtain documents, the timeframe for pursuing legal avenues would shrink. Uncooperative agencies would be free to stall while the deadline for the *Report* drew near.[161]

When the 9/11 Commission was created, the final version of the legislation stipulated the conditions for issuing subpoenas. A subpoena could only be issued if six of the ten 9/11 commissioners agreed to the necessity of a subpoena, or if the chair and vice chair agreed.[162]

Though the majority of commissioners felt it necessary to issue subpoenas to NORAD, Lee Hamilton voted no. He told the others "I've known Don Rumsfeld for twenty, thirty years. When he said 'I'm going to get that information for you,' I took him at his word."[163]

Besides waiving the customary option of issuing subpoenas, Lee Hamilton had an especially high view of executive privilege. Whenever the White House wanted to assert "executive privilege" as the reason why something the 9/11 Commission sought should not be made available, Hamilton would agree. The Bush Administration, including Vice President Dick Cheney and Secretary of Defense Donald Rumsfeld, were all greatly encouraged by Lee Hamilton's reflexes to side with the administration.[164]

That wasn't the only indication of the 9/11 Commission's bias. When it held its first hearing on March 31, 2003, Abraham Sofaer was called as an expert witness for his role as a member of the Hoover Institution. A proponent of "preemptive war," Sofaer was speaking just eleven days after the war in Iraq began on March 20. Sofaer told the commissioners "Bin Laden, Sadaam Hussein, and others like them have made very clear why they hate us."[165]

At the third hearing on July 9, 2003, Dr. Laurie Mylroie, a political scientist at the American Enterprise Institute, was called to the stand. Mylroie was author of *Study of Revenge: Saddam Hussein's Unfinished War Against America*. In it, Mylroie theorized that Iraq and al Qaeda were one and the same. Mylroie spoke before the 9/11 Commission to "demonstrate Iraq's link to the 9/11 attacks."[166] Mylroie claimed that Iraq attacked America on 9/11. She also said the idea that the attacks on the World Trade Center in 1993 and 2001 were examples of a new type of terrorism was "simply not true." Mylroie argued both events were the result of a state actor, Iraq.

The Bush White House, especially Vice President Cheney, promoted this as the reason America invaded Iraq in March 2003. At the time, over 80% of Americans believed that Iraq had attacked America on September Eleventh.

Lorie Van Auken confronted the 9/11 Commission Executive Director Philip Zelikow after Dr. Mylroie's testimony. She said to him, "that took a lot of nerve putting someone like that on the panel. Laurie Mylroie? This is supposed to be an investigation of September 11. This is not supposed to be a sales pitch for the Iraq War!" Though the director said nothing, Van Auken recalls, "he knew exactly what he was doing. He was selling the war."[167]

Despite the bias, the Family Steering Committee remained hopeful they would receive answers. During the life of the 9/11 Commission, the Family Steering Committee issued numerous formal statements. Thirty-one of these were sent to the Commission between May 1, 2003, and July 26, 2004. The FSC issued another 18 statements related to the implementation of the recommendations from *The 9/11 Commission Report*.

On May 1, 2003, FSC members met with eight of the commissioners, as well as the Executive Director and Deputy Director. The Deputy Director, Chris Kojm, was an assistant to Lee Hamilton in the Iran-Contra inquiry. The 9/11 Commission and the FSC agreed that when testimony that was inconsistent with what was publicly known was presented at the hearings, the commissioners wanted to "be advised" by the FSC.[168] Lorie Van Auken remembers that in response to what was unfolding early during the public hearings, "any time we saw something that was not right we would email commissioners ... telling them ... that somebody did not tell the truth about whatever we knew to be true. And we would send our evidence and research."[169]

FSC members were not alone in observing false statements made by witnesses who came before the inquiry. The 9/11 Commission's Senior Counsel, John Farmer, said in his book *The Ground Truth: The Story Behind America's Defense on 9/11* that "at some level of government, at some point in time ... there was an agreement not to tell the truth about what happened ... I was shocked at how different the truth was from the way it was described."[170]

The FSC also wanted the 9/11 Commission to provide them with "a list of individuals who will be testifying both publicly and in closed session." The request was made so they could compose questions for the Commission staff teams to include when interviewing witnesses.

On May 15, there was another meeting between commissioners, staff, and FSC members. To aid the investigation, it was suggested that the 9/11 Commission inform the public during the public hearings about how anonymous callers and whistle-blowers could pass on tips. The FSC also stressed that witnesses should be sworn in before testifying.

The FSC didn't stop there. At a meeting at FBI Headquarters on June 10, 2003 with FBI Director Robert Mueller, the FSC and other family groups discussed the FBI investigation into the attacks. After the meeting, the FSC reported: "Although family members had many questions regarding the FBI's knowledge about the terrorists, FBI communication with other governmental agencies and its actions prior to September 11th, Director Mueller declined to answer many questions on the basis that the answers may be integral to the government's prosecution of Moussaoui."[171]

In a press release on September 10, 2003, the FSC stated, "Some things about September 11th just don't make sense in light of intelligence gathered and established protocol and procedures in place prior to 9/11, so the Family Steering Committee has submitted questions to the Commission on a wide range of topics. To date, none of our questions have been answered."[172] They raised concerns about a possible cover-up, stating "since no substantive information about the investigation had been released, we are being asked to take on faith that an in-depth investigation is taking place and that it will not be a whitewash. But trust began to die when President Bush opposed an independent investigation for more than a year. We should not have had to fight our government for an independent commission."

The FSC was concerned about the exclusion of details that needed further examination. They felt the administration's posturing throughout the lead-up investigation and during its proceedings was contributing to "conjecture and discontent" and undercutting the government's "integrity."[173] The FSC reminded the 9/11 Commission and the Bush administration that the intent of the investigation was "pursuing the truth wherever it leads."[174]

The FSC also felt that the 9/11 Commission's application of its mandate to "identify, review, and evaluate the lessons learned from the terrorist attacks from September 11th, 2001," fell short. The lack of attention to such basic matters as the timeline of events surrounding the attacks was regarded as deficient.[175]

By September 2003, the 9/11 Commission had held only three public hearings. The FSC released a "Report Card" to motivate the Commission "to better serve the public interest" and "assure the American public that they are doing the job that needs to be done."

The FSC broke down their report into categories. Under "Investigative, Informative Open Hearings," they awarded the 9/11 Commission a "D" grade. They clarified: "FSC feels that expert witnesses invited to testify before the Independent Commission should hold valuable and pertinent information that will yield fruitful insights into the systemic government failures that occurred on 9/11. As an example, in the most recent open hearing, we had an 'expert' witness testifying on Iraq and no expert witness testifying about Saudi Arabia. The FSC would like to draw attention to the fact that 15 of the 19 hijackers were Saudi, and none were from Iraq. Additionally, the 900-page Joint Inquiry Report shows no Iraqi connection to 9/11."[176]

Also contributing to this grade was the FSC's disappointment that after nine months the 9/11 Commission had only held three open hearings. They reminded the Commission that at its inception it had promised to hold open hearings monthly.

The FSC stressed that the success of the hearings depended on asking relevant questions. They observed that "the Commissioners, individually and as a whole, did not carry out the necessary hard-hitting lines of questioning, cross-examination and crucial follow-up questioning all of which are critical in unearthing the truth," which further contributed to the low grade. Commissioner Tim Roemer told PBS that FSC members were regularly introducing new facts and evidence that he was unaware of. "That happens on pretty much a weekly basis. They're always telling me, 'We need you to kick down the doors. To be responsible. To be our prosecutor. And to get at the facts.'"

The FSC gave the 9/11 Commission a grade of "C-" for "Frequency of Meetings." In addition to more regular meetings, they had counted on the Executive Director issuing Interim Reports. This idea came from 9/11 families' participation in the Joint Inquiry, where its Staff Director Eleanor Hill had issued Interim Reports of their investigation from February to December 2002.

The FSC gave a grade of "D" to the 9/11 Commission for their "Structure and Conduct of Open Hearings." They wrote "The FSC is shocked with the use of 'minders' in the interrogatory process." Minders were staff from government agencies, including the executive branch, who were senior to those called to testify before the Commission. The FSC objected to their presence, considering it "a form of intimidation" of the witnesses. The 9/11 families determined "it does not yield the unfettered truth."[177]

The FSC was not alone in expressing concerns about these government minders. They noted that at previous open hearings, certain 9/11 commissioners objected to the presence of government minders, which they had expressed at a recent press conference. Nonetheless, the FSC observed "'minders' continue to be present during witness examination and questioning."

Three Commission staff sent a memo to the General Counsel of the 9/11 Commission, Dan Marcus, and his Deputy General Counsel on October 2, 2003, titled "Executive Branch Minders' Intimidation of Witnesses." They cited instances of minders answering questions directed to witnesses and preempting witness responses to questions posed by a commissioner, which was problematic.

Echoing FSC concerns, the Commission staff noted that also

in closed door testimony "minders have positioned themselves physically and ... generally have sat next to witnesses at the table across from Commission staff, conveying to witnesses that minders are participants in interviews and are of equal status to witnesses. Moreover, minders take verbatim notes of witnesses' statements, which we believe conveys to witnesses that their superiors will review their statements and may engage in retribution."[178] They noted they were not unique among staff observing intimidation by minders. Why were government minders concerned about what witnesses might say if they were allowed to speak freely?

In relation to the conduct of the open hearings, the FSC noted that the 9/11 Commission had yet to have any witnesses swear an oath before testifying. The FSC insisted, "Without sworn testimony, witnesses cannot be held accountable for what they testify about before the Commission." Although the FSC had been guaranteed by the 9/11 Commission's Executive Director that any witnesses who testified before the Commission would be admonished if they were later found to have made incorrect statements, the 9/11 families wrote "the FSC has been given no evidence that [this] has been done."[179]

Another factor that earned the Commission a "D" grade in this category had to do with the reluctance to subpoena witnesses. From the beginning, the FSC urged Commission to "subpoena early and often." Now, nine months into their mandate, the Commission hadn't issued a single subpoena. The FSC wrote "The Commission's failure to subpoena, while polite, prohibits the ultimate claim by the Commission that they, themselves, were the victims of "stonewalling" by the agencies, organizations and councils."[180] It was time for the Commission to make use of the assets it possessed to uncover all the factors that contributed to the nation's failure to avert the attacks. Subpoenas were an essential tool to ensure the 9/11 Commission brought before them crucial "information and access to witnesses needed to make their investigation a success."[181]

During the investigation, the Commission's access to many

documents was denied. For example, the Commission was not given access to the findings of the earlier Joint Inquiry, which had issued its final report in December 2002. The Commission wanted to know what the Joint Inquiry had discovered in its investigation into the intelligence community. This would ensure that they wouldn't have to start from square one.

A member of the 9/11 Commission, Tim Roemer, had even served on the Joint Inquiry. Roemer figured that since he'd sat on the Joint Inquiry, he at least could see the documents the 9/11 Commission needed. "But he was met by a pair of Justice Department lawyers who told Roemer that he wasn't allowed to see the documents. It didn't matter that he'd been part of the Joint Inquiry."[182] The Joint Inquiry's report was classified, and the White House wouldn't agree to 9/11 Commission requests to see it, citing executive privilege.

Arizona Senator John McCain got wind of the denial of access for Roemer. McCain appeared before the 9/11 Commission and expressed his disappointment. "I was disheartened that members of your commission were until recently denied access to the report of the joint congressional investigation into the September 11 terrorist attacks. Using the congressional committee's report as the baseline for your work would theoretically have allowed the commission to hit the ground running. Instead, you've been stuck in the quicksand of negotiating access to a document you should have been entitled to examine on a priority basis at the beginning of your tenure … While I don't want to believe such a basic lack of cooperation was intentional, it nonetheless creates the appearance of bureaucratic stonewalling."[183] Senator McCain was in a position to make the commissioners and the press sit up and listen.

On October 30, 2003, FSC member Bill Harvey told McClatchy Newspaper that he was a registered Republican and had voted for the President's father George H.W. Bush twice, and for George W. Bush in 2000. But, said Harvey about the younger President Bush, "He's obfuscated this investigation from Day One. I just don't understand why, as commander in chief and the person in charge of the security of this country, he's not interested in investigating how this was able to happen."[184]

With even staunch Republicans on the FSC frustrated with the White House, it was clear some of the lower grades given to the 9/11 Commission were worsened by stonewalling from the administration. The FSC issued a press release on November 13, insisting that "All ten Commissioners should have full, unfettered, and unrestricted access to all evidence ..." This was to include all Presidential Daily Briefings pertaining to matters related to the attacks.[185]

November 27, 2003, was the anniversary of President Bush signing the Act that created the 9/11 Commission. On that anniversary, the FSC issued another press release. They quoted Bush: "I also hope that the commission will act quickly and issue its report prior to the 18-month deadline ... for the security of our country." The FSC observed that meeting this deadline was now elusive, "Due to the untimely issuance of subpoenas to the FAA, NORAD, and the City of New York along with the access restrictions placed by the White House." Consequently, the FSC urged that the Commission be given an extension to finish its work.[186]

Eventually, the 9/11 Commission would be given a sixty-day extension. But 2004 was an election year. The White House didn't want the 9/11 Commission to continue its investigation during an election campaign. In the end, the government's own interests interfered with its ability to impartially investigate itself.

~ 5 ~

Executive Director Zelikow and Transition Briefings

"It is now apparent why there has been so little effort to assign individual culpability. We can now see that the trail would lead directly to the staff director himself."
~ Family Steering Committee to the 9/11 Commission,
March 20, 2004

When Chairmen Tom Kean and Lee Hamilton began working on the 9/11 Commission, they judged they had two initial tasks. The first was to establish a working relationship with the families of the 9/11 victims. The second was to appoint an executive director for the commission who could "start hiring other staff and setting up an infrastructure."

Although they were given many recommendations, Kean and Hamilton wrote in their memoir, *Without Precedent: The Inside Story of the 9/11 Commission,* "we seriously considered only one candidate: Philip Zelikow."[187]

Lee Hamilton first approached Zelikow by phone, and after a series of phone calls both Kean and Hamilton met with Zelikow at Drew University in New Jersey. Kean and Hamilton were excited about Zelikow's credentials as a historian. They were taken with his concept of a commission report written through the lens of a historian, "telling the authoritative story of what happened on September 11, 2001, so that our recommendations would emerge directly from the facts of the 9/11 story."[188]

However, there were concerns about Philip Zelikow from the moment he was considered for the position of 9/11 Commission Director. It was known that Zelikow had co-authored a book, *The Kennedy Tapes: Inside the White House During the Cuban Missile Crisis*, with fellow Commission staff member Ernest R. May. The book's questionable scholarship was called out in an article in *Atlantic Monthly* titled "What JFK Really Said." It pointed out that Zelikow's "flawed transcription" of White House recordings rendered meanings of transcripts into the polar opposite of what the originals actually meant. While it should be a simple matter to render a transcript from a tape to print material without error, the *Atlantic Monthly* contributor found Zelikow's work shocking. "What I discovered left me dismayed. The transcript abounds in errors that significantly undermine its reliability for historians, teachers, and general readers."[189]

Other red flags were brought to the attention of Kean and Hamilton regarding Philip Zelikow. White House Chief of Staff, Andrew Card, had warned Kean about Zelikow's abrasiveness and secretiveness. He fretted that he'd have to justify to the press any obvious conflicts of interest that could easily surface from having Zelikow as Director.[190]

Kean's own university staff complained about Zelikow's abrasiveness. They urged Kean not to hire him. Commissioners Max Cleland, Richard Ben-Veniste, Jamie Gorelick, and Tim Roemer were concerned that such a hiring would undermine the image of the 9/11 Commission as nonpartisan. Ben-Veniste recalls that the appointment of Zelikow was presented to the commissioners by Kean and Hamilton "as a fait accompli."[191] Lee Hamilton admits he was the only Democrat on the 9/11 Commission who wasn't "wary of Zelikow's appointment."[192]

The assistants to the director of the CIA were unimpressed early on with Zelikow's "come in with answers rather than questions" approach. Since Zelikow hired the staff for the Commission, he demanded that no phone calls from any of the ten commissioners were to be returned without his permission.[193]

Despite this, Thomas Kean and Lee Hamilton boasted, "we had full confidence in Zelikow's independence and ability ... A historian dedicated to a full airing of the facts ... Zelikow would not lead a staff inquiry that did anything less than uncover the most detailed and accurate history of 9/11."[194] They mused that Zelikow had "been much tougher ... than a lot of people would have liked him to be."[195]

On January 27, 2003, the 9/11 Commission issued a press release announcing Zelikow as its executive director, describing him as "a man of high stature."[196] As executive director, Zelikow decided which areas the 9/11 Commission would investigate, what briefing materials the commissioners would read ahead of interviews, what topics were chosen for hearings, who the witnesses would be, and what the lines of questioning were for those witnesses. Essentially, Philip Zelikow would run the investigation, while the commissioners presented its public face. Chris Kojm, who was an assistant to Lee Hamilton in the Iran-Contra inquiry, was named his Deputy Director.

When it was announced that Philip Zelikow had been chosen as the director of the 9/11 Commission, Richard Clarke, chairman of the "Counterterrorism Security Group," said "the fix is in." Clarke was dismayed, recalling that when Zelikow was a member of the Bush White House Transition Team, he'd placed Clarke and his Counterterrorism Security Group (CSG) in a peripheral role within the National Security Council. Consequently, all the agenda items of the CSG were virtually off the Bush administration's radar. And Zelikow was in the room when President Clinton's National Security Advisor Sandy Berger warned his successor, Condoleezza Rice, about al Qaeda and Osama bin Laden. Clarke was stupefied, since "Zelikow had been right there, sitting with her, listening with her."[197]

Further, the institutional design Zelikow helped to create impaired the Bush administration's ability to connect the dots in the months before the attacks.

Zelikow hired all eighty 9/11 Commission staff and divided them into nine teams. Each team only focused on their piece of the puzzle. While the staff teams only saw a fragment of what was unfolding through the Commission's work, Zelikow shaped the big picture.

Zelikow's administrative assistant, Karen Heitotter, had worked for US diplomats and embassies in the past, and maintained a high level of professional standards. This included keeping a log of the telephone calls Zelikow received. Beginning on June 23, 2003, at 4:40 p.m., she was astonished to pick up the phone and hear a voice saying, "This is Karl Rove. I'm looking for Philip." The 9/11 Commission was supposed to be an independent investigation, and yet they were receiving calls from President Bush's Senior Political Advisor. Rove would call again on June 24, September 4, and September 15.

Word of continuing communication between Philip Zelikow, Karl Rove, and National Security Advisor Condoleezza Rice confirmed the worst suspicions about just how "independent" the 9/11 Commission was from the White House.[198] Karl Rove was directly involved in consulting with Zelikow about the progress of the 9/11 Commission. According to Republican commissioner John Lehman, "Rove was the quarterback for dealing with the commission."[199]

Upon learning that his executive assistant was keeping a record of the 9/11 Commission's phone calls, Zelikow ordered her to cease keeping the phone log. His assistant was so troubled by this order that she met privately with the Commission's General Counsel, Dan Marcus. It was agreed that Zelikow's order "looks bad."[200] In the end, it was recommended that she not obey Zelikow's order and quietly continue keeping a phone log.

The scandal of Zelikow receiving numerous messages from Karl Rove and Condoleezza Rice came to the attention of FSC members Kristen Breitweiser, Lorie Van Auken, Patty Casazza, and Mindy

Kleinberg. They passed on the story to a *New York Times* reporter.

But when the reporter followed up to write a story, Chairmen Thomas Kean and Lee Hamilton downplayed the allegation. They'd been assured by Zelikow that the calls he'd received from Karl Rove were only connected with work he'd done previously at the University of Virginia's Miller Center of Public Affairs. With the appearance of impropriety called into question, the *New York Times* reporter shelved the story. It never went to print.[201]

Zelikow's White House connections went even further. In October 2003, the 9/11 Commission General Counsel, Dan Marcus, met privately with Thomas Kean and Lee Hamilton to present them with hard evidence that Zelikow had other conflicts of interest that hadn't been publicly made known when he was first hired. He informed them of Zelikow's large role in sidelining the Counterterrorism Study Group early in the new Bush administration. Zelikow was also a key contributor in the paper advocating preemptive war, which laid the intellectual groundwork for the reason to invade Iraq in 2003.

However, the 9/11 Commission's chairman and vice chairman brushed away Marcus' concerns about Zelikow's multiple conflicts of interest. General Counsel Dan Marcus found it incomprehensible that Lee Hamilton's view was that the "staffers" with the 9/11 Commission just weren't that important. Marcus observed that Lee Hamilton seemed to have a "misplaced confidence" in Zelikow, and had a penchant for minimizing any red flags.[202]

As the Commission's investigation got underway, Zelikow was presented with a list of people to interview. This list was compiled by Commission staff Mike Jacobson and Dana Lesemann, who had experience in the earlier Joint Inquiry. Commissioner Tim Roemer had recommended them to Zelikow. The interviews were intended to follow leads that suggested some of the alleged hijackers had the support of elements within the Saudi Arabian government. Instead, Zelikow told them to interview only half of those on the list.

Dana Lesemann, a former Justice Department lawyer, objected, telling Zelikow his decision was "very arbitrary" and "crazy." She declared, "Philip, this is ridiculous. We need the interviews. We need these documents. Why are you trying to limit our investigation?" Zelikow suggested that he was worried federal agencies might feel overwhelmed if there were too many requests for documents and interviews.

In April 2003, Dana Lesemann sought to obtain a file related to the 28 redacted pages from the Joint Inquiry's report. The pages related to a possible Saudi Arabian connection with the attacks on 9/11.[203] Zelikow fired her, signaling to all the 9/11 Commission staff that he would not tolerate anyone contradicting his directives.

In her book, *Wake-Up Call*, Kristen Breitweiser recalls she was doubtful about Zelikow from the start and this quickly grew into an aversion.[204] Members of the Family Steering Committee became increasingly uncomfortable with Zelikow as they learned more and more about him. Breitweiser learned that it would be Zelikow's responsibility to head an investigation that would involve probing into his own actions during the transition from the Clinton to the Bush administration. She observed that Zelikow's actions directly contributed to the miscalculations concerning the danger posed by al Qaeda and bin Laden.[205]

Breitweiser and other FSC members informally met with Zelikow at a Starbucks to convey their concerns. They learned that Zelikow was testifying before the 9/11 Commission about his leadership as part of the Bush transition team after the November 2000 election. Breitweiser was incredulous that Zelikow could be impartial and be responsible for approving the subsequent written report.[206]

Initially, the FSC had been hopeful that Zelikow, with his relationship with Condoleezza Rice and others in the Bush White House, might foster cooperation between the 9/11 Commission and the Bush administration. However, the FSC learned more about Zelikow's enmeshment with the Bush White House from a *Washington Post* story from February 2001, recently brought to their attention. The paper reported that in September of 2000 "Condoleezza Rice asked Philip Zelikow, a fellow staffer on the Scowcroft NSC ... to draft memos on organizing the NSC along Scowcroft's lines. Edited by Rice and others, the memos were further refined when Rice's deputy Stephen Hadley came on board, and Zelikow ... became part of the transition ... free to roam the halls of the Clinton NSC operation."[207]

On October 3, 2003, the FSC wrote to the 9/11 Commission to request Philip Zelikow's recusal from all commission work related to the National Security Council (NSC) and the President's Foreign Intelligence Advisory Board (PFIAB). Since the executive director's role included writing the report about the NSC and PFIAB, the FSC called for Zelikow to step aside from that part of the Commission's work to avoid a conflict of interest.

The FSC pointed to Commissioner Jamie Gorelick as an example. As the former US Deputy Attorney General under President Clinton from 1994 to 1997, Gorelick removed herself from all matters related to investigating the Justice Department. The FSC stressed that if Zelikow failed to recuse himself they wanted "his resignation as Staff Director from the 9/11 Independent Commission."[208]

The FSC weren't the only ones concerned with how the Commission was developing. Commissioner Max Cleland resigned from the Commission in late 2003. On December 3, 2003, Bob Kerrey replaced him. The FSC lobbied for Kristen Breitweiser to replace Cleland. But Tom Daschle appointed Committee for the Liberation of Iraq member Kerrey. Before Cleland resigned, he called the Bush administration's stonewalling and efforts to "slow walk" the Commission a "national scandal." He later complained, "there was a desire not to uncover bad news, a desire to leave rocks unturned—both in the White House and, to a certain extent, on the leadership of the Commission."[209] Both Chairman Thomas Kean and Vice Chairman Lee Hamilton had expressed concern to Senator Tom Daschle about Cleland's criticism of the Bush administration's cooperation with the Commission.

Meanwhile, on his first day as a commissioner, Bob Kerrey

uncovered a memo by Philip Zelikow, where the Executive Director detailed his ties to Condoleezza Rice. Kerrey said he "just could not believe" the extent to which Rice and Zelikow were intertwined. Kerrey was alarmed that Zelikow had downgraded terrorism as a priority and been the author of the preemptive war doctrine to get America into Iraq.

On December 9, 2003, Bob Kerrey threatened to resign from his new position of commissioner if Zelikow wasn't let go. Chairman Thomas Kean tried to assuage his concerns and convinced Kerrey to stay. Philip Shenon, author of *The Commission: The Uncensored History of the 9/11 Investigation*, notes "For Kean, it was hard to see which would be worse, the loss of Zelikow so late in the investigation or the angry resignation of a newly arrived commissioner because of Zelikow's conflicts of interest."[210]

On March 20, 2004, the FSC wrote a letter to the 9/11 Commission to express how "deeply disturbed" they were regarding Zelikow's conflict of interest. He could potentially be held culpable for failing to heed warnings about the threat al Qaeda posed prior to September Eleventh. This information came to their attention through interviews with Richard Clarke, former Chairman of the Counterterrorism Security Group, published in the *New York Times* and on CBS' *60 Minutes*. Clarke told the media he was "very explicit" with Philip Zelikow, National Security Advisor Condoleezza Rice, and her assistant Stephen Hadley about the threat al Qaeda posed when he met with them in person.[211] Zelikow failed to prioritize the threat.

Zelikow had also written a memo for the Bush White House articulating preemptive war against Iraq as a foreign policy strategy. It was titled "The National Security Strategy of the United States," and written in early 2002 at the request of Condoleezza Rice.[212]

The FSC had a press conference with "9-11 Citizens Watch" on March 22, 2004, where they stated: "It is clear that [Zelikow] should never have been permitted to be a member of the commission, since it is the mandate of the commission to identify the source of failures.

It is now apparent why there has been so little effort to assign individual culpability. We now can see that trail would lead directly to the staff director himself."[213]

The FSC called for Zelikow to resign immediately. They called for him to testify before the 9/11 Commission under oath. They called for the notes he'd taken during intelligence briefings with Counterterrorism Security Group Chairman Richard Clarke to be subpoenaed. They called on the 9/11 Commission "to apologize to the 9/11 families and America for this massive appearance of impropriety."[214]

Thomas Kean and Lee Hamilton declined the FSC's request to replace Zelikow as executive director. Kristen Breitweiser considered it ironic that the 9/11 Commission later attributed the failure to prevent the attacks on September Eleventh to being "nobody connected the dots." And yet, the Commission was run in such a way that no one except Zelikow was able to connect those dots.[215] The FSC stated that this information about Philip Zelikow called "into question the integrity of this Commission's investigation."[216]

Chairman Thomas Kean stood up for Philip Zelikow when Kean was a guest on NBC's *Meet the Press* on April 4, 2004. Kean described Zelikow as "one of the best experts on terrorism in the whole area of intelligence in the entire country." He added that the executive director was "the best possible person we could have found for the job."[217]

Two days later, *Salon* ran a story that revealed that of Zelikow's many articles, "only one article focused on terrorism." *Salon* also pointed out that Zelikow had written nothing about al Qaeda.[218] In hindsight, Chairman Kean's claims about Zelikow's terrorism expertise seemed like a lot of bluster.

National Security Advisor Condoleezza Rice was cleared by the Bush administration and Philip Zelikow to testify before the 9/11 Commission on April 8, 2004. She told the commissioners that the Bush administration had no warnings of any specific terrorist threat prior to September Eleventh.

In response, Commissioner Richard Ben-Veniste asked Rice about a Presidential Daily Brief (PDB) from August 6, 2001. Rice reluctantly offered that the title of the PDB was "Bin Laden Determined to Strike in US." When one and a half of the eleven pages of the August 6 PDB was released, it warned of an al Qaeda attack on "federal buildings in New York."

The World Trade Center contained a number of federal buildings, including the US Customs Service, United States Department of Commerce, the Central Intelligence Agency, Department of Defense, and the United States Secret Service, among others. It would seem that in 2001, with its iconic status (by 2001 it had been depicted in nearly 500 films) and notable occupants, the World Trade Center had sufficient federal offices to warrant putting it high on a list of likely targets.

During the inquiry, Commission staff learned that historian (and Commission advisor) Ernest May and Philip Zelikow had constructed a detailed outline of the 9/11 Commission's final *Report*—an outline created prior to the 9/11 Commission's first public hearings on March 31, 2003. The outline remained a secret, kept from commissioners and staff teams alike, until it was leaked to several staff. The whole investigation was conducted in a way that sought information to fill in the points of the outline. Any narrative from among the 1,200-plus people the 9/11 Commission interviewed that didn't fit neatly into the outline was excluded from the final report.

The outline consisted of sixteen chapters. Shenon wrote that "Zelikow shared the document with Kean and Hamilton, who were impressed by their executive director's early diligence but worried that the outline would be seen as evidence that they—and Zelikow—had predetermined the report's outcome. It should be kept secret from the rest of the staff, they all decided."[219]

May said he and Zelikow determined that the outline must be "treated as if it were the most classified document the commission possessed." Zelikow created a confidential way to assign all documents related to "the outline. He labeled it 'Commission Sensitive,' putting those words at the top and bottom of each page." [220]

Many Commission staff were alarmed that the plot of the terrorist attacks was already described in Zelikow's outline. Shenon noted, "A few staffers began circulating a two-page parody of Zelikow's effort entitled 'The Warren Commission Report—Preemptive Outline.' The parody's authorship was never determined conclusively. The chapter headings included 'Single Bullet. We Haven't Seen the Evidence Yet. But Really. We're Sure.'"[221]

Did the outline establish in advance what the 9/11 Commission *Report* would conclude? For Bob McIlvaine, whose son Bobby died on 9/11, the existence of an outline for the official story before the first public hearings were even held was scandalous. He said, "that's monumental news. The outline of the investigation of my son's murder was out before the first day they started the investigation."[222]

For anyone who examines the "Commission Sensitive" Outline of the 9/11 Report and puts it beside the Contents pages of the published *9/11 Commission Report* for comparison, the influence quickly becomes clear. The Outline's point 1 is "The Foundation of an Islamic Army," resembling the *Report*'s Chapter 2 heading "The Foundations of the New Terrorism." The Outline's point 2, "Counterterrorism Evolves," was the Commission's Chapter 3 heading.

Subheadings of the published *Report* in Chapter 3 were almost all the same as the Outline's point 2 subheadings: "From the Old Terrorism to the New," "Adoption—or Non-Adoption in the Law Enforcement Community," "the Intelligence Community," and "the White House" were the same. "The First World Trade Center Bombing" had formerly been "The Case of WTC1."

The Outline's points 3-6 were all the same as the published *9/11 Report*'s Chapters 4-7, each just one chapter behind. Point 6.5 of the Outline, "The Summer of Threat," became the title of the *Report*'s Chapter 8. Other chapter headings, like "Heroism and Horror" and "Wartime" also found their way, unaltered, into the Contents pages of the *Report*.

In the end, at least thirty-five of the chapter headings and sub-headings in *The 9/11 Commission Report* were either identical or only slightly altered from the original Outline created by Philip Zelikow and Ernest May.[223]

Zelikow's Outline for *The 9/11 Commission Report* was briefly mentioned by Kean and Hamilton on pages 270-271 of their 2006 book, *Without Precedent*. The Chairman and Vice Chairman acknowledged "there was a suspicion among staff that Zelikow and May would attempt to draft the entire report, which was a point of some tension, particularly because the prospective outline was not circulated to the staff teams."[224]

While all the commissioners had to approve the final text of the Report, May recalled that "no language appeared anywhere in the final text unless Zelikow or I or both of us ... had accepted it."[225]

~ 6 ~

An Open Letter to former Mayor Giuliani from the Family Steering Committee, May 22, 2004

"To suggest that an investigation is synonymous with attacking each other is a deliberate misrepresentation of the goals and work of the Commission."
~ Family Steering Committee

When commissioners tried to ask tough questions about failures in leadership, it backfired. The hearings held in New York City on May 18-19, 2004 in particular were a low point for the Commission. It illustrated the limits of getting answers and following leads wherever they led.

Republican commissioner John Lehman told Thomas Von Essen, New York City Fire Commissioner, "I think the command and control and communications of this city's public service is a scandal ... not worthy of the Boy Scouts, let alone this great city." Lehman added that the communication between the city's Police and Fire Departments was "a clearly dysfunctional system."

Hotly denying the criticism, the Fire Commissioner shot back, "You make it sound like everything went wrong on Sept. 11. I think it's outrageous that you make a statement like that."[226]

Family Steering Committee member Monica Gabrielle remarked after the hearing, "It just seems like there was just a lot of non-answers." She lamented the stance of city officials, who asserted that on 9/11 "Everything was wonderful. Everything worked well. We had a plan in place." She asked, "So why did nearly 3,000 people die?"[227]

The next day, the press jumped all over the grilling of the September Eleventh FDNY Fire Commissioner and NYPD Police Commissioner Bernard Kerik.[228] The morning tabloids decried John Lehman's questioning of the pair. One newspaper headline simply read "Insult." Within ten days of the acrimony between Lehman, the NYPD and the FDNY, Lehman apologized to the 2001 New York Mayor, Rudy Giuliani. No more fingers were to be pointed.

When Mayor Giuliani, *Time*'s Person of the Year in 2001, was before the Commission on May 19, he was commended for his leadership.[229] "New York City … in a sense was blessed because it had you as leader. It had somebody who was a great, great leader to take charge of a terrible, terrible event," exclaimed 9/11 Commission Chairman Tom Kean.[230]

Giuliani told the 9/11 Commission that the NYPD and FDNY members who were involved with rescue operations had all heard the call to evacuate. In his opening remarks before the Commission, the mayor explained that despite the evacuation order these first responders demonstrated "willingness, the way I describe it, to stand their ground and not retreat."

Giuliani noted that the terrorists' objective to kill as many as twenty-five thousand people at the World Trade Center was thwarted by the first responders. Their "initial heroism" meant that they interpreted "an evacuation order the way a brave rescue worker would interpret an evacuation order, which is first get the civilians out, and then get yourself out,"[231] said the mayor.

Mayor Giuliani's assurances that first responders made a conscious decision to stay in the Twin Towers contrasted with statements from the first responders themselves. Fire Lt. Warren Smith of Ladder 9 described what he saw as he descended down the stairs in the North Tower: "There definitely were firefighters that we were picking up on the way down that had no knowledge" that the South Tower had collapsed. Smith added: "They were like, they didn't believe us ... Knowledge of the fact that the other building went down ... I don't think a lot of guys did."[232]

Continuing his testimony, Giuliani described what he had done on the morning of the attacks. At one moment he looked up at one of the towers and "saw a man hurling himself out of the 102nd, 103rd, 104th floor. ... I said to the Police Commissioner ... we're in uncharted territory, we've never gone through anything like this before, we're just going to have to do the best we can to keep everybody together, keep them focused."[233]

Giuliani told the commissioners that he was with FDNY Chief of Department Pete Ganci that morning. The Chief "pointed to a big flame that was shooting out of the North Tower," Giuliani recalled. And the mayor explained that when the chief pointed to the tower he took it to mean that they couldn't manage any rooftop evacuation by helicopter because it was "too dangerous" and the "helicopter would explode."[234]

On the afternoon of September Eleventh, Giuliani was interviewed on ABC. Recounting the events of the morning, Giuliani said that they were in their temporary headquarters across the street from the South Tower when they were told, about fifteen minutes before it fell, "that the World Trade Center was going to collapse ... And it did collapse before we could actually get out of the building. We were trapped in the building for ten to fifteen minutes."[235] The people who told him were in the Office of Emergency Management, which was under the mayor's control.

Giuliani told ABC that when he was warned the towers were going to collapse, he was with the Police Commissioner, Fire Commissioner, and the Director of Emergency Management. Neither the mayor, Police Commissioner, Fire Commissioner, or head of Emergency

Management alerted first responders of their expectations that the towers would collapse.

However, during his testimony before the 9/11 Commission Giuliani neglected to inform the Commission that he had been warned of the twin towers' collapse. Instead, he told the 9/11 commissioners that he and his emergency management team left WTC Building 7 because he was afraid that it would collapse, "we were in danger in the building, that the building could come down."[236]

Richard Ben-Veniste was the first commissioner to question Mayor Giuliani. He praised the mayor for his "leadership on that day (that) ... gave the rest of the nation, and indeed the world, an unvarnished view of the indomitable spirit and the humanity, of this great city, and for that I salute you." He went on to ask Mayor Giuliani about the radios the first responders had. The mayor explained the firefighters and police "all had a radio system that would have allowed them to communicate with each other."[237]

Commissioner James Thompson followed by commending Giuliani for his "extraordinary leadership" and described the terrorists as "versatile, smart, entrepreneurial, and they don't fight the same war twice as we sometimes do."

Commissioner Timothy Roemer commended the mayor for his "brave and courageous leadership on September the 11th." He raised the matter of the August 6 Presidential Daily Briefing (PDB), which had been a focus of debate when National Security Advisor Condoleezza Rice appeared before the Commission on April 8, 2004.

Roemer asked Giuliani to comment on this PDB which specifically mentioned that bin Laden was determined to strike the United States. In the PDB it mentioned both "New York City or the World Trade Center three times" and "the recent surveillance of federal buildings in New York City" prior to 9/11. Roemer wondered why the FBI and CIA weren't sharing more of this information with the Mayor and the Office of Emergency Management when the CIA director was saying their "hair was on fire."

Giuliani told Roemer it was "hypothetical" to guess what he might have done if he'd known what was in the August 6 PDB.[238]

Commissioner Slade Gorton asked Rudy Giuliani about the rescue efforts. The Mayor replied "I know one firefighter whose family explained this to me. He was in the North Tower. He was evacuating people. He was given an evacuation order. He told his men to go, sent them down, they got out. But he was with a person in a wheelchair, and an overweight person having a hard time getting down, so he stayed with them. So how did he interpret that evacuation order? He interpreted that evacuation order, 'I'll get all my men out, but I'm going to stay here and help these people out.' And the fact that so many of them interpreted it that way kept a much calmer situation and a much better evacuation."[239]

The contention was too much to stomach for September Eleventh family members who had lost first responder loved ones. They held up signs that read "lies" and "liar." Family Steering Committee member Sally Regenhard held up a sign that read "FICTION."[240] She hollered, "My son was not told to get out! He would've gotten out! My son was murdered, murdered because of your incompetence and radios that didn't work!" Rosaleen Tallon, whose brother Sean Tallon, a rookie firefighter, was killed on September Eleventh, shouted at Giuliani "talk about the radios."

Commission Chairman Thomas Kean told the audience, "you're simply wasting time … I understand your feelings. I also understand that this hearing has to continue in an orderly manner. I ask you to conduct yourselves that way."[241]

The audience took more than that to settle down. When Jamie Gorelick began to question Rudy Giuliani, a member of the audience interrupted with a demand to put one of them on the panel, which was met with applause by the others attending the public hearing. Chairman Kean again had to intervene to let the hearing continue.

When it was time for Vice Chairman Lee Hamilton to question Rudy Giuliani, he began by saying "Mayor, we're running about twenty-five to thirty minutes late because of the interest the commission has in your questions and your answers. You'll be glad to know I'll not ask any questions. I did feel, however, it important that I simply express to you my appreciation, not just for your leadership, you've heard that a lot this morning. But also because of the cooperation you've given this commission and the candor with which you've responded this morning. And in the previous interview. We're deeply appreciative of that. And we may very well want to ask you further questions as we finalize our report. As a Midwesterner I might say to you I've been impressed time and again with the pride you've expressed in New York City. And I admire that greatly."[242]

At this point, Lee Hamilton was interrupted by other audience members. who yelled "Talk about the radios!" One, a fireman who was there representing one of his fallen FDNY brethren, stood up and said, "They were not killed because he was a great leader. 3,000 people murdered does not mean leadership. It is a vacuum of leadership. Don't arrest the whistleblowers. No more softball questions. No more kissing ass. My brother's a fireman and I want to know why 300 firemen died. Let's ask the real questions. Is that unfair? And what about the bunker? You didn't ask him about the bunker, the Office Of Emergency Management bunker on fire … Remember this, your government funded and trained al Qaeda!"

As this fireman was escorted away by security, Mayor Giuliani got up from his chair and walked out of the hearing. A woman in the audience responded, "You know what? My brother was one of the firemen that was killed and I think the mayor did a great job, so sit down and shut up."[243] Chairman Kean told audience members "if you want to be disruptive you will be removed from this room."[244]

After Giuliani's testimony, Monica Gabrielle told CBS "The commission blocked any real inquiry by cloaking everything in heroism." She described herself as "frustrated" and condemned the panel. She concluded: "they made a huge faux pas in letting Rudy Giuliani polish his crown."[245]

Beverly Eckert said of the heckling, "The commission members don't press hard at all." She told the *New York Post*, "I'm glad there was that interruption, because that was a very important message, that tough questions aren't being asked."[246]

The next day Mayor Giuliani spoke on the CBS News Early Show. He said he had anticipated the families' response. "Their anger I understand, because they went through just terrible loss. But I think the anger is misplaced. The anger should not be at the people who tried very, very hard, did the best they could to try to save their loved ones. Their anger has to be directed at the people who attacked us. Mistakes were made and those mistakes should be focused on. But not from the point of view of this kind of hatred and anger and blame being placed on some of the people who made these decisions, who I think were making these decisions in good faith in a terrible, terrible situation."[247]

On May 22, 2004, Monica Gabrielle, Sally Regenhard, Beverly Eckert, and other members of the FSC wrote "An Open Letter to former Mayor Giuliani from the Family Steering Committee." In their letter, they stated: "At the 9/11 Public Hearings you announced that all the anger and blame should be focused on the 19 terrorists who piloted planes. You went on in your press conferences to state that you understood that the comments from the crowd were due to misplaced anger from the grieving process. We respectfully disagree with you on both accounts."

In their letter, the FSC articulated a consensus that held throughout the duration of the 9/11 Commission. They asserted: "It is true that on September 11th, nineteen terrorists were responsible for murdering nearly 3000 people. But the terrorists could not have succeeded if there had not been loopholes, inefficiency, and lack of collaboration, communication and coordination in our national security system. Something went terribly wrong which allowed the terrorists to launch a surprise attack here in America, using hijacked airplanes. All the factors, which contributed to the death of so many on September

11th, must be identified and corrected. Certainly, the terrorists are at the top of the list, but there is much more to this story and it cannot be swept under the rug, as if it does not exist."[248]

The FSC letter to Giuliani continued, "Your statement, 'Our enemy is not each other, but the terrorists who attacked us,' implies that asking questions about our government's knowledge, preparedness and response prior to and on 9/11 is somehow wrong. To suggest that an investigation is synonymous with attacking each other is a deliberate misrepresentation of the goals and work of the Commission whose mandate is to tell the full story and make recommendations for correcting the problems."

The FSC reminded Giuliani that the nation's leaders' first obligation was to protect its citizens. Without an honest accounting of "what went wrong," the FSC warned that unaltered security and emergency response plans would result in future successes for terrorists.[249]

The FSC stressed that the venting by families who lost loved ones was not misplaced. Instead, it was the result of frustration that important topics, like the non-functioning firefighter radios, were not being discussed.

Significant issues were left unaddressed while commissioners lavished praise on the Mayor during each of their five minutes of allotted time to ask questions.[250]

By April 2007, while he was running a campaign for United States President, Giuliani had been forced to limit his appearances in New York City due to the increasing protests of family members of 9/11 victims, particularly police, fire and other emergency workers.[251]

While the former mayor of the nation's largest city was widely lionized for his post-9/11 leadership —"America's mayor" was Oprah Winfrey's assessment—city firefighters and their families were renewing their attacks on him for his performance before and after the terrorist attack.

"If Rudolph Giuliani was running on anything but 9/11, I would not speak out," said Sally Regenhard, whose firefighter son was among the 343 FDNY members killed in the terrorist attack. "If he ran on cleaning up Times Square, getting rid of squeegee men, lowering crime—that's indisputable. But when he runs on 9/11, I want the American people to know he was part of the problem." Regenhard told the *Daily News* in April 2007, "The bitter truth is that Rudy Giuliani is building a path to the White House over the bodies of 343 firefighters."[252]

John Walsh, 48 and a firefighter for 21 of those years, had been an early supporter of Giuliani. But now he complained, "He's been riding our coattails since 9/11 like he did something. He did nothing. He showed up to funerals. So what? He's a self-promoter. I told my wife, 'Anything that ever happens, I don't want him at my funeral.'"[253]

25-year FDNY veteran and battalion chief, Robert Keys, said of people outside New York City, "I think they assume that we all love him. He wound up with this 'America's Mayor' image. Those of us who had to deal with him before and after 9/11 don't share that same sentiment." Referring to Guilani's conduct at the Ground Zero pile, Keys added, "he treated firemen like they were common criminals."

Deputy Chief Jim Riches, who lost his FDNY son on September Eleventh, objected to the mayor's decision to remove firefighters from Ground Zero just weeks after the attacks. "We were finding bodies the week before ... The bodies didn't disintegrate. He just wanted to scoop them up, dump them in a truck and get out of there. Meanwhile, I'm down there on my hands and knees looking for my son and other firemen."[254]

Giuliani also had his supporters. Retired firefighter Lee Ielpi, whose 29-year-old son Jonathan Ielpi died when the towers collapsed, said he thought Giuliani was "solid and stayed to the point. We have to keep a clear mind that the job at hand of the commission is to make suggestions so that the events of 9/11 will not happen again. I can't change the past." He also wrote "Firefighters have no greater friend and supporter than Rudy Giuliani."[255]

Retired FDNY Capt. John Vigiano, who lost two sons on 9/11,

praised him, saying, "Rudy Giuliani was a great mayor for New York City, before Sept. 11, on Sept. 11 and afterward. Because of his efforts on behalf of my family, I never have to worry about my daughters-in-law or my five grandchildren.[256]

On September 11, 2011, when the 9/11 Memorial was established, Rudolph Giuliani was named an honorary trustee.[257]

~ 7 ~

The Final Report

"The Commissioners have concluded that September 11, 2001 resulted from a "failure of imagination." Although accountability was not assigned to specific individuals, it is clear that one solution is to hire new people with better imaginations."
~ Family Steering Committee, July 26, 2004

In the spring of 2004, the 9/11 Commission continued to suffer from partisan politics. House Republican leaders attempted to remove Democrat Commissioner Jamie Gorelick from the Commission. As Gorelick was the only commissioner who had full access to view the Presidential Daily Briefings (PDBs), the Family Steering Committee questioned the motives of the Republican house leadership. Gorelick's removal would leave the 9/11 Commission incapable of addressing Executive Branch knowledge of terrorist activities, and what actions were taken in response to the information contained in the PDBs President Bush received in 2001.

The FSC issued a statement to the 9/11 Commission and political leadership to stress the need for non-partisan cooperation. They underscored that the "Commission's work and its Final Report are of the utmost importance. We believe that the Commission's Final Report will serve as an excellent way to honor the 3,000 lives lost on 9/11, by proving that we can admit to, examine, and learn from our mistakes and failures of the past." [258] The FSC was still hopeful, despite all the stonewalling, denied access, and delayed subpoenas, that a helpful report would move America and its defense against terrorist attacks forward.

On May 11, 2004, Family Steering Committee members Kristen Breitweiser, Mindy Kleinberg, Patty Casazza, and Lorie Van Auken penned an op-ed in the *Wall Street Journal* titled "What Can A Citizen Do?" The article detailed the importance behind the struggle of receiving answers to vital questions about what went so terribly wrong on September 11, 2001.

The Jersey widows questioned how 19 hijackers could have been successful in attacking the World Trade Center and the Pentagon, given the "billions spent each year on defense and intelligence." Knowing what protocols were supposed to be in place to defend America's domestic airspace, these FSC members were puzzled why the "tragedy of 9/11 was not averted."[259] They cited numerous problems with the CIA, NSA, and FBI, and the lack of initiative on the part of agents, supervisors, Congress, the Executive Branch, and the media.

A month prior, the 9/11 Commission had heard testimony from Condoleezza Rice, who claimed that no one could have imagined planes crashing into buildings. The Jersey Girls stated, "our research revealed numerous indicators throughout our intelligence history illustrated the use, or intended use of planes as missiles. We found field reports, case files and studies, eye witness testimony, intelligence community threat matrices, and Department of Defense mock drills all addressing the 'planes as missiles' idea." In fact, a hijack scenario run on September 9, 2001 involved terrorists hijacking a plane to New York City.[260]

On August 31, 2001, the Department of Transportation conducted an exercise which an administrator described: "Ironically ... 12 days prior to the incident on September 11th, we were going through a tabletop exercise ... Part of the scenario, interestingly enough, involved a ... hijacked plane and someone calling on a cell phone, among other aspects of the scenario that were very strange when twelve days later, as you know, we had the actual event."[261]

Earlier that year, during the January-May 2001 trials of the 1998 bombings of United States Embassies in Nairobi and Dar es Salaam, it was revealed there was an interest in using suicide bombers to fly planes into the World Trade Center and the Pentagon. In 2004 *USA Today* ran an article revealing "NORAD Had Drills of Jets as Weapons." In the drills "one of the imagined targets was the World Trade Center."[262]

FSC members pointed out to the 9/11 Commission that Secretary Rice's contention that "no one could have predicted that planes could be used as missiles" was not true.

"Democracy cannot prosper on blind-faith. To work effectively, democracy's foundation—the people, must be well informed. And, in order to be more informed, more responsive, and more prepared for the challenges ahead, we must continue to ask questions to our leaders; that is our duty as responsible citizens." They argued for accountability and personal responsibility on the part of those entrusted to keep citizens safe.[263]

FSC members were perplexed during the open hearings of the 9/11 Commission. Lorie Van Auken reflected, "We went to every open hearing hoping the commissioners would ask tough questions. I can recall only a few instances during the 12 public hearings that we were actually pleased with the vigor of the questioning."[264]

Van Auken recalls that as witnesses appeared before the 9/11 Commission, commissioners were given brief allotments of time to interview witnesses. Yet, they choose to devote much of their time to friendly banter back and forth, camaraderie. "every time they spent five minutes saying how great the person was, their hairdo ... they were really taking time away from the point of the entire investigation ..."[265]

In addition, the Commission's executive director, Philip Zelikow, told the FSC "not to send [their] questions directly to the Commissioners." [266] Van Auken noticed that Zelikow scrubbed information that emerged in interviews if it didn't conform to the outline for the 9/11 Commission *Report* he created in March 2003 with Ernest May. She observed, "If information came up during an interview that didn't fit with what he had decided the storyline would be, he would not allow the new information to be investigated." [267]

Mindy Kleinberg said of meetings held by the 9/11 Commission in New York City, "The hearings in New York were such an extreme disappointment. No real questions were addressed."

The FSC issued a formal statement to the 9/11 Commission before the June 16–17 open hearings in 2004 with staff from NORAD, the FAA, and United States Strategic Command. They presented the commissioners with fifty-six categories of questions to direct their discussions.[268] But the questions weren't posed.

In reference to the upcoming hearings, which were to be held in Washington, DC, Mindy Kleinberg said, "People won't travel four hours to be frustrated and disappointed again." Commission Chairman Thomas Kean and Vice Chairman Lee Hamilton conceded the point. In their account of the inside story of the 9/11 Commission, *Without Precedent*, they wrote, "Those words rang true. We had less of a turnout at our final hearing than we had hoped. Several buses that had been chartered to bring family members down from the New York area were cancelled because people did not want to make the trip."[269]

9/11 Commissioner Tim Roemer had been a member of the earlier 9/11 Joint Inquiry. He was disturbed by the inconsistencies in the testimonies received on June 16–17 from the generals and the Secretary of Defense regarding what the Pentagon was doing on September Eleventh. Roemer recalls, "panel members so distrusted testimony from Pentagon officials that they referred their concerns to the Pentagon's inspector general … We were extremely frustrated with the false statements we were getting."

He and others on the 9/11 Commission wanted the Department of Justice to launch a criminal investigation into the Pentagon regarding the events of 9/11.[270] Some staff members and commissioners thought that emails and other evidence provided enough probable cause to believe that military and aviation officials violated the law by making false statements to Congress and to the Commission. "We to this day don't know why NORAD told us what they told us. It was just so far from the truth. … It's one of those loose ends that never got tied," Thomas Kean said later.[271]

On July 20, 2004, before *The 9/11 Commission Report* was published, the Family Steering Committee issued a formal statement to the Commission. They highlighted that from the very start the FSC had sought to cultivate a relationship by sharing with the Commission "our documented research, along with the questions it generated, and by communicating our concerns about the progress of the investigation." The FSC appreciated having staff liaise with them to ensure constant communication with the commissioners and staff. Yet they were underwhelmed by the final outcome. "While we believe that our concerns were acknowledged, we had also hoped that more of our questions and those of the American public would be fully addressed during the public hearings, or at the very least, discussed in the prepared staff statements. Yet today, many of our collective questions remain unanswered … These questions must be comprehensively addressed and clearly answered by the Commission in the final report."[272]

On July 22, 2004, around twenty Sept. 11 family members were invited to a private briefing with the 9/11 commissioners. During the briefing, they released to the families the *Final Report of the National Commission on Terrorist Attacks Upon the United States*. A team of reporters stood outside the briefing room, eager to get sound bites from the Sept. 11 families about their reaction to the *Report*.

In her book, *Wake-Up Call*, Kristen Breitweiser describes the scene. Once they were given their copies of *The 9/11 Commission Report*, many of the 9/11 family members jumped up to get the commissioners to sign their copies. Breitweiser remained in her chair. She flipped through pages in search of some nugget of information that suggested the attacks could have been prevented if vital information had been shared. On page 502 she found footnote 44. She showed it to Patty Casazza, Mindy Kleinberg, and Lorie Van Auken. The commissioners noticed the commotion in the front row and wondered what was up.

When the Jersey Girls walked into a scrum with the press, Kristen Breitweiser told the reporters that Footnote 44 "proved that the CIA deliberately withheld information from the FBI about two of the terrorists who would go on to become 9/11 hijackers." The two terrorists were Nawaf al-Hazmi and Khalid al-Mihdhar. On January 5, 2000, an FBI agent assigned to CIA Alec Station wrote a cable to notify the FBI that Khalid al-Mihdhar, one of the men who would later hijack an American Airlines flight on September 11, 2001, had a US Visa.

Under orders from the station chief, Tom Wilshire, the cable was blocked from within the CIA by Michael Anne Casey. Later that day, Casey sent out a false cable saying that the FBI had been notified. For 18 months the CIA withheld information from the FBI and the State Department about an al Qaeda sleeper cell in San Diego. Footnote 44 proved that "the CIA's failure to share information with the FBI was not a mistake or an oversight. It was done on purpose. And the CIA tried to cover up their malfeasance."[273]

As Breitweiser read the *Report*, she noticed it was disjointed, a print version of the shaky, hand-held camera techniques in independent cinema that create a sense of jerkiness and visual imbalance for the viewer. She observed "the book is choppy and disconnected. It is confusing, as the story line jumps back and forth through facts and history, making it very hard to keep track of the mounting failures that keep adding up."[274]

Later that day, with Kean and Hamilton at his side, President Bush told the press, "I want to thank these two gentlemen for serving their country so well and so admirably. They've done a really good job of learning about our country, learning about what went wrong prior to September 11th, and making very solid, sound recommendations about how to move forward."[275]

During his time as Chairman of the 9/11 Commission, Thomas Kean met a number of times with White House Chief of Staff Andrew Card and National Security Advisor Condoleezza Rice. Kean recalls that they wanted him to "stand up," not for the truth but to "stand up for the president." They wanted Kean to show "courage" by not following the trail of evidence about 9/11 wherever it might lead, but to prevent a "runaway commission" from concluding that Bush and his White House bore some responsibility for 9/11.[276] The published *Report* avoided any such suggestion. The reason for the attacks was due simply to a failure of imagination.

Kean and Hamilton framed the work of the Commission stating, "We were investigating a national catastrophe, not a White House transgression; this was 9/11, not Watergate."[277] For the co-chairmen it was "heinous" to suggest that anyone in government had fallen down on the job, had foreknowledge of the attacks, or might be complicit in the attacks. Consequently, any problematic documents or red flags that were raised by witnesses were avoided. The scope of inquiry began with absolute certainty regarding who was responsible. They summarized, "We started with teams looking at al Qaeda; intelligence; counterterrorism policy; terrorist financing ... The first team split into two, with one assessing al Qaeda and the other focused specifically on the 9/11 plot."[278]

As a result, when they posed the question "Who was the enemy who had perpetrated this attack?" it was not to seek information, as the questioners were already confident they knew the answer.[279] The unmentioned premise in the question drove the direction of the inquiry.

They professed an impartial "nonpartisan" approach to the investigation, and boasted their independence. Their mission was to "not miss the forest for the trees in the 9/11 story by looking solely for individuals to blame."[280]

Kean and Hamilton commented: "It is interesting that the 9/11 Commission was held in equal derision by [the] … far right, because we dared to ask questions about the war on terror and failed to draw a straight line from 9/11 to this or that Clinton administration policy; and on the far left, because we did not endorse heinous conspiracy theories assigning culpability for 9/11 to the Bush administration."[281]

Commission staffer Timothy Naftali wrote a book in 2005 titled *Blind Spot*. In it he stated, "after years of studying the intelligence and security world, I have come to believe less in the efficiency of conspiracies than I do in the inefficiency of government."[282] Naftali believed that no plot for nefarious purposes could be hatched within government. Conversely, any alleged foreign conspiracy was to be accepted on its face.

The 9/11 Commission paid Naftali to write *Blind Spot*. Naftali is at least the intellectual author of the 9/11 Commission's *Report* in its primary conclusion that the attack was a failure of intelligence and imagination: that was the thesis of *Blind Spot*.

On July 26, the FSC issued another formal statement to the 9/11 Commission, beginning with extending "its heartfelt gratitude to the 9/11 Commissioners and staff for their tireless work in producing the Final Report." They also congratulated the commissioners for directing the attention of Americans with the single focus of "making this nation less vulnerable to terrorists."

At the same time, the FSC reminded the commissioners "we have not yet completed our review and analysis of the report and its footnotes." The commissioners could count on various FSC members to keep holding their feet to the fire. They would remain vigilant in urging the passage of the *Report's* recommendations, comment on the *Report* itself and other emerging issues. The FSC also suggested explaining away the attacks of September 11 as a "failure of imagination" was another way of evading accountability. The FSC suggested to the

Bush administration and members of Congress it would be fitting to "honor the memory of our loved ones who perished on 9/11 to implement the Commission's recommendations."[283]

When the 9/11 Commission began its investigation, they saw it as their mandate "to provide the fullest possible account of the events surrounding 9/11."[284] However, when the Commission wrapped up their investigation and published their findings, they failed to answer or address seventy percent of the questions the Family Steering Committee posed.[285] Only nine percent of the questions were answered satisfactorily. Another twenty-one percent of the questions were touched upon.

In 2006, 9/11 Commission Vice Chairman Lee Hamilton was interviewed by the CBC. He was asked to respond to the charge that the 9/11 Commission failed to sufficiently address the 9/11 families' questions. Hamilton offered, "you can't answer every question when you conduct an investigation."[286]

The 567-page *9/11 Commission Report* received many rave reviews in the media after it was released.

Slate Magazine was effusive in its praise for the "exemplary" *Report*, approving of "its literary style and its allegiance to the truth."[287] *Slate* pointed to the care given to its detailed narrative and emotive accounts. *Slate* gave readers a synopsis of the *Report*'s thesis: "The core of the book backs up from the events of 9/11 and describes two parallel stories: the resolve and plans of Islamic fundamentalists to attack the United States, and the US government's well-intentioned but disorganized and ultimately doomed attempts to assess and cope with the threat."[288]

The *New Republic* commended the *Report* as a fine example of the fusion of "urgency" and "truth." The only fault that Ernest R. May, a senior advisor with the 9/11 Commission and contributor to its outline, found with the *Report* was the commissioners' "reluctance ever to challenge the CIA's walling off Al Qaeda detainees." As a result, Ernest R. May conceded, "we never had full confidence in the interrogation reports as historical sources."[289]

Time lauded the Commission for having "produced one of the most riveting, disturbing and revealing accounts of crime, espionage and the inner workings of government ever written," and for its thoroughness in scouring through 2.5 million documents.[290]

The New York Times called the *Report* "an uncommonly lucid, even riveting, narrative" and an "improbable literary triumph." However, the article cautioned that the *Report* pointed to something banal: "that it is almost impossible to take effective action to prevent something that hasn't occurred previously." It contended what Condoleezza Rice had basically testified before the 9/11 Commission: that it was unthinkable that al Qaeda would attack America by "infiltrating operatives into this country to learn to fly commercial aircraft and then crash such aircraft into buildings." [291] The article concluded that despite all the practical recommendations in the Commission's *Report*, there was likely little that could be done to prevent a future terrorist attack.

W.W.Norton & Company printed 600,000 copies of the *Report* in conjunction with its release. Another 500,000 copies were printed a week later to keep up with demand. By the end of March 2005, there were over two million copies of the *Report* sold, while an additional 6.9 million copies had been downloaded from the 9/11 Commission's website.[292] The 9/11 Commission's *Report* topped the Bestseller lists.

In addition to the praise the 9/11 Commission *Report* was receiving, which looked good for the Bush Administration, there were others who cited the *Report* in order to take the White House to task for its actions and inactions. *The Nation* magazine was not especially critical of the *Report*, but it did view its findings as bad news for President Bush, citing "the Bush administration's reaction to the threat reports of 2001," and "the alliance (or lack thereof) between al Qaeda and Iraq." The article recommended all the voters in the swing states read the *Report* before the November 2004 election.[293]

In his book, *The Greatest Story Ever Told: The Decline and Fall of Truth*, Frank Rich singled out the fake "yellowcake in Niger" and "mobile biological and chemical weapons labs" as two stories that led the US into a preemptive war against Iraq. Rich noted that 51 percent of Americans in 2003 believed that Iraqis were personally involved in 9/11. Not only were the "yellowcake" documents cited in Bush's State of the Union speech fake, Rich revealed that the White House then lied about those lies: *The 9/11 Report* revealed that the administration lied about a claim that Mohammed Atta met with a senior Iraqi official in Prague—and then lied about that lie.[294]

Harper's Magazine journalist, Benjamin DeMott, penned the lead story for the October 2004 issue titled "Whitewash as Public Service: How the 9/11 Commission Report Defrauds the Nation." After spending four days reading through the *Report*, DeMott concluded "The plain, sad reality … is that The 9/11 Commission Report, despite the vast quantity of labor behind it, is a cheat and a fraud. It stands as a series of evasive maneuvers that infantilize the audience, transform candor into iniquity, and conceal realities that demand immediate inspection and confrontation."[295]

The 9/11 Commission had abundant evidence brought before it that President George W. Bush had known that there were terrorists in the USA and there were specific plans to attack the nation. However, what Bush told the 9/11 Commission was that "nobody told me." Benjamin DeMott notes that the 9/11 Commission did backflips all the way through their *Report* to avoid calling the president a liar. The 9/11 Commission knew the president had been told on multiple occasions of imminent terrorist threats.

DeMott concluded that the Commission knew "that before 9/11, and in the frantic days afterward, departmental secretaries and undersecretaries were pressing—inexplicably but unrelentingly—for the bombing of Iraq, in meetings with, and in briefings written for, the president. And it knows that Bush himself was seeking justification, from his counterterrorism chief, for an attack on Saddam."

In seeking to write a *Report* where there was no one to blame for the monumental failure of defending the nation, the Commission succeeded in dangerously reenergizing "a national relish for fantasy," DeMott lamented. Instead of learning necessary lessons and distinguishing falsehood from truth, the *Report* provided entertainment. It scattered comments by officials throughout "like Hansel and Gretel breadcrumbs" that only served to leave its readers lost in the woods.[296]

FSC member Patty Casazza protested, "The Commission failed in its duty to learn all the lessons of 9/11 and squandered the opportunity to protect our country, our children, from terrorist harm."[297]

On January 30, 2008, MSNBC's reporters, Robert Windrem and Victor Limjoco, called out the 9/11 Commission for having "relied on more than 100 CIA interrogation reports. Its Executive Director Philip Zelikow admits that 'quite a bit, if not most' of its information on the 9/11 conspiracy 'did come from the interrogations.'"[298]

MSNBC found that 441 out of over 1,700 endnotes depended on torture of detainees under interrogation. MSNBC reported that much of *The 9/11 Commission Report* "about the planning and execution of the terror attacks on New York and Washington was derived from the interrogations of high-ranking al-Qaeda operatives. Each had been subjected to 'enhanced interrogation techniques.' Some were even subjected to waterboarding."

MSNBC said that most of the endnotes that cited detainee interrogations were from the Commission's "most critical chapters:" five, six, and seven. These were the chapters where *The 9/11 Commission Report* created its narrative about the plot to hijack the planes and attack the World Trade Center and the Pentagon on September Eleventh.[299]

MSNBC's report was concerned about the 9/11 Commission constructing a narrative that used tortured confessions to hold it together. One detainee was tortured "eight hours at a time, tying him tightly in stressful positions in a small chair until his hands feet and mind went numb. They retied him in a chair every hour, tightening the bonds on his hands and feet each time so that it was more painful.

He was often hooded and had difficulty breathing. They also beat him repeatedly, slapping him in the face, and deprived him of sleep." [300] In such circumstances, detainees agree with whatever statements of confession are required of them to stop the torture.

During the airing of the program, "9/11 Commission Controversy," MSNBC reporters interviewed Karen Greenberg, the director of the Center for Law and Security at New York University's School of Law. Greenberg said the revelations about *The 9/11 Commission Report* were disturbing. "It calls into question how we were willing to use these interrogations to construct the narrative."[301] The "9/11 Commission Controversy" news report on MSNBC gave viewers a reason to be skeptical of their government's account.

Although MSNBC had been harshly critical of *The 9/11 Commission Report* in 2008, five years later the network appeared to have forgotten its own investigative report. On April 24, 2013, MSNBC host Rachel Maddow mocked those who questioned the story of record regarding the attacks in a 13-minute commentary. She referred to *The 9/11 Commission Report* as the "definitive, official report." She told viewers, "the 9/11 conspiracies have not gone away because they are too ideologically, and I think emotionally, satisfying to the people who espouse them. They're too satisfying to let the fact that they have been thoroughly refuted get in the way of continuing to enjoy the way that conspiracy makes you feel."[302]

However, this was just Rachel Maddow's speculation on the motivations of anyone who questioned the official report. She might have read MSNBC's own reports by Robert Windrem and Victor Limjoco in 2008 to learn why her own network colleagues had questioned the official *Report*.

~ 8 ~

The 9/11 Commission's Recommendations

*"The office of the President of the United States is the most
important job in the world. Among its responsibilities, one takes
precedence over all others — protecting the American people."*
~ Family Steering Committee, October 20, 2004

The *9/11 Commission Report* offered 41 recommendations to confront
terrorism and make America safe from future terrorist attacks.
There were several categories of recommendations, including
terrorist sanctuaries, addressing the roots of terrorism, human rights
and civil liberties, weapons of mass destruction, terrorist financing
and travel, border and transportation security, allocating resources,
reorganizing the intelligence community, threat and risk assessment,
Congressional oversight, security clearances, intelligence budgets,
and information sharing.

The Family Steering Committee issued 17 formal statements to the
9/11 Commission concerning the progress of the implementation of
those recommendations. Many of these statements were also directed
at members of Congress, President Bush, Henry Kissinger, and the
CIA. In their formal statement on July 26, 2004, the FSC warned

them, "We intend to hold any elected official publicly accountable for any obstruction or opposition to the implementation of these recommendations. We will maintain a log on our website that will track the course of this legislation. We will in effect conduct our own oversight—'the people's oversight.' And we will actively lobby Congress and the White House until these important recommendations are in place."[303]

The United States House of Representatives created a Committee to Review 9/11 Commission Recommendations. It held its first hearings on August 3, 2004. Testifying before the committee were several members of the FSC.

In her testimony, Beverly Eckert spoke of how many American citizens "lost faith" in their government and its commitment to protect its citizens after the attacks. She urged: "Help us make these recommendations happen … Are you willing to implement reforms, before this year is ended, and thereby restore our nation's faith in its government?"[304]

When FSC member Robin Wiener spoke, she described it as "an honor" to be asked to testify at the hearings. She said that out of the tragedy of the attacks on September Eleventh emerged a united America. But that unity had dissipated "as response to the tragedy became political. Even the families were, at times, drawn into debates that had more to do with politics."

Wiener posited that the American spirit that "drives us to seek the truth" was evident in the sales of the bestselling *9/11 Commission Report*. She reminded the members of Congress that "unity and truth are very important." She urged the elected body to ensure that "the 9/11 Commission be kept alive" so that its recommendations could be properly implemented.[305]

As the 9/11 Commission's *Report* became a runaway bestseller, 9/11 family members began to read its contents and take exception to some of the conclusions it reached.

Speaking at the August 3 hearings, Sally Regenhard expressed her disquiet about one section in the *Report*. It related "to the evacuation orders of the North Tower on pages 322-323 ... and the corresponding endnote numbers 209. It is alleged that many of the firefighters in the North Tower heard the message to evacuate but chose to remain in the building prior to its collapse. ... I take specific exception to the section in the Commission Report which states: 'In view of these considerations, we conclude that the technical failure of the FDNY radios, while a contributing factor was not the primary cause of the many firefighter fatalities in the North Tower.'"

Regenhard reviewed with other experts the documentation provided in the *Report* and found it very weak. Reading from the *Report*, she quoted examples of flimsy arguments such as "it is very possible that at least some of these firefighters did hear the evacuation order" and the contention that firefighters were "likely to have known to evacuate." She described the statements as lacking foundation.

"Stating that the firefighters refused to evacuate the building (for whatever reason) and disobeyed such an important order simply cannot be confirmed and is a disservice to their memory. ... My son earned these medals for obeying orders as a Recon Marine Sergeant, during his five years of distinguished service in the USMC before joining the Fire Department. When a Marine receives an order, he follows it! If told by a superior officer to evacuate the World Trade Center on 9/11, he and others would have done so. If only their radio would have worked. All of those predominantly young firefighters lost at the WTC on 9/11 (with rare exception) would have chosen life—if only given the chance."[306]

On August 17, 2004, a number of FSC members were invited to speak before the US Senate Governmental Affairs Committee Hearing. Mary Fetchet said, "The Commission may not have answered all our questions, but its report does offer a much-needed overall strategy to develop a comprehensive foundation for creating a safer America."

In making this distinction, Mary Fetchet was advocating a pragmatic approach to what could be done now. The 9/11 Commission may not have addressed seventy percent of the Family Steering Committee questions, but what was important now was to pass the recommendations issued by the *Report*. She told the senators about her son Brad, who was directed by Port Authority officials to remain in the South Tower building. This kind of decision-making cost Bradley Fetchet his life, and was an example of what the recommendations could change in the future.

Mary Fetchet stated, "As a Mother, it didn't make sense to me why they were directed to remain in a 110-story building after the high rise building next door had been hit by a plane; had a gaping hole in its side and was engulfed in flames."[307]

At the hearing, Fetchet recounted some of the failures that made the attacks on September Eleventh possible: intelligence agencies declining to share information with other agencies; NORAD and the FAA failing to observe protocols on the day of the attacks; and the refusal to act on a report by Minneapolis FBI agent Coleen Rowley identifying terrorists.

Agent Rowley had been so frustrated by the sabotage of her efforts to pass on urgent information of terrorist activity that she wrote "jokes were actually made that the key FBI HQ personnel had to be spies or moles like Robert Hanssen who were actually working for Osama Bin Laden to have so undercut Minneapolis' effort."[308] Rowley had also complained that when she and fellow Minneapolis FBI agents reached out to the CIA for help, they were admonished by FBI superiors in Washington.

Now, almost three years after the attacks, the nation was placed under a heightened national terrorist alert. Fetchet commented, "We all recognize that we have experienced another Pearl Harbor now known as September 11th." She warned the senators, "Our enemies are preparing to strike us now and the longer we wait to move decisively, the greater advantages and opportunities they have to harm us." She also lamented, "Americans have lost faith in our government and its ability to protect us."[309] She told those assembled that the nation was sadly unprepared for a terrorist attack, even though it had been forewarned.

Kristen Breitweiser also spoke before the same committee—but only after she was vetted. Breitweiser recounted how, before she was allowed to speak to the committee, she had to speak to two senators in person, respond to their questions and endure their "candid warnings about turning their hearings into a 'political circus.'" Then she had to meet Senate committee staff, who wanted an assurance that Breitweiser would not make any unfavorable remarks against the president in her testimony.[310]

In her testimony, Breitweiser catalogued the deficiencies in the system that put Americans at risk of another terrorist attack. Public transportation systems, in particular, were an area of concern. In her memoir *Wake-Up Call*, she would elaborate that most of the cargo on commercial flights does not get tested. Breitweiser pointed out that it was ridiculous for passengers to go through extensive security and screening of their luggage, while cargo from businesses shipping items wasn't checked for bombs.[311]

Breitweiser assessed the intervening years and found that the danger terrorists posed remained. She told the Senators: "Three years post-9/11, al Qaeda has metastasized rapidly despite losing its sanctuary in Afghanistan. The attacks that have taken place in Indonesia, Thailand, and the Philippines illustrate the fact that the threat of terrorism in the US could be greater than it was in 2001 ... prior to 9/11 we had a clear and present danger presented by al-Qaeda that was clearly not fully appreciated." She noted intelligence agencies were slow to respond to the real threat al Qaeda presented.

Breitweiser urged the senators to create a position of a National Intelligence Director to coordinate all intelligence information gleaned from the many agencies. She pointed out the lack of checks in border security and proper vetting of US visa applications contributed to the success of the attacks on September Eleventh. The hijackers' visa applications variously contained false, incomplete, or inaccurate information that would have excluded their entry into America if the agents responsible had been alert.

Breitweiser underscored that the intelligence failures that led to the attacks on September Eleventh were continuing to steer the nation in the wrong direction. As an example, she cited "the faulty intelligence that provided the basis for the war in Iraq." She also detailed the many deficiencies in airline security. Acknowledging the sacrifices being made by those in the United States military overseas, she concluded by saying, "We have taken our unspeakable pain and made some good out of it by fighting for the creation of the 9/11 Commission. We are now urging you to act upon the Commission's recommendations."[312]

Henry Kissinger, who had to refuse the position of Chairman for the 9/11 Commission on grounds of conflict of interest, made a statement to the United States Senate on September 21, 2004 titled "Guiding Principles For Intelligence Reform." The statement was signed by a number of eminent persons, who all cautioned "racing to implement reforms."

Many of the signees were closely involved in the events surrounding the 9/11 attacks. One of those included former Oklahoma Senator David Boren, who became president of the University of Oklahoma in 1994. The university happened to house the Airman Flight School, where six of the nineteen hijackers had trained prior to 9/11.[313]

Boren was among the first to tell the media that Osama bin Laden was responsible for the attacks. Boren told shell-shocked viewers in an interview with PBS on September Eleventh, "I think you have to have bin Laden on the suspect list. You probably have some nation states that ought to be on the suspect list as well, Iraq, for example."[314]

Another signee was former CIA Director and future Secretary of Defense Robert Gates and former Secretary of Defense Frank Carlucci.

On September Eleventh, Carlucci was chairman of the private-equity investment firm, The Carlyle Group. A brother of Osama bin

Laden, Shafig bin Laden, was attending the Carlyle Group's annual investor conference the morning of the attacks; the bin Ladens had invested two million in the Carlyle Group.[315]

One of the other signees was former Deputy Secretary of Defense John Hamre. It was under Hamre's watch that NORAD ran an exercise named Vigilant Virgo 99-1 in 1998. The exercise had injected simulated missiles into NORAD's radar systems. The exercise was repeated on September Eleventh, putting false blips on radar screens that confused FAA and NORAD radar operators during the multiple hijackings.[316]

Kissinger, Boren, Carlucci, Hamre, Gates, and other signees of the statement argued that intelligence reform was "too complex" to revise with speed. Instead of harmonizing data gathering, Kissinger and others argued that "the best analysis emerges from a competitive environment." They asserted that the fall 2004 election campaign was a poor time to make decisions about reforming the intelligence community. Consequently, they recommended that Congress "return to this issue early next year ... to address these issues more comprehensively."[317]

In response, the FSC issued a statement two days later. They wrote, "we respectfully disagree with Dr. Kissinger's campaign to slow the process of creating a National Intelligence Director." The FSC pointed out that before the attacks of September Eleventh, the United States Congress had debated thirty-eight separate bills to reform the nation's Intelligence community. Sadly, not one of these bills had been passed into law.[318]

As the weeks dragged on, the United States Senate and House of Representatives found themselves getting into turf battles; they ended up adding on unrelated provisions that were sticking points for various lawmakers.

On October 18, the FSC wrote an open letter to the members of Senate and Congress tasked with amending their versions of 9/11 reform legislation. They urged the lawmakers to present a bill to both houses that would enact the key reforms recommended in *The 9/11*

Commission Report. They also pointed out that this was President George W. Bush's wish.[319]

In the following week, the FSC were "deeply disturbed" to learn that the CIA Inspector General's Report post-9/11 had not been released, even though it was conducted in 2002. The FSC urged the CIA to release their report so that lawmakers could address deficiencies and hold the agency accountable. They didn't want the agency to withhold information to shield errant CIA staff who may have failed in their duties to protect Americans from terrorists.[320]

That same day, October 20, 2004, the FSC wrote an open letter to President George W. Bush, reminding him that he had stated that he wanted something done "as soon as possible." Congress was now "on the verge of failing to reach consensus" on the legislation that would address the lapses in intelligence. They reminded President Bush his chief responsibility was "protecting the American people."[321]

The stonewalling of House Republicans prompted the FSC to issue a statement on October 21, 2004. They expressed extreme concern with the slow pace in reaching consensus between both houses in the nation's Capitol. They called out a faction of House Republicans for "thwarting the process" and derailing the possibility of much-needed intelligence reform. The FSC commented "we saw this same pattern when there was resistance to the creation of the 9/11 Commission, to funding for the Commission, and to the Commission's extension."

The 9/11 Commission Bill Conference continued being conducted behind closed doors. The FSC demanded that the process be open to the public so that Americans could "see who is holding up action on this critically important legislation." The FSC supported the wording in the Senate legislation, and urged Congress to align their legislation.[322]

But the House-Senate conference over the 9/11 Commission bill had stalled, and the White House had remained silent on this development for almost a week. On October 22 the FSC released another statement demanding that President Bush deal with the "obstructionists" among the House Republicans who had engaged in "back-room maneuvering and ... refused to schedule public hearings."

The FSC challenged President Bush to show that he was deserving of re-election. It was now time for the president to confront the maverick group within his party and ensure the passage of the 9/11 Commission's recommendations. They concluded by saying, "The American people entrusted the President with the responsibility to protect us and NOW is the time for him to show that he has earned that trust."[323]

On October 25 the FSC felt compelled to sound an alarm that "The same administration that failed to protect us on 9/11 is failing us again."[324] Senate and Congress had failed to agree on compatible wording for their legislation. The FSC called out specific elected officials as responsible for the failure, most notably President Bush for permitting members of the Republican party to "derail the legislative process."[325]

During this time, a number of FSC members were actively campaigning for Democratic candidate Senator John Kerry (D-MA) for president. While the White House and House Republicans were being obstreperous and slow-walking discussions about legislative reform, John Kerry told the press in late August 2004 that if he became president, he would act to implement all the recommendations of the 9/11 Commission. Kerry's endorsement was viewed by Breitweiser and others as a political move.

However, the tone at the Republican National Convention at Madison Square Garden from August 30 to September 2, 2004 scared her: in particular, the speeches by senators John McCain and Zell Miller. After watching their speeches, she "realized that the Republicans believed the only way to be safer post-9/11 was to blow up the rest of the world."[326]

On September 5, 2004, Kristen Breitweiser called Mindy Kleinberg, Lorie Van Auken, and Patty Casazza to let them know she had decided to come out in support of John Kerry's campaign for president.

She said, "I know you guys are going to be really upset with me for changing my mind, but the only way we are going to get these recommendations acted upon is with a new president."

After hearing her reasoning, Lorie Van Auken, Patty Casazza, and Mindy Kleinberg agreed to also campaign for Kerry.[327] When Kristen Breitweiser told the Family Steering Committee that she and the other three "Jersey Girls" were going to campaign for Kerry, numbers of people on the committee were furious.

From the start, FSC members had worked for a non-partisan steering committee and an independent Commission. Breitweiser understood the anger in the room since numbers of FSC members were worried their recommendations would be caught in the crossfire of partisan politics.[328] Explaining her decision, Breitweiser maintained that after appearing before the Senate Governmental Affairs Committee on August 17, the vetting process she had to undergo to testify, and what she was hearing about the views from the White House, she believed a new administration was the only way forward. "I knew that we needed a new president who understood that being safer from terrorists wasn't as simple as "going overseas to kill 'em all."[329]

On September 14, Family Steering Committee members Kristen Breitweiser, Lorie Van Auken, Mindy Kleinberg, Patty Casazza, and Monica Gabrielle went to Washington DC to endorse John Kerry for president. At the press conference, Breitweiser began by disclosing that she "had voted for George Bush four years earlier but could no longer support him." Patty Casazza, who had also voted for the Bush-Cheney ticket in 2000, spoke about how difficult it was for her to change her allegiance from Republican to Democrat. She said, "It has been a painful process to accept that President Bush failed us."[330]

During the campaign, Kristen Breitweiser would speak at rallies for John Kerry. Her speeches expanded on the "Ever Since" Kerry campaign ad where Breitweiser told viewers "My husband, Ron, was killed on September 11th. I've spent the last three years trying to find out what happened to make sure it never happens again. I fought for the 9/11 Commission, something George W. Bush, the man my husband Ron and I voted for, didn't think was necessary. And during the Commission hearings we learned the truth, we are no safer today. I want to look in my daughter's eyes and know that she is safe, and that is why I am voting for John Kerry."[331] Breitweiser often received tears and a standing ovation from her speeches.

The week before the 2004 election, President Bush and John Kerry were neck-and-neck in the polls. But four days before the election, Osama bin Laden appeared in a video that was broadcast on all the major TV stations. The video was scary. At the time, Bush's senior advisor, Karl Rove, was with the president in Ohio campaigning for the election. Rove said in response to the bin Laden video, "this has the feel of something that's not gonna hurt us at all."[332]

One of *Time* magazine's columnists said in response to the bin Laden video, "I find it hard to find any way that this helps John Kerry. What we've seen over and over and over again is that when terrorism is the topic, and when people are reminded of 9/11, Bush's numbers go up."[333]

The bin Laden video may have been a deciding factor in the outcome of the election. Although on the night of the election exit polls showed Kerry winning, President Bush ended up taking Ohio, and with that state in his column, he was elected for a second term.

There was also a heightened terror alert raised three days before the election. Tom Ridge, the Secretary of Homeland Security, would later accuse the Bush White House of pushing him to "raise the national security alert just before the 2004 Election" for political gain.[334]

After the 2004 election, FSC members learned from an interview with 9/11 Commissioner Bob Kerrey that the commissioners took an oath not to discuss any points of disagreement during the election campaign so that the *Report*, and its recommendations, could be heard by Congress.[335]

Mindy Kleinberg observed, "the 9/11 Commissioners made a decision collectively, apparently, to keep silent about any issues that they disagreed about. And to keep silent about any areas of accountability until the election. The problem with this is you're not telling the truth … When you have a Commissioner such as Bob Kerrey go on a television program after the election and say that he feels the administration had some responsibility and accountability for the failures that took place on 9/11, it's too late. It's too late to have that effect any change. … Doesn't that make him complicit in a system that is failing us?"[336]

The FSC issued five more statements between November 8 and 20. They continued to press the Senate, Congress, and President Bush to reconcile the bills for 9/11 intelligence reform and get the legislation passed.

Finally, on December 9, 2004, the two houses passed legislation. In an open letter to the 108th Congress the twelve FSC members wrote, "You have at last reached consensus on a bill that will implement the 9/11 Commission's recommendations. We believe this conference report accomplishes our main goal, which was to fix our nation's broken intelligence system. The passage of these reforms marks a critical point in a long, three-year journey."[337] The legislation was signed into law on December 17, 2004.

A final statement by the FSC was released on January 11, 2005. They thanked many who had supported them over the previous years. They promised that although the FSC would not continue as an official body, that individual FSC members would continue to address issues related to 9/11 that emerged.[338]

With over half of the recommendations in the *Report* adopted, some FSC members began to reflect on the many questions they'd asked the 9/11 Commission that went unanswered. While 9/11 commissioners were deferential in public statements toward the FSC, during the public hearings and in private testimony not open to the public, the commissioners ignored the FSC questions. For example, on September 10, 2003, in their "Family Steering Committee Press Conference Remarks," the FSC reminded the commissioners that "To date, none of our questions have been answered." With additional concerns about the secretive way the inquiry was being conducted, they said "we are being asked to take on faith that an in-depth investigation is taking place and that it will not be a whitewash."[339] Notwithstanding their joint efforts to get the recommendations passed, for numbers of FSC members fears about a whitewash remained. They also posted "excerpts from the list of questions" the FSC had submitted to the 9/11 Commission.

PART THREE: THE FAMILY STEERING COMMITTEE'S UNANSWERED QUESTIONS

~ 9 ~

Question to NORAD

"Why Weren't NORAD Jets able to Intercept the Hijacked Planes if they were Airborne Within Eight Minutes of Notification?"

Carol Ashley, a member of the Family Steering Committee, spoke before the 9/11 Commission on January 26, 2004 concerning aviation security.

At the start of her testimony, she told the Commission about her own family circumstances. "On September 11th, 2001, my beautiful 25-year-old daughter, Janice, was killed in the terrorist attack on the World Trade Center. She worked on the 93rd floor of Tower One. Janice's dad, her 18-year-old brother and I were devastated by her death. Like the families of nearly three thousand others killed, our world became surreal, controlled by overwhelming, mind-numbing grief. Our close-knit family was shattered. Many of our dreams for the future died with Janice that morning. She was a joy, a light in our lives for twenty-five years. My heart aches. The pain of losing her will be with me until the day I die.

"Our nation was traumatized by the enormity of the death toll, and the destruction, and by the stark realization of our vulnerability.

Across America there was anger at the unspeakable savagery of the attack which targeted unsuspecting, innocent people. From the beginning, there was dismay. And questions, so many questions. What had gone wrong? Why hadn't our government fulfilled its foremost obligation—to protect our nation? It was soon apparent to some that an independent investigation into the terrorist attack was needed. We were stunned when President Bush opposed such an inquiry."[340]

Carol Ashley and the other Family Steering Committee members posed over a thousand questions to aid in the investigation of the 9/11 Commission. The questions were intended to direct the focus of the inquiry, and ask those most directly involved what led to the failures on that day. They understood that it would not be the FSC members themselves asking the questions. Instead, they would be posed to witnesses by 9/11 commissioners in public hearings, or asked by Commission staff behind closed-door proceedings.

Some of these questions were directed at the North American Aerospace Defense Command (NORAD). One question the FSC asked the 9/11 Commission was: "Why weren't NORAD jets able to intercept the hijacked planes if they were airborne within eight minutes of notification?"[341]

NORAD was founded in 1957 as a joint command military organization between the United States and Canada. It was established during the Cold War to provide North America with forewarning and defense against nuclear and missile attacks, as well as any threat that may be posed by space vehicles. By 1960, there were 1,200 interceptor aircraft dedicated to responding to any threat from the Soviets.[342]

In the years prior to September 11, a 1994 report of the US General Accounting Office to the US Congress provided information about "Scramble Activity by Air Defense United and Alert Sites, 1989-92." The report stated that, "Overall, during the past 4 years, NORAD's alert fighters took off to intercept aircraft (referred to as scrambled) 1,518 times ... activity generally involved visually inspecting unidentified aircraft and assisting aircraft in distress."[343]

Canadian Brig-Gen. Jim Hunter, the Vice Commander of NORAD, commented to the *Calgary Herald* that in 2000, "jets were scrambled 129 times over US airspace."[344] In each of these 129 instances fighter jets successfully intercepted off-course flights promptly. As with the nearly 380 intercepts per year between 1989-92, the military was batting a thousand.

A NORAD spokesman confirmed, "At a NORAD operations center in Cheyenne Mountain in Colorado Springs, Colo., a noncommissioned officer listens to conversations on the FAA network from all over the United States."[345]

The FAA (Federal Aviation Administration) was created in 1958 to establish standards for air navigation and air traffic control. The catalyst for its creation was the 1956 Grand Canyon mid-air collision, where two commercial flights collided, resulting in 128 fatalities—the worst in history at that time. As this was one of several collisions of commercial flights, the flying public needed to be reassured that when they boarded a flight it wouldn't crash into another plane on route to its destination. Subsequently, the FAA made it mandatory for all planes to have approved flight paths tracked by radar. Their cruising altitude also had to be approved before take-off.

In 1961, hijacking protocols were put in place after the first two domestic hijacking incidents took place.[346] An Air Traffic Control Center binder from August 1998 counseled controllers that when a plane strayed from its approved flight path, or altitude assignment, it "will likely find two [jet fighters] on their tail within 10 minutes or so."[347]

Before 9/11, NORAD typically had five practices a month dealing with hijackings out of its Cheyenne Mountain Operations Center in Colorado.[348] With an average of one anti-hijacking training exercise taking place every six days since 1998, it would seem that NORAD should have been ready to respond promptly to the four hijackings on September Eleventh. Therefore, the FSC wanted to know why protocols weren't followed on that day? Why was NORAD zero for four?

The FSC was also aware of a NORAD plane that intercepted golfer Payne Stewart's Learjet in October 1999. They asked the 9/11 Commission: "Please draw up a chart of NORAD's response to the Payne Stewart Lear jet incident vs. the 9/11 incident. Why was protocol not followed on 9/11? What is the name of the individual who did not follow protocol? Where are the transcripts from the F-16s? Where is the log and record from NORAD?"[349]

In an article in October 2001, the *Calgary Herald* asked, "Where was NORAD, the multimillion-dollar, 24-hour eyes and ears of North American skies, when the hijacked planes embarked on their sinister missions? Ironically, NORAD was doing its job: peering 300 kilometres out into the Air Defence Identification Zone encircling North America. Its task: to help assess, within two minutes, if each of the 7,000 incoming aircraft every day is friend or foe ... When the second plane hit the other World Trade Center tower, NORAD swiftly shifted its attention to help prevent possible further attacks. NORAD was instrumental in getting fighter jets—normally on 15-minute alert—airborne within eight minutes."

In testimony before the Senate Armed Services Committee in March 2002, NORAD Commander General Ralph Eberhart explained that once the FAA suspects something is wrong with a flight over domestic airspace, "it takes about one minute" for them to notify NORAD. At that point, NORAD can scramble jets typically within 2.5 minutes to an altitude of 29,000 feet (or more) "to anywhere in the United States."

But the *Calgary Herald* and General Eberhart omitted part of NORAD's operations. In addition to assessing incoming foreign aircraft, its first mission was "surveillance and control of the [domestic] territorial air space" in the United States and Canada. In order to maintain "air sovereignty" in the continental USA, it created the Continental United States NORAD Region to "detect, identify and if necessary intercept aircraft" over American air space. And NORAD radar operators were tasked with initiating "phone contact with FAA officials about commercial aircraft," not just passively waiting to be informed.[350]

A NORAD spokesperson told the *Boston Globe* in September 2001 that typically two fighter planes are sent to intercept a hijacked flight. "When planes are intercepted, they typically are handled with graduated response. The approaching flight may rock its wingtips to attract the pilot's attention, or make a pass in front of the aircraft. Eventually, it can fire tracer rounds in the airplane's path, or, under certain circumstances, down it with a missile."[351]

If the jets NORAD had available were ready to scramble within eight minutes to intercept an errant flight, why did they not arrive in time to intercept any of the hijacked planes? McGuire Air Force Base in North Hanover, NJ, was about a 70-mile flight from the WTC. Once jets were scrambled, they could have been in Manhattan in 3 minutes. Together, the four hijacked planes passed over numbers of Air Force bases on route to their targets. A report in *New Scientist* noted that "US military radar can track space debris as small as 10 centimeters across miles up in space."[352] Consequently, the FSC's question to the 9/11 Commission.

It was reported that the hijackers had been considered by their flight school instructors to be variously "mediocre," "very poor," and "totally clueless" in their efforts to fly a 3-passenger Cessna 172 aircraft. None of the hijackers had ever flown a commercial airplane. The editor of Air Transport Intelligence told Dublin's *Independent* newspaper that "Flying an aircraft into a building is not a(sic) simple as it appears," and that it took considerable skill to steer planes into the World Trade Center."[353]

The *Telegraph* interviewed experts on September 12, 2001, who compared the targets of the WTC towers to "narrow runways tipped vertically." From "switching off the autopilot," the hijackers "would have to know how to control the aircraft and be able to find the target."

They said that "rag-trousered terrorists with no flying experience could not have hit" the Twin Towers. And a 767 pilot told the *Boston Globe* "To hit something with an airplane is easy only if you have been flying for 20 years."[354]

Therefore, FSC members wondered why experienced fighter jet pilots couldn't have prevented these rookie hijackers from reaching their targets, given the precision required to hit a skyscraper while flying at speeds of over 500 mph. Intercepting fighters would have been able to perform aerial maneuvers around the hijacked flights to force the hijackers off-course.

The Family Steering Committee had more questions about what NORAD was doing in response to having four planes hijacked on the same day. Given that NORAD was equipped to launch fighter jets within eight minutes to intercept any plane veering off its flight path, the committee asked the 9/11 Commission: "Why did NORAD wait until after the second plane hit the WTC to try and prevent possible further attacks?"

Adding confusion to NORAD's response on September Eleventh were the statements given by Air Force General Richard Myers. On September 13, Myers testified before the Senate Armed Services Committee. But his answers were vague and confused. Significantly, Myers asserted that no fighter jets were scrambled in response to the hijackings until after the Pentagon was hit.[355]

On September 17, 2001, NORAD officials met at the White House. The following day, NORAD published a timeline of what they were doing on September Eleventh, which conflicted with Myers' earlier statement. But even then, the timeline NORAD offered raised more questions than answers.

During the 9/11 Commission proceedings, Mindy Kleinberg commented on NORAD's lack of attention to their own protocols on September Eleventh. She stated, "Prior to 9/11, FAA and Department of Defense Manuals gave clear, comprehensive instructions on how to handle everything from minor emergencies to full blown hijackings.

These 'protocols' were in place and were practiced regularly for a good reason—with heavily trafficked air space, airliners without radio and transponder contact are collisions and/or calamities waiting to happen. Those protocols dictate that in the event of an emergency, the FAA is to notify NORAD.

Once that notification takes place, it is then the responsibility of NORAD to scramble fighter-jets to intercept the errant plane(s). It is a matter of routine procedure for fighter-jets to "intercept" commercial airliners in order to regain contact with the pilot."[356]

Next, Kleinberg pointed out that there were special exercises taking place in the skies of America on September Eleventh. They were meant to fine-tune NORAD's readiness to respond quickly to any hijacking. The North East Air Defense System (NEADS), a geographical sector of NORAD, "was several days into a semiannual exercise known as 'Vigilant Guardian.' Key officers were manning the operation battle center, 'fighter jets were cocked, loaded, and carrying extra gas on board.' Lucky for the terrorists none of this mattered on the morning of September 11," said Kleinberg.[357]

Kleinberg also referred to the data on public record about American Airlines Flight 11, the first plane to hit the World Trade Center. It flew out of Boston's Logan International Airport at 7:45 a.m. The plane's transponder lost contact early on, and radar showed the plane was off its FAA approved flight path. Its last communication with ground control was at 8:13 a.m.

Two flight attendants contacted the airline to alert them that a hijacking was in progress; the emergency protocols in place dictated that NORAD should have been immediately notified that a hijacking was unfolding. But according to NORAD's official timeline, no one was in touch with them until 8:40 a.m., and no jets were scrambled until 8:52 a.m.

Kleinberg urgently asked the 9/11 commissioners: "Why was there a delay in the FAA notifying NORAD? Why was there a delay in NORAD scrambling fighter jets? How is this possible when

NEADS was fully staffed with planes at the ready and monitoring our Northeast airspace?"[358]

Mindy Kleinberg's questions were echoed by the Family Steering Committee: "Why weren't the fighter jets that tailed flights 11 and 175 as they crashed into New York's WTC, rerouted to intercept flights 77 or 93, before they crashed into the Pentagon and Pennsylvania? At precisely what time was NORAD notified of each plane being hijacked? What was their response? What is the name of the individual who determined from which bases the F-16s should be scrambled? Whose decision was it to not fly the F-16s at maximum speed?"[359]

In order to connect the dots concerning what went wrong on September Eleventh, it was necessary to interview those persons directly involved in the decision-making process. If it was discovered that there were staff in important positions who weren't sufficiently competent, they needed to be replaced with those capable of defending the nation by following established protocols.

However, *The 9/11 Commission Report* never suitably answered these questions. It only described the "inaccuracies" in NORAD's official September Eleventh timeline. NORAD untruthfully asserted that NEADS was told at 9:24 a.m. that Flight 77, the plane that would hit the Pentagon, was hijacked. The 9/11 Commission claims NEADS notice was faulty, as Flight 77 "had not hit the World Trade Center and was heading for Washington DC."

The 9/11 Commission states "NEADS never received notice that American 77 was hijacked." Instead it was given notice at 9:34 a.m. that the plane was "lost. Then, at 9:36 a.m., NEADS was informed of an unidentified plane flying six miles southwest of the White House."

The 9/11 Commission also took issue with a claim NORAD made about sending fighter jets to intercept Flight 77. The whole response by NORAD, as described in the 9/11 Commission report, "was one failure after another." Instead, the Commission reported that the fighters were scrambled in response to an incorrect report that Flight 11 was still airborne and heading south.[360]

The Commission conceded that if two F-16 fighter jets had been contacted prior to 8:37 a.m., they could have reached New York City before Flight 11 crashed into the North Tower. Even after a plane had already hit the World Trade Center, there was still a sequence of postponements in notification and delays in scrambling fighter jets. Mindy Kleinberg pointed out that, according to the US military, jets were scrambled from Langley Air Force Base in Hampton, Virginia in response to Flight 77. This was instead of the closer Andrews Air Force Base beside Washington DC.

Mystified, Kleinberg observed, "Even more baffling for us is the fact that the fighter jets were not scrambled from the closest air force bases ... As a result, Washington skies remained wholly unprotected on the morning of September 11th. At 9:41 a.m. one hour and 21 minutes after the first plane was hijack confirmed by FAA, Flight 77 crashed into the Pentagon. The fighter jets were still miles away. Why? So the hijackers luck had continued. On September 11 both the FAA and NORAD deviated from standard emergency operating procedures. Who were the people that delayed the notification? Have they been questioned? In addition, the interceptor planes or fighter jets did not fly at their maximum speed. Had the belatedly scrambled fighter jets flown at their maximum speed of engagement, they would have reached NYC and the Pentagon within moments of their deployment, intercepted the hijacked airliners before they could have hit their targets, and undoubtedly saved lives."[361]

There were many varying reports of the scrambled jet fighter speeds. Pilots out of Otis Air Force Base in Cape Cod, Massachusetts, told ABC that they flew at "nearly 900 miles per hour."[362] Meanwhile, NORAD commander Major General Larry Arnold told MSNBC the Otis Air Force pilots rushed to New York City "at around 1,100 to 1,200 miles per hour."[363] Had this been the case the fighter jets from Otis could have intercepted Flight 175 and attempted to throw it off of its trajectory, missing the South Tower and saving lives in that building.

Yet NORAD issued its own timeline on September 18, 2001, stating that the fighter jets arrived at 9:11 a.m., taking 19 minutes to reach the World Trade Center, and flying at speeds below 600 miles per hour.[364]

Had NORAD scrambled fighter jets in time, their presence would be more than bluster and bluff. In fact, all options were on the table. Navy Commander Anthony Barnes later recalled that he was given permission to order the hijacked planes to be shot down.[365] And Vice President Dick Cheney told CBS "Well, I discussed it with the president. Are we prepared to order our aircraft to shoot down these airliners that have been hijacked? He said yes ... it was my advice. It was his decision."[366]

The Commission reported that the terrorists considered flying into nuclear facilities, but decided not to because they expected "that any plane would be shot down before impact." [367] Yet the Commission did not explain why the terrorists didn't expect a hijacked plane to be shot down if, for example, they targeted the Pentagon.

The FSC was perplexed that the 9/11 Commission failed to investigate the NORAD failures further. Even the media had taken to pointing out inconsistencies. The December 5, 2003 headline of New Jersey newspaper *The Bergen Record* read, "Atlantic City F-16 Fighters Were Eight Minutes Away From 9/11 Hijacked Planes." [368] The article described how there were two fighter jets from the Atlantic City International Airport based in Pomona, New Jersey, that were carrying out mock-bombing sorties only eight minutes away from Ground Zero.

FSC member Lorie Van Auken was astonished when she read *The 9/11 Commission Report* and discovered that this crucial detail was omitted from the report. "I'm frankly stunned by this ... If two fighters were only eight minutes away, the Commission should have done an exhaustive study on why they didn't get called. To leave them out of the official hearing record is unbelievable."[369]

9/11 Commission Chairman Thomas Kean stated in December

2003 that the attacks were completely preventable. At the time, Kean said, "This was not something that had to happen ... There are people that, if I was doing the job, would certainly not be in the position they were in at that time because they failed. They simply failed." Yet, the 9/11 Commission did not look into finding out which staff in the FAA or NORAD had delayed scrambling the jets. They didn't question these employees about what led to the breakdown, or why standard protocols were not followed.

Kean promised there would be major revelations in public testimony at the 9/11 Commission from the FBI, CIA, Department of Defense, and the NSA so that the lessons learned from the attacks would prevent any repeats.[370] However, these major revelations never came.

Kean also distrusted testimony by NORAD officials. "We to this day don't know why NORAD told us what they told us. It was just so far from the truth," he said.[371] Kean said Republicans on the 9/11 Commission blocked a request sent to the Department of Justice to investigate the Pentagon based on suspect or contradictory statements.

Paul Thompson, author of *The Terror Timeline*, commented that the 9/11 Commission considered a criminal investigation of NORAD and Pentagon officials who gave the inquiry seven different contradictory stories regarding the military response to the hijackings.[372]

The number of war game exercises being held on September Eleventh was unprecedented. These included Vigilant Guardian, which had previously run hijack exercises on October 25–27, 1998 and October 16–23, 2000.[373] There were also two field training exercises called Amalgam Warrior and Amalgam Virgo, which covered two NORAD regions. Amalgam Warrior was typically held in April and October.[374]

Linked to Vigilant Guardian and Amalgam Warrior was Global Guardian, sponsored jointly by the US Strategic Command, US Space Command, and NORAD. Apollo Guardian, linked to Global Guardian, also ran on the morning of September 11.[375] Was there a reason all these (normally separate) war games were being held on September

Eleventh? Could they have contributed to slower response times, or confusion in finding the hijacked planes on radar?

When 9/11 Commissioner Jamie Gorelick began to ask NORAD General Richard Myers questions, she was interrupted by several audience members at the hearing who wanted her to "ask about the war games that were planned for 9/11." Gorelick's only response was, "could you please be quiet, we only have a few minutes with General Myers, and I would like to ask a question." In the end, none of the 9/11 Commissioners asked General Myers, or any of the other generals from NORAD, about the war games on September Eleventh. When Myers said he had to leave, a member of the audience said that they, too, were leaving, because "this is a farce."[376]

The FSC issued a statement to the 9/11 Commission and the press on June 14, 2004. They pointed out: "Amalgam Virgo One, the NORAD exercise that took place June 2001, has a picture of Bin Laden on the cover." The photo of Osama bin Laden was accompanied by five photos of military planes around the terrorist.[377] The scenario for Amalgam Virgo One (a war game 3 months prior to the military's Amalgam Virgo exercise on September Eleventh) involved a suicide pilot attacking a military building. Another NORAD simulation, this one on August 4, 2001, was named Fertile Rice. It featured Osama bin Laden directing a drone filled with explosives to target Washington DC.

On September 11, 2001, two of NORAD's coincidental war game exercises, Vigilant Guardian and Global Guardian, had a photo of Osama bin Laden on the cover of their documents. The documents were created prior to 9/11. What can account for the coincidence of bin Laden's photo on these war game exercises? Was there an expectation that Osama bin Laden would hijack planes and use them as weapons?

Though Chairman Kean said from the outset: "Our purpose is to find out why things happened," this was not an avenue the commissioners chose to explore while questioning NORAD officers.

The FSC also asked the 9/11 Commission about a news report by Saudi-based Worldwide News Inc. They were named in a purchase order for a news service for the National Military Command Center from January 1, 2001, to September 30, 2001. The 9/11 families commented, "This order is for news wire services at our National Military Command Center. Why is any foreign owned news service permitted on the presumably secure premises? Is it possible that the hijackers somehow found out about the planned drill from reporters at the National Military Command Center?"[378] The questions were left unanswered in *The 9/11 Commission Report*.

~ 10 ~

Question to the FAA

Why were these four planes able to evade all radar?

On September Eleventh, radar operators with the FAA and NORAD weren't able to track the hijacked planes like they routinely track planes every other day of the year. Why was 9/11 different? The Family Steering Committee informed the Commission, "Even when the transponders are disconnected, a plane is still able to be located by its 'skin' on radar screens." [379] In her testimony before the 9/11 Commission, Mindy Kleinberg observed that regarding Flight 11 "radar indicated that the plane had deviated from its assigned path of flight." Since the United States military "was monitoring our Northeast airspace" why were Americans being told that the hijacked planes could evade all radar? [380]

Prior to the 9/11 Commission, FSC member Kristen Breitweiser spoke at the Joint Inquiry public hearing on September 18, 2002. She stated: "Soon after the attacks, President Bush stated that there would come a time to look back and examine our nation's failures, but that such an undertaking was inappropriate while the nation was still in shock. I would respectfully suggest to President Bush and to our Congress that now, a full year later, it is time to look back and investigate our failures as a nation.

"A hallmark of democratic government is a willingness to admit to, analyze and learn from mistakes … The families of the victims of September 11th have waited long enough. We need to have answers. We need to have accountability. We need to feel safe living and working in this great nation." She asked before the US Senate and Congressional members "Why was our Air Force so late in its response?"[381]

Radar stands for **RA**dio **D**etection **A**nd **R**anging. Experiments in the 1880s by European scientists proved the existence of electromagnetic waves and radio waves that would reflect off metal objects. Early uses for the discovery helped prevent ships from crashing ashore on coastlines during fog. The term *RADAR* was coined in 1939 by the United States Signal Corps as it worked on its development for the US Navy.[382] Radar is used to calculate the location and speed of an object in both marine and aviation contexts. All Air Traffic Control towers have radar, as well as the US military.

In its report the 9/11 Commission wrote, "On 9/11, the defense of US airspace depended on close interaction between two federal agencies: the Federal Aviation Administration and the North American Aerospace Defense Command."[383] On the morning of September Eleventh, the interaction between air traffic controllers and NORAD originated out of regional FAA control centers, including Boston, New York, Cleveland, and Indianapolis.

FAA testified that in the event of a hijacking, these air traffic controllers were required to "notify their supervisors, who in turn would inform management all the way up to FAA headquarters. FAA Headquarters had a hijack coordinator who was the director of the FAA Office of Civil Aviation Security or his or her designate."

In the event of a hijacking, Michael Canavan was responsible for making contact with the Pentagon's National Military Command Center (NMCC) and "the NMCC would then seek approval from the Office of the Secretary of Defense to provide military assistance.

If approval was given, the orders would be transmitted down NORAD's chain of command [to the interceptor pilots]."[84]

In its report, the 9/11 Commission stated that according to official accounts, the communication that NORAD received from the FAA didn't allow for enough time to intercept the hijacked aircraft. The Commission reported that "NEADS air defenders had nine minutes' notice on the first hijacked plane, no advance notice on the second, no advance notice on the third, and no advance notice on the fourth."[385]

According to *The 9/11 Commission Report*, at 8:25 a.m. air traffic controllers at Boston Center began notifying the FAA that a hijacking had taken place. Those notified included the FAA's New England Regional Operations Center in Burlington, Massachusetts, and the FAA Command Center in Herndon, Virginia.[386] *The 9/11 Commission Report* also says, "By 9:34, word of the hijacking had reached FAA headquarters."[387]

What can account for the gap between 8:25 a.m., when FAA offices knew of the hijacking, and 9:34 a.m., when FAA headquarters was alerted? Since CNN and other news networks had been reporting that a second hijacked aircraft had hit the South Tower at 9:03 a.m., is it feasible that no one on the job within FAA headquarters was aware that hijackings were in progress until 9:34 a.m.?

Even more peculiar, the 9/11 Commission maintains that FAA headquarters chose not to give notice to NORAD fighter pilots, charged with defending US airspace, until the final flight, United Airlines Flight 93, had crashed.

If this was an odd decision for the FAA to make, it was not a decision that the 9/11 Commission wanted to explore. Although the 9/11 Commission didn't pursue the matter, the Family Steering Committee asked them to find out: "What was the protocol of when and who would be notified in the event of a hijacking? Please indicate where in the sequence the FAA would contact NORAD, the Secret Service, the President, FBI, DOT, DOD, etc. Did the FAA follow protocol? Specifically, when did the FAA contact each?"[388]

A person in a position of key responsibility on September Eleventh was Lieutenant General Michael Canavan. He had assumed a new role as FAA Hijack Coordinator in January 2001. In the following months, Canavan relaxed the protocols governing the FAA. During that time, Canavan was in charge of running training exercises that were "pretty damn close to [the] 9/11 plot," according to John Hawley, an employee in the FAA's intelligence division who testified before the 9/11 Commission.[389]

In his comments to the 9/11 Commission, Canavan denied having participated in any such exercises. It didn't occur to the 9/11 Commission to resolve the irreconcilable comments it had received from Hawley and Canavan.

After a number of softball questions to Canavan, it was left to Richard Ben-Veniste to ask him what he was doing the morning of September Eleventh. Canavan said, "Here's my answer—and it's not to duck the question. Number one, I was visiting the airport in San Juan that day when this happened … I was down there also to remove someone down there that was in a key position. So when 9/11 happened, that's where I was. I was able to get back to Washington that evening on a special flight from the Army back from San Juan, back to Washington … when I got back it was, 'What are we going to do over the next 48 hours to strengthen what just happened?'"[390]

None of the commissioners asked Canavan who was tasked with the position of FAA Hijack Coordinator while he was in San Juan. Their report said nothing about the crucial role of the FAA Hijack Coordinator. Still, the FSC asked the Commission to discover "Why were these four planes able to evade all radar?"[391]

The 9/11 Commission concluded that NORAD had failed to do its job on September Eleventh; NORAD's decisions impaired the FAA radar operators' conduct.

General Eberhart was the head of NORAD on September 11, 2001. According to his testimony before the 9/11 Commission, Eberhart was at his Wyoming office in Peterson Air Force Base: the headquarters of the US Air Force Space Command. This is a half-hour drive from NORAD's Cheyenne Mountain Operation Center.

The Command Director at Cheyenne Mountain phoned Eberhart at 8:45 a.m. about several planes suspected of being hijacked. At that moment, Eberhart walked into his office and saw the news footage about the first plane hitting the North Tower.

After the South Tower was hit at 9:03 a.m., Eberhart attempted to get in touch with the Chairman of the Joint Chiefs of Staff, General Henry Shelton. Unfortunately, Shelton was on a flight to Europe to attend a NATO meeting. Eberhart told the 9/11 Commission there was "great confusion in the system."[392]

In a separate interview with the 9/11 Commission the NORAD Deputy Commander, a Lieutenant General of the Canadian Forces, told the commissioners there was "confusion as to how many, and which aircraft, were hijacked."[393]

This was because General Eberhart happened to be overseeing a number of war games that morning, including Vigilant Guardian. This war game, by coincidence, was scripted on a storyline where terrorists hijacked a plane in order to attack Manhattan.

During this time, NORAD's radar screens displayed the false tracks of the Vigilant Guardian war games, which were conducted "sim over live." This meant "the simulated hijackings were to be inserted into the live air traffic control system. As a result, NEADS personnel for some time were uncertain whether the radar tracks were real or simulated."[394]

Eberhart told the 9/11 Commission he recognized once the South Tower of the World Trade Center had been hit that a "coordinated terrorist attack" was occurring. He also knew that radar personnel at Cheyenne asked NEADS to "get rid of this goddamn sim." The "sim over live" was creating the confusion that the Canadian Lieutenant General had referred to.

However, Eberhart chose to let the war games proceed until after

10:00 a.m.; by then, the North Tower, South Tower, and Pentagon had been hit, and Flight 93 had crashed in Pennsylvania.[395] General Ralph Eberhart was questioned by the 9/11 Commission about how the Vigilant Guardian war games might have impeded NORAD's response to the hijackings. Eberhart "falsely claimed that they had 'at most cost us 30 seconds.'"[396]

Given that Eberhart realized America was under attack after the South Tower had been hit, the commissioners asked him why he had failed to implement a protocol known as the Security Control of Air Traffic and Air Navigation Aids, or SCATANA. This protocol mandated that all commercial and private planes would have to leave American airspace and fly to the nearest airport. Initiating SCATANA would have given the United States Air Force complete control of the American skies.

Eberhart claimed that NORAD's radar system was not in a condition on September Eleventh to be able to "control the airspace that day." [397] He believed SCATANA would only have compounded the crisis. Meanwhile, other NORAD officers urged Eberhart to put SCATANA in place immediately. Eberhart replied, "I will execute SCATANA once you have a modified SCATANA that ... doesn't cause a bad situation to become worse."

It was only by around 11:00 a.m. on September Eleventh that Eberhart succeeded in implementing the modified SCATANA.[398]

General Eberhart was also in charge of setting alert levels for Infocon, the alert system that defends the Pentagon. Infocon lets the Pentagon's communications networks know if an incoming hostile plane is approaching. For some unknown reason, Eberhart decided to lower the Infocon alert levels just prior to 9:00 p.m. the night of September 10th. Infocon was set at its lowest alert level on the morning the Pentagon was hit.[399]

General Eberhart's errors in judgment the morning of September Eleventh were reported in *Aviation Week & Space Technology*, Lynn Spencer's account in *Touching History: The Untold Story of the Drama*

That Unfolded in the Skies Over America on 9/11, and Eberhart's own testimony before the 9/11 Commission. Although these failures were General Eberhart's responsibility, he was promoted to Head of US Northern Command in May 2002.[400]

Eberhart's actions on the morning of September Eleventh may help to explain another of the FSC's questions: "Why weren't the fighter jets that tailed flights 11 and 175 as they crashed into New York's WTC, rerouted to intercept flights 77 or 93, before they crashed into the Pentagon and Pennsylvania?"[401] His actions may also address the question, "Why were these four planes able to evade all radar?"[402] General Eberhart's decision to maintain the Vigilant Guardian war games "sim over live" would have been a relevant line of inquiry for the 9/11 Commission to pursue. It would have helped the September Eleventh families answer these questions. But the Commission failed to follow up.

The 9/11 Commission also failed to interview Brigadier General Montague Winfield, director of the National Military Command Center (NMCC) located in the Pentagon. Winfield decided to be relieved of duty at 8:30 a.m. on September Eleventh. He would have normally been in command. The 9/11 Commission learned about Winfield's absence from the testimony of Winfield's deputy, Capt. Charles J. Leidig, who described himself as a rookie to the position as of August 2001. With Winfield absent, his deputy had "to stand watch as the Deputy Director for Operations in the NMCC" until Winfield took over after United Airlines Flight 93 crashed.[403]

Winfield wasn't the only person of authority not present during the time of the attacks. The acting head of the Joint Chiefs of Staff, General Richard Myers, was in an hour-long meeting about terrorism with Senator Max Cleland.[404] Nobody in the military thought to contact General Myers. After Myers left the meeting, he learned the Pentagon had been hit.

NORAD commander General Eberhart was unreachable for 45 minutes during the crisis while driving in his car. Eberhart explained in an interview on March 1, 2004, that he chose to be absent from the command post for 45 minutes while the attacks were unfolding because things had "quieted down."[405] However, at the time, there were reports of possibly eight hijacked planes.

So altogether: FAA Hijack Coordinator Lieutenant General Michael Canavan was in San Juan, Puerto Rico. Brigadier General Montague Winfield relieved himself of duty that morning. General Ralph Eberhart was overseeing war games before leaving his command post for 45 minutes. Chairman of the Joint Chiefs of Staff General Henry Shelton was on a plane to Europe. His acting head, General Richard Myers, was in a meeting that no one thought to interrupt. And Secretary of Defense, Donald Rumsfeld, alleges he was out-of-the-loop—that no one in the military or White House thought to inform him of the unfolding attacks.

The families of the September Eleventh victims wondered how it could be that every key person in a position of leadership in NORAD and the FAA was AWOL. All these military leaders were, apparently, uninformed by their colleagues, other agencies, and the White House on the urgency of the events unfolding that morning. Were there no cell phones?

In her testimony before the 9/11 Commission on March 31, 2003, FSC member Mary Fetchet asked, "Who should be held accountable?"[406]

Mindy Kleinberg commented on the coincidences that piled up. She stated in her testimony before the Commission: "With regard to the 9/11 attacks, it has been said that the intelligence agencies have to be right 100% of the time and the terrorists only have to get lucky once. This explanation for the devastating attacks of September 11, simple on its face, is wrong in its value. Because the 9/11 terrorists were not just lucky once; they were lucky over and over again ... Is it luck that aberrant stock trades were not monitored? Is it luck when 15 visas are awarded based on incomplete forms? Is it luck when Airline Security screenings allow hijackers to board planes with box cutters and pepper spray? Is it luck when emergency FAA and NORAD protocols are not followed? Is it luck when a national emergency is not reported to top government officials on a timely basis? To me luck is something that happens once. When you have this repeated pattern of broken protocols, broken laws, broken communication, one cannot still call it luck." [407]

A year after *The 9/11 Commission Report* was released, researcher Paul Thompson, who had compiled his thorough 9/11 online timeline, questioned the *Report*'s claim that by 10:00 a.m. there had been no attempt to send any military planes to defend Washington DC, although Flight 77 had gone missing at 8:56 a.m. Based on the standard military procedures that had been in place for decades, Thompson stated that what the 9/11 Commission was asserting "is just frankly impossible."

The *Report* claims that the Indianapolis Flight Center that was tracking Flight 77 remained unaware that any hijackings or attacks on the Twin Towers had occurred at all. And yet, "other centers such as theirs had been notified of the crisis long before the first plane even crashed into the World Trade Center." [408]

An additional problem concerned violation of standard procedure where a real emergency is declared once a plane is two miles off its approved flight path.[409] Flight 11 was dramatically off course by 8:20 a.m. Boston flight control assumed Flight 11 had been hijacked by 8:20 a.m., and notified other flight control centers by 8:25 a.m. NORAD radar operators would have seen this on their radar screens at 8:20 a.m., but didn't act. Although some reports suggested NORAD didn't learn about Flight 11 until 8:40 a.m. ABC reported on September 14, 2001, "There's a gap that will need to be investigated." [410]

As well, FAA Acting Deputy Administrator Monte Belger testified before the 9/11 Commission. His testimony undermined the talking point that the military were dependent on being notified by the FAA before they could respond to the hijacking emergency that was unfolding. Belger stated:

"There were military people on duty at the FAA Command Center.

They were participating in what was going on. There were military people in the FAA's Air Traffic Organization in the situation room. They were participating in what was going on." [411]

~ 11 ~

Questions to the CIA/SEC/FBI

Was the CIA monitoring the financial markets in the weeks preceding September 11ᵗʰ? To the CIA/SEC/FBI: What are the names of the individuals and the financial institutions who placed "put" orders on American Airlines and United Airlines for the 3 weeks prior to 9/11?

After the attacks, news stories alleged that there were people who made speculative bets in money markets that the price of airline stock would fall. These stocks happened to belong to the same airlines that were hijacked on September Eleventh. But on September 29, 2001, a new dimension to the story added to its significance. The *San Francisco Chronicle* reported: "there is evidence that a number of transactions in financial markets indicated specific (criminal) foreknowledge of the September 11 attacks on the World Trade Center and the Pentagon."[412]

This foreknowledge was evidenced by the increased number of United Airlines stock bought with a "put option." This gave the purchaser of the stock the ability to sell it at a predetermined set price in the event that the value of the stock fell. In other words, the purchaser of the stock *expected* the stock to fall, and profit if it did so.

The *Chronicle* article explained that the firm used to manage these "put option" contracts was Banker's Trust, a major US investment bank with ties to CIA Executive Director Alvin "Buzzy" Krongard, who used to be Vice Chairman of the board of Banker's Trust.

"Krongard's last position at Banker's Trust (BT) was to oversee 'private client relations' ... in a kind of specialized banking operation that has been identified by the US Senate and other investigators as being closely connected to the laundering of drug money. Krongard joined the CIA in 1998 as counsel to CIA Director George Tenet. He was promoted to CIA Executive Director by President Bush in March [2001]."[413] Did Krongard, third-in-command in the CIA, know anything about these unusual trades in his former investment banking firm, Banker's Trust?

The news that there was an unusually high level of put buying, placed with the expectation that United Airlines stock would fall after the attacks, should have interested the general public. At first glance, it seems odd that more US media sources did not pick up on the story. Alleged criminal foreknowledge of the September Eleventh attacks, and a possible link to the number-three person in the CIA, seems like big news.

But if the CIA didn't want news reports getting out, they had the means to prevent them. Former CIA agent, William B. Bader, once said "There is quite an incredible spread of relationships. You don't need to manipulate *Time* magazine, for example, because there are [Central Intelligence] Agency people at the management level."[414] Former CIA Director, William Colby, once bragged, "The Central Intelligence Agency owns everyone of any significance in the major media."[415] As it happened, the US mainstream media didn't pick up the CIA angle to the story.

When Kristen Breitweiser testified in front of the Joint Inquiry on September 18, 2002, she commented that "Our intelligence agencies routinely monitor sudden shifts in trading patterns with Promis software, which gives intelligence agencies the valuable ability to track and analyse market indicators that might hint at worldwide events and planned terrorist attacks."

Breitweiser learned that Promis software had the ability to register the irregular trading activity on stock for American Airlines and United Airlines, as well as the reinsurance companies and leaseholders of the World Trade Center immediately prior to September Eleventh. Breitweiser observed that since the intelligence agencies monitored these kinds of trades, she found it curious "that none of our Watchdogs noticed."[416]

The FSC asked the 9/11 Commission "How did Promis software end up in the hands of bin Laden? In what ways could Promis be useful to al Qaeda?"[417]

In a similar vein, the FSC noted, "There were an extraordinarily large number of stock puts on American and United airlines stock and others which were subsequently impacted by the terrorist attack. It is well documented that the CIA has long monitored such trades in real time … Was the CIA monitoring the financial markets in the weeks preceding September 11th? Please provide the names of those individuals, investment groups and others who purchased the stock puts in question and the reasons they gave for anticipating a drop in the stocks of companies which coincidentally happened to have been severely impacted on September 11th."

To the US Securities and Exchange Commission (SEC), the government agency that oversees investments and securities, they also asked, "What are the names of the individuals and the financial institutions who placed 'put' orders on American Airlines and United Airlines for the 3 weeks prior to 9/11? Who has possession of these monies?"[418]

Counterpunch Magazine also noted unusual stock trades. "Put options for Morgan Stanley and Merrill Lynch, two of the biggest occupants of the World Trade Center, also saw abnormal activity. Most of the investments in these put options originated in Germany through the Deutsche Bank. Deutsche Bank had earlier acquired

Banker's Trust, a investment banking firm whose Vice Chairman in charge of 'private client relations' in the late 1990's was A. B. 'Buzzy' Krongard."[419]

In September 2001, several European finance ministers stated that insider trading related to United Airlines, American Airlines, Boeing, and several banks had occurred before September Eleventh. The *Washington Post* reported on September 22, 2001, "The president of Germany's central bank said today there was mounting evidence that people connected to the attacks in New York and Washington sought to profit from the tragedy by engaging in 'terrorism insider trading' on European stock and commodity markets. Ernst Welteke, head of the Bundesbank, said a preliminary review by German regulators and bank researchers showed there were highly suspicious sales of shares in airlines and insurance companies, along with major trades in gold and oil markets, before Sept. 11 that suggest they were conducted with advance knowledge of the attacks. Welteke said his researchers came across what he considers almost irrefutable proof of insider trading as recently as Thursday, but he refused to release details pending further consultations with regulators in other countries. 'What we found makes us sure that people connected to the terrorists must have been trying to profit from this tragedy.' Welteke said."[420]

In 2011, a 46-page study on the question of insider trading concluded that there was evidence of abnormal trading surrounding September Eleventh that was "consistent with insiders anticipating the 9-11 attacks."[421] The people who made these trades anticipated the attacks on September Eleventh, but chose not to report what they knew in the last eleven days of August and the first ten days of September: the time frame for when these trades on airlines and financial companies were made.

The FSC asked the 9/11 Commission, "Were individuals with ties to terrorists or states which sponsor terrorism involved in shorting airline and other stocks which were impacted by the terrorist attacks on September 11th?"[422]

The 9/11 Commission stated that 95% of United Airlines stock puts "were placed by a single US-based institutional investor with no conceivable ties to al-Qaeda."[423] If this was the case, who was this institutional investor with no ties to al Qaeda but had advance knowledge the attacks were to occur?

Within a few weeks of the attacks on September Eleventh, the FBI had agents investigating the unusual trades. They identified two suspicious traders in an informal briefing with the 9/11 Commission on August 15, 2003. One concerned 56,000 shares of Stratesec Incorporated Strategic Security between September 6 and September 10, 2001. Stratesec provided security systems to airports, including Dulles Airport, the World Trade Center, and United Airlines. Its share price almost doubled after September Eleventh when Wall Street markets reopened on September 17, 2001.

The trades traced back to a couple whose names were redacted from the memo; however, they were easily identified from information that was not redacted. These traders were Mr. and Mrs. Wirt Walker III. Wirt Walker III is a relative of President George W. Bush, and a business partner of one of the president's brothers, Marvin Bush. Still, the FBI decided not to bother interviewing the Walkers because they "revealed no ties to terrorism or other negative information."[424]

Yet, Wirt Walker III was a board member of the Carlyle Group; several of his fellow board members were related to Osama bin Laden. That should have at least prompted the FBI to have an in-person interview with Wirt Walker III.

The FSC had questions for the FBI about who purchased the stock options and what led the purchasers to believe the stocks would go down. They observed "the FBI has concluded that there is 'no evidence that allies of Osama bin Laden were involved,' in unusual volume and ratio of stock puts to calls on American and United airlines stock and other agencies directly impacted by the terrorist attacks." The families asked the FBI: "What criteria were used to determine whether the purchaser of the stock puts is an ally of Osama bin Laden? Why would the FBI limit the investigation to only allies of bin Laden? Others, [for example, individual Saudis...or investment groups such as the Carlyle Group or Banker's Trust-AB Brown] could have had foreknowledge of the attack and should be thoroughly investigated." The FSC also asked FBI Director Robert Mueller "Did the CIA notify the FBI of unusual number of stock puts?"[425]

The FBI investigation into the trades included consulting with a German computer firm named Convar. The company performed analyses on damaged disk drives from the World Trade Center debris to see what they might reveal about the suspicious trading. Berlin-based IDG News Service reported "an unexplained surge in transactions was recorded prior to the attacks leading to speculation that someone might have profited from previous knowledge about the terrorist plot by moving sums of money. But because the facilities of many financial companies processing the transactions were housed in the ... World Trade Center, it has until now been impossible to verify that suspicion."[426]

Convar confirmed the put options to sell shares in United Airlines, American Airlines, Merrill Lynch, Morgan Stanley, and Marsh & McLennan Companies weren't just a coincidence; they involved foreknowledge of the attacks.

Reuters interviewed both the director at Convar, Peter Henschel, and the company's data retrieval expert, Richard Wagner. Henschel was asked about the importance of analyzing the data retrieved from the computer disk drives in the rubble at Ground Zero. He explained, "The suspicion is that inside information about the attack was used to send financial transaction commands and authorizations in the belief that amid all the chaos the criminals would have ... a good head start ... It could turn out that Americans went on an absolute shopping binge on that Tuesday morning. But at this point there are many transactions that cannot be accounted for. Not only the volume but the size of the transactions was far higher than usual for a day like that."

Henschel was grateful that the scanner they developed at Convar was able to retrieve data from the badly-damaged computers in the World Trade Center rubble. This included "100% of the data on most of the drives we've received." [27]

Convar's data retrieval expert, Richard Wagner, said "some people had advance knowledge of the approximate time of the plane crashes in order to move out amounts exceeding $100 million. They thought that the records of their transactions could not be traced after the main frames were destroyed." If Convar hadn't developed their scanner technology to retrieve data, it would have been impossible to gather.

Reuters reported Convar had provided the summary of what they had found, but "to date the FBI has yet to investigate." Since the FBI hadn't bothered to investigate, the FSC asked the 9/11 Commission, "Has the FBI requested records from Convar, the German Company which is attempting to retrieve data from damaged hard drives?"[428]

Trading related to the unusual "put" and "call" options was traced to the Marsh & McLennan data center on the 95th floor of the North Tower. This is the center of where the tower was hit on September Eleventh. Marsh & McLennan occupied the 93rd to the 100th floors of the North Tower. Were those responsible for the attack hoping that the data housed in Marsh & McLennan's offices would be destroyed to conceal an economic crime? [429]

On September Eleventh, the chief of Risk Management for Marsh & McLennan Companies was Paul Bremer. He'd served as the US Ambassador to the Netherlands from 1983 to 1986, and then as the Coordinator for Counterterrorism from 1986 to 1989 under the Reagan Administration. From there, Bremer became managing director of Kissinger and Associates from 1989 to 2000, working closely with Henry Kissinger.

After the attacks on September Eleventh, Paul Bremer went on to become the Administrator of the Coalition Provisional Authority of Iraq. In this capacity he reported directly to the Secretary of Defense,

Donald Rumsfeld. This put Bremer in charge of the occupation in Iraq.

This might not have taken place at all, given that Bremer's office was above where the North Tower was hit on September Eleventh. There, a conference call was proceeding, where Marsh & McLennan employees were raising concerns about mysterious transactions in the data center. But they all died when the building collapsed.

However, Paul Bremer wasn't in his North Tower office on the morning of September Eleventh. "I was diverted on a plane this morning. I was trying to get to New York and wound up in Baltimore," he told an NBC lunch hour host.

Just three hours after the first plane hit the World Trade Center, Bremer told NBC viewers "this is a very well planned, very well coordinated attack ... there are only three or four candidates in the world really who could have conducted this attack." The NBC news anchor said, "bin Laden comes to mind right away Mr. Bremer." To which Bremer replied, "bin Laden ... has to be a prime suspect, Iran and Iraq."[430]

Bremer, as Director of Risk Management, didn't mention in the interview that there were 1,700 employees of Marsh & McLennan Companies who were in their offices from the 93rd to 100th floor of the North Tower. As the North Tower had collapsed at 10:28 a.m., two hours before his 12:46 p.m. interview, Bremer's omission of this detail and lack of emotion is puzzling. The number of lives lost to the attacks would later total 295 employees and 63 consultants.[431]

During the interview, Bremer told viewers that in order to determine who might be responsible for the attacks, you have to consider "what you have to work with ... is motivations and capabilities. You have to start with what you know about the past and which groups have motives ... We have to identify the perpetrators."[432]

Bremer also said that America needed to ask, "What are the lessons we learned? What did we learn about the intelligence failure? What did we learn about the security failure? And how do we move forward in the future in those areas?" [433]

On September Eleventh, a fire raged in Seven World Trade Center (WTC7), floors 11 to 13. These housed Security & Exchange Commission records relating to multi-billion-dollar investigations.[434] The *Los Angeles Times* reported on September 17, 2001 that "an estimated 3,000 to 4,000 cases were destroyed. They included SEC's major inquiry into the manner in which investment banks divided up hot shares of initial public offerings (IPOs) during the high-tech boom." [435] The destruction of these files resulted in huge savings for the CEOs and corporations being investigated.

It wasn't the only strange economic happenstance surrounding the events of 9/11. In 1998, the Port Authority of New York and New Jersey agreed to privatize the World Trade Center they'd owned since 1973. On July 24, 2001, Larry Silverstein of Silverstein Properties, who already owned World Trade Center Building 7, signed a 99-year lease for World Trade Center Buildings 1 and 2 (the Twin Towers) and Buildings 4 and 5. The deal was unusual. The Port Authority carried only $1.5 billion in insurance coverage, and the World Trade Center had recently been valued at $1.2 billion. However, Silverstein insisted the World Trade Center be insured for $3.5 billion.

In addition, in the lease contract Silverstein Properties was given the right to rebuild the structures if they were destroyed and expand the amount of retail space if rebuilding did take place.

Starting on September 11, 2001, Silverstein sought to have the attacks construed as two attacks and not one. This way, his company could be awarded up to $7.5 billion.[436] Luckily for him, Silverstein Properties had written into the agreement six weeks previous that they would have insurance coverage for any terrorist attacks.[437]

In the end, his company was awarded $4.55 billion when it was judged that the World Trade Center had been the site of not one, but two terrorist attacks. After he won the insurance claims for the attacks, Silverstein sued United Airlines and American Airlines for more insurance money.[438]

The World Trade Center complex also had asbestos lawsuits

pending when Silverstein bought the buildings. After 9/11, he didn't have to spend billions to remove the asbestos. It all begs the question: before he made the purchase, did Larry Silverstein have information the World Trade Center had been targeted for a terrorist attack?

However, the 9/11 Commission wasn't interested in exploring leads about possible foreknowledge of the attacks. Regarding who helped fund the alleged 19 hijackers they stated, "To date, the US Government has not been able to determine the origin of the money used for the 9/11 attacks. Ultimately, the question is of little practical significance."[439]

~ 12 ~

Question to Mayor Giuliani

Why was the World Trade Center steel removed so quickly, without being examined, from the scene of a mass murder?

One of the members of the Family Steering Committee was Robin Wiener. After her brother died, Robin, a resident of Washington DC, became a board member of Families of September 11. She also became a member of Voices of September 11th, "Give Your Voice," and the "WTC United Family Group."

Trained as a lawyer, Robin was President of the Institute of Scrap Recycling Industries (ISRI) in Washington DC. She appeared before the "US House of Representatives Committee on Government Reform Hearings to Review 9/11 Commission Recommendations" on August 3, 2004. She introduced herself as the "sister of Jeffrey Wiener, who was killed that morning while working at his desk" for Marsh Risk Technologies on the 96th floor the North Tower. Jeffrey was 33-years-old.[440]

After he died, the Jeffrey Wiener Scholarship Fund was established to help graduates of Trumbull High School in Trumbull, Connecticut.[441] Jeffrey Wiener is one of a number of those who died on September

11 who is featured at the National Museum of American History's collection, *September 11: Bearing Witness to History*. The collection has been on display since 2002.

At 8:46 a.m. on September 11, when American Airlines Flight 11 struck the North Tower, Jeff's parents were in their car "driving north on the New Jersey Turnpike from where they could see the towers. They immediately called their daughter, Robin. She drove from Washington, DC, to New York to join the family in the search for her brother." The next morning Jeff's wife, his parents, Robin Wiener, and other family members "began distributing missing person posters, visiting hospitals, contacting police, and checking with relief organizations. Sadly, they never found Jeff alive."[442]

Jeffrey Wiener was thought to have died in the North Tower of the World Trade Center. But on February 2, 2002, the remains of his body were found on the roof of World Trade Center Building 5. The family wondered why it had taken so long to recover his body. They also wondered how a person dying in the North Tower could end up on the roof of WTC 5. If Jeffrey Wiener had jumped from the North Tower, he might have landed on the roof of WTC 6, the closest building to the North Tower. The roof of WTC 5 would have Jeffrey Wiener landing over 300 feet across the length of the World Trade Center complex. What could cause him to fly through the air and land on the roof of World Trade Center Building 5? Did no one go onto the roof of that building between September 11, 2001, and February 2, 2002?[443]

For the 9/11 families, the fallen towers at the World Trade Center was a crime scene in need of investigation. And they weren't the only ones who thought so. On September 19, 2001, Professor of Civil Engineering at the University of California at Berkeley, Professor Abolhassan Astaneh-Asi, arrived in New York. He was there to conduct a two-week scientific reconnaissance of the collapsed towers. He hoped to gain an understanding of how they had come down. His project was one of eight financed by the National Science Foundation to study the World Trade Center disaster.

Professor Astaneh-Asi said, "Where there is a car accident and two people are killed, you keep the car until the trial is over. If a plane crashes, not only do you keep the plane, but you assemble all the pieces, take it to a hangar, and put it together. That's only for 200, 300 people, when they die. In this case, you had … a major … manmade structure. My wish was that we had spent whatever it takes … Get all this steel, carry it to a lot … After all, this is a crime scene and you have to figure out exactly what happened."[444]

However, that was not to be the case for the scene at the World Trade Center. Official investigation teams, such as the Federal Emergency Management Agency (FEMA) and the FBI did not have access to the site. Within a few short weeks, steel from the Trade Center buildings was already being shipped to salvage yards and sold as scrap.

The Family Steering Committee asked the 9/11 Commission: "Why was the World Trade Center steel removed so quickly, without being examined, from the scene of a mass murder? Who ordered the removal of the steel?"[445]

The US House of Representatives Committee on Science met in 2002 and convened a hearing titled "Learning from 9/11: Understanding the Collapse of the World Trade Center." In their report, the Committee on Science stated that at Ground Zero there was "No clear authority and the absence of an effective protocol for how the building performance investigators should conduct and coordinate their investigation with the concurrent search and rescue efforts, as well as any criminal investigation. Early confusion over who was in charge of the site and the lack of authority of investigators to impound pieces of steel for examination before they were recycled led to the loss of important pieces of evidence that were destroyed early."[446]

The report chided the decision of the National Institute of Standards and Technology (NIST) for preventing FEMA's Building Performance Assessment Team from being on site before October 7 to begin the important work "of initiating analysis that could ultimately yield valuable information about the sequence of events and failures that resulted in the progressive collapse of the building."[447]

New York State Democratic Representative Joseph Crowley said the recycling of Trade Center steel without being examined would taint the investigation. Crowley concluded, "It is not only unfortunate, it borders on criminal."[448]

The 9/11 families agreed with Crowley's assessment that the shipping of debris from Ground Zero bordered on criminal activity. They asked the 9/11 Commission to inquire into the matter. The FSC stated: "Former FBI Acting Director Thomas Pickard said that the FBI wanted to take over Ground Zero and make it a crime scene as was done at the Pentagon. If that had occurred all materials from the scene would have been protected until an investigation was complete. Pickard also stated that you, Mayor Giuliani, would not allow the FBI access to the pit area. Is this accurate? If so, then what was your reason for keeping the nation's chief investigatory team—the FBI, out of Ground Zero?"[449]

After October 7, FEMA issued their assessment of the World Trade Center. FEMA's Building Performance Assessment Team reported in Appendix D of the assessment, "More than 350,000 tons of steel were extracted from Ground Zero and barged or trucked to salvage yards where it was cut up for recycling. FEMA did not have access to Ground Zero."[450]

FEMA identified four salvage yards that were contracted to process the steel after it was removed. They were:

- Hugo Nue Schnitzer at Fresh Kills Landfill, Staten Island, NJ
- Hugo Nue Schnitzer's Claremont Terminal in Jersey City, NJ
- Metal Management in Newark, NJ
- Blanford and Co. in Keasby, NJ.

In January 2002 *Fire Engineering Magazine*, the paper of record for the Fire Department of New York, ran an editorial titled "$elling Out the Investigation." The magazine's editor, Bill Manning, was an early champion of the September Eleventh families' efforts to have an inquiry into the attacks. In the editorial, he chastised the clean-up operations at Ground Zero, describing how for over "three months structural steel from the World Trade Center has been … cut up and sold for scrap." The systematic "destruction of evidence" demonstrated an "astounding ignorance of government officials to the value of a thorough, scientific investigation of the largest fire-induced collapse in world history." Nowhere in the national standards for a fire investigation "does one find an exemption allowing the destruction of evidence for buildings over 10 stories tall." Consequently, the editorial concluded, *Fire Engineering* has good reason to believe that the 'official investigation' … is a half-baked farce."[451]

The editorial underscored that legitimate questions about why the buildings fell virtually at free-fall speed needed to be accounted for. Some in the administration contended that steel frame buildings could collapse due to fire. But "the structural damage from the planes and the explosive ignition of jet fuel in themselves were not enough to bring down the towers." And if it was determined that steel frame buildings could collapse due to fire, this had huge implications for the safety of firefighters trying to rescue people in skyscraper fires.

Queens Fire Commissioner Chris Gioia of Franklin Square & Munson Fire Department spoke about these implications in an interview. He said that decisions by firefighters to enter burning skyscrapers since the early 20th century were made based on their collective experience that steel-frame buildings didn't collapse when they were on fire. If firefighters understood that a skyscraper could crumble to the ground in a matter of seconds, they wouldn't commit to entering the building.

Gioia said there were "plenty of examples" like One Meridian Plaza in Philadelphia in 1991 that burned for 19 hours. After the fire was extinguished city officials determined the skyscraper at no time was in danger of collapse. Gioia said that in his 32 years with the fire department, "firefighters had no reason to suspect that any skyscraper they entered would catastrophically fail due to fires." ~~While firefighters knew there were dangers entering a building when it was on fire, "complete and sudden building failure" was not one of them~~. Gioia added that firefighters were brave and were willing to take calculated risks, but were not suicidal.[452]

The 9/11 Commission itself confirmed that "none of the [fire] chiefs present believed that a total collapse of either tower was possible."[453]

Sally Regenhard, FSC member and co-founder of the Skyscraper Safety Campaign, was also mentioned in the *Fire Engineering* article. She "wants to know why and how the building fell as it did upon her unfortunate son Christian, an FDNY probationary firefighter. And so do we … a full-throttle, fully resourced, forensic investigation is imperative … from a moral standpoint." Since firefighters were always the first in and last out when rescuing those in harm's way, the editorial stated that knowing more "about the buildings' design and behavior in this extraordinary event must be learned and applied in the real world."[454]

This failure to follow protocol led the FSC to ask the 9/11 Commission: "A few short weeks after 9/11, tons of metal from the collapsed twin towers was sold to scrap yards in New Jersey. Thereafter, the steel was re-sold to other recyclers in the United States and overseas. Anecdotal evidence suggests that the 'scrap' has ended up in India, Japan, South Korea, China and Malaysia. It is the FSC's position that the thousands of pounds of debris was crime-scene evidence. It should have been examined, catalogued, and stored in a secure location. Why were the steel beams sold and shipped overseas and not retained as evidence? Was the material examined before it was sent overseas? If examined, then by whom? Were any diagnostic studies/tests performed? If not, then why? Whose responsibility was this?"[455]

The *Fire Engineering* editorial urged the federal government to cease the destruction and removal of the debris and "commission a fully resourced blue-ribbon panel to conduct a clean and thorough investigation of the fire and collapse, leaving no stones unturned."

The editorial also revealed that "numbers of members of the New York Fire Department who were first responders on 9/11 reported explosions from within both of the twin towers before and after the planes hit the tops of the towers. We have these reports from taped radiophone communications from firefighters stationed in the basement of tower one and tower two, and from firefighters participating in rescue efforts from floors 7 and 8, 10–13, and other floors as high as floor 78 in the North Tower. These reports raise very serious questions about what happened on 9/11. If explosives were planted in the Twin Towers, how did this happen?"[456] If there were explosives used to assist in the collapse of the towers at Ground Zero, metallurgists could examine the fragments of steel for evidence of it.

The FSC cited a story in the *New York Daily News* from April 2002, where it was reported that tons of steel from the Twin Towers were being sold to New York scrap dealers. It was then exported to China and Korea as quickly as it could be loaded onto ships, thereby removing the evidence. The paper reported "Some 185,101 tons of structural steel have been hauled away from Ground Zero. Most of the steel has been recycled as per the city's decision to swiftly send the wreckage to salvage yards in New Jersey. The city's hasty move has outraged many victims' families who believe the steel should have been examined more thoroughly. Last month, fire experts told Congress that about 80% of the steel was scrapped without being examined because investigators did not have the authority to preserve the wreckage."[457]

The *Telegraph* of London reported on September 29, 2001, "The pace of the steel's removal was very rapid, even in the first weeks after the attack. By September 29, 130,000 tons of debris—most of it apparently steel—had been removed." The *Telegraph* noted that "Controlled Demolition Inc. (CDI) appeared to be a key player in the expedient removal and recycling of the steel. CDI was retained by Tully Construction Co. Inc., one of the site's four cleanup management contractors."[458]

Controlled Demolition Inc. (CDI) was one of the major demolition companies involved in the removal of debris at Ground Zero. They first arrived at the World Trade Center site on September 13. The president of the company noticed "hot spots of molten steel in the basements ... at the bottoms of the elevator shafts of the main towers, down seven basement levels." The World Trade Center towers had 47 central support columns connected to the bedrock. When workers got to that area in the rubble in mid-October of 2001, they found hot spots of steel that had literally melted "three, four, and five weeks later, when the rubble was being removed." Molten steel was also found at World Trade Center Building 7. This was noted as odd by the president of CDI because construction steel has an extremely high melting point of about 2,800° F.[459]

A report on the Government Computer News website in Washington DC stated, "In the first few weeks when a worker would pull a steel beam from the wreckage, the end of the beam would be dripping molten steel. For six months after Sept. 11, the ground temperature varied between 600 degrees Fahrenheit and 1,500 degrees, sometimes higher."[460] *Johns Hopkins Public Health Magazine* reported in late October 2001, "Fires are still actively burning and the smoke is very intense. In some pockets now being uncovered, they are finding molten steel."[461]

An interview with a chaplain accompanying the FDNY at Ground Zero was published on September 8, 2002, in the Hudson Valley's *Times-Herald Record*. The chaplain recalled, "When I was there ... the remnants of the towers were still standing. It looked like an enormous junkyard. A scrap metal yard, very similar to that. Except this was still burning. There was still fire. On the cold days, even in January, there was a noticeable difference between temperature in the middle of the site than there was when you walked two blocks over on Broadway. You could actually feel the heat. Why? Because I felt more comfortable. I realized it was actually warmer on site. The fires burned up to 2,000 degrees underground for quite a while before they actually got down to those areas and they cooled off. I talked to many contractors and they said they actually saw molten metal trapped, beams had just totally been melted because of the heat."[462]

However, after the buildings' collapse wasn't the only time this phenomenon was noted. An employee at Merrill Lynch's US Cash Equities Group across from the World Trade Center, David Long, emerged from Fulton Street Station at 8:30 a.m. on September Eleventh. He was on his way to a meeting at the World Financial Center when he heard a loud boom. When he walked outside, Fulton Street was impassable, covered with debris.

Long looked up at the North Tower and noticed "long streams of molten metal coming out of the building. They were not coming from the area where the impact [later] was ... there was molten metal just coming out of the building like a stream from a welders torch ... These streams were probably two or three stories in length ... And they would go out into sparks and spread out as they went toward the ground. ... I remember [thinking] what the hell are those streams of metal coming out? ... That is not fire. That's not smoke. That is something hot enough to glow bright orange. And it's coming out in a stream. And there were probably at least three different places that it was coming out of the corners. ... I remember thinking, has somebody got a blowtorch up there? What is going on with this building? This is the strangest thing I've ever seen."[463]

The FDNY Battalion Chief Thomas Vallebuona, had a similar reaction. He recalled, "I couldn't believe what I was seeing ... I saw stuff coming out of the side of the building. It looked like a giant fountain."[464]

On September Eleventh, ABC News reported live to interview Mayor Giuliani. In the interview he told a reporter, "I went down to the scene and we set up headquarters at 75 Barkley Street, which was right there with the Police Commissioner, the Fire Department Commissioner, the Head of Emergency Management, and we were operating out of there when we were told that the World Trade Center was going to collapse." [465] No steel-framed building had collapsed because of fire prior to September 11, 2001. Why did those with Mayor Giuliani expect the towers to?

On April 1, 2003, the 9/11 Commission heard testimony from the Commissioner of New York City Department of Design and Construction. He told the inquiry that his staff were at Ground Zero in the days that followed the attacks. Though WTC Building 6 was not hit by a plane, Kenneth Holden reported that "Underground, it was still so hot that molten metal dripped down the sides of the wall from Building 6" [466] Jet fuel was not a factor in the condition of WTC Building 6. What could cause its steel beams on the sides of its wall to drip molten metal? Examining more steel samples, instead of removing the debris and shipping it off to scrapyards, would have yielded more clues. But the 9/11 Commissioners didn't follow up on that matter.

The 9/11 Commission's Vice Chairman, Lee Hamilton, was asked by the CBC, "Should the Commission have asked more questions about the removal of the debris?" Hamilton replied, "Look, you can say that about almost every phase of our investigation, 'you should have asked this, you should have asked that, you should have spent more time'—you're conducting an investigation, you have a time limit, you don't have unlimited time, you have a budget limit, you cannot go down every track, you cannot answer conclusively every question."[467]

In the end, the FSC also commented, "Mr. Giuliani, several members of the Family Steering Committee attended a meeting with you in 2002 at which time you told us that you were against, and would not support, the formation of an independent commission to examine the events of 9/11. Why did you oppose the creation of this commission? Given the revelations that have emerged during commission hearings, do you still regard their work as unimportant and unnecessary? Do you now believe it is beneficial to have the public well informed about the actions of the government, its agencies and its public officials?"[468]

The FSC also wanted the 9/11 Commission to ask: "Why did you ask to have your records as Mayor of New York City sealed for 25 years?"[469] Giuliani's records are sealed until 2026.

~13 ~

Question to President George W. Bush

*As Commander-in-Chief on the morning of 9/11, why didn't
you return immediately to Washington DC or the National
Military Command Center once you became aware that America
was under attack? At what time were you made aware that other
planes were hijacked in addition to Flight 11 and Flight 175?*

In her testimony before the 9/11 Commission on March 31, 2003,
9/11 widow Mindy Kleinberg recalls how her husband Alan started
his day on September Eleventh. "At 6:15 a.m., my husband Alan left
for work; he drove into New York City, and was at his desk ... with
Cantor Fitzgerald ... [in] Tower One [North Tower] of the WTC by
7:30 a.m. In contrast, on the morning of September 11, President Bush
was scheduled to listen to elementary school children read. Before
the President walked into the classroom NORAD had sufficient
information that the plane that hit the WTC was hijacked. At that
time, they also had knowledge that two other commercial airliners, in
the air, were also hijacked. It would seem that a national emergency
was in progress. Yet the President was allowed to enter a classroom
full of young children and listen to the students read."[470]

Mindy Kleinberg's testimony shone a light on the peculiar leadership decisions on the morning of September Eleventh. The FSC asked the 9/11 Commission to inquire of President Bush, under oath: "As Commander-in-Chief on the morning of 9/11, why didn't you return immediately to Washington DC or the National Military Command Center once you became aware that America was under attack?"[471]

On September 11, 2001, at 8:46 a.m., the first plane hit the North Tower of the World Trade Center. At that time, President George W. Bush was in a motorcade driving through Sarasota, Florida. The 9/11 Commission reported at that crucial moment "no one in the White House or traveling with the president knew that [Flight 11] had been hijacked [at this time]. Immediately afterward, duty officers at the White House and Pentagon began notifying senior officials what had happened."[472]

Yet, there were numerous reports to the contrary. James Bamford, in his book, *A Pretext for War*, highlights that President Bush wasn't informed about the airplane hitting the World Trade Center until his motorcade had arrived at the Booker Elementary School. This in spite of the presence of a secure phone in the president's limousine: meant for exactly an emergency of this kind. Oddly, there were reports that others in the president's motorcade were notified, even though the president was not.[473]

At 9:03 a.m., President Bush entered one of the Booker Elementary School classrooms. According to Sarasota County Sheriff Bill Balkwill, there was a Marine in charge of carrying the president's phone standing in an adjacent room. The Marine listened to someone speak to him over his earpiece. Then the Marine said to Balkwill, "Can you get me to a television? We're not sure what's going on, but we need to see a television."

Balkwill turned on a TV set in the front office just seconds before Flight 175 hit the South Tower. Balkwill watched along with the Marine, a SWAT team member, and three Secret Service agents. When

Flight 175 crashed into the World Trade Center, the Marine turned to Balkwill and said, "We're out of here … can you get everyone ready?"[474]

Even years later, it remained a mystery who made the decision for Bush to stay in the classroom. The Secret Service declined to comment.[475] Philip Melanson, author of *The Secret Service: The History of an Enigmatic Agency*, wrote, "With an unfolding terrorist attack, the procedure should have been to get the president to the closest secure location as quickly as possible, which clearly is not a school. You're safer in that presidential limo, which is bombproof and blastproof and bulletproof. … In the presidential limo, the communications system is almost duplicative of the White House—he can do almost anything from there but he can't do much sitting in a school."[476]

The FSC was astonished at the president's choice to remain in the classroom, as well as at the Secret Service for not initiating his removal. They asked the 9/11 Commission to ask the Secret Service these questions: "Why was President Bush not immediately evacuated from the Sarasota school, but rather was permitted to remain in the building after the second building was hit and this nation was under attack? Why was protocol not followed? Was President Bush deemed to be in the 'zone of danger'? If so, at exactly what time was he put in the 'zone of danger'? Where is the log and record of the Secret Service agents? Where is the incident report?"[477]

At 9:06 a.m., while sitting in the classroom, President Bush was told about the second crash at the World Trade Center. The second-graders were about to read a story called *The Pet Goat* when the president was told of the attack. A report by the *Tampa Tribune* relates that the classroom was silent for thirty seconds. Then President Bush picked up the book and read with the children "for eight or nine minutes."[478]

While this was occurring, White House Press Secretary Ari Fleischer stood at the back of the room, maintaining eye contact with the president. The press secretary held up a pad of paper with the words, "DON'T SAY ANYTHING YET," printed in big, block letters. Reporters who were present noticed the Secretary with this message.[479]

However, on December 4, 2001, President Bush made the following statement at a Town Hall meeting about the moment—9:01 a.m.—that he said he learned about the attack. "And I was sitting outside the classroom waiting to go in, and I saw an airplane hit the tower—the television was obviously on, and I use to fly myself, and I said, 'There's one terrible pilot.' And I said, 'It must have been a horrible accident.' But I was whisked off there—I didn't have much time to think about it."[480] This despite the fact that the *Washington Times* reported that President Bush didn't have access to a television until fifteen minutes later.[481]

A *Boston Herald* reporter reflected on Bush's statements. "Think about that. Bush's remark implies he saw the first plane hit the tower. But we all know that video of the first plane hitting did not surface until the next day. Could Bush have meant he saw the second plane hit—which many Americans witnessed? No, because he said that he was in the classroom when Andrew Card whispered in his ear that a second plane hit. How could the commander in chief have seen the plane fly into the first building—as it happened?"[482]

The Family Steering Committee noted from reports in the press, that at 8:55 a.m. Navy Captain Deborah Loewer, director of the White House Situation Room, told President Bush a plane crashed into the North Tower when his limousine arrived at the elementary school. They asked that Bush "Please explain the reason why you decided to continue with the scheduled classroom visit, fifteen minutes after learning the first hijacked airliner had hit the World Trade Center."

Lorie Van Auken recalls the morning of September Eleventh and her reaction to President Bush sitting in the Florida classroom. She had just heard a voicemail message from her husband, who was stuck in the North Tower above the impact zone. Black smoke was billowing out of the tower, and Kenneth Van Auken didn't know if he'd make it out alive.

Lorie turned on the TV to watch the live coverage. She recalls, "Then the second tower was hit. As I continued to watch the breaking news, they showed the President sitting in an elementary school classroom, juxtaposed with the footage of black smoke coming from the World Trade Center, along with people jumping to their deaths from the burning buildings. I screamed at the television. 'Get up, President Bush. Get up and do something,' but he remained seated in a classroom of small children. I watched as Andrew Card whispered something to the President, and yet, still my President remained seated in a classroom of small children when our country was so obviously under a terrorist attack. In between panic and hysteria, in between hoping that my husband would get out of the World Trade Center alive, and wondering how I would ever break the news to my children, I also wondered why the Secret Service was letting the President stay in the classroom full of children. Why didn't they whisk him away? It seemed as if every target in America was being attacked. So, wasn't the President, the leader of the free world, in danger of being fatally attacked as well? Weren't the children who were in the classroom with the President in danger, too?"[483]

Paul Thompson, researcher and author of *The Terror Timeline*, noted at "8:48 a.m. on the morning of September 11, 2001, the first pictures of the burning World Trade Center were broadcast on live television. The news anchors, reporters, and viewers had little idea what had happened in lower Manhattan, but there were some people who did know. By that time, the Federal Aviation Administration (FAA), the North American Aerospace Defense Command (NORAD), the National Military Command Center, the Pentagon, the White House, the Secret Service, and Canada's Strategic Command all knew that three commercial airplanes had been hijacked. They knew that one plane had been flown deliberately into the World Trade Center's North Tower; a second plane was wildly off course and also heading toward Manhattan; and a third plane had abruptly turned around over Ohio and was flying back toward Washington, DC. So why, at 9:03 a.m.—fifteen minutes after it was clear the United States was under terrorist attack—did President Bush sit down with a classroom of second-graders and begin a 20-minute pre-planned photo op?"[484]

President Bush departed the elementary school at 9:34 a.m. At this time, CBS news was reporting that there were as many as eight hijacked planes flying over American airspace.[485] Yet, the Secret Service didn't remove Bush from harm's way.

In contrast, the Secret Service showed no signs of inaction when it came to removing Vice President Dick Cheney that morning. The vice president was reported by President Bush's personal secretary as being "seized by the arms, legs and his belt and physically carried" out of his office at 9:03 a.m. by Secret Service agents. Cheney was taken to the Presidential Emergency Operations Center below the White House, where Secretary of Transportation Norman Mineta saw him prior to 9:25 a.m.[486] As Cheney describes it, the agents "hoisted me up and moved me very rapidly down the hallway, down some stairs."[487]

The Secret Service director, who was also ordering the roundup of top officials and members of the president's family, recalls, "There wasn't a lot of time for chit-chat, you know, with the vice president ... we knew there were unidentified planes tracking in our direction."[488]

If the Secret Service director in Washington DC knew there were unidentified planes tracking in the direction of the White House and the Capitol, why were Secret Service agents with the president so passive in their role?

The largest Secret Service Field Office was in World Trade Center Building 7. By the time the president arrived at the Booker Elementary School, the Secret Service agents in WTC 7 had all been evacuated.[489] Weren't Secret Service agents with the president in touch with their head offices in Washington and New York?

The Family Steering Committee wanted the 9/11 Commission to ask President Bush, "At what time were you made aware that other planes were hijacked in addition to Flight 11 and Flight 175?" [490] The Secret Service was able to see the FAA's radar, and there were multiple Secret Service agents traveling with Bush. Since the White House and the Secret Service Presidential Protective Division were in touch, the president should have been informed of what was happening over the skies of America as soon as the FAA let Otis Air Force Base know of the status of Flight 11 by 8:30 a.m.

Other planes were also reported as hijacked that morning. Given that the Secret Service had the ability to see the FAA's radar, the president should have been in the loop in real-time. The FSC posed their questions about when President Bush was made aware of the hijackings, but there were no comments offered on the subject in the Commission report. The 9/11 Commission simply omitted any discussion of this important detail.[491]

In front of the 9/11 Commission, FSC member Carol Ashley commented about how foreign intelligence agencies had warned the United States of an imminent attack. For instance, *The Telegraph* published a story on September 16, 2001, titled "Israeli Security Issued Urgent Warning to CIA of Large-Scale Terror Attacks." On May 21, 2002, *The New York Times* reprinted an *International Herald Tribune* story titled "The Road to Sept. 11: The US Ignored Foreign Warnings, Too."

Ashley noted that foreign intelligence agencies in at least eleven different nations provided very specific data to the United States government about a terrorist attack. This included anticipated attacks on the World Trade Center and the Pentagon. The warnings by these other intelligence agencies included the threat of using planes on suicide missions.[492]

FSC member Patty Casazza also spoke about how foreign intelligence agencies warned the US government about specific attacks. She said there were FBI and other intelligence officers who wanted to testify before the 9/11 Commission about the foreknowledge they had received regarding the date and location of the impending attacks.[493]

Carol Ashley informed 9/11 Commissioners, "on September 10, Pentagon brass suddenly canceled flights scheduled for the 11." She wanted to know why. What prompted this type of cancelation? What did some people in the Pentagon know that warned them not to fly on September 11? Ashley referred to other news stories, where San

Francisco Mayor Willie Brown was warned on September 10 to not fly to New York City. Attorney-General John Ashcroft had stopped flying on commercial planes in response to an FBI threat assessment. Why were ordinary American citizens kept in the dark?

She concluded her testimony before the 9/11 Commission, stating, "there were a lot of dots to connect. But look at what was known. Our intelligence agencies were tracking the hijackers. Eleven nations warned us of the attack. There was foreknowledge by some. Hijackings were predicted. The targets had been identified. It is heartbreaking and infuriating to think that there were clear warnings, yet, seemingly, preventive measures were not taken; that protocols were not followed which might have saved so many lives. Instead, innocent people were murdered in an unconscionable act of barbarism, shattering three thousand families, traumatizing our nation and horrifying the world. It should never have happened."[494]

So, the FSC requested the 9/11 Commission ask President Bush this question: "As Commander-in-Chief, from May 1, 2001 until September 11, 2001, did you receive any information from any intelligence agency official or agent that [Osama bin Laden] was planning to attack this nation on its own soil using airplanes as weapons, targeting New York City landmarks during the week of September 11, 2001 or on the actual day of September 11, 2001?"[495]

Newspaper headlines indicated Bush was warned. The *New York Post* ran a story on May 15, 2002, with the headline, "Bush Knew: Prez Was Warned of Possible Hijackings before Terror Attacks."[496] The *Guardian* published a story with the headline, "Bush Knew of Terrorist Plot to Hijack US Planes.[497] And a *New York Times* headline read, "Bush was Warned bin Laden Wanted to Hijack Planes."[498]

Carol Ashley asked the 9/11 Commission, "Why didn't President Bush, as Commander in Chief, assume command and order defensive actions to protect our nation as soon as he was told by his chief of staff, 'We are under attack'?"[499] Ashley wanted Bush to make statements before the 9/11 Commission under oath.

In a memorandum to the 9/11 Commission on February 16, 2004, the FSC wrote: "that President Bush should provide sworn public testimony to the full ten-member panel ... Before an audience of the American people, the Commission must ask President Bush in sworn testimony, the following questions."[500]

But, the meeting with Bush and Cheney took place in secret on April 29, 2004. It was not held under oath. No transcript was made available of their conversation with the commissioners. Nothing was learned about why the president remained at an elementary school during the attacks. Nothing was learned about what the president knew regarding foreign intelligence agencies forewarning the US. Nothing was learned about why the president had authorized America to prepare for war against Afghanistan in the days and weeks prior to the attacks on September 11.[501]

~ 14 ~

Question to the Port Authority/WTC/City of New York

What is the name of the individual who made the announcement in 2 WTC who told workers to return to their offices? Why were the roof access doors locked? Why was there no roof-top evacuation?

One of the questions the Family Steering Committee (FSC) wanted answers to concerned reports by Mary Fetchet's son Brad and others who were asked to either remain in their offices, or, if they were already evacuating, to return to their offices. The FSC asked: "What is the name of the individual who made the announcement in 2WTC who told workers to return to their offices?"[502]

FSC member Mary Fetchet noted that "Rick Rescorla, Director of Security for Morgan Stanley directed his employees to leave the building—to disregard the Port Authorities commands to evacuees to 'return UP to their offices.'" [503] Mary Fetchet was shocked that different employees in the South Tower "were receiving such conflicting information, which ultimately, senselessly cost my son's life and the life of 600 others ... No one in building two should be dead today. ... who is accountable?"[504]

Brian Clark, an executive with Euro Brokers, was the fire warden on the 84th floor of the South Tower. He recalls hearing the repeating message on the public address system, "Your attention, please, ladies and gentlemen. Building 2 [South Tower] is secure. There is no need to evacuate Building 2. If you are in the midst of evacuation, you may use the re-entry doors and the elevators to return to your office. Repeat, Building 2 is secure."[505]

The announcement was made by Philip Hayes, Deputy Fire Inspector for the South Tower, based on instructions from George Tabeek of the Port Authority of New York and New Jersey.[506] Why did George Tabeek of the Port Authority give the order to make these announcements in the South Tower? Individuals with bullhorns were telling frightened employees to return to their offices. All those who returned to their offices died.

There were numerous examples in the media of workers being told to stay in the building. John Howard, a man working on the 60th floor of the South Tower (WTC 2) felt the building shake when the plane crashed into it. He remembers that people were preparing to evacuate. Suddenly, there was a man with a bullhorn telling them to stop. Howard recalls, "He was telling us, 'Don't panic!' saying that we were safer in the building than leaving it."

Another employee was Jennifer. She was on the 92nd floor of WTC 2. She was in the midst of evacuating and had descended to the 52nd floor, where she encountered someone ordering her to return to her office. "Some jackass started yelling up at us through a bullhorn saying: 'This tower has been secured. You are in America. Return to your offices!'"[507]

The man with the bullhorn appealed to employees' sense of patriotism ("you are in America") as a way to motivate them to return to their desks. While John and Jennifer ignored the orders, others obeyed the directive to stay in their offices while the buildings burned. One of these employees was 9/11 widow Kristen Breitweiser's husband, Ron, who called to tell her, "Sweets, I'm okay ... They told us to stay in the building. I've got to go."[508]

Breitweiser and Patty Casazza wanted the 9/11 Commission to find out who was giving orders to World Trade Center employees to stay in the building.

On 9/11, WABC New York interviewed employees Michelle Scott and Evalle Sweezer outside the North Tower while the building was still standing. They reported a bombing in the tower. Michelle Scott told WABC, "We ran down the steps to the lobby. There was no lobby. Everything was torn up. And even the turnstile was burnt and it was sticking up. And they just told us to run."

Evalle Sweezer said, "My boss ran out of the office. He said one thing. 'Run.' Everybody just ran. And we ran down the stairs. They told us to come back up. And we were like 'come back upstairs? Are you crazy?' So we continued down the stairs. We came out into the lobby. There was no lobby. The lobby was gone."

They were asked by WABC, "Did you see other people?" Evalle Sweezer exclaimed, "There was a woman with her face blown off and as we were coming out we passed the lobby. There was no lobby. So I believe a bomb hit the lobby. And in a couple of seconds the first plane hit [the North Tower]."[509]

Here we have a report of a bomb going off "a couple of seconds" *before* the first plane hit the World Trade Center. Building management were encouraging employees to stay in the North Tower of the World Trade Center after these explosions. Anyone in America who had attended school knew from fire drills that when a building is on fire you MUST leave the building.

FSC member Mary Fetchet gave testimony before the 9/11 Commission on March 31, 2003. Her 24-year-old son Brad worked as an equity trader on the 89th floor of the South Tower. She told the commissioners that Brad had phoned and spoken to her husband, then tried to contact her. Brad wasn't aware the plane that had hit the North Tower was a commercial jet.

Mary received a phone message from Brad 14 minutes after the North Tower was hit: 3 minutes before the South Tower. She described how "The Port Authority directed my son's company to stay put in their office, 'that the building is safe and secure.' My husband (Frank) asked Brad to call me at home. Here is the recording of the message Brad left me around 9:00 a.m. Message: 'Hi Mom, it's Brad. Just wanted to call and let you know. I'm sure that you heard there was … or maybe you haven't heard that a plane crashed into World Trade Center One. We're fine. We're in World Trade Center 2. I'm obviously alive and well over here. But obviously a pretty scary experience. I saw a guy fall out of probably the 91st story, ah, all the way down, so (long pause, cleared throat) you're welcome to give a call here. I think we'll be here all day. I'm not sure if the firm is going to shut down for the day or what. But ah, give me a call back later. I called Dad to let him know. Love You.'" 510

Mary Fetchet never had a chance to call her son back "to say goodbye and tell him I love him." 511 The last phone call Brad made was to his girlfriend at 9:20 a.m., 29 minutes before the South Tower collapsed. From that last phone call, it was clear there were sirens in the background and "he was frantically trying to escape the building."

Mary was not alone. Other families were receiving calls from loved ones "who knew they were going to die, who were trapped above the fire, asphyxiated or injured and unable to escape."512

Given the perilous situation, Mary asked, "How is it that people were directed to remain in a 110-story building supposedly 'safe and secure' when its twin tower is billowing in smoke and people choosing to jump to their death in order to avoid a high-rise fire? How is it that Brad was unaware of the dangerous situation he was in 15 minutes after the 1st plane hit tower one? Precious time was wasted."

Mary recalled the World Trade Center bombing of 1993. She wondered what was learned from that attack? For those who listened to the Port Authority on September Eleventh and did not evacuate, "They died a horrendous death."

Donna Marsh O'Connor, whose daughter, Vanessa Lang Langer, was on the 93rd floor of the South Tower, spoke at the National Press

Club. Donna recalled that on the morning of September Eleventh Vanessa "five minutes after the first plane hit ... was on the phone to the Park Avenue office of Regis Business International where she worked ... [saying] that the Port Authority ... told [people in the building] they were safe, that they should stay at their desks. They were not safe."

O'Connor added, "Roughly, about the same time George W. Bush, the President of this country, walked into a school to lecture to children. He didn't rush to command central. He didn't order evacuations of any of our major skyscrapers, including, and especially Tower Two. My daughter was found ten feet from an alley, whole and intact. She wasn't crushed. She didn't fall. She had injuries, blunt trauma to her head, her neck, her femur. I have two sons. One of them, at the time, was her best friend. He was fourteen years old. And he spent September 12 researching all of the phone numbers of all of the emergency rooms of New York City because this was an impossibility. My daughter would have run for her life. My daughter would have run not to make her brothers the saddest human beings on the face of the planet." [513] Vanessa Lang Langer was found dead between World Trade Center Buildings 4 and 5.

Vanessa Lang Langer was four months pregnant when she died. Vanessa's husband, Tim Langer, fell into a spiral of alcohol abuse after the death of his spouse and dreams of a firstborn child were blown apart. He died of liver failure in 2005 at the age of 34.

FSC member Patty Casazza stated that her husband John told her that the rooftop doors were locked. This meant that all of the employees at the highest floors of the North and South Towers of the World Trade Center were prevented from the fastest possible evacuation route. In the 1993 bombing of the World Trade Center, police helicopters had landed on the Twin Tower roofs to help evacuate employees. Those who climbed to the roof were taken to the ground level by a series of helicopter flights.

The Family Steering Committee wanted the 9/11 Commission

to have Mayor Rudy Giuliani and his staff answer these questions: "On 9/11, rooftop doors to both of the World Trade Center towers were locked. Thus, rooftop rescue by helicopter was impossible. Who made the decision to lock the rooftop doors? When was this decision made? Why was this decision made?" [514]

In the North Tower, escaping down the stairs for employees above the 91st floor was not possible due to collapsed staircases. But could there have been a rooftop evacuation? During his testimony before the 9/11 Commission, Mayor Giuliani explained that he saw people near the top of the North Tower "hanging out the windows." He recalled asking FDNY Chief of Department Pete Ganci, "Can we get helicopters up on the roof and help any of those people?"

Giuliani said Chief Ganci "pointed to a big flame that was shooting out of the North Tower ... And he didn't say the rest of it, which was 'Do you see the flame, the helicopter would explode' ... I knew what he was saying."[515]

Giuliani and Ganci were at street level when this conversation reportedly took place. These conclusions weren't based on a visual inspection of the North Tower rooftop, but on the mayor's interpretation of Chief Ganci's nonverbal gesture. No one could ask Chief Ganci if he agreed with how the mayor interpreted his gesture; Ganci died on September Eleventh when the North Tower collapsed.[516]

The Smithsonian National Museum of American History details that the upper limit of the crash zone in the North Tower from Flight 11 was the 98th floor.[517] After the South Tower fell there were photos of flames shooting out of the North Tower as high as the 105th floor, but not as high as the rooftop.

While Giuliani told the commissioners a rooftop rescue wasn't possible, other accounts reported in the news contradicted that premise. FSC members had read these before submitting their questions to the 9/11 Commission.

In October 2001, the *Wall Street Journal* reported that two choppers from the Brooklyn Police Aviation Bureau had responded immediately after they got the radio call about an explosion at the North Tower. The helicopters were equipped with 250-foot hoists, and capable of rescuing as many as ten people at a time. Plan A would be to land a rescue helicopter on the North Tower rooftop helispot. The helispot was certified, meaning the Port Authority had gone to the trouble to have authorized a safe and legal place for helicopters to land in case of emergency. Plan B would be to hover over the roof and drop the hoist in order to lift people up to the chopper.

Each "three-man crew was specially trained for rooftop rescues." In fact, pilots in two of the helicopters had personally rescued people from the rooftop of the North Tower after a truck loaded with explosives was detonated in the basement of the tower in 1993. But on September Eleventh, pilot Greg Semendinger recalled as the Brooklyn choppers swooped in and "peered through a smoke-free area on the top of the North Tower they saw no one to save." A light northerly wind was keeping portions of the rooftop clear of smoke.

There were occupants who were still alive above the Flight 11 crash site, but the first pilot to reach the North Tower, said "there was nobody on the roof" to save. Semendinger told *The Wall Street Journal* that "he estimated that dozens of people could have been taken to safety before the tower collapsed."[518] He made his estimate based on his experience of rescuing 28 employees from the North Tower rooftop after the 1993 bombing.

However, according to an article in New Jersey's *Aviation International News Online*, the Port Authority decided to leave the rooftop doors locked to prevent "suicides, daredevil stunts and possible theft or vandalism of millions of dollars worth of broadcasting equipment on the roof."[519] An indignant FSC asked, "Whose responsibility was it to communicate to the building leaseholders and occupants that rooftop doors would be locked in the event of a catastrophe and/or emergency?"

When Flight 11 crashed into the North Tower, Stephen L. Roach was at his office on the 105th floor. He made several phone calls to his wife, but only got their home answering machine. Isabel Roach told the *Wall Street Journal* that one message her husband left was to tell her that he loved her. In the second message she said "she could hear the desperate shouts of her husband's coworkers at Cantor Fitzgerald yelling "Try the roof! Try the roof!" Her husband yelled back to his coworkers in the middle of his second answering machine message "There's no way out!"[520] FSC member Beverly Eckert said her husband in the South Tower, Sean Rooney, "thought that the rooftop was an option, and so they went up and they were trapped because the roof doors were locked."

There had been a successful rescue of 28 people immediately after the 1993 bombing of the North Tower. They were able to access the rooftop. Lives were saved! Since that time, the World Trade Center had only increased its security: in 1998, the NYPD created a citywide security plan in which it rated the World Trade Center at the top of its "vulnerability list"; in June 1999, Mayor Giuliani opened the New York Emergency Command Center in WTC 7, which was reinforced with bulletproof and bomb-resistant walls;[521] starting on September 4th, Mayor Giuliani's Office of Emergency Management began preparing for an exercise that simulated the "recovery of operations and business continuity in the Financial District after a terrorist attack";[522] and according to a security guard interviewed in *Newsday*, the World Trade Center had bomb-sniffing dogs on site—although on September 6, 2001, they were "abruptly removed."[523]

The Port Authority was offering an odd excuse. If the rooftop doors had been unlocked, would occupants accessing the rooftop in order to be visible for a helicopter rescue have chosen to vandalize broadcasting equipment instead of getting rescued and flown to street level? Why were the rooftop access doors accessible in 1993 but not in this atmosphere of heightened threat in 2001? If there really was a concern about vandalism, concurrent with high expectation of terrorist attacks, security could be assigned to both guard against vandalism and assist in an emergency.

The FSC were concerned that locked rooftop access doors constituted a breach and asked, "Did locking the rooftop doors violate New York City or New York State building codes?" The New York City Fire Code mandated that each "exit, exit access and exit discharge, shall be continuously maintained free from obstructions and impediments to immediate use in the event of fire or other emergency."[524] This included rooftop exit doors.

In her statement to the 9/11 Commission on November 19, 2003, FSC member Sally Regenhard commented that the "cloak of competence" was pulled off on the day of the attacks. She noted the Port Authority "had no evacuation procedures in place at all." Regenhard discussed the inadequacy of adherence to codes at the Port Authority. "But any discussion of the NYC codes is completely irrelevant to the WTC, because these buildings were above the law. The PA's buildings were totally immune from every single NYC building and fire code and were subject to their own codes which remains a mystery to this day, because no one has ever seen them. The PA repeatedly claims that they meet or exceed NYC codes, however, history has shown that this is a falsehood."[525]

~ 15 ~

Question to Vice President Dick Cheney

Did you have open lines with the Secret Service, NORAD,
the FAA and DOD? Who was in the Situation Room with you?

Before the attacks on September 11, 2001, Kristen Breitweiser liked Dick Cheney, the man who would be named as Vice Presidential running mate of George W. Bush. In the run-up to the 2000 presidential election, Kristen and her husband Ron tried to do their civic duty and inform themselves about the candidates vying for president. She recalls, her husband liked to watch political commentators on TV. "He loved Dick Cheney." Still, she was uneasy with George Bush's mediocre post-secondary grades and public statements like "Rarely is the question asked, is our children learning," and "I know how hard it is for you to put food on your family."[526] However, "Ron would allay my fears by saying that Cheney was a man who knew what he was doing and who would make sure George Bush didn't screw anything up."[527]

The Family Steering Committee requested the 9/11 Commission to inquire of Vice President Cheney: "Did you have open lines with the Secret Service, NORAD, the FAA and DOD? Who was in the

Situation Room with you?" [528] Vice President Cheney had nothing to say to the 9/11 Commission about these two questions.[529] However, a glimpse of what occurred that morning emerges from articles and documents published in the years since.

According to numerous reports, the vice president was taken to the Presidential Emergency Operations Center beneath the White House the moment the South Tower was struck at 9:03 a.m. At that time, Secret Service agent Nelson Garabito was at the Secret Service Joint Operations Center in the White House. Nelson Garabito was the designated Secret Service agent in charge of joint decision-making with the Federal Aviation Administration (FAA). Garabito's contact at the FAA informed him that there were four hijacked planes. Two had hit the World Trade Center and two others were headed toward D.C. According to documents obtained through the Freedom of Information Act in 2010, Garabito passed the information on to other Secret Service agents.[530]

However, *The 9/11 Commission Report* claimed Garabito was unsuccessful in getting his message to other Secret Service agents. The Commission wrote that Garabito's information was "either not passed on or was passed on but not disseminated."

The 9/11 Commission states that the Secret Service first learned of the attacks at 9:03 a.m. But Cheney's chief speechwriter, John McConnell, recalls being at the entrance to Cheney's office at 8:50 a.m. when Secret Service agents posted at the vice president's door told them that the plane that hit the North Tower of the World Trade Center was a commercial jet.[531] McConnell's recollection is consistent with what ABC reported: that at 9:03 a.m., Secret Service agents weren't just learning of the attacks; they were flying into action and telling Cheney "Sir, you have to come with us."[532]

The 9/11 Commission reported that Dick Cheney didn't arrive at the bunker until 9:58 a.m. This despite a US Secret Service memorandum that contradicted that timeline. The memo states, "VP Cheney was in the shelter when they were notified that a plane had hit the Pentagon."[533] Since the Secret Service sees the FAA radar in real time, they knew that Flight 77 hit the Pentagon at 9:37 a.m.

Dick Cheney seemed to be saying just as much in an interview on NBC's *Meet the Press* on September 16, 2001. Cheney said that at one point Flight 77 appeared to be heading toward the White House. Cheney added, "The Secret Service has an arrangement with the FAA. They had open lines after the World Trade Center was ..." and then he ended his thought, mid-sentence.[534]

According to a memorandum by the Secret Service's Technical Services Division (TSD) on September 12, 2001, Dick Cheney was in the bunker by or before 9:30 a.m. He was seen by Secret Service Assistant Division Chief Danny Spriggs, who arrived at 9:30 a.m. to find Cheney and his personal Secret Service Agent Anthony Zotto there. This was along with ten other staff connected to the president and vice president, including National Security Council Advisor, Condoleezza Rice.

On July 28, 2003, a document was created that detailed the Secret Service statements and interview reports to 9/11 Commission staff. The 9/11 Commission stamped these interviews as "Commission Sensitive." This account indicates that Special Agent In Charge, Carl Truscott, escorted National Security Advisor, Condoleezza Rice, to the Presidential Emergency Operations Center shortly before 9:30 a.m. When they got to "the White House Shelter Area" they met Dick Cheney, who was in the middle of a phone call, and Mrs. Lynne Cheney.[535]

In an article for *Washington's Blog*, "Secret Service Failures on 9/11: A Call for Transparency," Kevin Ryan summarized the Secret Service Technical Services Division's timeline of activities on September 11, 2001: "The TSD timeline states that at 9:18 am 'SAIC [Special Agent in Charge] Truscott learned that an aircraft had been identified en-route to the Washington area.' Therefore, there is officially prepared documentation that indicates Truscott was aware of a hijacked plane heading for Washington at least 18 minutes before the official account says the vice president was moved from his office. If this is true, the public deserves to know why the vice president was not moved to safety immediately. On the other hand, if he was moved earlier, that fact supports Mineta's astonishing and important testimony.[536]

Transportation Secretary Norman Mineta had arrived at the Presidential Emergency Operations Center at 9:20 a.m. Mineta observed that Dick Cheney was clearly in command. He saw an unidentified young officer come in and tell Cheney, "The plane is 50 miles out." According to Mineta, the young man keeps reporting to the vice president, saying, "The plane is 30 miles out." When he tells Cheney, "The plane is 10 miles out," the young man asks, "Do the orders still stand?" In response, Cheney "whipped his neck around and said, 'Of course the orders still stand. Have you heard anything to the contrary?'" Mineta told Lee Hamilton and the 9/11 commissioners that, "just by the nature of all the events going on," the order being referred to was a shootdown order. But as the young man kept asking if the orders still were in effect, Cheney's order may have been to *not* shoot down the Flight 77 which proceeded to hit the Pentagon, but to stand down.[537] Mineta's testimony to the 9/11 Commission was omitted from its *Report*.

Another agent who was in the bunker when Truscott arrived was Special Agent In Charge Anthony Zotto. It was Zotto who was totally responsible for Dick Cheney's safety. In the world of the Secret Service, with an assignment like that, wherever Dick Cheney went, Anthony Zotto was either one step behind or ahead of him, depending on what the circumstances required.[538] So, if Agent Zotto was in the bunker before 9:30 a.m., it would lend credibility to Norman Mineta's statements that Cheney was in the bunker by 9:20 a.m., when Mineta arrived.

However, Cheney told the 9/11 Commission that he was carried away from his office by the Secret Service at 9:35 a.m. According to *The 9/11 Commission Report* Dick Cheney didn't arrive at the Presidential Emergency Operations Center bunker until 9:58 a.m. Then, at 9:59

a.m. the South Tower of the World Trade Center collapsed. Everyone in the bunker watched the tower collapse on CNN.[539]

A year later on PBS, Dick Cheney told Jim Lehrer that when the South Tower collapsed it "was a shock to everybody, it certainly was to me."[540] But to others in the bunker, Cheney's reaction seemed at odds with their own. In a *Washington Post* story in June 2007, three witnesses described what happened in the bunker. "There was a groan in the room that I won't forget, ever," one witness said. "It seemed like one groan from everyone"—with the exception of Dick Cheney. He made no sound. One witness, who kept a diary of the events of that day, said, "I remember turning my head and looking at the vice president, and his expression never changed." The witness recalled that the moment the South Tower collapsed, Cheney closed his eyes against the image for one long, slow blink.

Three people interviewed by *Washington Post* reporters said "they saw no sign then or later of the profound psychological transformation that has often been imputed to Cheney. What they saw, they said, was extraordinary self-containment and a rapid shift of focus to the machinery of power. While others assessed casualties and the work of 'first responders,' Cheney began planning for a conflict that would call upon lawyers as often as soldiers and spies." Cheney next went about setting in motion the legal framework for expanding presidential powers.[541]

In May 2001, Cheney was put in charge of overseeing domestic terrorism. But when it came to discussing what he had done regarding domestic terrorism between May and September of 2001, Cheney could not recall. The Family Steering Committee asked the 9/11 Commission to find out from Cheney the answers to these questions: "In addressing the issue of domestic terrorism, which you were asked to oversee by President Bush in May, 2001, whom did you consult and/or from whom did you request briefings? What were your findings on the threat level? What recommendations for improved security resulted from your study of domestic terrorism? When were they made and to whom? What coordinated plans of action, directives or protocols developed as a result?" [542] But the vice president had no comment to make to the 9/11 Commission regarding these questions.[543]

In her book, *Wake-Up Call*, 9/11 widow Kristen Breitweiser cites her husband's enthusiasm for the vice president persuaded her to be open-minded toward Cheney. But she soon discovered Cheney was busy trying to sabotage any investigation. "He would call up congressional officials and threaten them ... Publicly, in his grumbling tone and with his glaring eyes that always shifted down and never made contact with anyone else's, he would ordain that the White House was opposed to any independent-style 9/11 commission because we were a nation at war and could not spare any resources."[544]

Was it just fiscal restraint that was the basis for Cheney's fierce opposition to the creation of an independent investigation of the events of 9/11? Was Cheney concerned there might be too much scrutiny over his whereabouts in the first critical hour after the North Tower was struck? Why was the story told by Cheney and the 9/11 Commission in conflict with so many other accounts of his arrival time at the bunker?

The Family Steering Committee asked the 9/11 Commission to get Cheney to account for the firsthand hostility they experienced toward having an investigation into the events of September 11: "Please explain your opposition to the creation of an independent commission to investigate 9/11 and your request that Senator Daschle quash an investigation."[545]

On May 8, 2001, there was an Executive Order signed by President Bush that placed Vice President Dick Cheney directly in charge of managing the "seamless integration" of all training exercises throughout the entire federal government and all military agencies, specifically all "training and planning."[546] This included oversight of Continuity of Government operations in the case of a national crisis. One of the things Cheney would have been responsible for authorizing was scheduling the five war game training exercises that took place the morning of September Eleventh.

An essay for *The Nation* in 2014 noted that behind Dick Cheney's blank expression, his calm, unwavering gaze, and "slightly lopsided frown—embodied a philosophy of power unapologetically, brutally simple: attack, crush enemies, cause others to fear, submit."[547] This reputation of Cheney was consistent with what the 9/11 Widows experienced. They found Cheney's vitriolic attacks and obstruction against any attempt to investigate the events of September Eleventh reliably belligerent.

~ 16 ~

Question to Secretary of Defense, Donald Rumsfeld

How is it possible that the National Military Command Center, located in the Pentagon and in contact with law enforcement and air traffic controllers from 8:46 a.m., did not communicate to the Secretary of Defense also at the Pentagon about the other hijacked planes especially the one headed to Washington?

On March 31, 2003, Mindy Kleinberg testified before the 9/11 Commission. She summarized some of the different comments the Secretary of Defense, Donald Rumsfeld, had made about his whereabouts that morning. Kleinberg then posed a set of questions the Family Steering Committee wanted investigated: "How is it possible that the National Military Command Center, located in the Pentagon and in contact with law enforcement and air traffic controllers from 8:46 a.m. did not communicate to the Secretary of Defense also at the Pentagon about the other hijacked planes especially the one headed to Washington? How is it that the Secretary of Defense could have remained at his desk until the crash? Whose responsibility is it to relay emergency situations to him? Is he then supposed to go to the war room?"[548]

It is reasonable to assume the Secretary of Defense would be notified of the attacks on the World Trade Center. Statements made by the Secret Service and CIA prior to, and shortly after, the North Tower was struck confirm this. FAA Acting Deputy Administrator, Monte Belger, recalled senior military personnel were in the FAA Command Center and FAA Air Traffic Organization situation room observing what was happening in real time. It would be expected, once it was clear a plane was headed toward the Pentagon, that the Secretary of Defense would be alerted. The first thing the FAA is supposed to do according to protocol, when there is a hijacking, is to notify the Secretary of Defense.[549] From discussion in the previous chapter, the Secret Service knew that a plane was headed toward the Pentagon by or before 9:18 a.m. And yet Rumsfeld was allegedly unaware a plane was heading toward the Pentagon up until the time it crashed.

Kristen Breitweiser discussed this enigma on the *Phil Donahue Show* on August 5, 2002. She said, "I don't understand how a plane could hit our Defense Department ... an hour after the first plane hit the tower. I don't understand how that is possible. I'm a reasonable person. But when you look at the fact that we spend a half a trillion dollars (a year) on national defense and you're telling me that a plane is able to hit our Pentagon ... an hour after the first tower is hit? There are procedures, are protocols in place in this nation that are to be followed when transponders are disconnected, and they were not followed on September 11."[550]

The New York Times reported on September 15 that "During the hour or so that American Airlines Flight 77 was under the control of hijackers, up to the moment it struck the west side of the Pentagon, military officials in a command center on the east side of the building were urgently talking to law enforcement and air traffic control officials about what to do." The paper told its readers that "there were procedures, first devised in the 1950's, over how to send fighter planes to shadow a hijacked plane on its way, perhaps, to Cuba."[551] But on September Eleventh, those procedures weren't followed.

CBS News reported that American Airlines Flight 77, which the government claimed was piloted by Hani Hanjour, "did a downward spiral, turning almost a complete circle and dropping the last 7,000 feet in two-and-a-half minutes. The steep turn was so smooth, the sources say, it's clear there was no fight for control going on. And the complex maneuver suggests the hijackers had better flying skills than many investigators first believed. The jetliner disappeared from radar at 9:37 and less than a minute later it clipped the tops of street lights and plowed into the Pentagon at 460 mph."[552]

However, *The New York Times*, in their news story, "A Trainee Noted For Incompetence," reported in 2002 that Hani Hanjour had no piloting skills at all. Hanjour had failed a number of piloting courses in Phoenix, Arizona, at the Pan Am International Flight Academy and JetTech Flight School. Staff at one of the flight schools told *The New York Times* that Hanjour was a poor student. A former JetTech employee said, "I'm still to this day amazed that he could have flown into the Pentagon. He could not fly at all."[553]

As Secretary of Defense, Donald Rumsfeld was number-two in the United States military command structure. He was working in the east side of the Pentagon on the morning of September Eleventh. The Pentagon is the headquarters of the US military: it has links to NORAD's most advanced communications control center at Cheyenne Mountain in Wyoming. And yet Rumsfeld told Larry King on December 5, 2001, that he knew nothing about either of the World Trade Center attacks until fifteen minutes before the Pentagon was hit.

According to Rumsfeld, even fifteen minutes before the crash he hadn't been told that a plane was headed for the Pentagon.[554] He claimed that no one bothered to tell the Defense Secretary of the United States of America that four jetliners had been hijacked; no one in the US military thought it pertinent to tell the Defense Secretary that two of the planes had flown into the Twin Towers, or that one of them was headed for the Pentagon. No one.

The *Fayetteville Observer* in North Carolina reported that on the morning of September Eleventh Rumsfeld was at a meeting in the Pentagon at 8:44 a.m. "Defense Secretary Donald H. Rumsfeld had some people in to talk about missile defense and the risk that terrorism, seen in the past, would happen again. 'Let me tell ya,' he said, 'I've been around the block a few times. There will be another event.' Two minutes later, a plane smashed into the first World Trade Center tower and proved him right."[555]

In her testimony before the 9/11 Commission, Mindy Kleinberg summarized the official story that Rumsfeld had cobbled together regarding his whereabouts on the morning of September Eleventh. "The Secretary of Defense, was at his desk doing paperwork when AA77 crashed into the Pentagon. As reported, Secretary Rumsfeld felt the building shake, went outside, saw the damage and started helping the injured onto stretchers. After aiding the victims, the Secretary then went into the 'War Room'."[556]

The story paints a picture of a hapless Rumsfeld left hopelessly out of the loop, with the whole of the US military fumbling its protocols and forgetting to notify Rumsfeld about what was unfolding. However, Assistant Secretary of Defense for Public Affairs, Victoria Clarke, says she told Rumsfeld after 8:46 a.m. that the first tower had been hit. She and others headed over to the National Military Command Center. But Rumsfeld stayed put, Clarke says, because "he wanted to make a few phone calls."[557] Clarke stated Rumsfeld was gone from the Pentagon for "about half an hour."[558]

Over time, Rumsfeld gave three different versions of what he was doing on the morning of September Eleventh.[559] Rumsfeld explained he was going to his fourth-floor office when the Pentagon was struck. He went to the Pentagon lawn and started assisting people, putting them on stretchers, and taking them to waiting ambulances. After "a while" he returned to his office to figure out what his next steps were.

The Department of Defense published this account on its website on September 15, 2001, clarifying that Rumsfeld was out on the Pentagon lawn "about a half hour."[560] But each side of the enormous

Pentagon is the length of three football fields: Rumsfeld's office was a brisk ten-minute walk to the Pentagon lawn. Rumsfeld could only have been at the crash scene for an extremely brief period; he did not have half an hour to spend before returning in the time he claims.

Later, Rumsfeld offered another version of what he did that morning, this time to the 9/11 Commission. To them he stated: "I was in my office with a CIA briefer ... At 9:38, the Pentagon shook with an explosion of then unknown origin ... I went outside to determine what had happened. I was not there long because I was back in the Pentagon with a crisis action team shortly before or after 10:00 a.m."[561]

Meanwhile, Richard Clarke, the National Coordinator of Counterterrorism, recalls Rumsfeld participating in a videoconference when Clarke arrived around 9:15 a.m. in the Presidential Emergency Operations bunker. When everyone participating in the videoconference learned of the attack on the Pentagon, Clarke could "still see Rumsfeld on the screen."[562]

According to Richard Clarke, the Secretary of Defense would not have been walking around on the Pentagon lawn when he first learned about the attacks on September Eleventh, but participating in a videoconference for at least 23 minutes prior to the attack.

Was Rumsfeld participating in a Presidential Emergency Operations Center videoconference with Vice President Cheney, Coordinator of Counterterrorism Clarke, National Security Advisor Rice, General Richard Myers, and others? If so, Rumsfeld was intimately in the know about what the FAA, Secret Service, and US military were aware of in real-time the morning of the attacks. Rumsfeld, together with Cheney, would then have been part of the elite few making decisions as the earth-shaking events of September 11, 2001, unfolded.

According to Richard Clarke, Rumsfeld was a participant in the videoconference, which began at 9:03 a.m.[563] Subsequently, Rumsfeld's actions outside the Pentagon were rehearsed, not spontaneous. He would have known in real-time that a plane was headed toward the

Pentagon at least 20 minutes earlier.

At his confirmation hearing before the Senate Armed Services Committee on January 11, 2001, Donald Rumsfeld had warned of the danger of a surprise attack like Pearl Harbor happening again. He announced, "We all know that history is filled with instances where people were surprised. There were plenty of signals, plenty of warnings, plenty of cautions. But they weren't taken aboard. They didn't register. They weren't sufficient to cause a person to act on those. We know that the thing that tends to register on people is fear, and we know that that tends to happen after there's a Pearl Harbor, tends to happen after there's a crisis. And that's too late for us. We've got to be smarter than that. We've got to be wiser than that. We have to be more forward-looking."[564]

ABC News would later comment on Rumsfeld's confirmation hearing address in the immediate aftermath of the attacks on 9/11: "eight months to the day after his warning of a surprise attack, Rumsfeld's fears became reality with the Sept. 11, 2001 terrorist attacks."

In his memoir, Donald Rumsfeld recalls that he wrote a note, in which he expressed his fear of the US experiencing a "modern-day version" of Japan's surprise attack on Pearl Harbor. Rumsfeld dictated the note to himself. He intended to include it when testifying before Congress. The note read: "In some future hearing, I am going to say that I do not want to be sitting before this panel in a modern-day version of a Pearl Harbor post-mortem as to who didn't do what, when, where, and why. None of us would want to have to be back here going through that agony."[565]

The day before the September Eleventh attacks, Donald Rumsfeld admitted that $2.3 trillion of Pentagon money was missing. Auditors had audited the 1999 fiscal year of the Department of Defense: of the $7.6 trillion, the auditors found $3.5 trillion was supported with the proper documentation. However, another $2.3 trillion was missing paperwork and thus unaccounted for. There was a further $1.8 trillion that the auditors were unable to review due to lack of time and proper staffing as a result of budgetary cuts to the US Army's financial/audit department.

During a speech he gave on the 10th, Rumsfeld stated, "some might ask how in the world could the Secretary of Defense attack the Pentagon in front of the American people? To them I reply, I have no desire to attack the Pentagon. I want to liberate it."[566] On September Eleventh, Flight 77 blew concentric holes through six walls and slammed into the newly-renovated US Army financial management and audit area. This was one of two main offices heavily destroyed in the Pentagon attack.

Casualties were heavy. The *Pittsburg Post-Gazette* later reported "One Army office in the Pentagon lost 34 of its 65 employees in the attack. Most of those killed in the office were civilian accountants, bookkeepers and budget analysts."[567] Was the attack on September Eleventh used as an opportunity to target the auditors investigating 2.3 trillion dollars missing from the Defense budget? Killing half the staff looking into the missing trillions is a good way to derail any discovery of criminal activity. Could there be Pentagon officials collaborating with the terrorist attack on the Pentagon? Or were the auditors specifically targeted by Osama bin Laden and al Qaeda? Did President George W. Bush have it all wrong—did al Qaeda actually not so much hate America's freedoms, but rather America's bookkeeping and accounting practices?

Since the reported $2.3 trillion went missing, the problem has grown steadily worse. In September 2012, the Pentagon Inspector General submitted a report that found out of $7.6 trillion in the budget, the US Army did not properly account for how it spent $5.8 trillion.[568]

In 2013, *Reuters* interviewed a retired worker from the Office of Defense Finance and Accounting Service, Linda Woodford, who provided an account of the waste and mismanagement at the Pentagon. Each month, numbers would come in with no explanation for how the funds were spent. Then, two days before a fiscal deadline, "staff were able to resolve a lot of the false entries through hurried calls and emails to Navy personnel, but many mystery numbers remained. For those, Woodford and her colleagues were told by superiors to take 'unsubstantiated change actions'—in other words, enter false numbers, commonly called 'plugs,' to make the Navy's totals match the Treasury's." The senior manager of the Office confirmed the pattern of falsifying numbers.[569]

The issue is not only that there is waste and inefficiency in the system. The Pentagon's failure to keep track of its budget has meant there is no way to determine how much money has been "stolen." In *Reuters'* three-part series on the breakdown of budget transparency at the Pentagon, they revealed that in 2013 the missing defense funds had climbed to $8.5 trillion.

CNN covered an interview with eyewitness Jamie McIntyre live from the Pentagon in front of the area where the auditors were killed. He told viewers, "I took a look at the huge gaping hole that's been in the side of the Pentagon in an area of the Pentagon that has been recently renovated … I could see parts of the airplane that crashed into the building, very small pieces of the plane on the heliport outside the building. The biggest piece I saw was about three feet long, it was silver and had been painted green and red, but I could not see any identifying markings on the plane. I also saw a large piece of shattered glass. It appeared to be a cockpit windshield or other window from the plane."

McIntyre was asked to clarify if the plane landed short of the Pentagon. McIntyre responded, "It might have appeared that way, but from my close-up inspection, there's no evidence of a plane having crashed anywhere near the Pentagon. The only site is the side of the building that's crashed in. And, as I said, the only pieces left that you can see are small enough you can pick up in your hand. There are no large tail sections, wing sections, fuselage, nothing like that anywhere around which would indicate that the entire plane crashed into the side of the Pentagon and then caused the side to collapse. Now, even though, if you look at the pictures of the Pentagon you see that the floors have all collapsed. That didn't happen immediately. It wasn't until almost about 45 minutes later that the structure was weakened and enough that all of the floors collapsed."[570]

Jamie McIntyre's comment was taken by some to imply that there was no plane that crashed into the Pentagon. But McIntyre was clarifying that there was no crash site on the lawn outside of the Pentagon. His earlier statement in his live report indicated that he had seen parts of the plane inside the damaged part of the Pentagon.[571]

The 9/11 Commission required no one to testify under oath, including eyewitnesses or Pentagon officials. Lorie Van Auken recalls an exchange between Commissioner Richard Ben-Veniste and Secretary of Defense Donald Rumsfeld. Ben-Veniste, a former prosecutor in the Watergate investigation, was a vigorous member of the 9/11 Commission. Other commissioners often asked softball questions. But Ben-Veniste cut to the chase. He asked "Mr. Rumsfeld, did you order jets scrambled to defend the Pentagon on the morning of 9/11?"

Rumsfeld smiled and kind of looked around at the room to the clock. And then he repeated the question: "Did I order jets scrambled on 9/11 to protect the Pentagon?"

That was when Chairman Thomas Kean banged the gavel and said, "Time's up. Next question."[572] That's as close as the 9/11 Commission got to finding out if the Secretary of Defense ordered jets scrambled on September Eleventh.

In a proper investigation, Rumsfeld would not have been able to avoid a question by simply repeating it back to a commissioner and run out the clock. If there needed to be a break when an important question was being addressed, Commissioner Ben-Veniste's question would have been dealt with after the recess. Consequently, the 9/11 Commission didn't get an answer from Rumsfeld to the questions FSC member Carol Ashley asked when she testified on January 26, 2004, "Why was Rumsfeld unaware that our nation was under attack? Why wasn't the Pentagon defended?"[573]

Treasury Secretary Paul O'Neill was with Donald Rumsfeld at a cabinet meeting on January 30, 2001, when the Defense Secretary spoke about the necessity for a regime change in Iraq. "Imagine what the region would look like without Saddam and with a regime that's allied with US interests ... It would change everything in the region and beyond it. It would demonstrate what US policy is all about," said Rumsfeld. O'Neill recalls that Rumsfeld argued that removing Saddam would "free the Iraqi people" and get rid of the "weapons of mass destruction."[574]

The Family Steering Committee wanted the 9/11 Commission to ask, "Why did Donald Rumsfeld, immediately after the September 11th attack, say that Saddam Hussein was involved?"[575]

~ 17 ~

Question to President George W. Bush

Who approved the flight of the bin Laden family out of the United States when all commercial flights were grounded ... a privilege not available to American families whose loved ones were killed on 9/11?

After September Eleventh, reports were made that members of the bin Laden family were flown from the USA to Saudi Arabia. At the time, all commercial and private flights were officially grounded. The only planes that were supposed to be in American airspace were US Air Force planes.

The Family Steering Committee asked the 9/11 Commission to investigate this question with President Bush, under oath: "Who approved the flight of the bin Laden family out of the United States when all commercial flights were grounded, when there was time for only minimal questioning by the FBI, and especially, when two of those same individuals had links to WAMY, a charity suspected of funding terrorism? Why were bin Laden family members granted that special privilege—a privilege not available to American families whose loved ones were killed on 9/11?"[576] However, during his interview with the 9/11 Commission, together with Dick Cheney,

President Bush chose not to address this question.

All flights were cancelled on September Eleventh, and there was a ban on private and commercial flights across the domestic airspace of the United States for several days. Donna Marsh O'Connor, whose daughter Vanessa Lang Langer was killed at the World Trade Center, was in Toronto at the time, away from her home in New York state. O'Connor wasn't able to book a flight home, or even get ground transportation back into the USA.

O'Connor recalls, "all I asked for, when the first news reporter from my local area in upstate New York came to tell me she was going to allow me to tell a beautiful story of my daughter, all I asked that day was why could I not fly home from Toronto, but Osama bin Laden's family and some Saudi nationals ... were flown out of the country in our airspace. I was grounded. They were not. I asked her [the reporter] that day: Where was NORAD? Where were our defense systems?"[577]

Donna Marsh O'Connor's story was a universal one for those who lost a family member on September Eleventh: they could not fly anywhere in the days that followed the attacks.[578] However, on September 13, a Lear jet left Tampa, Florida, on a private flight destined for Louisville, Kentucky. The flight took place through the defense contractor Raytheon on the outskirts of the Tampa airport. Every other commercial and private jet in America "was grounded due to safety concerns after the Sept. 11 attacks."[579]

Two armed bodyguards were hired to chaperone these clients out of the USA that day. The bodyguards on the Lear flight were private investigators Dan Grossi and Manuel Perez. Grossi had worked with the Tampa Police Department in internal affairs and homicide. He had just retired from the department in August of that year. Perez had worked for the FBI for over 29 years; he was a bomb technician and an expert in counterterrorism. Both Grossi and Perez had been guarding three young Saudi men since the attacks on September Eleventh.

Tampa police records indicate that the Saudi Arabian Defense Minister, Sultan bin Fahad, had made the request for a security detail to protect the young Saudis; they were frightened and wanted to get out of America. One of the men was the prince's son. All three were part of the bin Laden family.

The *Tampa Tribune* covered the story, and reported that Grossi received a call at 2:30 p.m. on September 13 regarding the flight to escort the young men out of the USA. "Grossi … was told the clearance came from the White House after the prince's family pulled a favor from former President Bush. Prince Sultan … was part of the coalition that fought the Persian Gulf War in 1991."[580]

Indeed, his royal highness, Prince Bandar bin Sultan Al Saud, had set up a hotline in Washington on September Eleventh. The Saudi Embassy hotline was ringing off the wall with calls from Saudi nationals arranging flights out of America. According to Craig Unger in his book, *House of Bush, House of Saud: The Secret Relationship Between the World's Two Most Powerful Dynasties*, the Prince was in "constant contact with Secretary of State Colin Powell and National Security Advisor Condoleezza Rice."[581]

Several Tampa Bay detectives brought the Saudis to the Raytheon airport, where Grossi met up with them. The pilot of the Lear jet had been given permission to fly in from Fort Lauderdale. "At 4:30 p.m., the twin-engine, eight-passenger jet lifted off." The detectives sensed the eeriness of flying in a sky empty of any other aircraft, except the occasional military patrol.

The flight from Tampa landed at the Blue Grass Airport in Lexington, Kentucky. There, the young Saudis were escorted by Saudi Arabian security officials to one of "several private 747s parked on the tarmac with foreign flags on the tails and Arabic lettering on the sides."[582] In subsequent days, other flights carried bin Laden family members, even as fighters escorted to the ground three other private planes attempting to fly.[583]

In the aftermath of the attacks on September Eleventh, 9/11 family members scanned the news to come to terms with the murder of their loved ones. The *Tampa Tribune* article was read with astonishment.

The FSC discovered that Prince Bandar bin Sultan Al Saud, the Saudi Arabian ambassador to the United States, had been making special arrangements for Saudi Arabian citizens from two powerful families in his kingdom to exit America after the attacks. The one family was the House of Saud, rulers of Saudi Arabia. The other was the powerful bin Laden family, friends of the House of Saud.[584] If the Saudis had stayed in America and been interviewed by the FBI, they might have been able to shed light on al Qaeda and provide leads for investigating the events of September Eleventh. Why would the White House make arrangements for the exodus of 140 potential witnesses, including around 25 relatives of the person the president said was the prime suspect in the attack?

The FSC wondered about this special privilege being granted the Saudis, and the bin Laden family especially. They asked the 9/11 Commission to find out from President Bush: "What is the connection between the Bush family and Bin Laden?"[585]

An article in *Vanity Fair* revealed that "before 9/11, coincidentally, President Bush had invited Bandar to come to the White House on September 13, 2001, to discuss the Middle East peace process. The meeting went ahead as scheduled."[586]

After he left the position of Coordinator of Counterterrorism in 2003, Richard Clarke told *Vanity Fair* about the exodus of the Saudis. Clarke said, "Somebody brought to us for approval the decision to let an airplane filled with Saudis, including members of the bin Laden family leave the country ... My role was to say that it can't happen until the FBI approves it. And so, the FBI was asked ... to make sure that they were satisfied that everybody getting on that plane was someone that it was OK to leave. And they came back and said yes, it was fine with them. So we said, 'Fine, let it happen.'" Although Richard Clarke didn't remember where the request to give the Saudis permission to leave the country came from, he speculates it was "either the FBI or the State Department." [587] Clarke repeated these details in his testimony before the Commission on March 24, 2004.

But should assurances from FBI staff that there was no one worth questioning have been taken at face value? This was the same FBI who had not acted when two of the alleged hijackers had been living for several years with an FBI informant in San Diego. This was the same FBI who had done nothing in response to the Phoenix memo sent to FBI headquarters concerning students at flight schools with possible terrorist links. America had just been attacked; wouldn't erring on the side of caution to question a few members of the bin Laden family before letting them fly to the Saudi kingdom make sense? After all, during the week of 9/11, no one knew that another terrorist attack wasn't imminent.

A twist in the story emerged on May 26, 2004, when Richard Clarke changed his story. He told *The Hill* that in fact it was neither the FBI nor the State Department that made the decision about the bin Laden family member flights. Clarke revealed that he was solely responsible for "approving flights of Saudi Arabian citizens, including members of Osama bin Laden's family, from the United States immediately after the attacks of Sept. 11, 2001." Clarke said, "I take responsibility for it. I don't think it was a mistake, and I'd do it again." The statement Richard Clarke made to *The Hill* contradicted his testimony to the 9/11 Commission when he said, "The request came to me and I refused to approve it."[588]

Seven days later, on September 18, 2001, a flight on a Boeing 727 out of Boston's Logan Airport was arranged for "at least five members of the bin Laden family back to Saudi Arabia."[589] More flights of bin Laden family members took place on September 19. Ironically, FBI counterterrorism agents who were trying to piece together how the terrorist attacks took place had been "unable to fly for several days." But now they were able to fly, although only in the capacity of chaperones for the bin Ladens according to FBI spokesman John Iannarelli.[590]

Some senior airport staff noticed that the exodus of Saudi nationals was being routed through two of the airports where the hijackings took place: Logan and Newark. At Logan International Airport, Aviation Director Tom Kinton recalls that senior management at Logan were appalled. Kinton said, "I wanted to go to the highest authorities in Washington ... But this was not just some mystery flight dropping into Logan. It had been to three major airports already, and we were the last stop. It was known. The federal authorities knew what it was doing. And we were told to let it come."[591]

While eleven more bin Laden family members were flying out of Logan Airport on September 19, President Bush declared the beginning of his global war on terror. Bush told the nation: "Our war on terror ... will not end until every terrorist group of global reach has been found, stopped, and defeated."[592]

The FBI has spent its time since the attacks of September Eleventh coaching informants on ways to entrap marginalized people. They've sent in *agents provocateurs* to manufacture most of the frightening terrorist plots that have been reported in the news over these post-9/11 years. They've infiltrated Muslim communities, befriended the unemployed, the mentally ill, and the loners. Hatching phony terrorist plots and prosecuting suspects has enabled the FBI to claim it is winning the War on Terror. The headlines tell the story of how the War on Terror is being won on the home front: "Key Witness in Seattle Terror Plot was Sex Offender";[593] "Suspect's Troubled Past: Rap Sheet, Hallucinations";[594] "Suspect's Life Marked by Mental Illness, Acquaintance Says";[595] "FBI Sting Foils Portland Terror Plot";[596] "Lawyer: FBI Entrapped Baltimore Bomb Plot Suspect";[597] "FBI Successfully Thwarts its Own Terrorist Plot";[598] "Terrorist Plots, Hatched by the FBI."[599]

Between September 11, 2001 and August of 2011, the US government prosecuted 508 defendants whom they judged to be terrorists. Trevor Aaronson, author of *The Terror Factory*, noticed "the US government was putting forward to the public people who seemed to have become terrorists only as a result of the prodding and inducements of FBI informants and undercover agents."[600] He investigated how many of the accused actually constituted a real threat, based on the evidence.

Aaronson combed through some 508 cases prosecuting alleged terrorists. Having poured over the transcripts of the trials, indictments, and news stories, Aaronson discovered "Of the 508 defendants, 243 had been targeted through an FBI informant, 158 had been caught in an FBI terrorism sting, and 49 had encountered an *agent provocateur*. Most of the people who didn't face off against an informant weren't directly involved with terrorism at all, but were instead Category II offenders, small-time criminals with distant links to terrorists. Seventy-two of these Category II offenders had been charged with making false statements. Another 121 of these offenders had been prosecuted for immigration violations ... Of the 508 cases, I could count on one hand the number of actual terrorists, such as failed New York City subway bomber Najibullah Zazi, who posed a direct and immediate threat."[601]

The FBI has gone to great lengths since September 2001 to win the War on Terror. But in the days immediately following 9/11, they allowed the easiest potential source of information to leave the United States when every other commercial and private plane was grounded. Of concern to the Family Steering Committee was a report on the BBC's *Newsnight* on November 1, 2001, "that the FBI was on the trail of other members of the Bin Laden family for links to terrorist organisations before and after September 11th."[602] The FBI's DC field office was on the trail of bin Ladens with terrorist ties, while another arm of the FBI passed on interviewing bin Ladens departing the USA in the days after the attacks. Someone wasn't connecting the dots.

~ 18 ~

Question To the CIA

Please explain the role of the ISI, Pakistan's intelligence agency, in aiding bin Laden and/or the al Qaeda from 1998 through the present.

During the Cold War, the CIA's task was to combat Communism globally with covert action operations. Richard Nixon once described covert action operations as "those activities which, although designed to further official US programs and policies abroad, are so planned and executed that the hand of the US Government is not apparent to unauthorized persons."[603]

Historians and political analysts have described how the CIA, together with US Special Forces, influenced the political and military developments in numerous countries. This included the overthrow of Guatemala's President Jacobo Árbenz in 1954 and the failed attempt to overthrow Cuba's Fidel Castro in the 1961 Bay of Pigs invasion. In 1967, they assassinated Ernesto Che Guevara in Bolivia. They overthrew Chile's President Salvador Allende on September 11, 1973, and installed dictator Augusto Pinochet. The CIA also sponsored the right-wing rebel group, known as the Contras, in Nicaragua after the revolution of the Sandinistas in 1979.[604]

1979 was also a watershed year for American support of another rebel group: Osama bin Laden's al Qaeda in Afghanistan, repelling the Soviet invasion in 1979.

Michael Scheuer was the CIA agent heading the Agency's first bin Laden unit. As reported by Scheuer, Osama bin Laden charity fronts had over six hundred million dollars pass through them from 1980 to 1989. The majority of these funds were funneled through a charity variously called Maktab al-Khidamat (MAK) or Al-Kifah. Funds typically came from wealthy contributors living in Saudi Arabia and other Persian Gulf states. The funds were used to help train, arm, and assist the mujahedeen in their war of resistance against the Soviet occupation of Afghanistan.

In his book, *Devil's Game: How the United States Helped Unleash Fundamentalist Islam*, Robert Dreyfuss cited a senior official in the Pakistani Intelligence Services, the ISI. The ISI official, Mohammad Yousaf, said the funds being funneled through the bin Laden charity fronts were a mix of Saudi, CIA, and other Persian Gulf donor money.[605]

In 1984, Osama bin Laden moved to the Pakistani border town of Peshawar. From there, he coordinated the charity front, MAK. He funneled money, arms, and fighters from the CIA, Saudis, and others to the resistance in Afghanistan.[606] In a 1998 program on MSNBC, viewers were told that "MAK [is] nurtured by Pakistan's state security services, the Inter-Services Intelligence agency, or ISI, the CIA's primary conduit for conducting the covert war against Moscow's occupation."[607]

Osama bin Laden's connections to the CIA were explored in an article in the Paris daily, *Le Monde*.[608] Its headline read, "The Most Dreaded Man of the United States, Controlled for a Long Time by the CIA." Significantly, the story ran in *Le Monde* on September 14, 2001, just three days after the attacks on September Eleventh. If two reporters for *Le Monde* could figure this out, surely the CIA would know of its own history using Osama bin Laden as a CIA asset.

The Family Steering Committee, on behalf of the families of the

September Eleventh victims, lobbied the 9/11 Commission to ask the CIA to "Please explain the role of the ISI, Pakistan's intelligence agency, in aiding bin Laden and/or the al Qaeda from 1998 through the present." They cited numerous news stories to support this line of questioning of the CIA. The FSC stated that "Between 1980 and the end of the Afghan/Soviet war in 1989, the CIA and Pakistan's ISI (Inter-Services Intelligence) recruited some 35,000 Muslim radicals join Afghanistan's fight. The US and Saudi Arabia gave up to $40 billion total to support the mujaheddin guerrilla fighters opposing the Russians. Most of the money is managed by the ISI, Pakistan's intelligence agency. At the same time, Osama bin Laden begins providing financial, organizational, and engineering aid for the mujaheddin in Afghanistan, with the advice and support of the Saudi royal family. The CIA, the ISI and Osama continued to work together against the Soviets until the end of the war."[609]

On November 8, 2001, a story for the *Laissez Faire City Times* in San Jose, Costa Rica, described a meeting in 1986 between a number of men at the Hilton Hotel in Sherman Oaks, California. One of the men was an FBI agent, and another was known for his work with aneutronic bombs. They were meeting with two men representing the Afghan resistance fighters, the mujahedeen. The topic under discussion was ways to get more armaments to the mujahedeen.

However, one of the two representatives didn't look like an Afghani. The article states, "he was a 28-year-old Saudi. Tim Osman… has recently become better known as Osama Bin Ladin. 'Tim Osman' was the name assigned to him by the CIA for his tour of the US and US military bases, in search of political support and armaments."[610] In the spring of 1986, Tim Osman's tour of the US included "receiving special demonstrations of the latest equipment" when he was on site at a number of US military bases.

In January 1998, Zbigniew Brzezinski, the former National Security Advisor to President Jimmy Carter, recalled the origins of the CIA's involvement with the mujahedeen in an article written in Paris' *Le*

Nouvel Observateur. Brzezinski explained that America wanted to force the Soviets to have their own "Vietnam" and draw them into a trap to fight a war in Afghanistan. He confided, "According to the official version of history, CIA aid to the Mujahideen began during 1980, that is to say, after the Soviet army invaded Afghanistan, [on] 24 December 1979. But the reality, secretly guarded until now, is completely otherwise. Indeed, it was July 3, 1979, that President Carter signed the first directive for secret aid to the opponents of the pro-Soviet regime in Kabul. And that very day, I wrote a note to the President in which I explained to him that in my opinion, this aid was going to induce a Soviet military intervention."[611]

This story, written in French, only came to light when it was translated in October 2001. It seems that the CIA was opening Pandora's Box and creating both an asset for certain anti-Soviet geopolitical goals and a bogeyman to rally Americans together against a common enemy.

In his book, *First In: An Insider's Account of How the CIA Spearheaded the War on Terror in Afghanistan,* former CIA station chief Gary Schroen recalls, "We were getting calls from CTC [the CIA's Counterterrorist Center], friends of the CTC in and around the building, that the World Trade Center, one of the towers had been struck." According to Schroen, there were "like, 30 of us standing around," and "as soon as the second aircraft smashed into the second tower, everyone said, 'Bin Laden. It was bin Laden ... This is the attack that bin Laden's been promising.'"[612]

At 8:50 a.m., four minutes after the aircraft hit the North Tower, CIA Director George Tenet was having breakfast at the St. Regis Hotel with his mentor, former Oklahoma Senator David Boren, three blocks from the White House. Boren had asked Tenet "What are you worried about these days?" Tenet replied, "Bin Laden," and told Boren the al Qaeda leader is going to do something big. When Boren expressed skepticism, Tenet emphasized "You don't understand the capabilities and reach of what they're putting together."

At that moment Tenet got a cell phone call from CIA headquarters about the crash into the North Tower. Tenet told others back in his office that Osama bin Laden was the one who had just attacked America. He said, "this has bin Laden's fingerprints all over it."[613] If CIA staff and Director George Tenet believed that Osama bin Laden had just launched a terrorist attack against America at 8:46 a.m., why did they not notify other agencies? What a difference it would have made that morning if someone in the CIA, certain America was under attack, had made a phone call to the Port Authority of New York and New Jersey.

If the Port Authority had been alerted that the plane that hit the North Tower represented a terrorist attack, the Port Authority would not have recommended that everyone in the Twin Towers stay at their desks. Secretary Rumsfeld, who maintains he wasn't notified by anyone in the Pentagon about the four hijacked planes, could have been notified by the CIA right after the first tower was hit. This could have ensured the US Air Force was guarding the nation's skies and scrambling fighter jets to intercept the planes headed for the South Tower and Pentagon.

Former CIA agent Michael Scheuer headed the CIA unit codenamed 'Alec' from 1996 to 1999. The task of the Alec unit was to kill or capture Osama bin Laden. Scheuer wrote the books *Imperial Hubris: Why the West Is Losing the War on Terror* and *Through Our Enemies' Eyes: Osama bin Laden, Radical Islam, and the Future of America*. In his writing, he states "that on 10 separate occasions his unit ... provided key policymakers with information that could've led to the killing or capture of Osama bin Laden. In each of those 10 instances, the senior policymaker in charge, whether it was Sandy Berger, Richard Clarke, or George Tenet, resisted taking action."[614] When 9/11 commissioners heard CIA Director George Tenet testify against this fact, most believed he was lying.

On the morning of September Eleventh, after breakfast with George Tenet, David Boren immediately identified Osama bin Laden as a "suspect" while he was interviewed on PBS. He added, "You probably have some nation states that ought to be on the suspect list as well, Iraq, for example." Boren said, "it's very clear—and I think this hopefully will give us leads to trace back and find and affix responsibility—the training that had to have been there by those who took over the aircraft, the ability to pilot the aircraft ... It was all carefully coordinated. So we're dealing with people with a lot of sophistication here. Some of that training and some of that preparation is bound to have left clues that hopefully we'll be able to thread through pretty quickly."[615] Boren didn't mention the Airman Flight School located at his university, where several 9/11 hijackers had trained, as one of these possible leads.

Prior to the *Report*, the 9/11 Commission was given a document from Pakistan claiming that Pakistani intelligence officers knew in advance about the 9/11 attacks.[616] The director of the Pakistan Inter-Services Intelligence (ISI), Lt. Gen. Mahmood Ahmed, had been in meetings in Washington DC since September 4, 2001, including some in the Pentagon with the National Security Council and CIA Director George Tenet.[617]

On September 12, 2001, Deputy Secretary of State Richard Armitage met with Ahmed and demanded Pakistan support the US or "or be prepared to live in the Stone Age."[618] Ahmed promised Armitage and Secretary of State Colin Powell that Pakistan would meet the non-negotiable demands they presented him. Those demands included giving America flight and landing rights for all US aircraft and access to Pakistan's airports, naval bases, and borders for operations against al Qaeda.[619]

On October 7, 2001, Lt. Gen. Mahmood Ahmed was replaced as ISI Director. This was as a result of US pressure after links were discovered between Mahmood, Saeed Sheikh, and the funding of the September Eleventh attacks. Mahmood Ahmed instructed Saeed Sheikh to transfer $100,000 into hijacker Mohamed Atta's bank account prior to September Eleventh. This was according to Indian intelligence, which claimed the FBI had privately verified the story.[620] Few in the western media covered this story. However, it was picked up in the *Wall Street Journal* on October 10 with the headline, "Our Friends the Pakistanis."[621]

On May 15, 2003, nine FSC members met with Chairman Kean and asked, "Why was General Mahmoud of Pakistan meeting with Senator Bob Graham and Rep. Porter Goss, the chairmen of the Senate and House Intelligence committees, on the morning of September 11 and what were they talking about?"[622]

~ 19 ~

Question to Mayor Giuliani

"On 9/11, no aircraft hit WTC 7. Why did the building fall at 5:20 PM that evening? ... Does "pull" mean demolished?"

Among the questions posed to the 9/11 Commission, the Family Steering Committee wondered about the collapse of World Trade Center Building 7: "On 9/11, no aircraft hit WTC 7. Why did the building fall at 5:20 PM that evening? Larry Silverstein is heard on a PBS tape saying 'I remember getting a call from the ... fire department commander, telling me that they were not sure they were gonna be able to contain the fire, and I said, "We've had such terrible loss of life, maybe the smartest thing to do is pull it." And they made that decision to pull and we watched the [WTC 7] building collapse,' said Larry Silverstein, WTC Leaseholder. – PBS (9/10/02) Does 'pull' mean demolished? What do you know about this?"[623]

Family Steering Committee members had reason to believe the word "pull" was common slang for demolishing a building. It raised other questions in their minds. If World Trade Center Building 7 came down in a controlled demolition when it suddenly collapsed in less than seven seconds at 5:20 p.m. on September 11, what contributed to the collapse of the Twin Towers when they similarly fell earlier in the day?

The term "pull" was routinely used by the company Controlled Demolition, who had a major contract to clean up the rubble from Ground Zero. Controlled Demolition used the term "pull" when announcing the completion of a demolitions project, which included imploding a building so that it would collapse.

In *Front Line*, a daily paper from Des Moines, Iowa, it was reported, "the City of Des Moines *subcontracted the implosion* of the Younkers Warehouse Building to Controlled Demolition Incorporated (CDI)." To implode the building, "CDI drilled over 500 holes in the supporting columns in the building and placed approximately 250 pounds of explosives. The explosives were detonated with a delay pattern that started in the southeast corner of the building and proceeded toward the northwest corner in a matter of seconds. This delay sequence allowed the explosive charges to detonate fractions of seconds apart …This delay allowed CDI to control the direction that the building would fall and resulted in the illusion that the building melted. CDI planned the implosion to pull it, the building, to the southeast and away from the intersection of SW 9th and Mulberry Streets."[624]

According to Controlled Demolition Inc. staff, the word "pull" is demolition jargon for demolishing a building. A 1997 NOVA show on PBS discussed the topic of controlled demolitions with Stacey Loizeaux. Stacey is the twenty-six-year-old daughter of the president of Controlled Demolition Inc. Her father taught her demolition work when she joined the explosives engineering firm in her teens. She told PBS, "There are a series of small explosions, but the building itself isn't erupting outward. It's actually being pulled in on top of itself. What we're really doing is removing specific support columns within the structure and then cajoling the building in one direction or another, or straight down."[625]

In order to have a successful demolition of a building, a sequence of small explosions must be timed just right in order for the building to fall on top of itself. Controlled Demolition published an article, "Demolition by Implosion," in the October 1995 issue of *Scientific American*. They described "the process of preparing a building for its five-second takedown as a process of carefully removing all non-essential (non load-bearing) materials, scanning blueprints, taking samples of concrete to determine its actual strength ... and even, in some cases, re-building parts of the structure in order to properly pull it down."[626]

"CDI has used this implosion method thousands of times around the world during the past 52 years to remove unwanted structures." [627] Therefore, the Family Steering Committee had reason to be curious when Larry Silverstein spoke about suggesting WTC 7 be pulled right before it became the third World Trade Center building to collapse on September Eleventh—in this case, within seven seconds.

The people who do not use the term "pull" at all are fire marshals in the Fire Department of New York City. Rudy Dent is a 32-year veteran of the FDNY, a member of the NYPD, and Vietnam veteran. He was at Ground Zero on September Eleventh, and retired shortly thereafter. He was trained as a fire marshal, equipped to investigate a fire's origin.

Dent commented in an interview on September 11, 2014, about what a fire marshal is trained to do and their capacity in investigations in America. He stated, "a fire marshal is considered an expert witness in court. He is like a forensic detective. He has the power ... to issue a subpoena ... A fire marshal is a highly trained person ... in the area ... of arson."[628]

When asked to comment on Larry Silverstein's reference to "pulling a building," Dent stated, "we have no term that says pulling buildings. That is not an area of expertise. We've never done that. We don't do that. For him [Larry Silverstein] to say that, I just don't know where he pulled that out of cause it's just not our area of operations."

Rudy Dent was asked his opinion about the explanation that WTC 7 collapsed due to office fires. He replied, "That's ridiculous.

First of all, our guys were up there [WTC 7]. They were calling for additional handlers to mop up the isolated pockets of fire. And let me explain to you one thing. Never in the history of high-rise skyscrapers has ever a skyscraper come down because of fire. And I'm talking massive fires … because fire does not burn by itself hot enough to compromise and melt steel. What we had in the World Trade Center, and I saw myself, was molten lava-like steel. I spent the night on the pile searching for bodies and saw that with my own eyes. So, who are you going to believe? Are you going to believe a bunch of government bureaucrats, or my fellow brothers of which I lost 343 guys that day?"[629]

Rudy Dent knew that firefighters wouldn't run into steel-frame buildings if they believed that steel melted from fire. If that had been the case, it wouldn't be safe for firefighters to enter any skyscraper to rescue people when it was on fire. But firefighters know steel disperses heat evenly and does not catch fire.

The first ever steel-framed skyscraper was the ten-story Rand McNally Building in Chicago, finished in 1889.[630] Between 1889 and 2001, the experience of fire departments across America and around the world was that steel-framed skyscrapers were safe for firefighters to enter in any rescue effort. This was because a steel building would not collapse due to fire, unlike wood-framed buildings.

Larry Silverstein had only begun to acquire the World Trade Center some months before September Eleventh. The World Trade Center had been privatized when the lease was purchased by the Silverstein Group for $3.2 billion. At the time, Silverstein had said of the World Trade Center, "we will seek to develop its potential, raising it to new heights." The purchase took place just after "the New York Port Authority lost an asbestos lawsuit and was ordered to remove all asbestos from the Twin Towers," which would have cost between $2 and $10 billion to achieve.[631] As a new purchaser, Silverstein would have been the one to spend those estimated billions removing the asbestos. This wouldn't have made the World Trade Center a great business investment. When the deal finally closed in July 2001, Silverstein acquired terrorist insurance on the World Trade Center.

In the month prior to Silverstein's purchase, the CIA Director and National Coordinator for Counterterrorism were sending emails to colleagues, including the National Security Advisor, to warn that the "threat level" of a major terrorist attack had "reached a crescendo," "the system was blinking red" and "a major terrorist attack" was impending.[632] The Bush administration received specific warnings about an al Qaeda terrorist attack involving hijackings, New York City, and skyscrapers from a dozen nations into the summer of 2001. Did someone in the loop about the terrorist threat give Silverstein a tip that the World Trade Center was an imminent target, encouraging him to make the purchase? Although he purchased the towers for $3.2 billion, he collected $4.55 billion in insurance after September Eleventh.[633]

Emergency Medical Services Division Chief John Peruggia of the FDNY told the World Trade Center Task Force (WTC Task Force) that around 9:00 a.m. he was on his way to the Office of Emergency Management at World Trade Center Building 7. (The WTC Task Force was established to preserve an official account of the experience of first responder FDNY members in their rescue efforts at the World Trade Center on September 11). Peruggia arrived within half an hour, and upon reaching the top of the escalators he encountered people running down. He recalls, "I questioned as to what the nature of the evacuation was. I was told it was not because of what was occurring across the street. No one feared that the building was in any danger as a result of two airplane attacks and subsequent fires, but that there were reports of a third plane that had been hijacked." Peruggia was told this was the basis for evacuating the building.[634]

On September 11, 2001, the *Associated Press* interviewed a survivor from World Trade Center 7. The *Associated Press* wrote: "After the initial blast, Housing Authority worker Barry Jennings, 46, reported to a command center on the 23rd floor of 7 World Trade Center. He was with Michael Hess, the city's corporation counsel, when they felt and heard another explosion. First calling for help, they scrambled downstairs to the lobby, or what was left of it. 'I looked around, the lobby was gone. It looked like hell,' Jennings said."[635]

Documentary filmmakers Dylan Avery and Jason Bermas were curious about Jennings' comments. In a February 2007 interview with them, Jennings recalled his time inside WTC 7. Jennings said he arrived just before 9:00 a.m. "When I came in there, the lobby had nice escalators." On the 23rd floor, he met with Michael Hess. They heard the crash of the South Tower and fled to get out of WTC 7. On their way down, the sixth-floor landing gave way from an explosion beneath them. They climbed up to the eighth floor. Jennings saw both Twin Towers collapse. Meanwhile, there were constant explosions going on inside WTC 7. The explosions occurred after 9:00 a.m. and before 1:00 p.m.

When he was rescued and saw the lobby, Jennings recalls, "It was totally destroyed, it looked like King Kong had been through it and stepped on it … It was so destroyed that they had to take me out through a hole in the wall, a makeshift hole … the fire department made to get me out."[636] He was then told by firefighters to get twenty blocks away from the area, because explosions were going off all over the World Trade Center complex.

Jennings told the documentary makers that he was trapped for several hours when both towers collapsed. "When they finally got to us, and they took us down to what they called the lobby, because when I asked [the firefighters], I said, 'Where are we?' [they told me] 'this was the lobby.' And I said, 'you've got to be kidding me.' I got into the building a little before nine. I didn't get out of there until … 1 p.m. I'm just confused about one thing and one thing only … why would World Trade Center 7 come down in the first place … I know what I heard. I heard explosions. The explanation that I got was that it was the result of the fuel oil tank. I'm an old boiler guy, if it was a fuel oil tank it would have been one side of the building."[637]

Still, the explanation that a diesel fuel tank was responsible for the fire in WTC 7 was repeated by *New York Times* reporter Philip Shenon in his book about the attacks. Shenon wrote, "it was determined that a fire that later destroyed WTC 7 on September 11 was probably caused by the rupture of the building's special diesel fuel tanks."[638]

The documentarians asked Jennings if he spoke with anyone about what he was telling them. Jennings said, "The 9/11 Commission. They called me down and asked the same questions you guys are asking me." Jennings told the 9/11 Commission about the bombs he had heard going off in WTC 7, which had begun before either Twin Tower fell and up until 1:00 p.m. on September Eleventh. But Jennings' private testimony never made it into their *Report*. He said, "the explanations that were given to me were totally unacceptable."[639]

FDNY Captain Ray Goldbach was interviewed by the WTC Task Force. He told them he went to WTC 7, where he was told Mayor Giuliani was in the Operation of Emergency Management command post. Goldbach was on the second floor of WTC 7 when he was told he "had to get out of the building. Everybody was evacuated in that building."[640]

A FDNY Emergency Medical Technician, DeCosta Wright, stated in his testimony to the Fire Department of New York: "I think the fourth floor was on fire ... We were like, are you guys going to put out that fire?" Wright asked the question after he and twenty-five other firefighters were ordered to leave WTC 7 at 11:30 a.m. At the time, they were told that Building 7 was going to collapse. A collapse zone was established. He remembers, "They measured out how far the building was going to come, so we knew exactly where we could stand (which was) five blocks away."[641]

Chief Thomas McCarthy said: "They were waiting for 7 World Trade to come down ... They had ... fire on three separate floors ... just burning merrily. It was pretty amazing, you know, it's the afternoon in lower Manhattan, a major high-rise building is burning, and they said 'we know.'"[642] Someone in the FDNY had instructed firefighters on hand not to put out the fire in WTC 7, even though it was only burning on a few of its 47 floors.

EMT Richard Zarillo informed other firefighters before the Twin Towers collapsed, "the buildings are going to collapse. We need everybody out." His colleagues were very confused. They said, "Who told you that?" Zarillo told them that Mayor Giuliani's Office of Emergency Management told him.[643] These reports were echoed by *The New York Times*, which reported: "By 11:30 a.m., the fire commander in charge of that area, Assistant Chief Frank Fellini, ordered firefighters away from it for safety reasons."[644] FEMA confirmed in a 2002 report regarding the WTC 7 collapse that "no manual firefighting operations were taken by FDNY."[645]

The BBC's Jane Standley reported WTC 7 had fallen as early as 10:45 a.m., six hours and 35 minutes prior to its collapse.[646] The building was still standing in the TV screen behind her in her afternoon report at 4:57 p.m. While she spoke, a headline at the bottom of the broadcast screen read: "The 47-storey Salomon Brothers building [WTC 7] ... has also collapsed."[647] September Eleventh family member Matt Campbell learned in 2014 that the prescient tip was phoned into the BBC by *Reuters*.[648]

Over at CNN Allan Dodds Frank told viewers at 11:07 a.m. that WTC7 had collapsed. "At a quarter to eleven there was another collapse or explosion following the 10:30 collapse of the second tower. And a firefighter who rushed by estimated that fifty stories went down."[649] Why were networks telling viewers WTC Building 7 had collapsed over six hours prior to its actual collapse?

NYPD Officer Craig Bartmer was a World Trade Center survivor, first responder, and rescue worker. He later became disabled from a respiratory illness caused by inhalation of toxic dust. He was close to WTC 7 when it collapsed at 5:20 p.m. Bartmer maintains, "I didn't see any reason for that building to fall down the way it did—I think we're being lied to. The only answer to get to the bottom of that lie is a new investigation. I think that the 9/11 Commission Report is a farce … There's not a word in it about Building 7. Why? … I walked around it. I saw a hole. I didn't see a hole bad enough to knock a building down, though. Yeah there was definitely fire in the building, but I didn't hear any … creaking, or I didn't hear any indication that it was going to come down.

"And all of a sudden, the radios exploded and everyone started screaming 'get away, get away, get away from it!' … I looked up, and it was nothing I would ever imagine seeing in my life. The thing started peeling in on itself … Somebody grabbed my shoulder and I started running, and the shit's hitting the ground behind me, and the whole time you're hearing boom, boom, boom, boom, boom. I think I know an explosion when I hear it. So, yeah, I want to know what took that building down … it had some damage … but nothing like what they're saying. Nothing to account for what we saw."[650] Craig Bartmer didn't get to testify before the 9/11 Commission.

CNN was reporting outside WTC 7 late in the afternoon of September Eleventh. Just when the building was about to come down, a CNN reporter's microphone picked up voices of emergency workers: "Keep your eye on that building, it'll be coming down." Then a second emergency worker says, "Building is about to blow up, move it back … Here we are looking back, there's a building about to blow up. Flame and debris coming down."[651]

At 5 p.m. on September Eleventh, Amy Goodman of *Democracy Now!* was across from WTC 7. In her book, *The Exception to the Rulers: Exposing Oily Politicians, War Profiteers, and the Media That Love Them,* Goodman said, "At 5:00 p.m., producer Miranda Kennedy and I walked outside and watched Building 7 go down. Seeing this forty-seven-story building just north of the Twin Towers crumple like a dollhouse was a surreal, sad moment. The building housed the mayor's multimillion-dollar eighth-floor bunker, built after the 1993 attack on the World Trade Center. The command center included 130,000 gallons of oil. As many pointed out … if the World Trade Center was attacked again, Mayor Giuliani's command center would blow up, endanger everything around it, and poison Lower Manhattan with PCBs. That's exactly what happened."[652]

However, that is not exactly what happened. Amy Goodman vastly overestimated the number of gallons of oil on site. On December 20, 2001, *The New York Times* reported that the fuel tank was not 130,000 gallons but a 6,000-gallon tank.[653] And the Mayor's bunker was on the 23rd floor, not the 8th floor as Goodman reported.

In 2002, FEMA's Building Performance Assessment Team released its *WTC Building Performance Study* to account for the damage to the buildings at Ground Zero. FEMA speculated that debris from the collapsing North Tower traveled a distance of 355 feet to WTC 6. Next, they hypothesized that this debris penetrated the outer wall of WTC 6 and smashed through about 50 feet of the building, including a concrete masonry wall. The debris then breached a fuel pipe in the north side of WTC 7. This caused a fire from the connecting fuel tank.[654] This fire, FEMA asserted, simultaneously made all the trusses in WTC 7 weaken to the point that they at once lost their strength and the building suddenly collapsed.[655]

Some firefighters and architects objected to this explanation, since no skyscraper prior to (or since) September Eleventh had collapsed due to fire.

In order to raise awareness of the need for a new investigation into the attacks on 9/11, on November 24, 2007, FSC members Lorie Van Auken and Patty Casazza spoke at a gathering at St. Mark's Church in lower Manhattan. The event was in support of a municipal ballot initiative to launch a new investigation into the attacks. Van Auken said, "The 9/11 Commission is silent on the collapse of WTC 7. Why? That building collapsed in exactly the same way that the WTC Towers 1 and 2 did, but WTC 7 was not struck by a plane. In a PBS interview Larry Silverstein, the buildings' leaseholder said: 'I remember getting a call from the Fire Department Commander telling me that they were not going to be able to contain the fire. I said, you know we've had such a terrible loss of life. Maybe the smartest thing to do is to pull it.' And they made that decision to 'pull.' And we watched the building collapse."

"Wouldn't we all have liked to have seen Larry Silverstein sworn in before the 9/11 Commission in order to explain what he meant? After all, Mr. Silverstein signed a 99-year lease for the WTC Towers One and Two, taking control of the buildings and insuring them in July of 2001, a mere six weeks prior to September 11, 2001. Why didn't the 9/11 Commission ever call upon Larry Silverstein to testify? Why didn't the 9/11 Commission answer any of the questions about WTC 7?"[656]

In 2008, the National Institute of Standards and Technology (NIST) ruled out diesel fuel fires, as theorized by FEMA, as a possible source for the collapse of WTC 7. The lead investigator for NIST told reporters, "WTC 7 collapsed because of fires fueled by office furnishings. It did not collapse from explosives or from diesel fuel fires."[657] In Chapter 14 of NIST's report it conceded that "fires for the range of combustible contents in WTC 7 ... on (the office) floors 7 to 9 and ... on floors 11 to 13, persisted in any given location for approximately 20 to 30 min."[658] NIST also speculated that there was no attempt to put out the fires between floors 7 to 9, and 11 to 13, due to a lack of available water to put out the fires.

But Chief Peter Hayden, in a formal legal interview under oath, testified that "there was water available" to extinguish fires at WTC 7. Hayden also confirmed that the standpipes to carry water were working in WTC 7 and "in service."[659] And video footage of the sprinkler systems spraying water on floors where fire had broken out confirmed that water was getting to the sprinklers in WTC 7, calling into question NIST's assessment that the sprinklers were out of commission.

"Architects and Engineers for 9/11 Truth" responded to NIST's claims. The group, which was made up of over 3,300 architects and engineers, cited a Freedom of Information Act document released in 2012 regarding the construction of WTC 7. Tony Szamboti, a mechanical design engineer with 27 years of experience in the aerospace and communications industries, disputed NIST's explanation. NIST claimed that the office fires made the beams on the floor expand due to the heat. This caused a girder on floor 13 to lose its connection to column 79, which pushed the girder off of its seat. According to NIST, when that happened, the whole building collapsed because now that the columns were unrestrained there was nothing to prevent them from falling loose.

However, Szamboti said the 2012 Freedom of Information Act document revealed NIST was wrong. The columns were not unrestrained. In fact, there were 3,896 shear studs holding those columns in place. Szamboti emphasized, "the beams could not expand far enough and if they could expand enough, those stiffeners would stop that girder from falling off. They were bonded."[660]

Official claims about the collapse of WTC 7 led the Franklin Square & Munson Fire Department on Long Island to pass a resolution in July 2019, asking for a new investigation given "overwhelming evidence … that pre-planted explosives and/or incendiaries … caused the destruction of the three World Trade Center buildings."[661] Franklin Square & Munson Fire Commissioner Chris Gioia, an ex-fire chief, said, "as a firefighter who has also had a career in construction, the official explanation for why WTC 7 fell makes no sense."[662]

Seventeen years after the Family Steering Committee asked the 9/11 Commission about the collapse of WTC Building 7, their questions were continuing to resonate with firefighters who lost fellow first responders. In 2020, the group "Firefighters for 9/11 Truth" released a documentary titled *Calling Out Bravo 7*. In addition to the FSC's unanswered questions, the documentary noted that, for some unknown reason, "Building 7's alarm system was put into test mode and deactivated at 6:47 a.m." of September Eleventh. This information came to light in a draft of a NIST study published in 2005.[663] Were terrorists responsible for deactivating the fire alarm system in WTC 7 on the morning of 9/11? *Calling Out Bravo 7* reports that "at least sixty firefighters were told WTC 7 was coming down. Some were told this, hours in advance."[664]

For instance, in April 2002, Chief Hayden told *Firehouse Magazine* that around 3:00 p.m. he informed firefighters in WTC 7 that they had to evacuate the building because "this building is going to come down, get back."[665] But the firefighters had no reason to suspect that the towers at the World Trade Center would catastrophically fail due to fires. Chief Hayden said the firefighters were committed to trying to put out the fires in WTC 7; they believed they were safe to remain. Hayden recalls, "We had to be very forceful in getting the guys out."[666]

Fire Commissioner Chris Gioia commented that firefighters only take "calculated risks when someone trapped by fire has their life at risk, and the first responder has a good chance of saving the lives of those trapped inside."[667] Since they have families, firefighters only commit to entering a building when they determine it is safe for them to do so.

On March 25, 2020, the University of Alaska issued a four-year computer modeling study on the collapse of WTC 7 titled "A Structural Reevaluation of the Collapse of World Trade Center 7." The study, led by Professor Leroy Hulsey, sought to examine the structure of the tower and its ability to withstand fire on September 11, 2001. They wanted to "Rule out scenarios that could not have caused the observed collapse" and identify what could have caused the 47-story steel-framed tower to collapse "as observed" in less than seven seconds.

The University of Alaska Fairbanks concluded that "fire did not cause the collapse of WTC 7 on 9/11." Instead, they posited it was the result of something that caused "near-simultaneous failure of every column in the building," which could be achieved by a controlled demolition.[668]

On April 15, 2020, citing the University of Alaska Fairbanks study, a formal request was sent to NIST. It was a "Request for Correction

Under the Data Quality Act to NIST's Final Report on the Collapse of World Trade Center Building 7." Those making the request included ten family members of September Eleventh victims, 58 architects, and 30 structural engineers. They wrote: "NIST was statutorily tasked with telling the 9/11 victims' families, the building and fire safety industries, the American people, and the US government how and why WTC 7 collapsed." The signatories were concerned that "NIST, through the NIST WTC 7 Report and the NIST WTC 7 FAQs, has disseminated inaccurate, unreliable, or biased information about the collapse of the WTC 7."[669]

Among the signatories were family members who lost loved ones on September 11, 2001. They were:

- Matt Campbell, brother of Geoff Campbell, who died on the 106th floor of the North Tower
- The family of Jean DePalma, who worked on the 100th floor of the North Tower: Francine Socozzo (sister), Jamie Gough (daughter), and Drew DePalma (son)
- Diana Hetzel, the widow of Thomas Hetzel, who was a firefighter in the North Tower on 9/11
- Barbara Krukowski-Rastelli, mother of William Krukowski, who was a firefighter on the scene of 9/11
- The family of Bobby McIlvaine Jr., who died after entering the North Tower lobby on route to a conference on the 106th floor: Jeff McIlvaine (brother), Bob McIlvaine (father), and Helen McIlvaine (mother)
- Kathleen Papa, daughter of Edward Papa, who worked on the 105th floor of the North Tower

All signed the request for NIST to correct the record of what caused the total collapse of WTC 7 on September Eleventh.

PART FOUR: ACCEPTANCE AND DISSENT

~ 20 ~

The Story of Record

"[Osama] bin Laden kept releasing videos, so we thought, 'Why don't we?' Because people are only hearing the terrorists' side of the story. We just thought we should fight fire with fire."
~ Carie Lemack

While the 9/11 Commission was into the final months of its inquiry, the War on Terror was in full swing, and the Iraq War was a year old. There were now color-coded, heightened terrorist alerts. Many families of the 9/11 victims looked to the Bush administration to make sense of what happened on September Eleventh.

In this mix, President Bush's campaign launched TV ads during March 2004 that "featured grisly images of firefighters carrying flag-draped coffins out of the rubble of the World Trade Center."[670] Debra Burlingame, whose brother "Chic" piloted the plane that crashed into the Pentagon, said of the ads, "These images honor those whose lives were lost." [671] Deena Burnett, whose husband, Tom, died on United Airlines Flight 93 when it crashed near Shanksville, Pennsylvania, applauded the ads as "a perfect reminder of what happened that day."[672]

But other 9/11 families objected. Rita Lasar, whose brother Abraham Zelmanowitz died in the North Tower on September Eleventh, said, "The idea that President Bush would rally support around his campaign by using our loved ones in a way that is so shameful is hard for me to believe. It's so hard for us to believe that it's not obvious to everyone that Ground Zero shouldn't be used as a backdrop for a political campaign. We are incensed and hurt by what he is doing."[673]

At the 2004 Republican National Convention, delegates heard from a number of 9/11 family members: Deena Burnett, who'd cheered the Republican TV ads earlier that year; Tara Stackpole, the widow of New York City firefighter Timmy Stackpole, who recalled how her brave husband "ran through the doors of the World Trade Center but did not walk out;"[674] and Debra Burlingame, who in her speech emphasized, "I want you to know that we were aware of what you did. We saw the spontaneous memorials, the cluster of candles on a front porch, the sign outside the Wal-Mart that said, 'Pray for the families.' We saw the flags on the office buildings, on storefronts, on kids' bikes. We saw your Web sites. We read your letters. We received the pictures your children drew. I'll also never forget the huge flag that was unfurled at the Pentagon just a few yards away from where the plane went in. I especially remember it lit up against the dark sky in the wee hours of September 12th. That was Chic's birthday. My heart fell into a million pieces as it brought back the memory, a sweet memory of my brother as a 9-year-old Cub Scout selling American flags door to door. He would have loved that tribute."[675]

The Republican party benefited from President Bush's tough stand against terrorism. Former Air Force Lt. Colonel Jim Ogonowski ran under the Republican banner for the Massachusetts 5th Congressional District in 2007. Ogonowski lost his brother John on 9/11. John Ogonowski was the pilot of American Airlines Flight 11, which was hijacked and flown into the North Tower of the World Trade Center, killing the 92 people aboard. Jim Ogonowski told the Associated Press that his brother's death on September Eleventh was a key factor in his decision to run for Congress as a Republican. Ogonowski garnered 45% of the vote, barely losing in a district that had elected a Democrat to office ever since 1974.[676]

Former Navy pilot Marc Flagg ran in the Republican primary in Florida's 22nd Congressional District in 2008. Flagg's site said that his parents perished aboard American Flight 77, which was forced into the Pentagon. The statement is repeated twice on the front of his website alongside his ensuing work on aviation security. His parents, United States Navy Rear Admiral Wilson "Bud" Flagg and Darlene Flagg, were headed to a family gathering in California. Flagg also mentioned his parents early in a video announcing his candidacy. He said he wouldn't be a candidate were it not for the events of September Eleventh, and that without national security nothing else matters. "Nine-eleven changed everything for me; I was quite happy being just a pilot," Flagg said. "For the last five years, I've helped this country. And I'd like to continue to do that because I see us going down a very different road than where we should be going."

In Arkansas, Deena Burnett had transformed her grief from losing her husband Tom into rallying Republicans to win elections. However, Burnett said she was not interested in being a candidate for elected office.[677]

Public opinion of international politics was also affected. After the attacks on September Eleventh, some families became convinced that Iraq was responsible. They cited articles published by Dr. Laurie Mylroie, who testified at the 9/11 Commission. Mylroie's book, *A Study in Revenge: Saddam Hussein's Unfinished War Against America*, was endorsed by neocon, Richard Pearle, as "splendid and wholly convincing." Mylroie credited Project for a New American Century signatory, Paul Wolfowitz, for providing "crucial support" in writing the book. And she thanked John Bolton and Vice President Dick Cheney's Chief of Staff Scooter Libby for their "generous and timely assistance."[678]

Mylroie's thesis was persuasive for the families of 9/11 victims George Eric Smith and Timothy Soulas. They sued and won a verdict on May 8, 2003, for $104 million against Saddam Hussein, the Iraqi government, Osama bin Laden, al Qaeda, and the Taliban.

The judge handing down the verdict was convinced by Mylroie's expert witness testimony. She said that Saddam Hussein, in addition to the attacks on 9/11, was also responsible for the World Trade Center bombing in 1993, the Oklahoma City bombing in 1995, and the US embassy bombings in the late 90s in Tanzania and Kenya.[679]

While the 9/11 Commission ultimately did not find any Iraqi complicity in the September Eleventh attacks, Executive Director Philip Zelikow attempted to bolster the Bush administration's false claim of a link between al Qaeda and Iraq. In doing so, he tried to change a 9/11 Commission staff report to state that the terrorist network repeatedly tried to communicate with the government of Saddam Hussein. This claim of cooperation had been cited by the Bush administration to justify the war in Iraq.

Statements made by members of the Bush administration after the attacks and at the start of the Iraq War gave many families of the 9/11 victims reason to believe Saddam Hussein was involved. The resolution Bush sent to Congress for approval of military action against Iraq included doing so as part of "the necessary actions against the international terrorist and terrorist organizations, including those nations ... who planned, authorized, committed or aided the terrorist attacks that occurred on September 11, 2001."[680]

Three years after *The 9/11 Commission Report* was released, by early 2007, about half of the 9/11 Commission's recommendations had been implemented. On January 9, 2007, former FSC members Carie Lemack, Carol Ashley, and Mary Fetchet testified before the Senate Committee on Homeland Security and Governmental Affairs. The Committee was meeting to discuss a bill on "Ensuring Full Implementation of the 9/11 Commission's Recommendations."[681]

Carie told the Senate committee about her mother, Judy Larocque, who died on American Airlines Flight 11 when it hit the North Tower. "Osama bin Laden was the mastermind behind my mom's murder," she told them. In her testimony, she referenced the bin Laden video the US military claimed they had found in an abandoned home in Afghanistan. For Carie Lemack, the bin Laden video, with the plump person said to be bin Laden "gloating" about the attacks, was trustworthy.

Reflecting on the passing years since the attacks, Lemack declared, "some experts are now telling us that it isn't as serious as we had thought. If al Qaeda are such a threat, why haven't we been attacked again? To answer that question, just ask the people of London, or Madrid, or Bali, or the other places where the terrorists have struck since 9/11. The US has not been attacked again. But we will be." [682] Lemack warned that bin Laden had issued a religious edict saying he was determined to kill over four million Americans, an allegation made by investigative reporter Paul Williams in his book, *Osama's Revenge: The Next 9/11: What the Media and the Government Haven't Told You.*[683]

Carol Ashley spoke before the Senate Committee and told senators Joe Lieberman and Susan Collins that she supported the bill before them. She spoke of the urgency of tightening security. Ashley worried that another terrorist attack was inevitable. Consequently, she wanted Congress to enact legislation to ensure that agencies in all governmental jurisdictions be "fully trained, equipped and prepared to respond cohesively" when terrorist plots emerged.

However, she was concerned to learn about the government's warrantless eavesdropping on US citizens. She cited a *New York Times* editorial from late December 2006. Ashley wondered why the Privacy and Civil Liberties Oversight Board, established by Congress upon recommendation of the 9/11 Commission, "didn't even get a formal briefing on the administration's eavesdropping on American citizens until October—almost a year after the warrantless surveillance program had been uncloaked."[684]

She agreed that it was important to put Americans who were suspected of terrorist activities under surveillance. Still, she argued "warrantless spying in which government agents listen in on the conversations and read the e-mails of Americans" was a violation of the Foreign Intelligence Surveillance Act (FISA) passed in 1978 and posed a danger to democracy. That legislation, Ashley said, was intended to protect "the privacy rights of Americans by requiring a warrant within 72 hours of the initiation of surveillance. Requiring warrants for surveillance does not prohibit government surveillance of suspected terrorists."[685]

Mary Fetchet told the senators that ever since her "son was senselessly murdered by terrorists on 9/11," she was dedicated to fix what was wrong with the system so that America could be safer. She told the senators, "It is my personal belief that almost six years later our country remains vulnerable, and although some progress has been made, much work remains ahead. We collectively—the administration, Congress, government agencies and interested individuals—have a moral obligation and responsibility to work together to ensure our government is taking the necessary steps to make our country safer." She cited a national survey conducted by Voices of September 11th that found 69% of Americans surveyed rated their nation's preparedness for a terrorist attack from "fair" to "poor."[686]

Also speaking before the Senate committee that day were 9/11 Commissioners Lee Hamilton, Slade Gordon, and Timothy Roemer.

Later that day, The Implementing Recommendations of the 9/11 Commission Act of 2007 passed in the House of Representatives by a vote of 299-128. This bill was necessary to harmonize with the pending Senate bill. Those voting against the resolution were Congressional Republicans.[687] Subsequently, on July 26, 2007, the United States Senate passed the Improving America's Security Act of 2007 by a vote of 85 to 8.[688]

Although the findings from the 9/11 Commission did bring about change, the lack of answers on some topics brought dissent. Conspiracy theories concerning the events of September Eleventh sometimes saw the support of 9/11 family members, while others spoke out against those who espoused such theories.

In 2011, 9/11 family member Bob McIlvaine appeared as a guest on talk show *Geraldo at Large*, part of Fox News. McIlvaine's son, Robert, had died in the North Tower. The topic of the day was the improperly explained collapse of WTC 7. The audience was shown a TV commercial titled "Building What?" which had been produced with four quick cuts of four 9/11 family members, including McIlvaine.[689] The commercial was a call to action, questioning the collapse of Building 7 and imploring the audience to join a ballot initiative and ask the city of New York to re-investigate the attacks. By October 2010, 81,000 signatures had been gathered.

Also on the show that day was engineer Tony Szamboti, who told the audience that WTC 7 had collapsed because of a demolition, not from fires caused by falling debris from the North Tower. When the host asked McIlvaine if he thought "9/11 was an inside job", McIlvaine replied, "I'm interested in finding out who murdered my son." Even the host of *Geraldo at Large*, Geraldo Rivera, admitted that there was much more to the 9/11 story than he'd realized.[690]

Rivera brought up the topic of discussion with another Fox News personality, Andrew Napolitano. Fox News was considering replacing one of their hosts with Napolitano. However, this received push-back from a number of 9/11 family members because of Andrew Napolitano's previous appearance on a conspiracy radio show, the *Alex Jones Show*. There, Napolitano told the radio audience, "it's hard for me to believe that [World Trade Center Building 7] came down by itself." He claimed that "twenty years from now, people will look at 9-11 the way we look at the assassination of JFK today. It couldn't possibly have been done the way the government told us."[691]

Board member of Families of September 11 Nancy Aronson, who lost her sister-in-law Myra Joy Aronson aboard the plane that flew into the North Tower, said, "It is disappointing when a major network would put on someone who would espouse a view that is so involved in personal aggrandizement. I would be disappointed Fox would do that. I would hope [removing] Glenn Beck would mean stepping in the direction of having what they say is 'fair and balanced' coverage. That [appointing Andrew Napolitano to replace Glenn Beck] is certainly not a step in that direction."[692] Another family member, Charles Wolf, whose wife Katherine died in the North Tower, warned that views like the ones Napolitano supported were unwelcome, and Fox should be careful.

Despite some issues of dissent, many families of September Eleventh victims have come together to spearhead support and memorial initiatives. Voices of September 11th, a family group founded by former FSC member Mary Fetchet, began hosting an annual "Always Remember Gala." Panel discussions included topics like "Resilient But Still Healing After All These Years: Group Interventions for Ongoing Recovery," and "Responders and Survivors—Update on the World Trade Health Program."

At their third annual gala in 2010, they had former British Prime Minister Tony Blair give a keynote address. Blair told Voices of September 11th, "It is a privilege to be able to meet with the families of the victims of 9/11. Their strength and dignity is inspirational. 9/11 was an attack on us all. America took the brunt of the terrorist outrage but 90 countries felt the impact as the honour roll shows. The evil of that day must never be forgotten. The innocent victims we honour at this benefit are continually in our thoughts and prayers. I am genuinely honoured and humbled to be supporting this event and inspired by those who work to ensure we never forget."[693]

Secretary of State Hillary Clinton was keynote speaker for the sixth annual Always Remember Gala in 2013. That year, NYPD Police Commissioner Ray Kelly received the Building Bridges award from Voices of September 11th. He told the audience that "with good police work and a little bit of luck, we were able to stop 16 planned terrorist attacks since 9/11/01."[694] These and other events held consistently to the narrative told by the 9/11 Commission. Former 9/11 Commission

Chairman Thomas Kean is a member of the Voices of September 11th Senior Advisory Board, while former FSC member Carol Ashley is a Community Board Advisor.

Mary Fetchet, also a former FSC member, helped to spearhead the "Living Memorial Project" for a memorial at Ground Zero. In that effort, a team of social workers listened to the stories of over 1,600 families, who each brought photos of a loved one who was lost on September Eleventh. Mary said, "There's a story with every photograph the families share." She added, "We've learned about the people that died through the people that survived."[695]

Another initiative of the 9/11 families was to create a National September 11 Memorial & Museum. The museum was officially opened to the public on May 21, 2014.[696] The Board of Directors currently includes one survivor of the attacks and eight family members who lost loved ones, such as board member Thomas Roger, who lost his daughter Jean Roger, a 24-year-old flight attendant, on American Airlines Flight 11.

When the 9/11 Memorial & Museum was being established, former FSC member Sally Regenhard asked, "Whose truth is going to be in that museum?" The museum held a series of discussions about the decisions the museum had to make. But Regenhard referred to some of the participants as "fat cats, VIP's and stuffed shirts." She said they personified "pure and simple tokenism" instead of legitimate family input.[697] But Mary Fetchet, who served on the 9/11 Memorial & Museum's advisory board, was content to donate her recording of her 24-year-old son Brad's last phone call while he was in the South Tower.

The 9/11 Museum's guiding principle is for its exhibits to explore "a factual presentation of what is known of the terrorists, including their methods and means of preparation." The narrative told in the museum starts with the Soviet invasion of Afghanistan, the emergence of radical Islamic fighters and Osama bin Laden, the American support of these radicals, and the rise of al Qaeda.[698]

For some, a thorough and factual explanation still does not exist, even after *The 9/11 Commission Report* was released. For others, this was less of an issue than the actions taken afterward. Debra Burlingame, whose brother "Chic" was the pilot of the hijacked Flight 77, was one of these. Ironically, her brother developed anti-terror strategies for the Navy prior to retiring to fly for American Airlines. "Chic" Burlingame drafted the Pentagon's emergency response plan in case it was hit by a civilian airliner.[699]

Coming to terms with the loss of her brother, Debra co-founded "9/11 Families for a Safe & Strong America" with Tim Sumner. She believes that criticism of leadership officials over what they were doing on 9/11 is a distraction and wastes energy by not fighting the terrorist threat. In late June 2004, Burlingame called the Jersey Girls "the rock stars of grief," saying, "I've practically been thrown out of meetings. They've gotten very angry with me. But I've decided it's very important that another voice is heard in the September 11 debate."[700]

Burlingame has authored articles in support of torture practiced by the CIA, maintaining that it has saved American lives.[701] A frequent guest on network news shows, she is also a strong believer in the good being done by keeping Guantanamo Bay open forever and continuing "preventive detentions." In a column on December 11, 2009, she described the Obama administration's plan to close the prison a "security nightmare" and "nothing more than moral vanity and rank political theater aimed at satisfying his liberal soul-mates at the ACLU and Human Rights First."[702] She serves on the Board of Directors for the "National September 11th Memorial Foundation."

Burlingame was also on the three-person board of "Keep America Safe," an organization founded in 2009 by Dick Cheney's daughter, Liz Cheney. The goal of Keep America Safe was to remind Americans "the United States remains a nation at war," and that America must be "feared and respected by our enemies."

Former FSC member Lorie Van Auken told the *New York Daily*

News: "You start to wonder why Liz Cheney would be organizing the 9/11 families. It's just a funny connection."[703]

Burlingame's organization is far from the only politically-charged September Eleventh family group. For instance, "9/11 Families for a Secure America" was launched in 2003. The group advocates keeping "illegal aliens" out of America, sending them back to their home countries, and denying them "any and all benefits."[704]

On June 2, 2007, 9/11 Families for a Secure America group founder Peter Gadiel wrote a column for the White Nationalist website, VDare, titled "Impeach Now."[705] Gadiel's son James died in the North Tower, where he worked for Cantor Fitzgerald on the 103rd floor.[706] Gadiel spoke out against building an Islamic Center and a mosque two blocks from Ground Zero, promoting an interfaith dialogue. He remarked, "Attack, destroy and erase the prior culture and build, literally and figuratively on the ruins. This is the history of Islam. The proposed mosque near the site of the 9/11 mass murder is a continuation of this violent history."[707]

Plenty of other controversies have surrounded the 9/11 attacks and organizations' reactions to them, including government organizations. In March 2019, Democratic Minnesota Congresswoman Ilhan Omar spoke in front of the Council on American-Islamic Relations banquet in suburban Los Angeles. In her speech, she said that on September Eleventh "some people did something." The comments were taken by many as dismissive toward the gravity of the attacks. Outside the California banquet protesters shouted, "Burn the Koran" and "Ilhan Omar go to Hell."[708]

Six months later, on the 18th anniversary of the attacks, 9/11 family member Nicholas Haros Jr. was motivated to respond. His mother, Frances Haros, was on the 89th floor of the South Tower on September Eleventh.[709] Haros appeared on stage wearing a T-shirt with the phrase "Some people did something." After reading his mother's name, Nick Haros Jr. said, "Today I am here to respond to you, exactly who did what to whom. We know who and what was done, there's no uncertainty about that. Our constitutional freedoms were attacked and our nation's founding on Judeo-Christian principles were attacked. That's what some people did—got that now? We are here today, Congresswoman, to tell you ... just who did what to whom."[710] Haros told CNN that Omar's remark "hurt me personally, my family," and other families of "victims of 9/11 ... I felt as a son of a victim to step up and set the record straight."[711]

Many others wanted to speak out about the specific act of terrorism itself. Former FSC member Carie Lemack founded the "Global Survivors Network" in 2009 to "work with victims of terrorism around the globe to help them speak out against terrorism—and we want to our voice to be louder than those who advocate for terrorism."[712] After the organization's launch, Lemack supported events in harmony with her network's vision in Jordan, Pakistan, and Indonesia.

Lemack also produced a documentary called *Killing in the Name*. Lemack was frustrated with the videos being broadcast by al Qaeda in the years after 9/11. She explained, "bin Laden kept releasing videos, so we thought, 'Why don't we?' Because people are only hearing the terrorists' side of the story. We just thought we should fight fire with fire."

The documentary centers on Ashraf Al-Khaled, a Jordanian Muslim who lost 27 members of his family after an al Qaeda suicide bomber detonated a bomb at his wedding. Al-Khaled challenges the father of the suicide bomber, and later speaks to the man who recruited the bomber. The film also includes interviews with women widowed after the bombing at Paddy's Pub in Kuta Beach, Bali on October 12, 2002.

Killing in the Name was accepted into the Cannes Film Festival and won an Academy Award nomination for Best Documentary (Short Subject) in February 2011. Lemack reflects, "I feel like the one thing my mom gave me in her murder was the moral authority to make a difference. And I need to use that moral authority very carefully;

to go out there and make sure what happened to us doesn't happen again."[713]

Al-Khaled and Lemack saw the film as part of their mission to prevent young Muslims from becoming radicalized. "We can penetrate them [terrorists] and we can stop their manpower if we speak to the kids. We have to clean our house by our hands, so this is why I am speaking out," said Al-Khaled.[714]

In an Op-Ed in the *Washington Post* in May 2011, Carie Lemack reflected on her journey nearly ten years after the attacks. Lemack recalls that when she co-founded Families of September 11 with her sister "our goal was simple: to meet the needs of the victims' families and to make sure that what had happened to our loved ones would never happen again ... I knew that bin Laden was still out there and still a risk to my family and others, and by engaging with world leaders and inserting myself into America's national security debates, I was doing all I knew how to do to counter him."[715]

More recently, Carie Lemack has become a visiting fellow at the Center on Global Counterterrorism Cooperation. She has been a term member at the Council on Foreign Relations (2009-2010) and in 2018-19 served on the Council's Studies Committee. The primary goal of the Council on Foreign Relations "is to start a conversation in this country about the need for Americans to better understand the world."[716] Inviting political literacy is a vital first step.

~ 21 ~

Cover-up?

"This report was supposed to provide the definitive account of what had transpired on September 11, 2001. We hoped that our thousands of unanswered questions would be addressed and answered. Yet, incredibly, we have found that the Commission's definitive final report had yielded more questions than answers."
~ Lorie Van Auken, July 22, 2005

In the weeks following the release of *The 9/11 Commission Report*, many family members bought copies and read it from cover to cover. They wanted to make sense of what had happened, and they hoped the *Report* would answer their questions. But for many, the *Report* only raised more concerns.

Just before the third anniversary of the attacks, on September 9, 2004, former Rep. Cynthia McKinney, along with 9/11 family members and citizen researchers, held what were called the "9/11 Omissions Hearings" convened by "The 9/11 Citizens' Commission" in New York City. The event was scheduled for the seventh week after the release of *The 9/11 Commission Report*. It featured 9/11 family member Bob McIlvaine as one of its commissioners, who heard witness testimony and asked questions. The event began with hearing the testimony that former FSC member Mindy Kleinberg gave to the 9/11 Commission.

One of the people who spoke at the hearings was Barry Zelman. His brother, Kenneth, was on the 99th floor of the North Tower when he died on September Eleventh. After the attacks, Barry was full of grief, and began to ask questions about what had happened. He wondered how the world's mightiest military could fail on so many counts as it was described on the TV news.

Zelman said to the 9/11 Citizens' Commission, "I really was never into politics ever in my life. It was a rude awakening, my brother's murder three years ago. He was my best friend, my only brother ... four airplanes an hour and half between the first impact and ... [last] impact with zero military response in the United States? It didn't happen that way. It couldn't have happened that way. You're talking about the most intelligent agencies that we have on the face of the earth. State of the art agencies ... And there was zero military response? ... It's very transparent that our own president did not want to investigate this tragedy. And I'm standing before you today for one reason. The only thing that I can give my brother is the truth. That's it."[717]

On July 22, 2005, a year after the release of *The 9/11 Commission Report*, US House Representative Cynthia McKinney convened an event titled "The 9/11 Commission Report One Year Later. A Citizen's Response: Did The Commission Get It Right?" The proceedings were entered into the Congressional Record. Former FSC members Lorie Van Auken, Monica Gabrielle, and Mindy Kleinberg were in attendance.

Lorie Van Auken reflected, "The 9/11 Commission's report is one year old today. This report was supposed to provide the definitive account of what had transpired on September 11, 2001. We hoped that our thousands of unanswered questions would be addressed and answered. Yet, incredibly, we have found that the Commission's definitive final report had yielded more questions than answers. Moreover, there are still so many areas that remain unexplained or only vaguely touched upon by the 9/11 Commission, so much so that it was difficult for me to decide where I should start my testimony to you today."[718]

Van Auken cited numerous patterns in the *Report* that illustrated how testimonies that the Commission knew would shine a light on deficiencies in various agencies were omitted. Countless national security whistleblowers were either prevented from testifying by their agency or had their calls left unreturned by the Commission. These included:

- Mark Burton, senior analyst for the NSA, volunteered to testify and was rebuffed.
- FBI Counterintelligence agent John M. Cole had vital information connecting Afghanistan, Pakistan, and the 9/11 attacks. However, the Commission chose not to follow-up.
- Sibel Edmonds, former translator for the FBI, indicated that she was gagged because she knew that the US government was aware of the date and method of the 9/11 attacks prior to September Eleventh.[719] The 9/11 Commission knew this from her testimony, and omitted the information she gave them in their *Report*.
- FBI agent Mike German let the 9/11 Commission know he had key information to share;[720] he was working on a case concerning the terrorist cell in Florida before 9/11. He discovered that FBI senior management falsified records, failed to properly handle evidence, falsely discredited witnesses, and failed to adhere to laws and regulations about electronic surveillance.
- Coleen Rowley tried to warn her superiors in the FBI about terrorist Zacarias Moussaoui. She asked in a memo to FBI Director Robert Mueller, "Why would an FBI agent deliberately sabotage a case?"[721] The 9/11 Commission chose not to interview her. Instead, they solely relied on her testimony before the Congressional Joint Inquiry.

- Behrooz Sarshar, an FBI language specialist, learned in April 2001 about the al Qaeda plans to use airplanes as missiles and slam them into skyscrapers. He reported this information to his FBI superiors at the time.[722]
- FBI agent Robert Wright was investigating terrorist financing, which was stifled by his FBI superiors. But the 9/11 Commission failed to subpoena him as well.[723]

There were dozens and dozens of whistleblowers willing to testify. Of these, only Behrooz Sarshar and Sibel Edmonds were called before the 9/11 Commission, and both their testimonies were omitted from its *Report*. Van Auken concluded that only an honest re-evaluation of the 9/11 attacks could provide a way forward for the nation.[724] She wondered, "Why is it that the Commission refused these key witnesses an opportunity to tell what they knew? How could the Commission be trusted to make right decisions without obtaining all the pertinent information? Worse yet, what happens when the Commission actively and knowingly ignores that information?"[725]

Van Auken also questioned the 9/11 Commission's soft approach toward pursuing those leads that they did follow. While Kean and Hamilton bent over backward to not be "confrontational" and issue subpoenas to the government, there were other pieces of information they could have obtained from private sources.

An example she cited was the crash at the Pentagon. It was common knowledge that there were security cameras at the Sheraton Hotel overlooking the Pentagon and at a nearby gas station, and that both had footage of the crash. In both cases, the Commission told Family Steering Committee members they had not subpoenaed for this evidence. Although it was easily obtainable, the Commission chose to issue document requests that were met with no reply.

Van Auken observed, "This seeming lack of persistence on the part of the Commission to collect all known evidence is worrisome. Again, if in fact they were unwilling to go after easily obtainable evidence, what other critical and more difficult pieces of the story were they missing? How was one to feel comfortable with their investigation knowing that they were not aggressively pursuing the most tangible of evidence and information?"[726]

Kean and Hamilton would later write in their memoir, *Without Precedent: The Inside Story of the 9/11 Commission*, "We reserved our subpoena power for when people were unwilling or unable to produce what we asked for."[727] However, as Van Auken highlighted, there were numbers of incidents where their follow-up evaporated, or they never asked to start with.

Looking back, Lorie Van Auken said once the 9/11 Commission issued their *Report* it only raised more questions. "We always said if there are conspiracy theories out there then it is the government's fault because they did not ever really explain, or show, or want us to know what happened … We lived it and nothing really ever made sense, ever. It just wasn't conducted the way that something should be conducted if you want to get to the bottom of something, to learn what happened."[728]

Although America had suffered an unprecedented attack, *The 9/11 Commission Report* omitted discussion of the president's opposition to the investigation, who then stonewalled and sabotaged it after it was underway. Senator Joe Lieberman said the Bush White House had "resisted this inquiry at every turn."[729]

Monica Gabrielle told the 9/11 Omissions Hearings, "while the terrorists did perpetrate this heinous crime, they could not have done so without the total failures of our local, state, and federal agencies."[730] For Gabrielle, the official story told about those failures didn't add up. To simply blame the terrorists and leave the mountain of coincidental gaps in readiness to be prepared was unacceptable. A year after *The 9/11 Commission Report*, Monica Gabrielle was still waiting for a full and credible account of how those failures took place.

John Judge representing "9/11 Citizens Watch" addressed the hearings. His group worked closely with the Family Steering Committee to press the Bush administration for an investigation into the attacks on September Eleventh. After reading the *Report*, Judge expressed concern about the secrecy of its footnotes. He stated, "The Final Report is essentially self-referential, since the hundreds of pages of footnotes at the end relate to 2,000 interviews, numerous documents and evidence which is all classified and beyond public scrutiny."[731]

In August 2005, a number of articles appeared in the press about a secret military intelligence unit named Able Danger. The intelligence unit had identified Mohammad Atta and three other hijackers as living in Brooklyn in early 2000. However, the official story was that the government didn't know Atta or the other hijackers were in the country before the attacks happened. Able Danger intelligence officer, Lt. Col. Anthony Shaffer, met with three members of the 9/11 Commission's staff in October 2003. In January 2004, he phoned the office of the Executive Director, but his call was not returned. Shaffer phoned again two weeks later and was told: "Dr. Zelikow tells me he does not see the need for you to come in. We have all the information on Able Danger."[732]

On August 12, 2005, Thomas Kean and Lee Hamilton hastily issued a press release in relation to Able Danger, stating, "None of the documents turned over to the Commission mention Mohammad Atta or any of the other future hijackers."[733] Days later, Shaffer responded to Kean and Hamilton's press release. "I'm told confidently by the person who moved the material over, that the Sept. 11 commission received two briefcase-sized containers of documents."[734]

In reference to this omission in the 9/11 Commission Report, FSC member Sally Regenhard told the *Village Voice*, "I think that we have to look at these alternative groups and these alternative people who are continuing to make films and bring their research to the public. Maybe people thought they were fringe groups or crazy but these are the only people left."[735] Regenhard suggested it would be beneficial to create an academic facility in New York where people could research and study 9/11.

Many people who've been involved in pressing the United States government for accountability concerning the attacks on September Eleventh began by wanting to trust their President. Janette MacKinlay lived across from the World Trade Center and wrote in her memoir, *Fortunate: A Personal Diary of 9/11*: "The people that died are one thing, but the people that lived are another. The people that lived are haunted, absolutely haunted."[736]

At first Janette wanted to fight back: to save her country and join the US Army. She created a sculpture with a big gun and bin Laden in the crosshairs of the rifle sight. She was caught up in the wave of patriotism and flag waving that swept the nation.[737] MacKinlay became a member of the Commonwealth Club to understand the political context for the events of September Eleventh. She was very open to learning from the 9/11 commissioners and their *Report*. On August 17, 2004, she attended a presentation about the *Report* by 9/11 commissioners Slade Gordon and Richard Ben-Veniste at the Commonwealth Club in San Francisco.

Janette had hoped that *The 9/11 Commission Report* would settle her unanswered questions. She hoped that she could be at peace with herself and everything she'd gone through. She hoped she would at last learn why America's defenses had so utterly failed to keep the nation safe on September Eleventh. As such, she was looking forward to hearing the 9/11 commissioners explain their findings. But the presentation gave rise to more questions than answers. She recalls, "as a matter of fact, there were no answers. Every answer to every question at the Question and Answer period was the same answer. And that answer was 'that's classified information.' Everything was classified. The issue that bothered me the most was that there was no accountability ... The Commissioners themselves said the 'Commission was set up to fail.'"[738]

The gathering in San Francisco to hear 9/11 commissioners present their *Report* invited the general public to hear the commissioners "provide the fullest possible account of the events surrounding 9/11."[739] Yet, for each question the commissioners were asked by those in the audience, the reply was always the same: "that's classified information."

Speaking at an event in Northern California in May of 2009, Janette MacKinlay told her audience, "I have never felt safe since that day [September Eleventh]. My whole sense of security was shaken. And I was counting on *The 9/11 Commission Report* to give us the information so that we could fix the system ... what needed to be fixed. Unfortunately, they did not give us the information that we needed."[740]

Janette's apartment, which was across from World Trade Center Building 4, filled with dust from the collapse of the Twin Towers. Dust also filled her lungs. Her close proximity to the World Trade Center caused her to ingest the ultrafine dust particles and other substances. It shortened her life. In her book, *Fortunate: A Personal Diary of 9/11*, she wrote, "I am going to be haunted by the dust for the rest of my life." Her sense of how it had pervaded her body was intuitive. Early in 2010, she was diagnosed with brain cancer. Her grandson, named Huxley, was born, and Janette was able to hold him before she was paralyzed with a stroke. Janette MacKinlay died on December 9, 2010.[741]

In 2006, a documentary was released titled *9/11 Press For Truth*.[742] The documentary told the story of how the Family Steering Committee lobbied the White House, Congress, and US Senate for an investigation. It featured archival news reports from a variety of mainstream news centers, and featured the story of the "Jersey Girls:" Kristen Breitweiser, Patty Casazza, Mindy Kleinberg, and Lorie Van Auken. There were interviews with Family Steering Committee members Monica Gabrielle and Sally Regenhard, as well as the moving comments made by FSC member Mary Fetchet to the 9/11 Commission about the loss of her son, Brad. September Eleventh family member Bob McIlvaine was also interviewed.

The 9/11 Commission had held its hearings and delivered its *Report*. Yet the story of the 9/11 family members who had forced their government to investigate what went wrong was not well known. *9/11 Press For Truth* told the background story that went beyond the news clips of individual family members reading the names of their loved ones on memorial anniversaries. It also critiqued the media's handling of the events of 9/11. Mindy Kleinberg observed, "somebody has to be out there connecting the dots. And we don't have that."[743]

Bob McIlvaine mentioned that the press was one of the main obstacles in getting to the truth of what happened. Rebecca Abrahams, an assignment editor with ABC News, was interviewed in the documentary. Commenting on the state of the media in America since September Eleventh, she said, "I think news reporting has drastically changed since 9/11. … now, there is always use of caution in how we cover a story. We are everyday kicking and screaming in the newsroom trying to get stories out. … we could do a story, but it might not make air. You have someone from the corporation making editorial decisions. These are not journalists."

She cited the 1970s Watergate scandal and the 1990s Clinton-Lewinsky affair as two instances where Americans had been lied to. In both cases, Americans were told to trust the government. Abrahams observed, "just because something is the official story of record does not mean we should not delve further and to see if really it is the actual story."[744]

Ironically, *9/11 Press For Truth* only aired once in the USA at KBDI in Denver, June 2009. In a press release, KBDI stated that "due to viewer response to the program" it was going to air the documentary three more times.[745] *9/11 Press For Truth* was also broadcast in Spain, Poland, and Australia.

In contrast, between September 10 and 11, 2006, ABC aired a six-hour mini-series titled *The Path to 9/11*. Thomas Kean served as both a consultant and co-executive producer. He had the power to say "this scene is not accurate and we need to make changes." But Kean declined to object to any fictional or false depictions, and didn't bother to see the final cut. ABC described the mini-series as "a dramatization, not a documentary."[746]

9/11 Commissioner Richard Ben-Veniste wondered how the mini-series that purported to reflect the findings of the *Report* could be hampered by so much misinterpretation. Two retired FBI agents told the *New York Times* they had rejected advisory roles on *The Path to 9/11* due to discomfort with its many inaccuracies: the first quit after only a month, stating "there were some of the scenes that were total fiction." His fellow agent recalls: "they sent me the script, and I read it and told them they had to be kidding."[747] ABC aired the mini-series without commercials.

In 2006, Kristen Breitweiser published her memoir *Wake-Up Call: The Political Education of a 9/11 Widow.* Her deeply-moving account detailed her journey from wife to widow to political activist, and provided much-needed insight into the journey of September Eleventh advocates. Breitweiser recalled that the opposition encountered by 9/11 family members seeking cooperation from the White House included most Republican senators and congressional representatives.[748]

Breitweiser's memoir was called "eye-opening, valiant, and heartbreaking" by *Kirkus Reviews.*[749] *Psychiatry Online* recommended the book as an inspiring example of one person's capacity for "resilience" and "recovery from adversity." [750] *RoadtripAmerica.com* commended the book for revealing that "Mistakes and intentional cover-ups occurred more often than the American public knew."[751] But the *Christian Science Monitor* gave it a brief notation, describing Breitweiser's book as an "angry memoir."[752]

Breitweiser was far from the only one frustrated by the opposition families seeking the truth faced. Gordon and Kathleen Haberman, whose daughter, Andrea Lyn Haberman, died on the 92nd floor of the North Tower, wrote that a "wall has been placed between the truth and us. What we have learned, and what we believe, is that September 11, 2001 could have been prevented ...I am concerned that the national security of this country has suffered by preventing honest and decent people, employees within our own government, sworn to protect us, from speaking freely, without fear of recrimination. Elected officials who publicly talk of honoring those who died on 9/11, should truly honor our loved ones and protect the American public by their actions."[753]

Their daughter, Andrea, had been on her first scheduled business trip to the North Tower on September Eleventh. Andrea and her fiancé "had a little competition every weekday morning. Whoever called the other one first after 7 a.m. would win. There was no real prize. The victor simply got proof that he or she was the first to think of, and call, the other—even though most days they'd only been separated for an hour and were at jobs no more than 20 to 30 miles apart."[754] Andrea won the competition that morning, having called her fiancé just as she walked into the North Tower at 8:00 a.m. American Airlines Flight 11 would strike the North Tower, one floor above where her meeting was taking place, forty-six minutes later.

Four years later, her parents reflected, "It is too late for Andrea. It is not too late for the truth. The dead are owed it, the living deserve it. Our government, rather than attempting to prevent the truth from being spoken and released, should welcome it; Learn from the truth and adjust its practices where necessary."[755] Gordon and Kathleen Haberman concluded that their government was more interested in preventing the truth from surfacing than discovering what it was.

On October 5, 2006, the Habermans signed a petition requesting the United States government release information, transcripts, and documents concerning the meeting on July 10, 2001 between former CIA Director George Tenet and National Security Advisor Condoleezza Rice. The petition included the signatures of FSC members Carol Ashley, Patty Casazza, Monica Gabrielle, Mindy Kleinberg, Sally Regenhard, and Lorie Van Auken.

The petitioners also sought the release of the 28 redacted pages of the Joint Inquiry, as well as the CIA Inspector General's report regarding the 9/11 attacks. In support of the petition, Gordon Haberman said, "The 'failure of imagination' has become the 'failure of investigation' and the 'failure to recollect' ... The dead: who speaks for them? An investigation under oath with serious probing questioning, rather than being offered the option of reading a prepared statement of what they were doing on the morning of 9/11 or being asked leading questions based on political party lines is needed." Haberman said it wasn't good enough for officials to contend "It wasn't my fault," or "I did my job."[756]

Former 9/11 commissioner Bob Kerrey gave a number of interviews after the *Report* was released, especially after the November 2004 election. Kerrey expressed frustration with the incomplete work of the Commission. He said the testimonies of some officials who spoke during its proceedings were dubious. "I think the basic facts here indicate that these attacks occurred as a consequence of a conspiracy ... There are ample reasons to suspect that there may be some alternative to what we outlined in our version." As a result of his concerns, Bob Kerrey announced that he was asking for the creation of a "permanent 9/11 Commission."[757]

Senator Bob Graham, co-Chairman of the Joint Inquiry, commented on the pattern of decision-making with regard to Saudi Arabian citizens before and after September Eleventh. He told a reporter that there were people in the United States government who knew something was going on before the attacks. He said there was evidence in the 28 redacted pages that the FBI knew of Saudi Ambassador Bandar's links to al Qaeda terrorists before the attacks.

Speaking to a reporter on the fifteenth anniversary of the attacks, Graham said, "It was so pervasive ... virtually all of the agencies of the federal government were moving in the same direction, from a customs agent at an airport in Orlando who was chastised when he denied entry into the United States to a Saudi, to the president of the United States authorizing large numbers of Saudis to leave the country, possibly denying us—forever—important insights and information on what happened. You don't have everybody moving in the same direction without there being a head coach somewhere who was giving them instructions as to where he wants them to move."

Graham said there were instructions being given to move key Saudis, including bin Laden family members, out of the United States. Graham complained that after September Eleventh people in the United States government took action to aggressively deceive the general public that such instructions never occurred.[758]

Over the years, Kristen Breitweiser has been one of many 9/11 family members pressing for the release of these 28 classified pages from the Joint Inquiry Report. The Joint Inquiry put the spotlight on Saudi Arabia: not Iraq, Afghanistan, Iran, Syria, or Pakistan. Breitweiser criticized President Obama's lack of engagement in the issue. She reminded readers that 9/11 Commission executive director Philip Zelikow blocked any investigation into a possible Saudi connection with the attacks.

Nonetheless, a formerly-classified FBI document was submitted on September 4, 2002, to the 9/11 Commission. On the top it was marked "Secret/Noforn/Orcon." It was dated August 28, 2000. The FBI document showed that hijackers Nawaf Al-Hazmi and Khalid Al-Mihdhar met with the Los Angeles Saudi consular official Fahad Thumairy.[759] The Saudi consular official also helped bring al Qaeda commander Khallad bin Attash (aka Tafwiq bin Attash/Walid bin Attash) into the United States to meet with the two hijackers nine months before September Eleventh.

In a 2017 column for the *Huffington Post*, Kristen Breitweiser asserted: "The Kingdom of Saudi Arabia provided operational and financial support to the 9/11 hijackers. That is a fact. And, the US government has been covering up that fact for fifteen years—even to this very day. And that is a crime."[760] At the bottom of her article former FSC members Monica Gabrielle, Mindy Kleinberg, Lorie Van Auken, and Patty Casazza signed their names.

Other investigators also disagreed with the universal attempt to manipulate information during the investigation. Former 9/11 commissioner Max Cleland had resigned out of frustration, in part, because of the refusal to question the White House's insistence in connecting the September Eleventh attacks and the need for the Iraq War.

Others alleged the White House never wanted the 9/11 Commission to succeed. 9/11 Commission Vice Chairman Lee Hamilton conceded that this was especially problematic. He told the CBC, "We got started late. We had a very short time frame ... we did not have enough money ... We had a lot of people who strongly opposed what we did. We had a lot of trouble getting access to documents and to people ... So there were all kinds of reasons we thought we were set up to fail."[761] However, 9/11 families objected that a major reason the 9/11 Commission had trouble getting access to documents was that they either didn't ask for them or failed to issue subpoenas for them.

Bill Doyle, head of the largest 9/11 family group—"Coalition of 9/11 Families," which represented over 7,000 families—said that over half of the family members in his group believed there was government complicity in the attacks. Doyle said, "There are still too few answers to too many questions even as promotions and medals are handed out rather than pink slips or prosecutions. Excessive secrecy and redactions still cover-up the truth and leave us in the dark about terrorist financing from still unnamed foreign nations, suspicious pre-9/11 stock market activity, pre-9/11 warnings to the President, the Attorney General and others, the infamous 28 pages of the Joint Inquiry Report ... faulty NYFD radios that didn't work in '93, Ground zero toxins breathed by thousands, a 9/11 narrative derived from torture induced testimony ... No American who believes in his country should settle for being in the dark about all this."[762]

In 2016 Terry Strada, whose husband died on the 104th floor of the North Tower, was among those pressuring the United States Senate to pass the Justice Against Sponsors of Terrorism Act. The bill made foreign states liable if they aided terrorists who committed atrocities in the United States. The act allowed a lawsuit by 9/11 families that alleged terrorist sponsorship by Saudi Arabia in the attacks.[763]

In March 2018, lawyers representing Saudi Arabia requested a lawsuit be thrown out because it alleged the nation conspired with terrorists to plot the attacks on September Eleventh. In accordance with the Justice Against Sponsors of Terrorism Act, the judge denied the dismissal.[764] In October 2018, the Department of Justice instructed the FBI to produce formerly-classified documents for the prosecution of the case. But before the midnight deadline on April 16, 2020, Attorney General William Barr and the acting Director of National Intelligence, Richard Grenell, brought four sealed statements before a federal court. It was argued before a judge that revealing anything more about "Saudi connections to the 9/11 plot would imperil national security ... the administration insisted in court filings that even its justification for that secrecy needed to remain a secret." Barr himself said to the judge that their revelation "would reveal information that could cause the very harms my assertion of the state secrets privilege is intended to prevent."[765]

The claim is all the more mysterious since the matter in question concerns two Saudi officials: one a Los Angeles consulate official, and another an alleged Saudi spy living undercover as an exchange student in San Diego. The involvement of these two Saudi nationals with several of the alleged hijackers has already been detailed in *The 9/11 Commission Report*. In what way does Attorney General William Barr mean that national security would be imperiled? How could details of possible Saudi complicity in the attacks of September Eleventh embarrass the United States government, or worse, harm the nation?

~ 22 ~

The Missing Accounts: FDNY

I thought [the South Tower] was exploding actually. That's what I
thought for hours afterwards, that it had exploded ... because the
debris from the tower shot out far over our heads. ...
It seemed the thing had blown up.
~ John Coyle, FDNY, December 2001

O n September 11, 2001, Thomas Von Essen, the fire commissioner
of New York City, ordered that oral histories be gathered from
first responders, firefighters, and medical workers. He wanted to
preserve the accounts of what they experienced at the World Trade
Center. In the weeks and months following 9/11, 503 oral histories
were taken. However, they were not released to the public. The 2002
mayor of New York City, Michael Bloomberg, and his administration
refused.

The Family Steering Committee asked the 9/11 Commission why
the Port Authority and the City of New York refused to release the
9/11 tapes.[766] But the Commission failed to address their question. So,
The New York Times and 9/11 families filed suit for the release of these
oral histories. FSC member Patty Casazza was especially interested in

uld reveal since her husband, John, told her there
ig off in the building during his final phone call from
of the North Tower.[767] *The New York Times* made first
estimonies available with a few redactions allowed. But
the f these oral histories didn't make the print edition. Instead,
the paper published them online on August 12, 2005. The pages of
oral history exceeded 12,000.

Many of these accounts included descriptions of explosions—
heard, felt, or the after-effects seen—*before* the towers collapsed. The
9/11 Commission was silent on the matter of reported explosions at
Ground Zero with one exception. On page 306, the *Report* mentioned
that there were first responders on the upper floors of the North
Tower who thought a bomb had gone off when the South Tower
fell.[768] This statement implied that the only first responders who
thought bombs had gone off in the Twin Towers were mistaken due
to their view of the South Tower being obscured.

However, the accounts of first responders at Ground Zero
counteract this assumption. For instance, FDNY firefighter John
Coyle was in the South Tower. During his interview, he recalled how
certain he was about the explosions all around him, even when he
called his father to let him know what had happened. "I finally got
through to my father and said 'I'm alive. I just wanted to tell you, go
to church, I'm alive. I just so narrowly escaped this thing.' He said,
'Where were you? You were there?' I said, 'Yeah, I was right there
when it blew up.' He said, 'You were there when the planes hit?' I
said, 'No, I was there when it exploded, the building exploded.' He
said, 'You mean when it fell down?' I said, 'No, when it exploded.'
… I totally thought it had been blown up. That's just the perspective
of looking at it, it seemed to have exploded out."[769]

And it wasn't just in the South Tower that explosions were
experienced. Standing outside, Captain Karin DeShore saw a sequence
of orange and red flashes coming from the North Tower. DeShore
noted that concussive blasts followed immediately after these

242

flashes. She recalled, "Initially it was just one flash. Then this flash ... kept popping all the way around the building and that building started to explode ... These popping sounds and the explosions were getting bigger, going both up and down and then all around the building." Later, while rescuing people inside the North Tower, DeShore experienced the explosions firsthand. "All I know is I had to run because I thought there was an explosion. ... Whatever this explosion was simply sucked all the oxygen out of the air. You couldn't breathe and the feeling of suffocation ... These popping sounds and the explosions were getting bigger and louder ... here was another explosion ... and this wave of force."[770]

Keith Murphy with the FDNY reported seeing extensive damage to the South Tower lobby walls, ceilings, and elevators. He noticed that parts of the ceiling had fallen, and whole marble walls were severely cracked. Two- and three-foot pieces of the wall had split, and others had fallen on the floor. Murphy stated, "There was tremendous damage in the lobby ... like something had exploded out. ... the whole area around it was maybe 25, 30 feet of really severe damage ... I got up close to see it."[771]

Murphy described seeing elevator doors that usually stood on a plumb line, vertical with the walls, hanging at angles. Next Murphy said, "The lights went out. Completely pitch black ... I had heard right before the lights went out ... a distant boom, boom, boom, sounded like three explosions. ... All of a sudden, I could feel the floor started to shake and sway. We were being thrown like literally off our feet, side to side, getting banged around."[772]

Assistant Commissioner Stephen Gregory said that prior to the South Tower collapsing, "I saw low-level flashes ... [at] the lower level of the building. You know like when they demolish a building?"[773] EMT Michael Ober reported seeing an "explosion ... one floor had blown completely outside."[774] And Firefighter William Reynolds remembers hearing a "large explosion" in the South Tower and seeing "fire ... shooting out a couple of hundred feet in each direction..."[775]

Concerned about possibility of bombs going off in the Twin Towers, firefighters debated the ongoing rescue efforts in the North Tower once the South Tower collapsed. Firefighter Christopher Fenyo told WTC Task Force interviewers: "At that point a debate began to rage because the perception was that the building looked like it had been taken out with charges ... many people ... felt that ... explosives had taken out 2 World Trade, and officers were ... debating whether or not to go immediately back in or to see what was going to happen with 1 World Trade."[776]

And it wasn't just the first responders who described explosions at Ground Zero: newscasters were reporting them as well. Three television networks, four cable news channels, and four local TV channels in New York City were all reporting explosions at the World Trade Center. The extensiveness of such reporting was analyzed in a July 2020 article titled "How 36 Reporters Brought Us the Twin Towers' Explosive Demolition on 9/11."[777] After examining over 70 hours of television coverage between eleven news channels, researchers Ted Walter and Graeme MacQueen found that the dominant explanation reporters gave to their viewers about the collapse of the Twin Towers was as a result of explosions and demolition.

Those viewing NBC on the morning of September Eleventh heard Pat Dawson reporting live with the headline on the screen: "Third Explosion Shatters World Trade Center." Dawson explained, "Shortly after 9 o'clock ... Albert Turi, the Chief of Safety for the New York Fire Department, received word of the possibility of a secondary device, that is another bomb going off. He tried to get his men out as quickly as he could, but said that there was another explosion which took place ... he thinks that there were actually devices that were planted in the building. One of the secondary devices ... that took place after the initial impact he thinks may have been on the plane that crashed into one of the towers. ... Albert Turi said that he probably lost a great many men in those secondary explosions."[778]

NBC's Ann Thompson reported, "I tried to leave the building. But as I got outside, I heard a second explosion, and another rumble and more smoke and more dust. I ran inside the building. The chandelier shook and again black smoke filled the air. Within another five minutes we were covered with more soot and more dust. And then a fire marshal came in and said 'we had to leave,' because if there was a third explosion this building might not last."[779]

At NBC's sister cable station, CNBC, *Wall Street Journal* reporter John Bussey told network anchors, "I looked up at the south building, the second World Trade Center to be hit, and explosions were coming down the building. It looked as if charges had been set on each floor and they were in succession going off … When I saw the floor-by-floor explosions happening, I dove out of the office where I was because the windows looked directly over the World Trade Center."[780]

And on NBC's cable station MSNBC, reporter Rick Sanchez described the challenges firefighters were facing because of "the second and third explosions" wreaking havoc on the "command centers."[781] While local NBC affiliate WNBC reporter Walter Perez described explosions in the South Tower as separate and prior to the collapse. "But on the far side of the building, there seemed to be another explosion and also on the right-hand side, there was also another explosion."[782] In all, eight reporters at NBC or their affiliate cable or local stations told viewers about explosions in the Twin Towers.

ABC viewers heard reporter Cynthia McFadden describe the challenges of first responders rescuing victims in the "blast site," as she referred to the World Trade Center. She described how "the first wave of rescue workers who went in were trapped, many of them killed by the second blast."[783] Seven reporters for ABC and its local affiliate stations told viewers about explosions at the World Trade Center.

Over at CBS, the principal "Ground Zero" reporter on the morning of September Eleventh was Mika Brzezinski. At 10:05 a.m. she described explosions as separate events from the collapse of the towers: "we saw it all after the first two hits. We saw the explosion and also the collapse of the tower."[784]

Shortly after the South Tower collapsed on the morning of September Eleventh, WCBS reporter Marcia Kramer told viewers, "CNN is now reporting that there was a third explosion at the WTC probably an explosion from the ground that caused WTC1 to collapse on top of itself. Again, there was a third explosion. It is unclear what caused it whether it was a bomb or whether the first plane that crashed into the tower had somehow been booby trapped with a bomb that was timed to explode later after the crash had occurred."[785] Eight reporters on CBS and its local affiliates reported about explosions.

Viewers who turned on CNN that morning had four reporters detailing explosions at the Twin Towers. One of these, Rose Arce, described how "every few minutes you'll hear a small sort of rumbling sound … an explosion … and another chunk of it (the building) will come flying down into the street." Then the shaking of the North Tower was a catalyst for people to jump. "I'm about a block away. And there were several people that were hanging out the windows right below where the plane crashed, when suddenly you saw the top of the building start to shake, and people began leaping from the windows in the north side of the building … and then the entire top of the building just blew up."[786]

The live coverage by 36 reporters across eleven American news channels, plus BBC reporters live on scene, all substantiated the explosive testimony of over one hundred first responders. Reporting for the BBC, Stephen Evans, standing outside the North Tower, exclaimed, "There was another big, big explosion in the other tower (South Tower). Flames coming out. This billowing gray smoke. People still not panicking…. an hour later … we had that big explosion, from much, much lower. I don't know what on earth caused that." [787] Afterward, he told the *Guardian*, "I was at the base of the second tower … There was another big, big, explosion … The base of the building shook... Then there was a series of explosions."[788]

However, in the following days American news channels omitted mention of explosions or demolition as being a catalyst for the collapses of the Twin Towers. The revised explanation given reflected what just one reporter in all the live coverage said on the day of the attacks: that the collapses were fire-induced.

ABC's Don Dahler told news anchor Peter Jennings at 10:00 a.m. "The second building that was hit by the plane has just completely collapsed. The entire building has just collapsed as if a demolition team set off—when you see the old demolitions of these old buildings." News anchor Peter Jennings next told viewers: "The southern tower, 10:00 eastern time this morning, just collapsing on itself. This is a place where thousands of people work. We have no idea what caused this. If you wish to bring—anybody who's ever watched a building being demolished on purpose knows that if you're going to do this you have to get at the under infrastructure of a building and bring it down."

But Dahler, who told Jennings "I grew up on military bases," interjected. He quickly revised his earlier explanation, stating: "What appeared to happen from my vantage point, the top part of the building was totally involved in fire, and there appeared to be no effort possible to put that fire out. It looked like the top part of the building was so weakened by the fire the weight of it collapsed the rest of the building. That's what appeared to happen … It all appeared to start at the top and then just collapse the rest of the building by the sheer weight of it. There was no explosion or anything at the base part of it. But I did see that the top part of it started to collapse."[789]

Corroborating first responder accounts, numerous employees at the World Trade Center also reported encountering explosions. Longtime anchor with *ABC World News Tonight*, Peter Jennings, interviewed World Trade Center carpenter Marlene Cruz, who was recovering in the hospital. She had been injured in the basement of the North Tower and was the first casualty from the World Trade Center to arrive at the Bellevue Hospital. From her hospital bed Cruz said, "I work for the Trade Center. I'm one of the carpenters. And I was gonna go do a job. And I got on the elevator, the freight elevator. And I heard the first explosion. And the elevator blew up. The doors blew up.

And it dropped. I was lucky that the elevator got caught between two floors ... The B Levels, the basement levels. After the first explosion I was laying on the floor about 40 minutes."

Having been on staff for fifteen years, Marlene Cruz had worked at the World Trade Center during the bombing in 1993. She said, "When I heard that explosion that's the first thing I thought was, here we go again, another bomb."[790] Since she had experienced the bombing in 1993, Cruz could have been a key witness for the 9/11 Commission. She could have been asked to testify about her experience of bombs going off in the North Tower on September Eleventh, and compare that with her experience of the World Trade Center attack in 1993. However, Marlene Cruz was never asked to testify before the 9/11 Commission.

Anthony Saltalamacchia was a maintenance supervisor at the World Trade Center. While he was handing out work assignments to employees in the North Tower sub-basement B1 he heard a "massive explosion that was in the World Trade Center about 8:46 a.m. ... The explosion ... came from the Mechanical Room ... below us in a lower sub-basement. Then we heard a series of other explosions ... 14 to 15 people came running and screaming into our office ... Then right after that the floor started shaking. The tile from above started coming down, falling on us ... A man came into the office ... in shock. He had multiple wounds. His arms were bleeding. Skin was peeling off. You could basically see his flesh. It was a very tough thing to see. And as we were standing there, more explosions were happening ... from 8:46 a.m. until the time we got out was ... at least ten."[791]

Construction worker Phillip Morelli was three floors below on the fourth sub-basement. He told a reporter: "There was a loud explosion and I was thrown to the floor. I got up and about a minute later there was another powerful blast that threw me to the floor again. This time the walls of the fourth sub-basement were blown out and the tiles from the ceiling began falling down."[792]

Two floors below that, "deep underground, in an area surrounded by solid bedrock," Stationary Engineer Mike Pecoraro was working with a grinder when he was interrupted by a co-worker. He recalls: "the whole building seemed to shake and there was a loud explosion." [793] White smoke filled the room, and the pair climbed to sub-basement C to a machine shop. But the whole place was demolished. "There was nothing there but rubble. We're talking about a 50-ton hydraulic press. Gone!"

Pecoraro climbed with his buddy to a parking garage that was also demolished. Pecoraro observed: "there were no walls, [and] there was rubble on the floor." When they got to the B level, they saw a steel and concrete fire door that weighed about 300 pounds wrinkled up on the floor "like a piece of aluminum foil." Once they got to the North Tower lobby he noticed "elevator doors were missing ... 20 by 10-foot section of marble [was] gone from the walls. The west windows were all gone ... These are tremendous windows. They were just gone. Broken glass everywhere, the revolving doors were all broken and their glass was gone. Every sprinkler head was going off."[794]

Shortly before 8:45 a.m. maintenance worker Kenny Johannemann was in the basement of the North Tower waiting for an elevator. He told a *Sydney Morning Herald* reporter what happened next. "The lift door exploded open. There was a man inside half burnt. His skin was hanging off. I dragged him out of the lift and somebody helped me get him out of the building."[795] Johanneman next took the blast victim to an ambulance. He told the *Sydney Morning Herald* about his heroics ten minutes after the South Tower was hit.

Below Johannemann, William Rodriguez was in the sub-basement of the North Tower when he experienced multiple explosions. Rodriguez recalled, "I was talking to my supervisor when I heard 'boom', very loud, and everybody in the room was pushed upwards." The impact shook the whole building, and all 15 people in the office started screaming. Later, William Rodriguez received a commendation from President George W. Bush for his heroism when he rescued co-worker

Felipe David, who had been restocking the vending machines in front of a elevator when a fireball burst out of the elevator shaft and he caught on fire.[796]

William Rodriguez met with the 9/11 Commission staff and told them about the bombs and secondary devices going off before the first plane hit the North Tower. Commenting on *The 9/11 Commission Report* he said, "what really upsets me is that my story never appeared in the 9/11 Commission report after I told it to them behind closed doors ... They never followed up with verifying my testimony and ... when the report came out, there was no mention of my statements and the other evidence of a basement explosion when they decided only airliners brought down the towers ... How could anybody not believe there was a massive explosion below ground level after talking with me and the other 14 people who witnessed the very same thing?"[797] Rodriguez said his story refutes the narrative of the commission's *Report*. He called his interview with the 9/11 Commission behind closed doors a "travesty."

Reports of explosions were not confined to the lobby or the sub-basements. Other first responders and eye-witnesses reported bombs and secondary devices going off in over a dozen floors above the North Tower lobby.

Kim White, who worked at a financial tech company on the 80th floor of the North Tower, was evacuating down the stairwell. She recalls, "All of a sudden the building shook, then it started to sway. We didn't know what was going on .... We got down as far as the 74th floor .... Then there was another explosion ..."[798]

Bob McIlvaine was critical of the 9/11 Commission's omission of FDNY testimony and ample public statements by reporters and World Trade Center occupants of explosions. He insisted: "my son died from an explosion. He didn't have burns on him ... he had postmortem slight burns, meaning that a detonation killed him, then the heat coming afterwards put some burns on him." Doctors who were on the scene told McIlvaine that they found people who "were blown into hundreds of pieces." He exclaimed, "How can that happen with fall down fire and a building falling straight down? These buildings came down from explosions."[799]

Although *The New York Times* published online the testimony of over 100 first responders who stated they encountered explosions at Ground Zero, this was not persuasive enough for one of the paper's reporters, Philip Shenon. In 2008 Shenon wrote it was "outrageous" to suggest "that the Twin Towers were brought down by preplanned explosives." He assured readers "Independent scientists and engineers had plausible explanations for the physical collapse of the Twin Towers" and World Trade Center 7.[800] 9/11 Commission co-chairman Lee Hamilton dismissed reports of explosions at the World Trade Center buildings in an interview with the CBC in 2006, saying there was "no evidence."[801]

Vice President Dick Cheney's Deputy Chief of Staff, Eric Edelman, was in the Presidential Emergency Operations Center with Cheney on the morning of September Eleventh. Edelman told *Newsweek* about the moment the South Tower began to fall. "Some of us I think were a bit stunned by how, the way it came down. ... it almost looked like ... charges on each floor to bring it to the ground. Some of us were speculating that maybe ... there was some kind of charge on the ground or in the building." Edelman recalled Cheney immediately insisted that what people were seeing were not explosives but the floors of the towers "pancaked" one on top of the next, causing the lower floors to collapse.[802]

However, what Cheney described is not what happened, at least to the 81st to 110th floors of the South Tower. TV helicopters caught aerial video of a most unusual phenomenon. As the tower began to collapse, the top 30 floors tilted, broke off from the rest of the building, began to rotate and then reverse itself as it was tipping. Physicist Steven Jones observed this from watching video footage in slow motion. He said of the top 30 floors of the South Tower, "They begin to topple over, not fall straight down .... this block turned mostly to powder in *mid-air!*"[803] The gut reaction of those in the bunker with Cheney, that the tower was imploding because of explosives, was astute.

The president of Controlled Demolition, Mark Loizeaux, told a reporter with *New Scientist* that he could make "doomed structures dance or walk" as they began to topple. He explained that by "differently controlling the velocity of failure in different parts of the structure, you can make it walk, you can make it spin, you can make it dance. We've taken it and moved it, then dropped it or moved it, twisted it and moved it down further – and then stopped it and moved it again. We've dropped structures 15 storeys, stopped them and laid them sideways.[804] We'll have structures start facing north and end up going to the north-west." Loizeaux's description of what demolition experts were capable of resembled the mid-air dance the top 30 stories of the South Tower did at 9:59 a.m., as was witnessed by those observing its collapse.[805]

Late on the morning of September Eleventh, Mayor Giuliani was asked by a reporter, "Do you know anything about the cause of the explosions that brought down the two buildings yet? Was it caused by the planes or by something else? There were second [sic] explosions." Giuliani replied, "We believe it was caused by the after effects of the planes hitting the buildings. We don't know of an additional explosion after that."

While responding, Giuliani turned his head around to New York City Police Commissioner Bernard Kerik for apparent confirmation. Kerik shook his head and muttered: "no, nothing like that." Giuliani had also told reporters that he knew the South Tower was going to collapse at least fifteen minutes before it fell. Yet, firefighters in the tower were unaware of the danger.[806]

At 9:48 a.m., eleven minutes before the South Tower collapsed, Deputy Chief Orio Palmer was in radio communication with some of his men, who had reached the 71st floor. From these and other audio evidence of the last ten minutes of radio communications, it is clear firefighters were responding throughout the tower. Battalion

7 had reached the 79th floor. Battalion 15 had reached the 78th floor. Battalion 7–Alpha had reached the 55th floor. Rescue teams only encountered small, isolated pockets of fire and numerous wounded survivors. The structure of the tower was not melted or deformed. Rescue teams were climbing up uncompromised staircases. Elevators were operational and in use up to the 40th floor.[807] Jet fuel fires were not sufficient to hamper these rescue operations. Yet, two minutes later, the South Tower collapsed in less than ten seconds.

On November 26, 2002, *Newsday* Magazine on Long Island released a transcript of the 9/11 radio transmissions of the North Brunswick Volunteer Fire/Ladder #3, including the text of radio messages between firefighters in the South Tower. In their radio communications, they were tracking numerous explosions in the twin towers. They reported bombs going off at 9:18 a.m., 9:24 a.m. and 9:32 a.m.[808] The firefighters were in radio communication with each other, and these details of secondary devices exploding were shared to warn their fellow firefighters of dangers they might face as they ascended the stairs of the Twin Towers.

On September 15, 2006, President George W. Bush told reporters that during interrogations, "Khalid Sheikh Mohammed described the design of planned attacks of buildings inside the US and how operatives were directed to carry them out. That is valuable information for those of us who have the responsibility to protect the American people. He told us the operatives had been instructed to ensure that the explosives went off at a high—a point that was high enough to prevent people trapped above from escaping." [809] Were terrorists setting off bombs in the World Trade Center to prevent people from escaping? If so, how could they have planned to set explosives without being detected? Who were the operatives with explosives President Bush was speaking about?

Nothing in this vein was ever clarified. In fact, even the transcripts of the FDNY interviews that had been released to *The New York Times* were censored. Nearly forty of the FDNY interviews contained over ten lines of testimony that were blacked out for security reasons. A few of these were matters of personal health, such as impaired vision, respiratory ailments, and PTSD. But others followed comments where a firefighter or EMT was discussing explosions.

Patricia Ondrovic was an EMT with Battalion 8. She was interviewed in 2006 about her oral testimony with the FDNY. She noticed that her mention of "flashes and explosions going off in the lobby of WTC 6" and descriptions of "depth charges going off in the building" no longer appeared in the transcript of her FDNY interview. She had also told her interviewers that she had heard explosions going off in WTC Building 5.[810] But these comments in her account were blacked out in the online post by The New York Times.

During his interview, Lt. Rene Davilla described being in the Millennium Hotel, where he saw that the lobby of the hotel was demolished. He also encountered explosions in the hotel. Over 200 lines from his FDNY interview were blacked out before they were published in The New York Times.[811]

Not many of the general public were aware of this. The testimony of FDNY first responders was only published online. Most of the New York Times' readership didn't go to the page with the names of 503 first responders and follow the links to their testimony.

With the online release of the FDNY accounts, many 9/11 families had more questions. Why had the testimony of 503 first responders over the fall and winter of 2001 not been reflected in The 9/11 Commission Report? FBI agents had been present at many of these interviews. News stories of other eyewitnesses escaping the towers and describing explosions had been published, or reported on local TV stations, in the months after the attacks.

FSC member Monica Gabrielle asked, "Why did the buildings fall? How could skyscrapers just crumble to the ground in ten seconds?"[812] This was at the heart of the Skyscraper Safety Campaign started in 2002 by Gabrielle and fellow FSC member Sally Regenhard. The buildings hadn't fallen due to the impact of planes crashing into the buildings. The National Institute of Standards and Technology stated in 2005 that the Twin Towers "have been investigated and found to be safe in an assumed collision with a large jet airliner (Boeing 707—DC 8) traveling at 600 miles per hour. Analysis indicates that such collision would result in only local damage which could not cause collapse or substantial damage to the building."[813]

Was it due to the temperatures from fires confined to the crash zones? CNN reported that "the fire was very, very intense and burned for a long time."[814] How long? The South Tower collapsed 56 minutes after the plane crashed, as the fires were dying down. The North Tower collapsed after one hour and 42 minutes. And NIST said, "The initial jet fuel fires themselves lasted at most a few minutes."[815]

How hot were the fires? Survivor Brian Clark was on the 84th floor of the South Tower when United Airlines 175 crashed. Clark said that when he got down to the 78th floor, "You could see through the wall and the cracks and see flames ... just licking up, not a roaring inferno, just quiet flames ... and smoke sort of eking through the wall."[816] When he descended to the 74th floor, the air was fresh and the lights were on.

Survivor Stanley Praimnath was on the 81st floor of the South Tower when the plane crashed into his floor. He could see "a piece of the plane wing ... stuck in the doorway, twenty feet from where I am."[817] Minutes before the South Tower collapsed, firefighter Orio Palmer had reached the 78th floor and was letting other first responders behind him know it was safe to proceed.

Many family members of September Eleventh victims wondered how the fires in the Twin Towers compared to other skyscraper infernos. In 2004, a fire in the 50-story Parque Central in Caracas, Venezuela, raged for seventeen hours. It utterly decimated the skyscraper's top twenty floors, and was hot enough to break windows. Still, it didn't collapse.[818] In contrast, fires in the Twin Towers didn't extend far beyond either crash site, and the windows outside the crash zones didn't break.

Fox News showed footage of a World Trade Center employee Edna Cintron standing on a steel beam at the crash site on the 93rd floor of the North Tower, signaling for help minutes before the tower's collapse.[819] Officially, the fire was hot enough to melt steel, yet it was not too hot for an employee in the North Tower to stand on a beam. The paper passports of alleged hijackers Mohamed Atta and Satam Al-Suqami were reported to be found at street level in the rubble of the World Trade Center, unsinged.[820]

The Twin Towers consisted of 200,000 tons of steel including 236 perimeter and 47 core steel columns, 425,000 cubic yards of concrete, and 600,000 square feet of glass. Being made of primarily nonflammable substances, the World Trade Center buildings were especially fire-resistant. An executive from Underwriters Laboratories, Kevin Ryan, confirmed that the steel used to build the Twin Towers met the requirements to withstand fires.

In a 2005 report NIST admitted that the few steel samples saved showed "only three columns had evidence that the steel reached temperatures above 250°C [482°F],"[821] not even close to the temperatures required to melt commercial steel, which is nearly 3000°F. NIST advanced a theory that the fastening of exterior columns to each floor was substandard, but it omitted mentioning the extensive cross-bracings that were welded and bolted to the vertical frames. NIST reported that when the planes crashed into the Twin Towers all the fireproofing simultaneously popped off the towers' perimeter and core columns, from top to bottom.[822]

In an interview with the *New York Times*, Sally Regenhard questioned NIST's findings. "We have had no access to the process by which those conclusions are reached." When Monica Gabrielle spoke to the *New York Times* in November 2004, she offered a challenge to NIST. "You have one job, and one job only—to find out the truth of what happened to those buildings and to report to the public about it. ... You owe it to the public—the truth, no matter where it goes."[823]

Near the eighteenth anniversary of the attacks, on July 31, 2019, financial and Libertarian blog Zero Hedge ran this headline: "New York Fire Commissioners Call For New 9/11 Investigation Citing 'Overwhelming Evidence of Explosives.'" Fire commissioners of the Franklin Square & Munson Fire District, 18 miles east of New York City, had discussed a resolution that was drafted and introduced by Commissioner Christopher Gioia. He and fellow Commissioner Philip Malloy were among the many members of their department who searched for survivors at Ground Zero after the towers fell. The resolution passed unanimously.

The blog stated that the attacks on 9/11 "are inextricably and forever tied to the Franklin Square & Munson Fire Department." It highlighted those first responders who died at the World Trade Center, and the reasons for petitioning a new, independent investigation. It added: "the overwhelming evidence presented in said petition demonstrates beyond any doubt that pre-planted explosives and/ or incendiaries—not just airplanes and the ensuing fires—caused the destruction of the three World Trade Center buildings, killing the vast majority of the victims who perished that day."

The Fire Commissioners judged that there had never been a complete investigation of the attacks on September Eleventh. Consequently, they resolved that their Board "fully supports a comprehensive federal grand jury investigation and prosecution of every crime related to the attacks of September 11, 2001, as well as any and all efforts by other government entities to investigate and uncover the full truth surrounding the events of that horrible day."[824]

After the resolution was passed unanimously, Commissioner Dennis Lyons acknowledged the loss the Franklin Square community had suffered on September Eleventh. "We have a memorial—a piece of steel from the World Trade Center with 28 holes where the nuts and bolts used to go. Every year on the 11th, we put a rose in each hole for the 24 Nassau County firefighters and four Franklin Square residents who died on 9/11."[825]

Present at the Fire Commissioners' meeting were the families of fallen 9/11 Franklin Square firefighters Thomas "Tommy" J. Hetzel and Robert Evans. Commenting on their presence, Commissioner Gioia said, "The Hetzel and Evans families were very appreciative of the proceedings. They know it's an uphill struggle. But at least they have hope, which is something they haven't had in a long time."

Of the losses of September Eleventh, Gioia stated: "we've been trained that when you fight the fire, you go in. You don't go in alone. You go in with your brother or your sister. You go in together, and if something happens, you come out together. You don't leave that person behind … We're not leaving our brothers behind … These were firefighters, cops, EMS, and they were just ordinary people who went about their business that day … We're not forgetting about them. They deserve justice, and we're going to see that justice is done."[826]

~ 23 ~

Campaigns for a New Independent Investigation

"I feel, frankly, abandoned. If I question anything about the official
story I'm called a conspiracy theorist."
~ Donna Marsh O'Connor, mother of Vanessa Lang Langer, 29

Colleen Kelly, co-founder of September 11th Families for Peaceful Tomorrows, was the sister of Bill Kelly Jr. Kelly recalled, "My brother, Bill Kelly Jr., died in Tower 1. He wasn't supposed to be there. He didn't work at the Trade Center. Ironically, Bill's prior visit to Windows on the World was in December 2000 to receive an employee recognition award. Who knew that the one-day conference Bill was attending on September 11th, the conference he cajoled his boss into letting him attend, would be an event from which he would never return."[827]

In January 2004, the 9/11 Commission was over half a year away from issuing their final *Report*. But Colleen Kelly had witnessed enough of the proceedings to write an endorsement for a book alleging a cover-up and calling for a new investigation. The book was titled *The New Pearl Harbor*, by David Ray Griffin.

In his book, Griffin highlighted the multiple opportunities the CIA had to kill Osama bin Laden. The al Qaeda leader was America's "most wanted" criminal. And yet he was in the American Hospital in Dubai in July of 2001 and safely visited by CIA agent Larry Mitchell.[828]

Griffin also wondered why FBI HQ had ignored a memo sent by Phoenix agent Ken Williams about Middle Eastern men taking flight lessons in 2000. He wondered why FBI HQ had blocked agent Coleen Rowley in Minneapolis, agent Robert Wright in Chicago, and the FBI office in New York City from properly reporting evidence of terrorist plotting. He wondered why the FBI, who had soon-to-be-hijacker Mohamed Atta under surveillance, did nothing to prevent Atta from re-entering the United States three times in 2001, despite his expired visa. Why had US officials obstructed these kinds of investigations? [829]

Griffin's questions resembled many of the questions the Family Steering Committee had raised. Consequently, Colleen Kelly endorsed *The New Pearl Harbor* stating, "It will be painful … to turn the pages of this thoughtful and meticulously researched book. But turn we must."[830]

For Griffin's subsequent book, *The New Pearl Harbor Revisited: 9/11, the Cover-up, and the Expose,* former FSC member Monica Gabrielle wrote this endorsement. "Mr. Griffin has again painstakingly laid bare the many lingering questions and inconsistencies of the official story regarding the horrific attacks of September 11, 2001. Sadly, millions of taxpayer dollars have been squandered on investigations that yielded no accountability, few answers, and fewer reforms. Yet, the attacks of September 11, 2001 have been wantonly used as political and policy fodder. Without truth, there can be no accountability. Without accountability, there can be no real change. Without change, we remain at risk."[831]

After the 9/11 Commission released their *Report* in July 2004, many people were eager to read its contents. In it, some people found omissions and distortions. Three months after the *Report*'s release, the website *911truth.org* ran a story with the headline, "Respected

Leaders and Families Launch 9/11 Truth Statement Demanding Deeper Investigation into the Events of 9/11."[832] Those calling for a new investigation included one hundred prominent American citizens, from authors to those who have served in former US administrations, the CIA, and military, as well as over fifty-five 9/11 family members.[833]

The signatories also included several members of the Fire Department of New York. One of these was Kevin Shea. On September Eleventh Shea was assigned to the Upper West Side with the FDNY Hazmat Operations. He was off-duty that morning when he chose to respond to the incident. Shea was in the South Tower lobby before it collapsed. During the collapse he says, "I was blown towards Albany and West. Sustained serious injuries including a broken neck and multiple trauma. Crawled 200 feet till surrendered to condition. Was found unconscious at intersection of Albany and West. Was rescued and evacuated for medical treatment."

Twelve of Shea's fellow firefighters from his fire station died trying to rescue people at the World Trade Center. Shea survived despite having "suffered a broken neck, multiple trauma, loss of part of his right thumb and other injuries."[834] Shea had no recollection of the first responders who rescued him. The last thing he remembered on September Eleventh was being in the South Tower lobby.

Part of Shea's rehabilitation was physical. He spent weeks at a Long Island hospital where he practiced exercises that returned him to almost full strength.[835] By September 2002, Shea no longer needed a neck brace and was back on the job. But the other part of Shea's rehabilitation was mental. He had questions about how he was blown out of the South Tower, what he told the others who rescued him, and how he'd survived. Shea felt *The 9/11 Commission Report* was insufficient. He wanted a deeper investigation into the events that took the lives of his twelve brothers at the station.

In their 9/11 Truth statement, Shea and the other petitioners asked "Why did the 911 Commission fail to address most of the questions posed by the families of the victims?"[836] Shea was an example of those most directly impacted by the attacks who felt the whole truth of what happened was not addressed. Shea and his fellow signatories were concerned that "people within the current administration may indeed have deliberately allowed 9/11 to happen, perhaps as a pretext for war."[837]

This was far from the only call for a new investigation. On the fifth anniversary of the attacks, Donna Marsh O'Connor spoke at the National Press Club in Washington DC. The occasion was the release of the documentary, *9/11 Press For Truth*. O'Connor held up a photo of her daughter, Vanessa Lang Langer, who had been working on the 93rd floor of the South Tower when the aircraft struck her building. Looking at the photo of her daughter, O'Connor said to the press, "This is my motivation. George W. Bush says 'God bless America.' He [God] already did. Blessed us over and over and over again. And on that day, on that day, it was men who cursed us, not God. And it has been in the hands of men ever since, to investigate everything; the events leading up to, during, and the events post-9/11. I know, on a daily basis, the press covers the event post-9/11. But I feel, frankly, abandoned. If I question anything about the official story, I'm called a conspiracy theorist ... I am not a theorist. I was a theorist at Syracuse University for twenty-two years when I taught writing and rhetoric and American public discourse and I can't do that anymore. I haven't seen my daughter in five years, except that she is the screen saver in my mind ... I am asking you for exposure. We are not crazy. We have questions. We demand answers."[838]

O'Connor appeared alongside two other 9/11 family members that day: Michelle Little and Christina Kminek. Michelle Little's brother, David Weiss, was a firefighter who lost his life trying to rescue others on the day of the attacks. Christina Kminek's sister, Mari-Rae Sopper, was a passenger on American Airlines Flight 77, which crashed into the Pentagon.

Christina Kminek said to the National Press Club, "Here we are five years later ...We are still left with unanswered questions, unaccountability and facts that come to light that beg new questions or reaffirm unresolved issues during the 9/11 investigation. There needs to be a new investigation." Kminek underlined how the Commission's report resolved nothing, and even raised new questions that it was supposed to have put to rest.

Michelle Little also expressed her support for a new investigation into September Eleventh stating: "I am here today to call for the facts of September 11, 2001 to be released to the American public ... The time is now to call upon all the Americans to lobby local media to cover this story and to pressure members of Congress to support legislation by reopening this investigation. We must hold those involved accountable for this atrocious tragedy. My brother, David, and ten brothers from his unit were murdered on 9/11. For them and for all of our mothers and fathers, sisters and brothers, aunts and uncles that died that day, it is imperative for their lives to know the truth."[839]

These 9/11 family members spoke before the National Press Club in order to increase awareness of the 9/11 families' unanswered questions. Yet, the press didn't report the 9/11 families' call to action that day. They weren't given the exposure.

As Donna Marsh O'Connor mentioned in her speech, when family members raise questions about the events, whether it's with the press or on an individual level, they are often branded as conspiracy theorists. In 2007, Boise State University researchers Ginna Hustings and Martin Orr described how the rhetorical device of calling someone a conspiracy theorist works. "If I call you a conspiracy theorist, it matters little whether you have actually claimed that a conspiracy exists or whether you have simply raised an issue that I would rather avoid ... I twist the machinery of interaction so that you, not I, are called to account. By labeling you, I strategically exclude you from the sphere where public speech, debate, and conflict occur."[840]

This phenomenon can be seen occurring beyond the 9/11 families in difficult conversations about the attacks between friends and family members across America. Dorothy Lorig, a counseling psychologist in Denver, had been practicing reevaluation counseling for over 12 years by 2001. When the attacks on September Eleventh occurred, Lorig remembers immediately suspecting that "the Arabs" had attacked America.

On the first anniversary of the Iraq War, Lorig, still a practicing psychologist, had a conversation with her brother about the attacks of September Eleventh. He told her that there were suspicions of persons within the United States government who were responsible for the 9/11 attacks. Lorig remembers: "when my brother told me this, I immediately felt such a sense of revulsion and distaste, it was as if he had exposed himself to me. And I just felt it was completely beyond the bounds of decency and good taste for him to have said something like that. And so, I changed the subject. I didn't ask any questions about it. I just didn't want to hear about it."

Reflecting on that conversation and her reaction over the following week, she said, "If we can think of our worldview as our mental and emotional home, I think all of us will do just about anything to defend our homes and families. And so, I see that with people, and I saw that with myself when my brother tried to talk with me about it."[841]

Lorig recalls that her response to her brother was basically to tell him, "Don't mess with me. Don't mess with my home. Don't mess with my comfort with how things are."

Because he was her brother, a week later Lorig sat down to read an article he had given her. At the time, she was on a lunch break at the office of her private practice. The article her brother had given her was a scholarly rebuttal to the official version of events. It led Lorig to reluctantly conclude that whatever the truth might be, the official version of events could not be accurate. She recalls, "I was in my office at the time and I sat there and I felt my stomach churning. And I thought maybe I was going to be sick. And I leaped out of my chair and I ran out the door. And I took a long walk around the block, around several blocks, and just broke down. I understand now that what was happening to me was that my worldview about my government as a protector, almost a parent, had been dashed. ... It was like being cast out into this wilderness, I think is the closest way to describe that feeling. And I sobbed and sobbed. I felt like the ground had completely disappeared beneath my feet."[842]

The government's official stance only solidified the conspiracy label. During his United Nations address on November 10, 2001, President Bush warned that he would not 'tolerate outrageous conspiracy theories.' Bush framed the conversation to imply that the government's official conspiracy was not outrageous, but that all other possible explanations were. Therefore, five years after the attacks, when 9/11 family member Donna Marsh O'Connor and others tried to question the official story about what happened, they were called conspiracy theorists.

In his book, *Among the Truthers*, Jonathan Kay told his readers that people who believe in any alternative view about what happened on September Eleventh are among a larger group of people who are afraid of vaccines and fluoride, deny the Holocaust, doubt the NASA moon landing ever took place, and don't believe President Obama was born in America. Kay wrote, "many of the most prominent boosters of the Truther movement—including some of the so-called Jersey Girls—have themselves been 9/11 Widows or first responders (a psychological phenomenon I describe in the "damaged survivor" subsection of Chapter 5)." In this fifth chapter, Kay mentioned 9/11 advocates Bob McIlvaine, Manny Badillo – who lost an uncle that had Thomas Joseph Sgroi A 9-11 Memorial Way in Brooklyn named in his honor – and the Jersey Girls. Kay surmised that "damaged survivors are particularly effective as recruiters for conspiracist movements because the spectacle of their grief short-circuits our intellectual faculties."[843]

Kay was not alone in expressing animosity toward those who were still asking questions after losing loved ones on September Eleventh. Ann Coulter said of the Jersey Widows, "I have never seen people enjoying their husbands' death so much."[844]

It's ironic that the media would label anyone who questions the official versions of events as a conspiracy theorist when the media themselves regularly report that persons in high places have been charged with conspiracy. Charges of conspiracy are so numerous, a law office in Philadelphia advertised that they had a full-time "Philadelphia Defense Attorney for Federal Conspiracy Charges."[845] And yet the press censors those who are concerned there could be a conspiracy concerning the attacks on September Eleventh; this despite the 9/11 Commission report itself referring to the attacks as a result of a "plot," which is a synonym for conspiracy.

The term "conspiracy theory" originated in papers discussing criminal cases. According to Lance deHaven-Smith, the term was almost unheard of in the media to strengthen an editor's or reporter's argument in their news story, editorial, or column. He clarifies that the term conspiracy theory "did not exist as a phrase in everyday American conversation before 1964."[846]

Between 1870 and 1960, the term conspiracy theory was used in the press on only thirty occasions. Most of the time it was used in reference to criminal trials. The rate of usage shot up in the 1960s from three times a decade to 46 times a decade in the *New York Times* alone. Most of these uses occurred after 1967. The CIA chose to introduce the term "conspiracy theory" in response a wave of books and articles about (what were then more neutrally regarded as) assassination theories critical of the Warren Commission's conclusions about the 1963 assassination of President Kennedy.

Between 2000 and 2009, the usage of conspiracy theory jumped up to 728 invocations and continued to exponentially grow. In a much shorter timer period between March 2011 and 2014, a LexisNexis search of news program transcripts uncovered 2,469 uses of "conspiracy theory/theories."[847]

The explosion of the negative use of the term "conspiracy theory" in American media is ironic considering that America began as a nation of pilgrims and pioneers "fearful of secret plots by political insiders to subvert constitutional governance." Those who use the term "conspiracy theory" to shut down discussion have forgotten that "the United States was founded on a conspiracy theory."[848]

Lance deHaven-Smith offers this background on the United States Declaration of Independence. "The Declaration of Independence claimed that 'a history of repeated injuries and usurpations' by King George proved the king was plotting to establish 'an absolute tyranny of the states.' ... The document signers claimed it was a 'design to reduce them under absolute despotism.'" This gave them the right and obligation as citizens seeking to create a democratic society to "throw off such government."[849]

Moreover, the Founders considered that power in political circles was absolutely corrupting. As a result, it was viewed as almost inevitable that political conspiracies contrary to the interests and liberties of the general public would be hatched, from time to time, by those in high office. Consequently, the Founders "repeatedly and explicitly called for popular vigilance against anti-democratic schemes in high office."[850]

Considering America was founded in reaction to the plots of King George III of England to oppress the colonists, Lance deHaven-Smith makes a timely assessment of what ordinary individuals began to wonder as the dust from the Twin Towers began to settle. "It is only natural to wonder about possible chicanery when a president and a vice president bent on a war in the Middle East are warned of impending terrorist attacks and yet fail to alert the American public or increase the readiness of the nation's armed forces. Why would Americans not expect answers when Arabs with poor piloting skills manage to hijack four planes, fly them across the eastern United States, somehow evade America's multi-layered system of air defense, and then crash two of the planes into the Twin Towers in New York City and one into the Pentagon in Washington DC? ... It is only natural to question the motives of the president and vice president when they drag their feet on this seemingly inexplicable defense failure, and then, when the investigation is finally conducted ... insist on testifying, together, in secret, and not under oath. Certainly, citizen distrust can be unwarranted and overwrought, but often citizen doubt makes sense."[851]

On August 30, 2006, CBC host Evan Solomon interviewed Bob McIlvaine, the father of Bobby McIlvaine, who died in the North Tower. In the interview, McIlvaine counted himself among the Americans who alleged that the US government was complicit in the attacks on September Eleventh. He told Solomon, "I believe 100% that the US orchestrated 9/11 with the help of other agencies around the world. But my blame goes to the United States because it happened in the US. There's people within the US that knew it happened, that planned this to happen."

Solomon clarified, "You believe there are people inside the US at high levels of government that were involved in orchestrating 9/11?" McIlvaine exclaimed, "Absolutely. I'm 100% sure." Solomon gave McIlvaine room to qualify his statement, asking, "Not just let something happen, not just let their guard down but were part of the planning?" Bob McIlvaine reiterated, "No. Part of the planning." When Solomon asked, "You think your son was therefore murdered by Americans?" McIlvaine said "absolutely."[852]

In a phone interview, Bob McIlvaine said that the price of asking questions has been enormous for families who lost loved ones on September Eleventh. "The Jersey Girls were just brutalized by Ann Coulter," he said. "And I've had a number of harassing phone calls, including one from someone who told me 'I hope someone puts a bullet through your head.'" Despite the animosity, various forms of law enforcement have told McIlvaine there is nothing they can do without a direct threat (such as a caller saying "I am *going to* put a bullet through your head."). "It's very stressful," McIlvaine said.[853]

Despite this, many family members push on. In March, 2009, former FSC members Patty Casazza, Monica Gabrielle, Mindy Kleinberg, and Lorie Van Auken wrote a letter to Senator Patrick

Leahy, Chairman of the Senate Judiciary Committee. They called on Senator Leahy to put a new investigation into the events of September Eleventh on the top of his list of "matters to be examined." They said that prior to the investigation "the 9/11 Commissioners agreed amongst themselves that their role was to fact find, not fault find." One consequence of this was that everyone just carried on. In the cases of persons who fell down on their jobs, who did not follow protocols laid out to keep America safe, these "incompetent" persons "were left in their positions, or worse, promoted."[854]

The widows' letter to Leahy stated, "At the 9/11 Commission hearings, little actual evidence was ever produced. Many individuals were not sworn in, critical witnesses were either not called to testify or were permitted to dictate the parameters of their own questioning, pertinent questions were omitted and there was little follow-up. Whistleblower testimony was suppressed or avoided all together."

Because of the omissions and distortions that occurred by cherry-picking what to include and who to interview, "the 9/11 Commission was doomed to fail as a real investigation." They reminded Leahy that Congress itself made no attempt to hold the 9/11 Commission accountable for its *Report* to the nation. They concluded their letter by asking the Senate Judiciary Committee to start a new investigation. "It could be surmised that holding no one accountable was more important than uncovering and disclosing the truth."[855]

Patrick Leahy did begin lobbying to establish a "Truth Commission." He wanted it to look into the events of September Eleventh, detainee torture at Guantanamo Bay, domestic surveillance, and other things that were kept hidden by the Bush White House. A *Gallup* Poll showed over 60% of Americans supported the establishment of such a Commission.[856] However, President Barak Obama said he was staunchly opposed to creating a "Truth Commission." With the promise of a Presidential veto, the initiative died.[857]

That year, there was an initiative to place a referendum on the ballot for the November 3, 2009, municipal election in New York.

If passed, the referendum would mandate the creation of a local commission with subpoena power tasked with investigating the attacks of September Eleventh.[858] This initiative was spearheaded by the New York City Coalition for Accountability Now (NYC CAN). NYC CAN was comprised of 9/11 family members, first responders, and survivors of the September Eleventh attacks. Supporters included Manny Badillo, who lost his uncle Thomas Joseph Sgroi; Bill Doyle, who lost his son Joseph Doyle; Donna Marsh O'Connor, who lost her daughter, Vanessa Lang Langer; and Bob McIlvaine, who lost his son, Bobby McIlvaine. Many 9/11 family members endorsed the ballot initiative, including Christine O'Neill, widow of John O'Neill. John O'Neill was killed on his first day on the job as head of Security for the World Trade Center. O'Neill was the former New York FBI Counterterrorism Chief, and was responsible for the investigation into Osama bin Laden. O'Neill had been hired by Jerome Hauer, WTC Emergency Manager, who later identified his body.

One of the people signing the 2009 petition was Jane Pollicino. She was a board member of the September Eleventh family organization "Tuesday's Children." The organization provided a variety of services to support both families and first responders. In a local interview she said, "On 9/11, I lost my husband Steve, who was 48 years old and my husband of 23 years. I was part of an average family almost eight years ago. And today I spent a day … in a city office trying to compare signatures so that we might be able to get the investigation that never was done, that we're all entitled to. I really think that we all deserve answers … I'm sorry this is only for city people to sign these petitions. Everybody all over our country should have the right to say we need an investigation now."[859]

To raise awareness, in May 2009, a September Eleventh family group created an ad to support the initiative. The ad was shown on local TV stations in the New York City area in the spring, summer, and fall of 2009. Four family members were featured in the film.

One of these was Jean Canavan, sister-in-law of Sean Canavan.

Sean was a carpenter working on the second day of a new contract on the 98th floor of the South Tower. Jean Canavan told viewers of the ad, "I lost my brother-in-law, Sean Canavan, on 9/11. I'd like to know why no one has ever been held accountable in any level of government for the countless failures leading up to and on 9/11. Why did the military lie to the 9/11 Commission?"[860] This was a question that even the commissioners had been asking. Chairman Thomas Kean had earlier admitted to the press "We to this day don't know why NORAD [the North American Aerospace Command] told us what they told us. It was just so far from the truth."[861]

9/11 survivor Janette MacKinlay also was featured. In the ad MacKinlay stated, "I was counting on the 9/11 Commission *Report* to give us the information so we could fix the system ... Unfortunately, they did not give us the information that we needed."[862]

However, the New York City Ballot initiative didn't proceed. They met with opposition when City Hall required all 81,000 signers of the petition to come to the municipal offices to ensure their signatures were valid. Even so, the threshold of total number of signatures required to place a ballot initiative before city residents was met. Over 80,000 New York City residents presented government ID to City Hall officials in person to verify that their signature on the petition was legitimate. However, staff in the legal department determined that the City of New York "had no interest" in investigating the attacks.[863]

On September 11, 2010, one of the NYC CAN signatories, Manny Badillo, spoke at the Ground Zero ceremony in memory of his uncle, Thomas Joseph Sgroi. He said, "Uncle Tom you remain the light of our lives, a loving man who teaches us still. Your smile, your humor, you are the rock defined. Your sister is here for the first time this year. Just last year eighty thousand New Yorkers petitioned for the comprehensive investigation into your murder that we all need. Without the truth there can be no justice. And we know the truth of this unsolved crime saves countless lives and brings us all toward the justice and accountability we all deserve. We miss you dearly and love you so very much Uncle Tom."[864]

Badillo was not alone among September Eleventh family members who were still pressing for an investigation into the attacks. The World Trade Center United Family Group represented over 7,000 family members. Its founder, Bill Doyle, lost his 25-year-old son, Joey, on 9/11. On a radio show he called the attacks a "cover up beyond belief," saying, "about half" of the families in his group agreed.

Questions about the collapse of three World Trade Center Buildings led to the creation of "Architects and Engineers for 9/11 Truth (AE911Truth)." In February 2010, former FSC members Patty Casazza, Monica Gabrielle, Mindy Kleinberg, and Lorie Van Auken endorsed their efforts. They wrote, "We must applaud Mr. Richard Gage and his colleagues, Architects & Engineers for 9/11 Truth, for their tenacity in seeking to answer lingering questions concerning the total destruction of the World Trade Center complex, in particular Buildings 1, 2, and 7 ... As family members of 9/11 victims, we have been seeking truth and transparency since 2001. Many years later, in spite of the NIST Investigation and the 9/11 Independent Commission, a vast majority of our questions remain unanswered." They looked forward to what more AE911Truth could do to address "the myriad oddities" involved the World Trade Center buildings' collapses.[865]

That four members of the Family Steering Committee would, six years after the release of *The 9/11 Commission Report*, endorse this organization is significant. AE911Truth stood in the forefront of groups questioning the government's official explanations of how the three World Trade Center skyscrapers had collapsed. AE911Truth stated on their website "we encourage those who seek the truth about the events of September 11, 2001, to ask the elementary question: 'Who had the means, the opportunity, and the motive?' Or in two simple Latin words, 'Qui bono?' That is 'Who benefited?' from this crime of the century."

The four 'Jersey Girls' reminded those reading their endorsement of AE911Truth that they had always been hopeful that the government would adhere to a complete, transparent accounting of what transpired on September Eleventh. They wrote of *The 9/11 Commission Report* and subsequent NIST report, "It was always our hope that both of these government investigations would uncover the cause of the WTC destruction and any loopholes or lapses in security protocols that could be remedied to protect us in the future. In this case, it was of utmost importance to determine what actually caused the collapses to ensure the future safety of high-rise buildings. Since the government failed to do that, we applaud Mr. Richard Gage and the many other professionals who are spending their own time attempting to seek the truth."[866]

But if the four Jersey widows were endorsing this "9/11 Truth" organization, the press were in no mood to give exposure to their applause. Like so many other press releases by the 'Jersey Girls' in the years following the release of *The 9/11 Commission Report*, the public was the last to know these women still had something to say.

In a similar vein to AE911Truth, a Highrise Safety Initiative was championed by September Eleventh family members in 2014, including the NYC Coalition for Accountability Now (NYC CAN). If approved by voters, it would have required the NYC Department of Buildings to investigate high-rise collapses in New York City that occurred on, or any time after, September 11, 2001. The initiative precluded investigating the collapses of the Twin Towers. But it would include the collapse of World Trade Center 7 and "any high-rise collapse that may occur in the future."

Editor of *Fire Engineering Magazine* of the FDNY, Bill Manning, endorsed the campaign on the group's homepage, stating, "Comprehensive disaster investigations mean increased safety. They mean positive change."

Bob McIlvaine also endorsed the campaign: "I support the High-Rise Safety Initiative because it represents our best opportunity yet to obtain a new investigation into the events that took my son's life."[867]

On June 25, 2014, *Crain's New York Business* reported that the campaign was a "9/11 conspiracy group's" petition.[868] This despite local New York NBC4 TV reporting that by mid-July 2014 this latest petition by NYC CAN gathered over 67,000 signatures—enough to get it on the municipal ballot—and was ready to add another 15,000 to the total.[869] Mayor Bill de Blasio told reporters that the initiative was "inappropriate, after all the suffering that went on 9/11 and since. It seems to be this is a very insensitive and inappropriate action."[870]

In response to Mayor de Blasio's comments, Bob McIlvaine and Valerie Lucznikowska, who lost her nephew Adam Arias on September Eleventh, asked in an open letter to the mayor, "Mr. Mayor, how can a campaign led by 9/11 family members be 'insensitive'? How were the signatures of 67,000 New Yorkers 'inappropriate'?"[871] A member of September 11th Families for Peaceful Tomorrows, Lucznikowska told reporters: "I watched what was going on very closely and I was very dissatisfied with the findings. I am a native-born New Yorker and I spend a great deal of my time in tall buildings and when NIST said it caught fire from the other buildings it disturbed me. If a building can just fall down like that, that is something that should be really investigated for the future."[872]

By September 2014 the campaign had gathered over 100,000 signatures. However, in October 2014, the question was not allowed to be placed on the municipal ballot. The New York Supreme Court ruled that the proposal, which involved authorizing the city to impose a 0.9% surcharge on construction permit fees in order to pay for the investigation, could be construed as a "tax" that the City was not authorized to impose.[873]

In 2017, there was another effort to investigate the attacks called the Bobby McIlvaine World Trade Center Investigation Act. If passed by US Congress, the act "would establish a select committee to reinvestigate the disaster."[874] Bob McIlvaine and Richard Gage, of Architects and Engineers for 9/11 Truth (website *www.ae911truth.*

<u>org</u>), launched the petition to pass the act at the National Press Club in Washington DC on September 11, 2017.

In an interview, Bob McIlvaine said there had been over three million people who had visited the website about the Act. On the website is a photo of Bob McIlvaine beside the quote, "I'm not a conspiracy theorist, I'm a father." Although most Congress members' eyes glaze over when he told them about the act, he did have one 45-minute conversation with a receptive Republican. The congressman told McIlvaine they had "never heard … anything about explosions in the North Tower" and what McIlvaine had learned from talking to the coroner's office, EMTs, and World Trade Center employees. McIlvaine said this congressman was "very interested and sympathetic" with what the Act was calling for. But the congressman told him candidly that he had no power. His first priority was to serve his constituents. If he endorsed the Act, that would be the end of his political career. Once the media reported that a member of Congress was questioning the official story about September Eleventh, he would be "crucified."[875]

In 2008, Bob McIlvaine had met with the doctor who examined his son's body at the morgue. He learned that his son, Bobby, was entering the North Tower lobby when he was killed by a blast from a detonation. Bobby had lacerations all over his chest from flying glass. The blast was strong enough to blow Bobby out of his laced shoes. "In a detonation, the blast is first and then followed by the heat," said McIlvaine. He concludes his son "was walking into the building, and before he got into the building there was a huge explosion, and … the force of it just threw him back into the open area. That's why he was picked up so quickly, because the EMTs came down there so quickly. Someone had gotten him out of there and to the morgue before the towers came down."[876]

McIlvaine said the official explanation is that a fireball was responsible for the blast in the North Tower lobby. He quoted *The 9/11 Commission Report*, which states: "The fireball exploded onto numerous lower floors, including the 77th and 22nd; the West Street lobby level; and the B4 level, four stories below ground." McIlvaine exclaimed, "it even destroyed parts of the PATH [rail] station more than 200 feet away. For one fireball to do all that, well, that's one powerful fireball."

McIlvaine also pointed out that each of the Twin Towers had 99 passenger and 7 freight elevators. There were elevators from the lobby to the 44th floor, and another set of elevators—across the landing—that operated between the 44th floor and the 78th floor. Finally, a third set of elevators across the landing on the 78th floor took passengers up as high as the 110th floor. The fireball would have had to jump in and out of elevators on the 78th and 44th floors, and cross whole lobbies, to continue on to the ground floor. The lobby in the North Tower was a huge area: 208 by 208 feet. McIlvaine said *The 9/11 Commission Report*'s explanation that one fireball did all this damage is "absurd."[877]

Bob McIlvaine states that testimony from other first responders shows that his son wasn't the only one blown out of the North Tower lobby. After the North Tower was struck, Firefighter Thomas Spinard pulled up "right in front of the building." In an interview he recalled, "We had two civilians blown out to the middle of West Street on the divider ... They were just blown up there."[878] Firefighter Fernando Camacho remembers after one of the explosions in the North Tower, "I must have flown 30, 40 feet through the air."[879]

On September 10, 2016, the CBC interviewed Bob McIlvaine and referred him as a "truther." McIlvaine didn't care for the label. In the interview, it was pointed out that according to the *New York Times* obituary, McIlvaine's son, Robert, died on the 106th floor of the North Tower.[880] To McIlvaine, the official story doesn't add up. American Airlines Flight 11 crashed into the 93rd to 99th floors of the North Tower. Some of those on the 91st floor and below were able to escape, but those above the point of impact all died there.[881]

However, McIlvaine's son was among the first ten bodies found, adjacent to the lobby. Bobby McIlvaine's corpse was taken to a local morgue and examined before the North Tower collapsed. No rigor mortis had set in. His corpse wasn't in the condition of a body that might have jumped from 106 floors up. If he'd jumped from the 106th floor, Bobby McIlvaine's bones would have shattered. But his bones were not reflective of trauma from a fall of over 1,200 feet. Further, knowing his son, Bob McIlvaine agreed that he would have phoned to say goodbye to his mom and dad if he had been on the 106th floor and planning to jump.[882]

In 2011 a panel of 23 experts, established as the "9/11 Consensus Panel," engaged in a six-year peer review project to analyze the verifiable evidence presented by the American government concerning the events of September Eleventh. Their expertise included backgrounds in the United States government, military, physics, aeronautical engineering, journalism, air crash investigation, academics, film, and a lawyer for the September Eleventh families. The panel examined fifty-one claims in the official narrative and voted by secret ballot on each claim.

In 2018 they published their findings in a report called *9/11 Unmasked*. They concluded that the claims made by the American government surrounding September Eleventh were not true. They observed "the official account, as summarized in *The 9/11 Commission Report*, gave false accounts of the behavior of political and military leaders on 9/11, including the vice president, the secretary of defense, the acting chairman of the Joint Chiefs of Staff, and the commander-in-chief of NORAD."[883] The panel noted that when people have raised questions about the official account of September Eleventh, instead of investigating those queries, the press has routinely attacked the questioners.

The Consensus Panel assembled their data "to provide a ready source of evidence-based research to any investigation that may be undertaken by the public, the media, academia, or any other investigative body or institution." This compendium of facts, drawn from long-available public source material, includes validation of the observations made by longtime CBS news anchor, Dan Rather, who reported shortly after the collapse of WTC Building 7 at 5:20 p.m. "For the third time today, it's reminiscent of those pictures we've all seen too much on television before, where a building was deliberately destroyed by well-placed dynamite to knock it down."[884]

Family Steering Committee member Lorie Van Auken offered an endorsement for *9/11 Unmasked*, stating, "The truth is out there in 'plane' sight: in videos, government reports, FOIA documents, and in physical evidence. This book highlights many issues that the American people should know more about. We owe a debt of gratitude to these fine people for 17 years of continuing to seek the difficult truth about 9/11."[885]

Were the events of September Eleventh only the acts of Osama bin Laden and 19 Arab hijackers, or were more powerful people involved? Former Underwriters Laboratories employee and author, Kevin Ryan, asked this question in his book *Another Nineteen: Investigating Legitimate 9/11 Suspects*. With the support of victims' families, Ryan examined others who had the means, motive and opportunity to accomplish the attacks.

Ryan contends a proper inquiry should have expanded the list of 9/11 suspects to investigate the actions and inactions of vice president Dick Cheney, Secretary of Defense Donald Rumsfeld, CIA Director George Tenet, Chairman of the National Commission on Terrorism Paul Bremer, Deputy Secretary of State Richard Armitage, FAA Hijack Coordinator Michael Canavan, NORAD Commander in Chief General Ralph Eberhart, New York City Mayor Rudy Giuliani, Secret Service Agent Carl Truscott, and others. Instead of seeking to provide "the fullest possible account of the events of 9/11," the 9/11 Commission was determined to exonerate the US Government of any taint of complicity. Its official name, the "National Commission on Terrorist Attacks Upon the United States," assumed the only 9/11 suspects to be identified and investigated were foreign.

Ryan's book was endorsed by three September Eleventh family

members. Bob McIlvaine stated: "Finally a comprehensive and meticulously researched book that thoroughly details what occurred before and on 9/11. Without a doubt, *Another Nineteen* should be required reading for those who want the real story." Lorie van Auken wrote that Ryan's "book reminds us that the attacks of September 11, 2001, and their details have never really been investigated." While Donna Marsh O'Connor said the lack of a proper investigation has "left each and every citizen of the world responsible for filling in the gaps. Kevin Ryan is doing his civic duty .... his work ... will be an important part of the mosaic that will one day be the pertinent facts of the morning of 9/11."[886]

Continuing to ask fundamental questions without flinching is a difficult task among those voices omitted or derided by government spokespeople and mainstream media. But without addressing fundamental questions, how can we truly understand, or remain informed, about the issues surrounding the events of September Eleventh? In a modern world of media spin, the idea of civic literacy becomes more important than ever.

~ 24 ~

September Eleventh Narratives

"Whose truth is going to be in that museum?"
~ Sally Regenhard, mother of Christian Michael Otto Regenhard, 28

The most enduring visible response to the attacks of September Eleventh has been the creation of the 9/11 Memorial and Museum. President Barak Obama dedicated the museum, saying it was a symbol that says of America "Nothing will break us." He added that it pays tribute to "the true spirit of 9/11—love, compassion, sacrifice."[887] Its website states "the 9/11 Memorial and Museum is the country's principal institution concerned with exploring 9/11, documenting its impact, and examining its continuing significance. Honoring those who were killed in the 2001 and 1993 attacks is at the heart of our mission."[888]

Former Family Steering Committee member Mary Fetchet was one of the driving forces behind the creation of the new World Trade Center site. Voices of September 11th, which Fetchet co-founded, worked in partnership with the 9/11 Memorial to catalogue photos of those who died and other images from the events of the day. While Mary Fetchet and a few other members of the FSC have been involved in the 9/11 Memorial and Museum, other FSC members have chosen not to visit.

The 9/11 Memorial and Museum is colossal. Its size makes one feel like a Lilliputian beholding the giant's lair. Upon arrival, a guide takes visitors through the Memorial first, explaining that "fires weakened the buildings." Guides tell different stories about the people who died horrible deaths on the day of the attack. Anecdotes, such as how one woman was a collector of Beanie Babies and another liked to eat gummy bears, are offered to remind visitors that the people who died were ordinary and had hobbies like anyone else.

The names of those who died are found on the bronze parapet perimeters of the two giant waterfalls inside the footprints of the North and South towers. The names are not in alphabetical order, but in panels proximate to where they are believed to have been when the attacks occurred. The random order of names resembles the chaos of the day. One panel includes the names Kenneth W. Van Auken, Alan David Kleinberg, and John Francis Casazza. Another has Christian Michael Otto Regenhard. On their birthday, 9/11 Memorial & Museum staff place a white rose by the name of each person who died. Family members who have lost loved ones can have a photo of the white rose beside the name sent to them by request.

A glass building stands adjacent to the Memorial: the 9/11 Museum. Upon entering, visitors go through security screening like one does when in an airport. No one wants an act of violence to occur in this place of remembrance. Proceeding along a hallway are two 60-70 ton rusted steel "tridents"—three-pronged forks—which are visible for onlookers standing on the Memorial plaza. Past the information signs, visitors to the Museum enter a hallway where a map is mounted on the brown wall to their left. The map illustrates the hijacking of four planes and the flight path of each to the World Trade Center, the Pentagon, and Shanksville, Pennsylvania.

Next, a montage of video imagery, audio tape, news footage, photographs, artifacts, and interactive technology engage visitors.

This includes snippets from news anchors and interviews with scared ordinary people. They provide pieces of a puzzle for visitors to try to make sense of the confusion and terror on the day of the attacks.

Further along a descending hallway is what the museum has named the Foundation Hall. From the view over the railing, visitors can observe the massive spot-lit 'Last Column,' which was the final piece of steel that was marked by fire and police crews, covered with memorabilia and ceremoniously taken from site. The hallway continues to descend to a large photo of the Twin Towers before they were hit.

Elsewhere, there is a timeline of the events of September Eleventh, complete with footage of planes crashing into the Twin Towers and people jumping from the burning buildings. There are huge beams from the towers, a crushed fire engine, a damaged fire truck from Ladder 3, a broken elevator, and first-person testimony of what happened as the day unfolded. There are stories of the rise of al Qaeda and a biography of Osama bin Laden. An exhibit titled "Revealed: The Hunt for Bin Laden" describes the ten-year effort to track down the person President Bush immediately concluded was the prime suspect behind the attacks.

One of the most moving parts of the Museum is the Memorial Exhibition: In Memoriam. It presents photographs of all 2,977 individuals murdered on September Eleventh, as well as the six people who were killed in the terrorist attack on February 26, 1993.

Another exhibit tells the story of the shift from grief at the loss to the effort of imagining and building a new World Trade Center site. It also tells the stories of people directly affected by 9/11 and their journey with grief, loss, and healing since the attacks. Lastly, it details the Mohawk ironworkers who helped build the Twin Towers, assisted in recovery operations at the World Trade Center, and gave their labor to build the new site. Visitors are reminded to keep a watchful eye in their daily lives, heeding the motto familiar at airports: "If you see something, say something."

At the end of the exhibit is the Museum store. There, tourists can buy tribute fridge magnets, one of a variety of 9/11 mugs, leafy necklaces that display the 'survivor tree,' T-shirts, baseball caps, tote bags, jewelry, commemorative coins, framed prints of the Twin Towers, and many other items.

The 9/11 Museum costs sixty million a year to operate. As it receives no funding from municipal, state, or federal sources, it relies on its tours, admission fees, and gift purchases from a steady stream of tourists.

Assistant Director of Education for the 9/11 Memorial & Museum, Jennifer Lagasse, explains, "The Museum has a dual mission. It wants to accurately tell the history of what happened on September 11th, and also to honor and memorialize the victims of the attack." In some ways, the 9/11 Memorial and Museum accomplishes this very well. But there are others in which the Museum's efficacy is debated.

The first half of the Museum's mission, to tell an accurate history of the events, is contended by some. Like the 9/11 Commission, the Museum tells its history by making choices about what background to provide in its presentation of different parts of the narrative surrounding the attacks, and omitting other information. Concerned about how the museum was being shaped, FSC member Sally Regenhard asked "Whose truth is going to be in that museum?"

The Twin Towers' collapse "because fire weakened the buildings" is the reason given by the Museum, but the accuracy of this statement is disputed. Critics also ask how the museum can accurately convey events when it fails to mention all of what occurred that day? The North and South Towers fell, yes, but in addition, at 5:20 p.m., the 47-story WTC Building 7 collapsed in under seven seconds. No plane hit that building. Yet, there is no exhibit in the 9/11 Museum dedicated to this historical incident.

The unmistakable message from visiting the Museum is that the loss of life on September Eleventh was the result of a foreign attack. In 2009, a *New York Times* article was printed while the museum was being constructed. It was written by the president and chief executive of the 9/11 Memorial and Museum. He told the paper, "We will not, and we do not, want to hide the truth of what happened, and identifying those who did it is core to that. It answers the question of who did this. Let's show the world the 19 individuals who boarded planes and murdered so many. To not do that would be a major disservice to the public."[889]

Yet, on September 20 and 27, 2002, then FBI Director Robert Mueller told CNN that there was "no legal proof to prove the identities of the suicidal hijackers." The FBI's task of confirming who boarded Flights 175 and 11 from Boston Logan, for example, was frustrated by the absence of any video cameras at the airport.[890]

In fact, of the 19 alleged hijackers, many were reported as alive variously in the *Washington Post, New York Times*, BBC, *Los Angeles Times,* and elsewhere, in late September of 2001.[891]

- Saeed al-Ghamdi, alleged to have been on United Airlines Flight 93, was reported to be alive and living in Tunis
- Salem al-Hazmi, alleged to have been on American Airlines Flight 77, was reported to be alive and working at a petrochemical complex in Saudi Arabia
- Khalid al-Mindhar, alleged to have been on American Airlines Flight 77, was reported to be alive by *The Guardian*, which also noted "he never entered the country [America]"
- Ahmed al-Nami, alleged to have been on United Airlines Flight 93, was reported to be alive and working as an administrative supervisor with Saudi Arabian Airlines in Riyadh, Saudi Arabia
- Abdulaziz al-Omari, alleged to have been on American Airlines flight 11, was reported to be alive; he had visited the US consulate in Jeddah to demand an explanation
- Mohand al-Shehri, alleged to have been on United Airlines Flight 175, was reported to be alive and living in Saudi Arabia. The Saudi embassy in Washington DC protested his alleged involvement

- Wail M. al-Shehri, alleged to have been on American Airlines Flight 11, was reported as alive by a Saudi Arabian official
- Waleed M. al-Shehri, alleged to have been on American Airlines Flight 11, was reported to be alive in Casablanca working as a pilot for Royal Air Maroc.

The FBI didn't bother to change the names, backgrounds, or mug shots of the alleged 19 hijackers, even after forty percent of them were reported as still alive. The 9/11 Commission published these photos and names in their *Report*, despite the accounts from mainstream news sources. The information the 9/11 Commission gathered about the hijackers came from statements made by Guantanamo Bay detainees under torture, and thus should be suspect.

When the 9/11 Museum opened, it posted the original list of alleged hijackers submitted by the FBI. It would have been more accurate to have large question marks in place of many of the suspect mugshots.

The second half of the museum's dual mission is to honor and memorialize the victims. Personal accounts have been provided by 9/11 families for visitors to read or listen to. High up on one wall of the museum are these words by FSC member Beverly Eckert: "I think about that last half-hour with Sean all the time. I remember how I didn't want that day to end, terrible as it was, I didn't want to go to sleep because as long as I was awake, it was still a day that I'd shared with Sean."

Elsewhere in the museum, Eckert says in an audio recording, "There was a building in flames underneath him, but Sean didn't even flinch. He stayed composed, just talking to me the way he always did. I will always be in awe of the way he faced death. Not an ounce of fear—not when the windows around him were getting too hot to touch; not when the smoke was making it hard to breathe. I wanted to use the precious few minutes we had left just to talk. He told me to give his love to his family, and then we just began talking about all the happiness we shared during our lives together, how lucky we were to have each other. At one point, when I could tell it was getting harder for him to breathe, I asked if it hurt. He paused for a moment, and then said, 'No.' He loved me enough to lie. I told him that I wanted to be there with him, but he said, no, no, he wanted me to live a full life. I just wanted to crawl through the phone lines to him, to hold him, one last time."

Beverly Eckert is just one of many whose recollections from the attacks of September Eleventh are memorialized in the Museum. Although the pain of that day is recorded, there is no mention in the museum that Eckert and others did not accept a cash settlement. She sued her government, having to resort to legal proceedings to aid in the search for truth. On February 6, 2009, she met with President Obama and asked for Guantanamo Bay to be closed. Tragically, she died in a small plane crash near Buffalo on February 12.[892]

Personal accounts are not the only means the museum uses to honor the victims. Down a flight of stairs from the Foundation Hall is a giant wall of multi-colored blue, blue-green, and lavender squares. They surround an equally-giant quote by the 1st century BCE Roman poet, Virgil: "No Day Shall Erase You From The Memory Of Time." The letters are 15-inches tall and made of steel from the ruined towers. Each of the nearly 3,000 tiles represents a person who died on September Eleventh. The colors are meant to represent the sky that morning.

However, there is some debate to be had surrounding the use of that particular quote. An article in *The New York Times* pointed out that Virgil's quote originated from his epic poem the *Aeneid*, and was a tribute to two Trojan soldiers, Nisus and Euryalus. These soldiers had just slaughtered enemy Rutulians in a camp "in an orgy of violence, skewering soldiers whom [they] ambushed in their sleep." [893] But moonlight reflects off the polished metal of the spoils they stole. This alerts Rutulian horsemen who, in revenge for the massacre, decapitate the pair. Their heads are impaled on spikes.[894] The article concludes, "Clearly, 'you' does not fit the profile of Sept. 11 victims."[895]

Helen Morales, a classics professor at the University of California, reflects on the quote in its 9/11 Museum context. "If we take into account its original context, the quotation is more applicable to the aggressors in the 9/11 tragedy than to those honored by the memorial. So, my first reaction is that the quotation is shockingly inappropriate for the US victims of the 9/11 attack."[896]

Defending the selection of the quote, museum director Alice M. Greenwald asserts, "The quote speaks to the indelibility of our memories. In selecting this quote, our focus was not on the specific narrative of the classic story nor its characters. What resonated with us, and with everyone who reviewed its use in the context of the museum, was the reference to a single day not being able to erase the memory of those we love."[897]

As an event with so many victims, it is little wonder that there are so many differing points of view and opinions. Distinct from the museum, there have been a number of dissenting perspectives told through exhibits or plays, but these are not permanent. They are temporary efforts by artists, leaving no lasting footprints.

Sarah Van Auken, daughter of former FSC member Lorie Van Auken, is one of those artists who shares her reflection on the events. She was only twelve when her father, Kenneth Van Auken, died in the North Tower. After high school, she attended college at the University of Arts in Philadelphia. She became an actress and a playwright. She wrote the play *This Is Not About 9/11*, which premiered at the Philadelphia SoLo Festival in June 2014.

The trailer for her play announced: "soon there will be a museum located inside One World Trade Center, A.K.A. 'The Freedom Tower.' As a tribute to the victims of September 11, 2001, the museum is interested in collecting tragic stories from all of their children. Interview number 5,234 is Sarah, a young woman with a different story to tell."

A review in *The Declaration* describes her 45-minute one-woman performance, responding to a faceless 9/11 Museum interviewer. At the start of the performance, the audience meets a spartan stage containing a swivel chair and a white folding screen with "9/11:

Never Forget" painted in bold, black lettering. The article describes the opening where: "A 25-year-old woman enters, rolling a packed suitcase onto the stage, prepared to give an interview for a video-taped oral history project as part of the unveiling of One World Trade Center."

Although the play is about a child who loses her father on September Eleventh, the article explains, "Hers is a tale about so much more than that, though: being manipulated by a news media bent on wringing every last tear out of 9/11 families in service to a grotesque faux-patriotism, while failing to actually *listen* to what these families have learned from tragedy." It adds *"This Is Not About 9/11* avoids browbeating the audience, using the spaces in between words to say so much more, and concluding with a *coup de grace* that will have you in tears not just for this young woman's loss, but perhaps more importantly, a lesson she desperately wants to impart, one a post-9/11 America refuses to learn."[898]

Sarah Van Auken transformed her grief by refusing to hold it in and bringing it to the stage. She told a reporter: "It freed me as a person and as an artist, cause the line is very blurred."[899] Sarah said that in the play "I'm challenging the audience to think about other aspects of how 9/11 has affected their lives."

In the play, Sarah expects the 9/11 Museum to be interested in her unique perspective. But, as the play unfolds, it becomes clear that the museum interviewer is less curious about Sarah's story—which encompasses more than her trauma from losing her dad—than it is in airbrushing Sarah's story with sentiment and its potential to pull on the heartstrings of 9/11 Museum visitors. The interviewer isn't interested in the story of her mother's advocacy, nor of the other Family Steering Committee members who successfully established the 9/11 Commission.

Of course, *This Is Not About 9/11* does, in fact, address the trauma of those who lost loved ones. Sarah told reporter Margaret Eby, "The pain that people feel, specifically the pain that family members feel on the anniversaries, myself included, is very real and very valid. It is not to be taken lightly. That being said, I'd like to simply shift the conversation."[900]

The play concludes with Sarah opening up her packed suitcase which contains actual memorabilia including quilts, photo albums, and programs from school productions. After the performance, the audience is invited to come on stage and take a look. Near the end of the play, she is asked what she has learned from the attacks and her experiences in the ensuing years. Her reply to the 9/11 Museum interviewer is "do your research." Her challenge to her interviewer doubles as an invitation for audience members returning home from the theater to do just that.

In an interview with _HelloGiggles.com_, Sarah Van Auken commented that her play "encourages people to think about how the world has changed, not just in the larger ways, but in the subtler ways, as well—and then, formulating a point of view about said changes. Educating one's self about what's happening in the world as a result of 9/11 is another way to pay tribute to those who died that day. Perhaps then it's possible to live in a place of awareness instead of fear, or worse, apathy."[901]

Bob McIlvaine saw _This Is Not About 9/11_ in Philadelphia. He said, "I laughed, I got angry, and I cried. There is some 'truth telling' in the play. Overall, it's really a fantastic play." Sarah Van Auken says of her play, "I want to highlight the fact that it isn't about 9/11, it's about us. We are all a part of what happened because it happened to all of us. What I'd like to encourage audiences to do is to involve and attune themselves to what's happening in the post-9/11 world."[902]

In a similar vein is the play _A Blanket of Dust_ by Richard Hopkins Squires. The play opened in June 2018 with the tagline, "The Truth Is in the Ruins." The play's central character is a 9/11 widow named Diana Crane, who is portrayed as the daughter of a United States senator. Her husband, Sam, dies in the North Tower, while having breakfast in the Windows on the World restaurant with a colleague.

In the play, Sam tries to reassure Diana that he will be fine, but then phones her back to tell her he's descended to the offices of Cantor Fitzgerald. He tells Diana, "There's not so much smoke here. It's eerie; the phones still work …. They're talking to the fire chief." [903] After Sam's murder on September Eleventh, hardly anyone can handle Diana's questions about what really happened on the day of the attacks. Her struggle for truth and justice drives her to the edges of mainstream society.

On June 27, 2018, a Question & Answer session about *A Blanket of Dust* was held. Among those on the Q&A panel were 9/11 family member Bob McIlvaine and architect Bill Brinnier, whose best friend Frank DiMartini was a World Trade Center construction manager before he died rescuing people trapped in the top floors of the North Tower. [904]

Since its premiere, *A Blanket of Dust* has had a staged reading at the Theaterhaus Mitte in Berlin in 2019. A run in Washington DC in the spring of 2020 was postponed due to the coronavirus pandemic. R.E. Griffin, with the 9/11 Truth In Action Project, described *A Blanket of Dust* as "the quintessential play for members of the 9/11 Truth Community … It speaks directly and forcefully without hesitation or apology to the painful truths, and the personal consequences and dilemmas facing them. Those in the 9/11 Truth Community will see and feel themselves so well on the stage that the line between art and life blurs. This play is a breakthrough moment for the 9/11 Truth movement." [905] Bob McIlvaine said *A Blanket of Dust* accurately portrays what happens to 9/11 family members "if you don't accept the official story, and the resistance you get." [906]

Plays aren't the only artistic medium being used to examine the events of 9/11. On September 11, 2018, the Feldman Gallery in SoHo opened an exhibition by Frederic Riskin expressed in print, canvas, video, and sound. It reflected "on the mystery, unseen political nuances and dark pain of the 9/11 attack as it remains an unhealed wound in the American psyche." The exhibition "explores the trauma" from this unhealed wound, and "examines our individual, collective, and government's response to this catastrophe. It is the subsequent debasement of American values that gives the exhibition its title, *9/11: The Collapse of Conscience.*"[907]

Visitors to this exhibit first encountered five HDTV monitors showing an assortment of video excerpts of what Americans saw unfolding on their TVs on September Eleventh. Next, visitors encountered 43 wall-mounted panels, each with images and accompanying text. The panels invited people to revisit alarming and ominous details surrounding the attacks. There are photos of the twin towers with black smoke billowing, a collapsing World Trade Center Building 7, a photo of Osama bin Laden, another of a hijacker clearing security, and the assertion that the buildings collapsed because of explosives.

Meanwhile, on the Upper East Side, the Met Breuer hosted an exhibit titled *Everything Is Connected: Art and Conspiracy.* The exhibit ran from September 18, 2018 to January 6, 2019. It was advertised as an "alternate history of postwar and contemporary art that is also an archaeology of our troubled times." Seventy works by thirty different artists "explored the hidden operations of power and the symbiotic suspicion between the government and its citizens that haunts Western democracies."

One of the Met Breuer curators commented: "this is the first exhibition that I know of about artists interested in conspiracy as a subject." The artists were working as citizen journalists, questioning the official stories of record between 1969 and 2016. Another curator of the exhibit, Ian Alteveer, detailed in a promotional video some of the pieces on display: sculpture, video, drawings, and questions of who killed JFK; revelations about the black sites used by US government agents for torture; New York real estate records in the 1970s detailing the practices of the slumlords; the attacks on the Black Panther movement by the US government; the AIDS crisis and subsequent response of the Reagan administration, and more. A series of paintings by Sue Williams showed the Twin Towers with the word "nano-thermite," somewhat smudged out, hovering almost playfully above them.[908]

The curators of the exhibit praised the artists for unearthing "uncomfortable truths." They alerted visitors that "the exhibition reveals, not coincidentally, conspiracies that turned out not to be theories at all, but truths." Seventeen years after the attacks, artists were inviting the general public to be skeptical about official narratives. They encouraged the public to ask more questions.

In response to these art exhibits, *The Nation* magazine penned a commentary with the headline "Conspiracy Theories Are Not Entertainment: New York's Art World Explores the Paranoia Haunting American Politics." The article chides *The Collapse of Conscience* exhibit for suggesting that the ten-second collapse of the Twin Towers contravened the laws of physics, and was "likely prompted by something other than the plane crashes."

The Nation cited an MIT Civil Engineering Department study by Thomas W. Eagar and Christopher Musso. The MIT study theorized that the cause of the twin towers' collapse was "the ignited jet fuel leaking out of the crashed airplanes" which "became hot enough to weaken the steel support beams until they bent under pressure, forcing each subsequent floor to collapse like a column of vertiginous dominoes."[909]

The same author also scolds the *Art of Conspiracy* curators for valuing the pursuit of "scavenging through the most contested chapters of American history to find plausible alternatives to today's hard truths." The article is a prime example of the phenomenon where a journalist presents their beliefs as "hard truths," while anything they distrust is a characterized as "conspiracy theory."

The Met Breuer exhibit takes issue with who decides what constitutes a "conspiracy." Commenting on the inspiration for the exhibit, the curator declared, "I would like to bring back the idea of art as a way of jolting people to get rid of their preconceived notions and hopefully question more."[910]

CONCLUSION

"I think the basic facts here indicate that these attacks occurred as a consequence of a conspiracy."
~ Bob Kerrey, 9/11 Commissioner

The story of the 9/11 Commission raises a fundamental question: can governments investigate themselves? The purpose articulated on the US Senate floor in December, 2001, by Senator Joe Lieberman was the need "to understand what happened without preconceptions about its ultimate finding."

However, prior to the first public hearings, Executive Director Philip Zelikow co-wrote a chapter-by-chapter outline of what the *Report* would find. Family Steering Committee members expressed concern that the investigation avoided following any leads that conflicted with the outline's assumptions. When staff from one 9/11 Commission team submitted a report portraying Condoleezza Rice's performance as "amount[ing] to incompetence, or something not far from it," Zelikow vetoed its inclusion.[911]

Over half of the 9/11 commissioners stated after the inquiry that it was either "set up to fail," or part of "a cover-up." They believed NORAD officials lied to them, and many wanted the DOJ to prosecute the organization. CIA Director George Tenet also lied in testimony before the Commission.

The most publicly-defiant member of the 9/11 Commission was Max Cleland. Highly critical of the White House's stonewalling, as well as Chairmen Thomas Kean and Lee Hamilton's failure to issue subpoenas, Cleland said the Commission was "compromised." Subsequently, Kean and Hamilton worked to get Cleland appointed to the Export-Import Bank, forcing his resignation.[912]

When commissioners toured to present and sell the *Report's* findings, members of the general public were told in answer to almost every question, "that's classified information." However, after initial critiques of the *Report*, the media chose to regard it as "definitive." 9/11 family members who expressed disappointment with the *Report* became *persona non grata*; the press wasn't interested in exploring questions the *Report* left unanswered.

When the press did acknowledge the existence of people questioning the *Report*, it painted dissenters as "conspiracy theorists," including 9/11 family members. The dictionary defines a theorist as "someone who considers given facts and comes up with a possible explanation." *The 9/11 Commission Report* failed to consider many of the given facts. In the face of its many omissions, Lorie Van Auken said, "if there are conspiracy theories out there then it is the government's fault, because they did not ever really explain, or show, or want us to know what happened." Bob Kerrey, who replaced Max Cleland on the 9/11 Commission, stated in 2008, "I think the basic facts here indicate that these attacks occurred as a consequence of a conspiracy."[913]

In 2008, Swiss historian Daniele Ganser told a Swiss audience that a conspiracy is "a secret agreement between two or more persons to engage in a criminal act. As 9/11 was a criminal act which was definitely not planned or carried out by one single person alone, but by at least two or more persons who agreed on the plan before it was implemented, 9/11 must be classified as a conspiracy."[914] Ganser contended that both the official conspiracy theory offered by the

9/11 Commission (that the attacks were a surprise) and dissenting narratives (that the government had foreknowledge and let it happen, or that elements within the government made it happen) must be evaluated based on the best evidence.

In 2016, a former co-chair of the Joint Intelligence Committee, Senator Bob Graham, told Real News Network reporter Paul Jay, "I no longer use the words *cover up* to describe what's going on. I find more accurate the words *aggressive deception*. The federal government has attempted to rewrite the narrative of 9/11 in order to exclude the role of the Saudis from that horrific story."

Once the 9/11 Commission was disbanded, 9/11 family members variously chose to focus on the *Report*'s recommendations, find comfort in its conclusions, point out its failings, and/or press for a new investigation. For some, it was hard enough to have to deal with the grief of losing loved ones from a terrorist attack: the spectacle of a government resisting any attempt to investigate the attacks, stonewalling the investigation, and starving it for the funds necessary to succeed was sobering for many 9/11 families. Yet, other 9/11 family members wanted only to trust their government's allegations and looked to the *Report* as definitive.

Some September Eleventh family members attended the open hearings of the 9/11 Commission. Most relied on media coverage to make sense of the inquiry. And many September Eleventh family members bought copies of the *Report* and subsequently drew their conclusions.

Since its publication, well over half of the 9/11 families agreed with the findings of the 9/11 Commission. In a 2011 interview, former FSC member Carie Lemack said, "Osama bin Laden killed not just three thousand people on 9/11, but he's killed people in East Africa, he's killed people in Jordan, Pakistan and Indonesia." Ten years after the attacks of September Eleventh, she didn't want to focus on "the perpetrators like bin Laden," but on victims like her mom.[915]

In the years after the *Report* was published, there was no consensus among September Eleventh families about its conclusions.

They disagree over whether the *Report* was definitive, whether it pointed to a cover-up, or whether its omissions justify the need for a new investigation.

Nearly two decades after the attacks, 70% of the questions the Family Steering Committee asked remain unanswered. These include questions posed to the following individuals and organizations:
- The North American Aerospace Defense Command (NORAD)
- The Federal Aviation Administration (FAA)
- The Central Intelligence Agency (CIA)
- New York Mayor Rudy Giuliani
- President George W. Bush
- New York City Port Authority
- Vice President Dick Cheney
- Secretary of Defense Donald Rumsfeld

Reflecting on the work of the 9/11 Commission, Chairman Thomas Kean said of the Family Steering Committee, "I doubt very much we would be in existence without them." [916] However, two decades after family members lobbied to have an investigation, many ordinary citizens are either unaware, or only vaguely aware that these families had anything to do with the 9/11 Commission. Of course, a majority of Americans don't remember much about the 9/11 Commission itself. And for many, the events of September Eleventh still have a traumatizing impact. Many just don't want to know.

Mindy Kleinberg contended in her testimony before the 9/11 Commission that it was wrong to presume that the terrorists were lucky. She said luck happens once or twice, not over and over again. The events related to the day of the attacks involved an ever-growing list of coincidences. Some of these have been discussed in this book:
- Coincidentally, President George W. Bush remained in an elementary school classroom reading a story about a pet goat, while Secret Service and other White House personnel failed to promptly remove him, in case he was a terrorist target in that first chaotic hour after the North Tower was struck and

America was caught by surprise.

- Coincidentally, Vice President Dick Cheney's story, about where he was on the morning of the attacks, was contradicted by multiple sources who saw him at the Presidential Emergency Operations Center over a half an hour before he claimed to have arrived.

- Coincidentally, no one in the US military thought to contact the Secretary of Defense, Donald Rumsfeld, and alert him that four planes had been hijacked and one was headed for the Pentagon.

- Coincidentally, the major area destroyed when the Pentagon was struck was the accounting/audit area, killing most of the auditors who were investigating the missing $2.3 trillion from the Pentagon's budget.

- Coincidentally, the United States military was engaged in five separate war game exercises on the morning of 9/11, with simulated phantom planes on live radar screens confusing radar operators.

- Coincidentally, the FAA Hijack Coordinator, Lieutenant General Mike Canavan, who was in charge of running training exercises in 2001 that were almost identical to the attacks that took place, was in Puerto Rico on the morning of September Eleventh, and it was unclear if he was replaced while he was away.

- Coincidentally, the United States military was unable to follow any of its standard protocols to intercept hijacked planes for 109 minutes, even though it routinely intercepts any flight two miles off its approved flight path hundreds of times a year with military precision.

- Coincidentally, the head of the Joint Chiefs of Staff, General Richard Myers, was in a meeting at the US Senate with Senator Max Cleland and recalled "nobody informed us" that the South Tower was hit and there was a national emergency. Myers said he was still on Capitol Hill when the Pentagon was hit, though this is contradicted by Richard Clarke who claims Myers was already at the Pentagon in a teleconference by 9:10 a.m.

- Coincidentally, NORAD Commander in Chief, General Ralph Eberhart, set the Infocon alert levels to defend the Pentagon at its least protective level the night before the attacks.

- Coincidentally, after the South Tower was struck and he believed a plane was possibly headed for the Sears Tower in Chicago, and another plane was headed toward the White House, NORAD Commander in Chief, General Eberhart, decided to take a drive around 9:30 a.m. (EST) for 45 minutes and was unreachable, having concluded that things had "quieted down."[917]

- Coincidentally, at 8:50 a.m. CIA Director George Tenet was certain the crash into the North Tower represented a terrorist attack by Osama bin Laden. However, Tenet didn't think to have the World Trade Center or Port Authority informed of his convictions and have them order an immediate evacuation.

- Coincidentally, New York City Mayor Rudy Giuliani told the press 15 minutes before the South Tower collapsed that he was informed steel-frame skyscrapers were going to catastrophically collapse for the first time in history, but made no effort to inform first responders of his foreknowledge.

- Coincidentally, soon to be named co-chairman of the Joint Inquiry, Porter Goss was meeting in Washington DC on the morning of September Eleventh with the head of Pakistani Secret Service, General Mahmood Ahmed. It was Ahmed who was reported in the press to have wired over $100,000 to the alleged ringleader of the terrorist plot, Mohamed Atta. Ahmed also met with CIA Director George Tenet earlier that week.

- Coincidentally, New York City Mayor Rudy Giuliani ordered the speedy removal of the debris from the fallen towers before sufficient samples could be obtained to determine the reason for the towers' collapses.

- Coincidentally, in the weeks prior to the attacks of September Eleventh, individuals placed financial bets that stocks of key companies impacted by the attacks would fall in the days after. One of these was President Bush's cousin and business associate of his brother Marvin, Wirt Walker III. However, the FBI saw no need to investigate evidence of foreknowledge, Walker's relationship to a flight school in Oklahoma where alleged terrorists trained, or being a Carlyle Group board member with other bin Laden family members.
- Coincidentally, no one thought to interview any of the dozens of members of the bin Laden family before flying them out of America when all other flights were grounded, even though they were related to the accused prime suspect Osama bin Laden.
- Coincidentally, the prime suspect for the attacks, Osama bin Laden, was reported in numerous books and articles to be a CIA asset, as a *Le Monde* headline declared: "The Most Dreaded Man of the United States, Controlled for a Long Time by the CIA."
- Coincidentally, a 47-story tower at the World Trade Center that had not been hit by a plane collapsed in under seven seconds at 5:20 p.m. on September Eleventh, and was reported on the BBC and CNN to have already collapsed over six hours prior to its actual collapse.
- Coincidentally, on the morning of the attacks over one hundred FDNY first responders reported they witnessed explosions in the Twin Towers, which they later testified to their superiors. But the 9/11 Commission omitted their testimony from its *Report*.
- Coincidentally, Boston Logan Airport had no security cameras to verify that the alleged hijackers were in the departure lounges or that they boarded either American Airlines Flight 11 or United Airlines Flight 175, the flights that crashed into the Twin Towers.

Mindy Kleinberg said to the 9/11 commissioners: "To me luck is something that happens once. When you have this repeated pattern of broken protocols, broken laws, broken communication, one cannot still call it luck." [918]

What was going on? These and other myriad oddities related to the attacks linger. Reflecting on her experience of the 9/11 Commission, and those who testified, Patty Casazza made this observation. "Yes, they lied. They all lied. Whether consciously or unconsciously. It happened. Now we need to look into why they lied and what were the results of those lies."[919]

At a symposium in West Hartford, Connecticut, in 2007, Casazza recalled "one of the reasons we still continued to fight for the commission, even as we knew it was a farce, is we wanted their words, their lies down on paper. We wanted to make them go ... through this exercise. And even if it came down to the annals of history, that the truth will come out." She believes without the efforts of the September Eleventh families, "more people in the future might not run out of a burning building; that they actually might listen to a recording that says 'You're safe in the building. Remain seated, or you could be fired.'" Casazza counselled, "I think we have to start thinking for ourselves."[920]

News stories many Family Steering Committee members read prior to formulating their questions remain available at _historycommons._ _org_. For twenty years ordinary citizens have learned that if they have any interest in educating themselves by reading mainstream news stories (like those researcher and author Paul Thompson archived), it gets them marked as a "conspiracy theorist."

The media's framing of this phenomenon renders all the questions the September Eleventh families asked as the stuff of conspiracy. Consequently, society has, by default, agreed that no questions can be asked when a crisis occurs. It is as if we are all frozen in time, back in the White House Press Room listening to press secretary Ari Fleischer tell us to "watch what we say" and "trust us."

Democracy depends on a social agreement that we assume wins universal approval. That agreement is that there is such a thing as truth. In an open society, we know facts may be constrained and slanted in the midst of debate. However, truth is the ground from which the constraint and slanted speech begin. Democracy depends upon accountability. This requires citizens being able to distinguish truth from falsehood. In order to be able to tell truth from falsehood, there must to be a social agreement that truth matters. If the ground of democracy is truth, the ground of autocracy is assertion. In an autocratic state, reality belongs to those who have enormous power to dominate and control others, including access to information.

For some, politicians must always be believed in a time of crisis: it is when a nation's citizenry feels most vulnerable. Consequently, statements by politicians and government reports must be treated with near-religious veneration. Lest we forget Watergate and the Clinton-Lewinsky scandal: simply trusting the words of government leaders *carte blanche* is a poor template from which to fashion a democracy.

Therefore, *The 9/11 Commission Report* gave rise to the "9/11 Truth Movement." Some in the movement recalled 20th Century political theoretician, Hannah Arendt, who observed that political leaders "determined to commit crimes find it expedient to organize them on the ... most improbable scale ... because the very immensity of the crimes guarantees that the murderers who proclaim their innocence with all manner of lies will be more readily believed than the victims who tell the truth." [921] Others recalled President James Madison's words to Thomas Jefferson in 1798, "perhaps it is a universal truth that the loss of liberty at home is to be charged to provisions against danger, real or pretended, from abroad."[922]

Some in the 9/11 Truth Movement examined the possibility that elements within the government itself might be complicit in the events that led to the attacks, either by letting them happen or by making them happen. Others contend that the government was wrong in its explanations. But for many Americans this conclusion was unspeakable.

French philosopher Rene Girard has noted it is a habit in human societies to find scapegoats when faced with a crisis. "Everywhere and always, when human beings either cannot or dare not take their anger out on the thing that has caused it, they unconsciously search for substitutes, and more often than not they find them."[923] Are the events of September Eleventh applicable to Girard's observation?

While some in the 9/11 Truth Movement presumed government complicity from the start, others remained neutral on the matter. But they wanted to verify government claims, demanding that the government produce evidence and make it public.

The Family Steering Committee's advocacy posed questions and asked their government for accountability. They had no agenda; they sought only a trustworthy account of what happened. They wanted to know why the Pentagon failed to defend its citizens, despite its multi-layered defense system meant to guard the nation's skies. They wanted to make America safe again.

The goals for the 9/11 Commission, as stated by Senators John McCain and Joe Lieberman, were to "thoroughly investigate all evidence surrounding the attacks." President George W. Bush and Commission Chairman Thomas Kean echoed these sentiments. However, the 9/11 Commission fell far short of a proper investigation, resulting in critique from the FSC.

Members of the Family Steering Committee were initially praised for holding the government to account. But when some continued to ask questions, especially after the 9/11 Commission issued their *Report*, they were attacked. FOX News commentator Bill O'Reilly called the Jersey Girls—Kristen Breitweiser, Mindy Kleinberg, Patty Casazza, and Lorie Van Auken—shrews, and suggested they pose for *Playboy*. In 2012, Patty Casazza looked back on their years of advocacy, saying, "I couldn't believe the politics. We thought we were doing things to protect people, by finding out what happened and making sure it never happened again. It was a harsh lesson to learn."

FSC member Monica Gabrielle said in 2012, "I don't have time to think about 9/11 now. I put my life on hold for years and now it's time to do something else." Shunning publicity and invitations to comment on the experience of her activism, in 2012 Mindy Kleinberg declined to return numerous phone calls from reporters at the Newark newspaper the *Star-Ledger*.[924]

Two decades after 9/11, the unanswered questions the FSC asked remain valid. From the 9/11 families' questions and research, we can obtain much-needed literacy about the events of September Eleventh. Such literacy is essential in a society too easily beguiled by headlines, media spin, and a history of forgetting. This includes forgetting that the 9/11 Commission was derelict, and failed in its duty to "make a full and complete accounting of the circumstances surrounding the attacks."

For some FSC members, the 9/11 Commission got it right. For others, the *Report* only raised more questions, especially about government nonfeasance. For them, the *Report* has contributed to a lack of trust in government, in particular concerning its lack of vigilance when protecting its citizens after being forewarned.

Fire Commissioner Christopher Gioia stated in an interview that he wants justice for his fallen comrades at the Franklin Square & Munson Fire Department. Gioia said the recording of Chief Orio Palmer's radio dispatch is significant. "In it, he said that he only needed a couple of hoses to put out the small isolated fires in the South Tower. If Orio had thought what he was encountering was going to be a danger, he would have gotten word to the other firefighters behind him to pull back and regroup." Gioia explained that Palmer's dispatch meant that he believed there was time for the firefighters below him to take an elevator to the 40th floor, climb up to the 78th floor, put out the fires, and tend the injured.

According to Gioia, it doesn't make sense that we are "being told that steel columns melted from the fire, but a firefighter could reach the 78th floor and be unharmed," by the heat.[925] Minutes before the

South Tower collapsed, Palmer observed nothing to suggest that the building was weakening. Palmer was on a mission to rescue people. He only conveyed a sense that he was equipped to do whatever was needed. He expected other firefighters could reach him, and together they could put out the "small pockets of isolated fires."

Questions are asked by those who want to ensure the story we tell does not bear false witness to what actually occurred. In late 2006, a sequel documentary to *9/11 Press For Truth* was released, titled *In Their Own Words: The Untold Stories of the 9/11 Families*. In it, Lorie Van Auken stated: "our perception of what happened on September 11 is very different from the general public's perception, I'd say for the most part." Mindy Kleinberg said, "I believe the public is still uninformed about most of the issues that are surrounding 9/11. I think that they still believe in the myth that there was nothing that we could do about it. That we were caught unaware and that today we would be better prepared." Patty Casazza said, "I still don't think ... that I have come to terms with how September 11 happened, why it happened and who actually perpetrated these crimes that day."[926] These comments by Family Steering Committee members are a call to revisit our assumptions about what we've been told.

In contrast, Kristen Breitweiser is certain that those who perpetrated the attacks were "the 9/11 hijackers and al Qaeda." But she wants "one of the largest co-conspirators of the 9/11 attacks, the Kingdom of Saudi Arabia," to be made accountable for its involvement in a court of law.[927]

In America, most citizens are very patriotic. September Eleventh Family member Donna Marsh O'Connor recalled, "When I was a kid and I would be in assembly, I had this really horrible problem. I couldn't sing any of the 'America' songs without crying. I was so infused with whatever this land was under me, that I grew up my entire life loving our paradoxes, loving our contradictions, loving even our sins. Because, here we could talk about them ... And still I loved this country. And no one will ever be able to call me anything but a patriot." It is out of Donna Marsh O'Connor's sense of patriotism, and desire for America to be its best, that she asks her questions about what happened on September Eleventh. Since the attacks, it has been her experience "that most people in this country do have some questions." She told her audience: "the only resources we have ... are reasonable arguments. Go out into the world and be reasonable, and just ask the fundamental questions of that day."[928]

Donna Marsh O'Connor's challenge is one readers would do well to consider. It is one that is as relevant today as when she posed it to her listeners in 2007: to ask fundamental questions of this time in our society. Citizen advocacy, holding government leaders to account—and to vigilantly scrutinize their claims—should be seen as exemplary. One day, perhaps, vigorous inquiry will be welcomed as the norm when one's nation faces a crisis and one's leaders offer explanations.

Each person who acts to uphold the value of formal education, scholarship, and encourages civic literacy brings society closer to this goal. These qualities are necessary for citizens to think for themselves and examine evidence. Such literacy is required in order to uphold standards of judgment. And so, the September Eleventh families' legitimate unanswered questions should be reflected upon, against the silencing odds.

The odds to be faced include the preference of many to rely on headlines and soundbites. Ridicule and ignorance trump critique and thoughtfulness, which deforms discussion. When someone notices problems with the official account concerning the events of September Eleventh, and tries to hold those in power accountable, it often results in being mocked, if not outright indignation. "Questions? Questions!? What questions? How could the 9/11 families have questions?" In this way, the 9/11 families' questions get labeled as "conspiracy theory."

Lorie Van Auken noted in her endorsement of *9/11 Unmasked* that there is an elephant in the room. The markings of a cover-up beg for further investigation, including plausible complicity on the part of some government officials. But defenders of the official narrative will brook no dissent from their assumptions. Daniel Patrick Moynihan once said "Everyone is entitled to his own opinion, but not to his own facts."

But in relation to the events of September Eleventh, Moynihan's statement is turned on its head. Public discussion about what facts to agree on—and continuing calls for government accountability—predictably devolve into outrage and name-calling. Consequently, no one is allowed to air an opinion that others disagree with. And no facts can be introduced to create common ground if these facts vary from approved orthodoxy.

Considering the persistent, toxic climate that impairs civil discourse, it is a miracle that the Family Steering Committee ever got to ask their questions to the 9/11 Commission back in 2003. Or that their questions were, at the time, regarded as legitimate. The chances of a new inquiry twenty years after the attacks remain remote, with truth, the whole truth, and nothing but the truth, its chief casualty.

In 1965 Trappist monk Thomas Merton wrote about "the presence of the Unspeakable." He was trying to describe a form of evil he understood as a "void that gets into the language of public and official declarations at the very moment when they are pronounced." The "Unspeakable" contradicted all the universal aspirations a generation pins its hopes on, making them ring hollow. For Merton, the "Unspeakable" signaled "a climax of absolute finality in refusal, in equivocation, in disorder, in absurdity which can be broken open again to truth only by miracle."[929]

The possibility that evil, which we do not wish to see or acknowledge, may be enmeshed in the events of September Eleventh is something many do not wish to contemplate. The implications are too terrifying. Monica Gabrielle points out that the families "wanted a commission that was going to be independent, nothing to do with the government, because we were going to have to investigate the government."[930] Instead, 9/11 Commission staff constructed a narrative for how the attacks happened and who was responsible prior to starting the inquiry. This didn't put these matters to rest. The 9/11 Commission failed in its mandate, repeatedly leaving stones unturned, important testimony it received out of its *Report,* and ignoring the families' questions.

Researcher Paul Thompson has called the events of September 11 "a scandal of tremendous proportions. It makes Watergate look small. There's a strange lack of interest on both the left and on the right. Nobody seems to want to uncover the truth and just follow the leads wherever they may go. 'Cause I think it goes to a lot of really damaging places."[931]

What does one do when few are willing to become familiar with the unanswered questions of the 9/11 families—including the 9/11 Commission itself? One option is to shift the conversation. Sarah Van Auken's play, *This Is Not About 9/11,* proposed an excellent way to honor those who were murdered on September Eleventh: to "do your research;" to unflinchingly explore the September Eleventh families' questions. History teaches us that the rush to reach conclusions about the story of record, usually based on assurances from those in authority, has not served democracy well. It is understandable to want to trust what politicians tell us in the midst of a crisis. Yet, it is equally important to verify and scrutinize those claims. Such scrutiny may lead us to some damaging places. Or it may instill new confidence in those in charge.

Regardless, two decades after the attacks, taking seriously the September Eleventh families' unanswered questions is a task still waiting for the majority to tackle. It is a challenge given their lack of exposure, proper framing, and the fading memory of their plight by those entrusted to engage the public in informed discussion. It's time to shift the focus. Acknowledge the discrepancies. Question without judgment. Research the facts. And press for an accurate historical report which the 9/11 Commission failed to provide: "the fullest possible account of the events surrounding what happened on September Eleventh." Let there be a new inquiry in the full light of day.

Afterword

On September 11, 2001, I was in Joshua Tree, California. Just before dawn I woke to go for a walk in the desert to see the sunrise at about 6:25 a.m. (PST). As the sun rose from behind the hills of the Mojave Desert, a plane flew overhead heading east. After about fifteen minutes, I headed over to a meeting hall where there was a session about to begin with stretching and yoga for the sixty participants in the retreat in which I was enrolled.

In my secluded setting there were no televisions. Near the end of the session the leader of the program had the group gather and stand in a circle. We were told she had just been on a phone call. We were informed that there had been an attack at the World Trade Center and on the Pentagon. She told us four planes had been hijacked. Both of the Twin Towers had collapsed. I remember the reaction of people in the room, including one couple who had a money manager who worked in one of the Twin Towers. Some people in the circle began to shriek. Others began to sob. Everyone was in shock, disbelief.

On a visit from Toronto in the spring of 1981, I had been to the Windows on the World restaurant on the 106th floor of the North Tower with friends from Bloomfield, New Jersey. My friends and I had enjoyed watching the sunset and seeing the Statue of Liberty at a distance. Over a decade later, a friend of mine in Toronto told me that his friend, John DiGiovanni, had died in the truck bombing incident in the North Tower on February 26, 1993. Now, on September 11, 2001, in my retreat setting in Joshua Tree, California, I felt a flood of feelings—horror, anger, fear, concern ... Having been to the World Trade Center, it seemed incredible to me that such massive buildings could crumble to the ground. And the loss of lives where many thousands worked was unspeakable.

In the days that followed, my flight back to Vancouver, Canada, was cancelled. All international flights and domestic flights were cancelled. I ended up getting one of the first flights out of John Wayne International Airport in Ontario, California, on September 14. After touching down in Seattle, I took a bus to Vancouver. After three hours of Canada Customs thoroughly screening everyone, the bus crossed into Canada and I was back home.

With the attacks of September Eleventh still on everybody's mind, I went to hear former Canadian Foreign Affairs Minister, Lloyd Axworthy, speak at Vancouver's Central Library. He urged that the response to capture Osama bin Laden should be a police and intelligence agency response. Axworthy cautioned against the rush to go to war in Afghanistan. I remember looking at a news story with photos of the 19 hijackers in September 2001. Seeing a photo of Mohamed Atta, I recall thinking 'so this is the face of evil.'

There was a blizzard of news about the war in Afghanistan, the war in Iraq, the War on Terror, the Anthrax attacks. In 2003 I happened upon a book in a Toronto bookstore by Thierry Meyssan titled *9/11: The Big Lie*. I looked at photos and diagrams suggesting that a missile had hit the Pentagon. And I remember thinking 'this is crazy.' I didn't buy the book.

In the winter of 2003-2004 a friend showed me a book review in the *Catholic New Times* by theologian Rosemary Radford Ruether. The headline read: "The New Pearl Harbor: Was the Bush Administration Complicit in 9/11?" I had met Ruether and knew her to be a solid thinker. Her review of David Ray Griffin's *The New Pearl Harbor* was chilling and sobering. I ended up buying Griffin's book, and with some skepticism I said under my breath 'this better be good.'

I went through *The New Pearl Harbor* using skills I'd learned at the University of Toronto as a student of political science. For every endnote I could reference online, I read the article, or read a section of the book. Sometimes this meant going to a local library to check out the book in question. I found to my surprise that Griffin's scholarship was very solid, and his references were used in context. Clearly, there was a case to be made that there could be other explanations for what really happened on the day of the attacks on September 11, 2001.

But life went on. I saw Condoleezza Rice speak before the 9/11 Commission. Otherwise, I had no other exposure to the proceedings of that inquiry. And I don't recall hearing anything about the release of its findings in late July 2004.

By chance in an airport bookstore, in 2007, I happened to notice a memoir by Kristen Breitweiser titled *Wake-Up Call: The Political Education of a 9/11 Widow.* Flipping through the table of contents I learned there had been families who lost loved ones involved in pressing for an investigation into the attacks. I wondered why, as someone who followed the news closely, I hadn't ever heard of Kristen Breitweiser. Why hadn't the news that I relied on introduced me to the Family Steering Committee for the 9/11 Independent Commission?

Breitweiser's book led me to discover the documentary *9/11 Press For Truth,* and to hear interviews of other members of the FSC. I got a copy of Paul Thompson's *The Terror Timeline.* Then I began to read and eventually compile over several thousand news articles. I listened on YouTube.com to Lorie Van Auken and Patty Casazza make comments to a gathering in Manhattan in November 2007 in support of a new investigation into the attacks of September 11. I viewed testimony of hearings convened by Rep. Cynthia McKinney in 2005, and other statements by family members at conferences, seminars, and interviews. I also read Janette Mackinlay's moving *Fortunate: A Personal Diary of 9/11.* While I was learning about members of the Family Steering Committee, I discovered they were not all in agreement—at least based on public statements.

I hadn't planned on writing a book.

But over the years I was struck by how off-the-radar all this material was. I knew a wide range of people across North America. Hardly anyone I knew was raising the topic of what the September Eleventh families had done to force an investigation; or knew of the series of campaigns by September 11 families for a new investigation.

I also noticed that books like *Fortunate: A Personal Diary of 9/11* were now out of print. YouTube videos I'd watched could not be found. Searches for articles I'd read now led me to "Page Not Found" or "404 Error." I started to paste and save articles, knowing I couldn't count on them remaining available online.

So, I decided to chronicle what I had discovered. I wrote. And as I was not part of any group, this was a very solitary exercise. I took my manuscript to several editors. While my dad had cancer from 2010 to 2014, I let the "book" sit on the shelf. After over a dozen years the shape and focus of this book changed substantially. Meanwhile, I visited the Family Steering Committee website hundreds of times. I thought more about their press releases, FSC member testimony, and their unanswered questions.

Initially, I was reluctant to question the official account. But after over a dozen years of researching this story, I have had to conclude the official account is dubious. In tackling just eleven of the Family Steering Committee's unanswered questions in Part Three of my book, I have only scratched the surface. I hope that what I have written will help others give themselves permission to seriously question if the 9/11 Commission got it right.

Appendix

The FSC website has remained online since March 2003. But in August 2020 it was altered. A new article titled "Hello World!" had no text. One tab read "9/11 Commissioners MESSY." All links led to "Page Not Found," deforming the site's value. Web browsers listed the FSC website as an unsafe site. Readers wanting to view more FSC unanswered questions would be stymied. So, a sample is provided here:

- To president Bush: "What defensive measures did you take in response to pre-9/11 warnings from eleven nations about a terrorist attack, many of which cited an attack in the continental United States?
- To president Bush: "Please discuss the National Security Presidential Directive presented for your approval on September 9, 2001, which outlined plans for attacking al Qaeda in Afghanistan."
- To vice president Dick Cheney: "Were you given Cipro on the evening of September 11? If so, why?" (Cipro is a medication given to people to treat anthrax exposure).
- To National Security Advisor Condoleezza Rice: "Prior to September 11, did the National Security Council ever consider alerting the American people to the internal threat from al-Qa'ida? What happened?"
- To CIA Director George Tenet: "Is the October 31, 2001, story by *Le Figaro* true which wrote of Osama bin Laden meeting with a CIA officer in Dubai in July 2001? If so, why wasn't he taken into custody?"
- To FBI Director Robert Mueller: "On the FBI's Ten Most Wanted Fugitive poster, revised Nov. 2001, why isn't the September 11th terrorist attack listed as one of [O]sama bin Laden's crimes?"

- To FBI Director Robert Mueller: "Please explain how the passports of Mohammed Atta and Satam al-Sugam, both on Flight 11, survived the inferno to be found on the street near the World Trade Center?"
- To FBI Director Louis Freeh: "Why weren't the flight schools shut down, or the terrorists deported, if the 'FBI Knew Terrorists Were Using Flight Schools' for years, as reported in the *Washington Post*, September 23, 2001.
- To Airport Security personnel on duty on September 11th at Logan, Newark and Dulles Airports: "Why were the hijackers able to pass through security with box cutters and mace or pepper spray which were specifically banned under FAA rules?"
- To Secretary of Defense Donald Rumsfeld: "Why did Donald Rumsfeld, immediately after the September 11th attack, say that Saddam Hussein was involved?"

Acknowledgments

This book could not have been written without the help of a broad range of people. The primary inspiration for writing this book came from reflecting on the testimony and unanswered questions posted on the website of the Family Steering Committee for the 9/11 Independent Commission. The questions they wanted the 9/11 Commission to address have remained posted online, although their work officially concluded in 2005. Not only their questions, but the formal statements by the Family Steering Committee to the 9/11 Commission helped me chronicle their own unfolding responses to the work of the Commission. In addition, a number of the Family Steering Committee kept themselves in the public eye in the years that have followed, appearing at government proceedings, conferences, on television, radio programs, writing columns, and featuring in countless news stories.

I am grateful to Kristen Breitweiser, whose book, *Wake-Up Call: The Political Education of a 9/11 Widow*, introduced me to her story and the September Eleventh families' quest for answers. Without discovering Breitweiser's book at a bookstore, I might never have learned about the Family Steering Committee for the 9/11 Independent Commission. This is because their work, in conjunction with the 9/11 Commission proceedings, was scarcely covered in Canada.

I am also grateful to the many who lost loved ones on September Eleventh for their diverse public engagement of how to respond to the 9/11 attacks. I am very appreciative of a number of first responders and September Eleventh victims' family members for their input. This includes Matt Campbell, Bob McIlvaine and Fire Commissioner Chris Gioia.

I am also grateful to Paul Thompson's *Terror Timeline* and the *historycommons.org* website. Thompson's work was an invaluable

315

source of mainstream news stories detailing the consistencies, and inconsistencies, of the government's account. There are many other authors whose work I have referenced that are found in the endnotes of this book. The range of viewpoints they represent has added much in chronicling the story of the 9/11 families' questions.

I have many people to thank for their comments on the manuscript in various stages. They include Keri Aguirre, Melba Burns, Sue Cook, Laurie Green, Gail Irvine, Anne Marie Konas, Lino Laure, Victoria Lynne, Susan McCaslin, Alice McGinnis, Doug McGinnis, Vivian Meyer, Mary Beth Nelson, Bert Sacks, Leo Santana, Celeste Snowber, Goichi Terachi, and Evan Tran.

I have Donaleen Saul to thank for our many years of friendship and for editing my first draft. I am grateful to Jim Douglass for his encouragement and suggestions, as well as introducing me to that great restaurant in downtown Birmingham. I am appreciative of the editorial work Elizabeth Woodworth gave to the second draft of my manuscript, and tea at her splendid home. I am indebted to Gordon Thomas for his receptiveness and care to review my manuscript and give it a final edit. His suggestions and direction have been invaluable in getting this book to print.

I am thankful to Susannah Greenberg for sharing her wisdom as a publicist, and her astute suggestion for a revision of my book title. And to John Cobb, I am very grateful for his advice in structuring this book, and for his foreword. As well, I enjoyed meeting others in his circle who were keen to hear about my emerging manuscript. And for providing leads on several fronts, my thanks to Jon Gold.

The Family Steering Committee published many unanswered questions. My task as an author was to decide which questions to explore. Given the limits of space, the chapters I devoted to their unanswered questions is only a beginning.

Endnotes

INTRODUCTION

1. Nick Clark, "Agatha Christie: Mystery of Crime Writer's Disappearance Tackled in Kate Mosse Story," *Guardian*, September 14, 2015.

2. Kristen Breitweiser, *Wake-up Call: The Political Education of a 9/11 Widow,* (Warner Books, 2006), 101.

3. Colin Powell, "NBC's 'Meet The Press' with Tim Russert," Interview by Tim Russert, NBC, September 23, 2001.

4. White House, press briefing, "America's New War: Daily White House Press Briefing by White House Press Secretary Ari Fleischer," September 24, 2001.

5. Seymour Hersh, "What Went Wrong," *New Yorker*, October 8, 2001.

6. Bill Carter and Felicity Barringer, "In Patriotic Time DissentIs Muted," *New York Times*, September 28, 2001.

7. Breitweiser, *Wake-up Call,*101. (See note 2.)

8. Family Steering Committee for the Independent 9/11 Commission *http://911independentcommission.org*

9. Dereliction of Duty, Wikipedia, *https://en.wikipedia.org/wiki/Dereliction_of_duty*

10. "Statement of Stephen Push," National Commission on Terrorist Attacks Upon the United States, New York, March 31, 2003.

11. Ray Nowosielski, director, "Interview with Mindy Kleinberg," *9/11 Press For Truth*. Banded Artists/Standard Issue Films, 2006.

12. Peter B. Collins, "Boiling Frogs: 'Jersey Girl' Lorie Van Auken Still Looking for Truth About 9/11," Boiling Frogs, Podcast Show #51, August 26, 2011.

13. Timothy Snyder, *On Tyranny: Twenty Lessons From theTwentieth Century,* (Tim Duggan Books, 2017), 65.

14.   Declaration of Independence, United States Congress, July 4, 1776.

15.   United States Constitution Article 2 Section 4, United States Senate, March 4, 1789.

16.   Dylan Matthews, "No, really, George W. Bush lied about WMD's," Vox, July 9, 2016. And Peter Sullivan, "Poll: Four in 10 think US found WMDs in Iraq," *The Hill*, January 7, 2015. In 2015 42% of Americans still believed that America found weapons of mass destruction in Iraq. And when asked in a survey in 2006 to explain their presence in Iraq, 85 per cent of American soldiers said that the "main mission" was "to retaliate for Saddam's role in the September 11 attacks." See Martin Amis, "The Real Conspiracy Behind 9/11," *The Sunday Times*, London, UK, September 2, 2006.

17.   President Bill Clinton, "White House News Conference," White House, January 26, 1998.

18.   Fred Emery, *Watergate: The Corruption of American Politics and the Fall of Richard Nixon*, (Touchstone, 1995).

19. "Nicholas Katzenbach Dead at 90," Associated Press, May 9, 2012.

20.   Martin Waldron, "F.B.I. Chiefs Linked To Oswald File Loss," *New York Times*, September 17, 1975.

21.   The House Select Committee on Assassinations concluded in its 1978 report that "on the basis of the evidence available to it, that President John F. Kennedy was probably assassinated as a result of a conspiracy." They stated that "scientific acoustical evidence establishes a high probability that two gunmen fired at President John F. Kennedy." The HSCA was "unable to identify the other gunman or the extent of the conspiracy." However, it did discover evidence to suggest that anti-Castro Cubans were involved in the assassination. For example, an undercover agent heard Nestor Castellanos tell a meeting of anti-Castro Cubans, "We're waiting for Kennedy (on) the 22nd. We're going to see him in one way or another."The HSCA concluded that "individuals active in anti-Castro activities had the motive, means, and opportunity to assassinate President Kennedy." See also "LBJ Reportedly Suspected CIA Link in JFK's

Death," *Washington Post*, December 13, 1977.

22.   Ron Nessen, *It Sure Looks Different From the Inside*, (Playboy Press, 1978), 58.

23.   Joint Committee On The Investigation of The Pearl Harbor Attack, Investigation Of The Pearl Harbor Attack Report, July 1946, United States Congress; James Perloff, "Pearl Harbor: Hawaii Was Surprised, FDR Was Not," *New American*, December 7, 2019. Perloff summarizes, "Comprehensive research has shown not only that Washington knew in advance of the attack, but that it deliberately withheld its foreknowledge from our commanders in Hawaii in the hope that the 'surprise' attack would catapult the US into World War II. Oliver Lyttleton, British Minister of Production, stated in 1944: 'Japan was provoked into attacking America at Pearl Harbor. It is a travesty of history to say that America was forced into the war.'" See also Robert Stinnett, *Day Of Deceit: The Truth About FDR and Pearl Harbor*, (Free Press, 2001).

24.   Amy Goodman and Juan Gonzales, "Flashback: A Look Back at the Church Committee's Investigation into CIA, FBI Misuse of Power," *Democracy Now!*, April 24, 2009.

25.   Lawrence E. Walsh, *Firewall: The Iran-Contra Conspiracy and Cover-Up*, (W.W. Norton & Company, 1998); David Johnston, "Bush Pardons 6 in Iran Affair, Aborting a Weinberger Trial; Prosecutor Assails 'Cover-Up': Bush Diary At Issue, 6-Year Inquiry Into Deal of Arms for Hostages All but Swept Away," *New York Times*, December 24, 1992.

26.   Mary Fetchet, "Testimony to the Commissioners for the 9/11 Independent Commission," 9/11 Commission, New York City, March 31, 2003.

27. Committee on Governmental Affairs United States Senate, To Establish The National Commission On Terrorist Attacks Upon The United States, And For Other Purposes, (US Government Publishing Office, 2002) 1.

28. Ibid.

29. James Gourley, editor, "Testimony of Laurie Van Auken and Bob McIlvaine to the Toronto Hearings," *The 9/11 Toronto Report*, (International Center for 9/11 Studies, 2013), 14.

1 - CALAMITY

30.   Frank Williams, "Arthur Barry, 35, Firefighter, Traveled Through North America," *Staten Island Advance*, October 1, 2001.

31.   Kathryn Carse, "Paul Keating, 38, Firefighter, Was Known for his Jokes," *Staten Island Advance*, October 3, 2001.

32.   Janette MacKinlay, *Fortunate: A Personal Diary of 9/11*, (Janette MacKinlay and Friends, 2003), 46.

33.   Ibid., 23-24.

34.   Ibid., 29-31.

35.   Ibid., 38-40, 59-60, 65-66, 69.

36.   In an author interview on January 25, 2020, Fire Commissioner Chris Gioia spoke about Tommy Hetzel's parents learning about their son's last moments. This included Louie Cacchioli telling reporters a blast stopped the elevator from moving that he and Tommy Hetzel were in. Cacchioli told *People*: "On the last trip up a bomb went off. We think there was bombs set in the building." (See "United In Courage," *People,* September 12, 2001). In the same article, administrative assistant Kim White told *People* she heard "another explosion" on the 74th floor. The story about both Lou Cacchioli and Kim White mentioning bombs in the towers was reported again by *People* in late September. (See "Hell On Earth," *People,* September 24, 2001). There were no corrections published by *People* in relation to either story. However, three and a half years later, Cacchioli told *Popular Mechanics* he was misquoted. (See "Debunking the 9/11 Myths: Special Report," *Popular Mechanics*, March 2005). Then on July 21, 2005, it was reported in the *Arctic Beacon* – after "an extended telephone conversation" with Cacchioli – that Tommy Hetzel was "his best friend." Cacchioli described three separate explosions in the North Tower. "Tommy [Hetzel] was with me and everybody else also gets out of the elevator when it stops on the 24th floor … There was a huge amount of smoke. Tommy and I had to go back down the elevator for tools and no sooner did the elevators close behind us, we heard this huge explosion that sounded

like a bomb. It was such a loud noise, it knocked off the lights and stalled the elevator." Cacchioli recalled there was "another huge explosion like the first one … about two minutes later." When Cacchioli got "down [to] the 23rd stairwell" he "hear[d] another huge explosion like the other two." In the chaos Cacchioli and Hetzel were separated. (See Greg Szymanski, "NY Fireman Lou Cacchioli Upset That 9/11 Commission 'Tried To Twist My Words'; A True Hero, He Vows To Stick To The Truth, Something Lacking In The 9/11 Investigation," *Arctic Beacon*, July 19, 2005). Lou Cacchioli was a very public face of first responders, appearing on the cover of *Faces of Ground Zero: Portraits of the Heroes of September 11, 2001* (*Life*, 2002). In an author interview on July 23, 2020, Fire Commissioner Chris Gioia said he tried to contact Cacchioli on behalf of the Hetzel family. They wanted to learn directly from Cacchioli about his being with Hetzel in the North Tower. But Gioia's calls to Lou Cacchioli were not returned. This author attempted to reach Fireman Cacchioli, but there was no reply.

37.   "Interview: Firefighter Thomas Turilli," World Trade Center Task Force, January 17, 2002, p. 4. Turilli mentions being with firefighters from Tommy Hetzel's Ladder 13, along with Cacchioli.

38. James Gourley, editor, "Testimony of LaurieVan Auken and Bob McIlvaine to the Toronto Hearings," *The 9/11 Toronto Report*, (International Center for 9/11 Studies, 2013), 1-3.

39.   Sherri Day, Anthony Depalma, Jonathan Fuerbringer, Kenneth H. Gilpin, Constance L. Hays, Lynette Holloway, Tina Kelley, and Melina Ryzik, "A Nation Challenged: Portraits Of Grief: The Victims; A Loving Family, a Solid Best Friend, a Bride-to-Be, an Ardent Traveler," *New York Times*, February 10, 2002; "Georgetown's Missing Faces," *Georgetown Voice*, Washington DC, November 1, 2001.

40.   Carie Lemack, "The Journey to September 12th: A 9/11 Victim's Experiences with the Press, the President, and Congress," *Studies in Conflict & Terrorism*, Vol. 30, Issue 9, August 14, 2007.

41.   Lemack, "The Journey to September 12 …". (See note 40.)

42.   Breitweiser, *Wake-up Call*, 52-53. (See note 2.)

43.	Breitweiser, *Wake-up Call*, 53, 57. (See note 2.)

44.	Marti Hopper, "Why People Reject 9/11 Truth: Psychologists Speak Out," *wakeupfromyourslumbers.com*, Boulder, Colorado, September 2011.

45.	Lemack, "The Journey to September 12 …". (See note 40.)\

46.	"Patty Casazza interview," *9/11 Press For Truth*.

47.	Richard Simon, "Congress OKs Airline Aid Package, *Los Angeles Times*, September 22, 2001.

48.	Breitweiser, *Wake-Up Call*, 76. (See note 2.)

49.	Bob Kemper, *Rubble: How The 9/11 Families Rebuilt Their Lives And Inspired America*, (Potomac Books, 2011), 78-79.

50.	Peter Slevin, "Libya Accepts Blame in Lockerbie Bombing," *Washington Post*, August 17, 2003.

51.	Lemack, "The Journey to September 12th…". (See note 40.)

52.	Ibid.

53.	Skyscraper Safety Campaign: A Project of Parents & Families Of Firefighters & WTC Victims, *http://www.skyscrapersafety.org*

54.	"Christian Michael Otto Regenhard: Determined to Follow Father," *New York Times*, October 16, 2001. See also "Regenhard, Christian Michael Otto," Obituary, *New York Times*, October 24, 2001.

55.	September 11th Families for Peaceful Tomorrows, *peacefultomorrows.org*.

56.	Nicholas Levis, "Interview with Beverly Eckert," *911Truth.org*, March 3, 2004.

57.	Rita Lasar, "Letters to the Editor," *New York Times*, September 17, 2001.

58.	"Rita Lasar, 1937-2017," *90 Cubed Rule*, January 2017. *http://www.90cubedrule.com/rita-lasar-1931-2017/*

59.	Emma Reynolds, "9/11 Hero Who Lost Half His Foot Fighting For Ground Zero Workers," *New Zealand Herald*, March 7, 2018.

60. Ibid.

61. Breitweiser, *Wake-Up Call*, 72. (See note 2.)

62. Kemper, *Rubble*, 86-87. (See note 49.)

63. Breitweiser, *Wake-Up Call*, 74. (See note 2.)

64. Breitweiser, *Wake-Up Call*, 81-82. (See note 2.)

65. Gourley, "Testimony of Lorie Van Auken," *The 9/11 Toronto Report*, 14. (See note 29.)

66. Oliver Burkeman, "Legal Action Jeopardizes 9/11 Compensation," *Guardian*, London, UK, September 20, 2002.

2 -THE SEARCH FOR ANSWERS

67. Beverly Eckert, "Silence Cannot be Bought," *USA Today*, December 19, 2003.

68. "Louis Neil Mariani," *New York Times*, September 10, 2002.

69. Bill Plante, "Bush Opposes 9/11 Query Panel," CBS, May 23, 2002.

70. Mike Allen, "Bush Seeks To Restrict Hill Probes Of Sept. 11; Intelligence Panel's Secrecy Is Favored," *The Washington Post*, January 30, 2002.

71. Lemack..."The Journey to September 12th...". (See note 40.)

72. Breitweiser, *Wake-Up Call*, 67. (See note 2.)

73. Ibid., 121.

74. Howard Fineman, "The Battle Back Home," *Newsweek*, February 4, 2002. Philip Shenon, *The Commission: The Uncensored History of the 9/11 Investigation*, (Twelve Books, 2008), 29-30.

75. Breitweiser, *Wake-Up Call*, 208. (See note 2.) "We had tried to work in a nonpartisan way throughout the life of the commission ... But every battle we had fought had been triggered by the Republicans."

76.   Andrew Jacobs, "Traces of Terror: Survivors; Trade Center Widows Lobby for Independent Inquiry," *New York Times,* June 12, 2002

77.   Ibid.

78.   Ibid. See also Nowosielski, "Mindy Kleinberg comments on June 11, 2002," *9/11 Press For Truth.* (See note 11.)

79.   Dave Tobin, "Syracuse University Remembers Victims of Pan Am Flight 103 Disaster," *Post-Standard,* Syracuse, New York, October 11, 2013.

80.   Andrew Jacobs, "Traces of Terror," *New York Times,* June 12, 2002. Also, Gourley, "Testimony of Lorie Van Auken ..." *The 9/11 Toronto Report,* 5. (See note 29.) Van Auken stated, "many people couldn't, or more likely didn't, want to hear the difficult questions regarding 9/11 that were emerging."

81.   Lemack..."The Journey to September 12th...". (See note 40.)

82.   Press Release of Intelligence Committee, "Senate and House Intelligence Committees Announce Joint Inquiry into the September 11th Terrorist Attacks," February 14, 2002.

83.   Statement of Kristen Breitweiser, Co-Chairperson September 11 Advocates, "Concerning the Joint 9/11 Inquiry," Senate Select Committee on Intelligence, September 18, 2002. *https://www.intelligence.senate.gov/hearings/joint-inquiry-intelligence-community-activities-and-after-terrorist-attacks-september-11-0#*

84.   US Congress, The House Permanent Select Committee on Intelligence and the Senate Select Committee on Intelligence, *Testimonies of Stephen Push, Kristen Breitweiser, Eleanor Hill,* 107th Congress, 2nd Session, September 18, 2002; Jim Miklaszewski, "US Had 12 Warnings of Jet Attacks, Family Members of Those Who Lost Loved Ones Testified, Angrily, That They Hold the Intelligence Community Responsible," MSNBC, September 18, 2002.

85.   "Statement of Kristen Breitweiser," Joint 9/11 Inquiry, September 18, 2002.

86.   Michael Isikoff and Daniel Kleidman, "Why The White House Said Yes to a 9/11 Inquiry," *Newsweek,* September 22, 2002. Also, Alabama Republican

Senator, Richard Shelby, had given his support to the idea of an independent commission earlier in September. Shelby sat on the Senate Select Committee on Intelligence. Interviewed by James Risen of the *New York Times*, Shelby said of the Bush White House, "you know, we were told that there would be cooperation in this investigation, and I question that. I think that most of the information that our staff has been able to get that is real meaningful has had to be extracted piece by piece." James Risen, "White House Drags Its Feet on Testifying at 9/11 Panel," *New York Times*, September 13, 2002.

87.   Mary Jacobs, "9/11 Inquiry's Success Surprises Skeptics," *St. Petersburg Times*, (Florida), September 29, 2002.

88.   Bootie Cosgrove-Mather, "Bush Backs Independent 9/11 Probe," CBS, September 24, 2002.

89.   David Firestone, "Threats and Responses: Toward an Inquiry; White House Blocks Deal by Congress on 9/11 Panel," *New York Times*, October 11, 2002. Lorie Van Auken recalled on the tenth anniversary of the attacks that, once the "final language for a bill that would give us the 9/11 Commission was almost agreed upon, we began to notice a lot of foot dragging. Vice President Dick Cheney had clearly been against having an inquiry from the start and was working behind the scenes to keep things from moving forward …. It became painfully apparent to everyone that it was the Bush-Cheney White House that was causing the stalemate." Gourley, '"Testimony of Lorie Van Auken …," *The 9/11 Toronto Report*, 6-7. (Note 29.) See also Breitweiser, *Wake-Up Call*, 128-135. (Note 2.)

90.   Dana Bash, "Congress OKs 9/11 Special Commission: 'We Are Excited We Have A Deal'," CNN, November 15, 2002.

91.   "The Kissinger Commission," *New York Times*, November 29, 2002.

92.   Joel Roberts, "Kissinger to Head 9-11 Commission," CBS, December 12, 2002.

93.   Howard Zinn, *A People's History of the United States*, (HarperPerennial, 1980), Chapter 20.

94. "The Kissinger Commission," *Chicago Tribune*, December 5, 2002.

95. Clarence Page, "Kissinger's Shady Record Is A Bad Omen For His New Job," *Chicago Tribune*, December 1, 2002; And Flora Botsford, Spanish Judge Targets Kissinger, BBC, April 18, 2002.

96. "Kissinger Wrong For The Job," *Los Angeles Times*, November 29, 2002.

97. Shenon, *The Commission*, 12-13. (Note 74.) Breitweiser, *Wake-Up Call*, 138. (Note 2) Breitweiser describes the heat in the meeting room being turned up to about "ninety-five degrees."

98. Dan Eggen, "Kissinger Bitterly Resigns From Sept. 11 Inquiry Panel," *Seattle Times*, December 14, 2002.

99. Breitweiser, *Wake-Up Call*, 140. (See note 2.)

100. "Kissinger Resigns as Head of the 9/11 Commission," CNN, December 13, 2002.

101. Amy Goldstein, "9/11 Panel Gets New Chairman: Ex-NJ Governor Kean Named to Replace Kissinger," *Washington Post*, December 14, 2002. Thomas Kean was not without his own conflicts of interest as an appointment to chair the 9/11 Commission. Kean was "a member of the Board of Directors of the oil company, Amerada Hess, which joined with Delta Oil of Saudi Arabia – one of the companies in the Cent Gas consortium – to form Hess-Delta." Consequently, Kean's appointment might have slanted the way the report would be written to omit "information that could create problems for US-Saudi relations, and information suggesting that the war in Afghanistan had something to do with allowing CentGas pipeline project to go forward." See David Ray Griffin, *The 9/11 Commission Report: Omissions and Distortions*. (Olive Branch Press, 2005), 285-286. See also, Kevin Kniffin, "Serving Two Masters: University Presidents Moonlighting on Corporate Boards," *Multinational Monitor*, November 1997.

102. Thomas H. Kean and Lee H. Hamilton, *Without Precedent: The Inside Story of the 9/11 Commission*, (Vintage Books, 2007), 45.

103. Timothy J. Burger, "9-11 Commission Funding Woes: Questions Arise Concerning the Administration's Funding of the Congressional Investigation

into the September 11 Attacks," *Time*, March 26, 2003.

104. "Undercutting the 9/11 Inquiry," *New York Times*, March 31, 2003.

105. Thomas Kean, "Opening Remarks," National Commission on Terrorist Attacks Upon the United States, New York, NY, March 31, 2003.

106. Lee Hamilton, "Commissioners' Opening Statements," National Commission on Terrorist Attacks Upon the United States, New York, NY, March 31, 2003.

107. "Statement of Stephen Push," National Commission on Terrorist Attacks Upon the United States, New York, NY, March 31, 2003. *https://govinfo.library. unt.edu/911/hearings/hearing1/witness_push.htm*

108. Nicholas Levis, "Interview with Beverly Eckert," *911Truth.org*, March 3, 2004. See also Thomas Donnelly, "Rebuilding America's Defenses," The Project for the New American Century, Washington DC, September 2000, 50-51. *https:// www.visibility911.org/wp-content/uploads/2008/02/rebuildingamericasdefenses.pdf.* Other Co-authors of the Project For A New American Century document in the Bush White House included: Peter Rodman, Assistant Secretary of Defense for International Security affairs in 2001; I. Scooter Libby, Chief of Staff to the Vice President of the United States; Zalmay Khalilzad, President Bush's special envoy to Afghanistan after the fall of the Taliban as well as his special envoy to the Iraqi opposition to Saddam Hussein; Jeb Bush, brother of George W. Bush and Governor of Florida, whose controversial election results in November 2000 gave the presidency to George W. Bush and not to Al Gore; and Richard Pearle, Chairman of the Defense Policy Board, United States Department of Defense. Eckert's concerns about the Project For A New American Century were expressed in several of the questions the Family Steering Committee asked the 9/11 Commission to pose to President George W. Bush.

109. "Statement of Commissioner James Thompson", 9/11 Commission, March 31, 2003. Similarly, Commissioner Timothy Roemer stated: "A central function of democracy is to allow a free people to drag realities out into the sunlight and demand a full accounting from those who were permitted to hold power. As our Declaration of Independence proclaims, those holding power, 'Deriving their powers from the consent of the governed,' should be accountable to their

citizens. That's what we are going to do on this Commission." Statement of Commissioner Timothy Roemer, 9/11 Commission, March 31, 2003.

110. Breitweiser, *Wake-Up Call*, 67. (See note 2.)

3: THE COMPLETE 911 TIMELINE

111. Jon Gold, "Lorie Van Auken – September 27, 2014," *We Were Lied To About 911: The Interviews*, (*wewereliedtoabout911.com*, 2018), 148.

112. "Patty Casazza and Mindy Kleinberg interviews," *9/11 Press For Truth*.

113. Gold, 149. (See note 111.)

114. "Patty Casazza interview," *9/11 Press For Truth*.

115. "Paul Thompson interview," *9/11 Press For Truth*.

116. Ibid.

117. Gold, "Lorie Van Auken – September 27, 2014," *We Were Lied To About 911*, 155-156. (See note 111.)

118. Family Steering Committee, "Meeting with Chairman Kean, Deputy Director Kojm, and Family Liaisons Emily Walker and Ellie Hartz," Madison, New Jersey, May 15, 2003. Absent from the meeting were FSC members Carie Lemack and Robin Wiener.

119. Dan Balz and Bob Woodward, "America's Chaotic Road to War," *Washington Post*, January 27, 2002.

120. President George W. Bush, "Letter to Congress," Congressional Record, March 18, 2003

121. PBS Frontline Transcript, "The War Behind Closed Doors," PBS, February 20, 2003.

122. Robert D. Novak, "Beyond Pearl Harbor," *New York Post*, September 13, 2001.

123. Glenn Kessler, "US Decision on Iraq Has Puzzling Past: Opponents of

War Wonder When, How Policy Was Set," *Washington Post*, January 12, 2003.

124. George Arney, "US 'Planned Attack On Taleban'," BBC, September 18, 2001.

125. Tim Russert, "Interview with Colin Powell," *Meet the Press*, NBC, September 23, 2001.

126. "America's New War: Daily White House Briefing by White House Press Secretary Ari Fleischer," CNN, September 24, 2001.

127. "Taliban Says Bin Laden Denies Role in Attacks," *Reuters*, September 13, 2001.

128. "Aide says Bin Laden Denies Role in US Attacks," *Irish Times*, September 13, 2001.

129. "Bin Laden Says He Wasn't Behind Attacks," CNN, September 17, 2001.

130. Tom Bowman, Mark Matthews, and Gail Gibson, "Taliban Face Ultimatum," *Baltimore Sun*, September 17, 2001.

131. NBC, Transcript, "The Vice President Appears on Meet the Press with Tim Russert," *Meet the Press*, NBC, September 16, 2001.

132. Ed Vulliamy, Patrick Wintour, and Kamal Ahmed, "After September Eleventh Terrorist Attacks in America 'It's Time For War,' Bush and Blair tell Taliban. We're Ready to Go: PM. Planes Shot at Over Kabul," *Guardian*, London, UK, October 7, 2001

133. "Bush Rejects Taliban Offer to Hand Bin Laden Over," *Guardian*, London, UK, October 14, 2001.

134. John Pilger, "This War of Lies Goes On," *Daily Mirror*, London, UK, November 16, 2001.

135. Seymour M. Hersh, "The Getaway: Questions Surround a Secret Pakistani Airlift," *New Yorker*, January 28, 2002; Paula Zahn interview with Seymour Hersh, "New Report Claims Secret US Airlift of Pakistani Military Advisors Out of Afghanistan Was Also an Escape Route for Enemy," America Morning with Paula Zahn, CNN, January 21, 2002

136. "Responsibility for the Terrorist Atrocities in the United States," Office of the Prime Minister, London, UK, October 4, 2001

137. Ibid.

138. "The Investigation and the Evidence," BBC, October 5, 2001

139. "Pentagon Releases Bin Laden Videotape: US Officials Say Tape Links Him to Sept. 11 Attacks," NPR, December 13, 2001

140. Steve Morris, "US Urged to Detail Origin of Tape," *Guardian*, London, UK, December 15, 2001. See also Brian Whitaker, "Swiss Scientists 95% Sure That Bin Laden Recording Was a Fake," *Guardian*, London, UK, November 30, 2002.

141. Dr. Sanjay Gupta, "Bin Laden Would Need Help if on Dialysis," CNN, January 21, 2002. See also Transcript: "Bin Laden Video Excerpts," BBC, December 27, 2001.

142. Toby Harnden, "US Casts Doubt on bin Laden's Latest Message," *Telegraph*, London, UK, December 27, 2001.

143. "Report: bin Laden Already Dead," FOX, December 26, 2001. Also, "News of Bin Laden's Death and Funeral 10 Days Ago," al-Wafd, Cairo, Egypt, December 26, 2001, Vol. 15, No 4633.

144. "Pakistan's Musharraf: Bin Laden Probably Dead," CNN, January 18, 2002.

145. Dan Rather Interview with Barry Petersen, Transcript of CBS report, "Hospital Worker: I Saw Osama," CBS, January 28, 2002.

146. "Naming Names or Not," *Washington Post*, October 1, 2002; PBS Frontline, "An Axis of Evil, State of the Union Speech," January 29, 2002

147. Philip Smucker, "How bin Laden Got Away, a Day-By-Day Account of How bin Laden Eluded the World's Most Powerful Military Machine," *Christian Science Monitor*, March 4, 2002.

148. "President Bush Holds a Press Conference," James S. Brady Briefing Room, White House, March 13, 2002.

149. On May 2, 2011 it was reported US Navy SEALs broke into a compound in Abbottabad, Pakistan. They killed Osama bin Laden and buried his body in the North Arabian Sea. See "Osama bin Laden is Dead," CBS, May 2, 2011. On September 9, 2012, *60 Minutes* interviewed SEAL Team 6 member Mark Owen who said the subject he shot did not look like bin Laden. Asked "Did you recognize him?" Owen replied, "No. You know, everybody thinks it's like, you know it's him. No. To us, at that time, it could have been anybody. Maybe this is another brother. Maybe this is a bodyguard. It doesn't matter." (Scott Pelley, "Killing Bin Laden," *60 Minutes*, CBS, September 9, 2012). Republican Massachusetts Senator Scott Brown said in an official briefing regarding bin Laden's reported killing, he'd been shown photos of bin Laden that were "doctored images." (Michael Levenson, "Faked bin Laden Photo Dupes Brown: Hoax Pictures Also Fooled Other Senators," *Boston Globe*, May 5, 2011). New Hampshire Republican Senator Kelly Ayotte said she was shown fake photos that had been photoshopped from scenes in the film *Blackhawk Down*. They were flipped around and enhanced with bin Laden facial images. It was not known why these photos were shown at official intelligence briefings to members of the United States Senate Committee on Armed Services. A *Guardian* headline later on May 2, 2011 exclaimed "Osama bin Laden Corpse Photo is Fake." On November 21, 2012, an *Associated Press* headline reported "No Sailor Witnesses to OBL May 1st Burial Says State Department." The article explained: "US military officers indicate that no sailors watched Osama bin Laden's burial at sea from the USS Carl Vinson …. the Defense Department said in March [2012] that it could not locate any photographs or video taken during the raid or showing bin Laden's body. It also said it could not find any images of bin Laden's body on the Vinson …. The Pentagon also said it could not find any death certificate, autopsy report or results of DNA identification tests for bin Laden."

150. Al Hunt, "General Myers Interview," Evans & Novak, CNN, April 6, 2002.

4 - FAMILY STEERING COMMITTEE REPORT CARD FOR THE 9/11 COMMISSION SEPT 2003

151. Breitweiser, *Wake-Up Call*, 144-145. (See note 2.)

152. Shenon, *The Commission*, 33, 72. (See note 74.)

153. Stephen Engelberg, "Washington Talk; Justice," *New York Times*, May 11, 1989.

154. Breitweiser, *Wake-Up Call*, 150-151. (See note 2.)

155. Author interview with September Eleventh family member Bob McIlvaine, March 5, 2020. In my phone interview with McIlvaine he concurred with Kristen Breitweiser's concerns that Lee Hamilton was a "gatekeeper."

156. Kean and Hamilton, *Without Precedent*, 16. (See note 102.)

157. Ibid., 41-42.

158. Ibid., 43.

159. "Statement of Mary Fetchet," National Commission on Terrorist Attacks Upon the United States, Public Hearing, (Washington DC), March 31, 2003. *https://govinfo.library.unt.edu/911/hearings/hearing1/witness_fetchet.htm*

160. Breitweiser, *Wake-Up Call*, 151. (See note 2)

161. Shenon, *The Commission*, 201. (See note 74.)

162. Gourley, "Testimony of Lorie Van Auken," *The 9/11 Toronto Report*, 8. (See note 29.)

163. Shenon, *The Commission*, 207. (See note 74.)

164. Shenon, *The Commission*, 177. (See note 74.)

165. Statement of Abraham D. Sofaer to the National Commission on Terrorist Attacks Upon the United States, March 31, 2003.

166. Statement of Laurie Mylroie to the National Commission on Terrorist Attacks Upon the United States, July 9, 2003

167. Shenon, *The Commission*, 134. (See note 74.)

168. Family Steering Committee Statement, May 1, 2003, Washington DC.

169. Gold, "Interview with Lorie Van Auken, September 27, 2014," *We Were Lied To About 9/11: The Interviews*, 161. (See note 111.)

170. Gordon Duff, "The 9/11 Commission Rejects Own Report as Based on Government Lies," Salem-News, Salem, OR, September 11, 2009.

171. Family Steering Committee Statement, June 10, 2003, Washington DC.

172. Family Steering Committee Press Conference Remarks, September 10, 2003.

173. Ibid.

174. Ibid.

175. Family Steering Committee Report Card for the 9/11 Commission, September 2003.

176. Ibid.

177. Ibid.

178. Kevin Sheid, Col. Lorry Fenner, and Gordon Lederman, "Executive Branch Minders' Intimidation of Witnesses," 9/11 Commission Team 2, October 2, 2003. The memo stamped "Commission Sensitive" was addressed to General Counsel staff of the 9/11 Commission Dan Marcus, and Deputy General Counsel of the 9/11 Commission Steve Dunne. *https://www.scribd.com/document/13279605/9-11-Commission-Memo-Executive-Branch-Minders-Intimidation-of-Witnesses*

179. Family Steering Committee Report Card for the 9/11 Commission, September 2003.

180. Ibid.

181. Ibid.

182. Kemper, *Rubble*, 146-147. (See note 49.)

183. Statements by Sen. John McCain. "Statement of John McCain to the National Commission on Terrorist Attacks Upon the United States," May 22, 2003.

184. James Rosen, "White House Stonewalls Relatives of 9-11 Victims," McClatchy Newspapers, Sacramento, CA, October 30, 2003.

185. Family Steering Committee, "Statement Regarding Access to Presidential

Daily Briefings (PDBs)," November 13, 2003. The stonewalling of access to documents by the Bush administration had precedents. After the attack on Pearl Harbor, "Senator Arthur Vandenberg (R-Michigan) ... joined with the House Naval Affairs Committee and proposed a full inquiry into the Pearl Harbor raid." Instead, President Roosevelt appointed "a five-man board of inquiry" called the Roberts Commission. In the space of a month the Roberts Commission produced a 13,000-page report on January 24, 1942. During their inquiry "None of the US Navy's intercept operators testified or produced their radio logs and documents. Nothing was revealed about them." The Roberts Commission scapegoated Pacific Fleet Admiral Husband Kimmel and Lieutenant General Walter Short, charging them with dereliction of duty. Admiral James Richardson said of the report, "It is the most unfair, unjust, and deceptively dishonest document ever printed by the Government Printing Office." George C. Dyer, *On The Treadmill To Pearl Harbor: The Memoirs of Admiral James O. Richardson*, (Department of the Navy, History Division, 1973), 453.

186. "Family Steering Committee Statement Regarding the One-Year Anniversary of the National Commission on Terrorist Attacks upon the United States," November 27, 2003.

5 ~ STAFF DIRECTOR ZELIKOW AND TRANSITION BRIEFINGS

187. Kean and Hamilton, *Without Precedent*, 28. (See note 102.)

188. Ibid., 28-29.

189. Sheldon Stern, "What JFK Really Said," *Atlantic Monthly*, May 2000.

190. Shenon, *The Commission*, 65. (See note 74.)

191. Ibid., 69.

192. Ibid., 69-70.

193. Ibid., 60, 69, 79, 84.

194. Kean and Hamilton, *Without Precedent*, 29. (See note 102.)

195. Shenon, *The Commission*, 263. (See note 74.)

196. 9/11 Commission press release, "9/11 Commission Convenes, Names Executive Director," Washington DC, January 27, 2003.

197. "Condi's Inside Man," *Sydney Morning Herald*, Sydney, Australia, March 15, 2008.

198. Shenon, 105-107. (See note 74.)

199. Ibid., 175-176.

200. Ibid., 172.

201. Ibid., 172-173.

202. Ibid., 170-171.

203. Ibid., 109-113.

204. Breitweiser, *Wake-Up Call*, 145. (See note 2.)

205. Ibid., 146.

206. Ibid., 147.

207. Karen DeYoung and Steven Mufson, "A Leaner and Less Visible NSC Reorganization Will Emphasize Defense, Global Economics," *Washington Post*, February 10, 2001.

208. "FSC Requests Staff Director Zelikow's Recusal," Family Steering Committee for the Independent 9/11 Commission, October 3, 2003.

209. Eric Boehlert, "The President Ought To Be Ashamed," *Salon.com*, November 22, 2003.

210. Shenon, *The Commission*, 164-165. (See note 74.)

211. Philip Shenon, "Clinton Aides Plan to Tell Panel Of Warning Bush Team on Qaeda," *New York Times*, March 20, 2004. Chris Strohm, "Groups Call for the Resignation of Sept. 11 Commission Director," *Government Executive*, Washington DC, March 22, 2004.

212. Amy Goodman, "New Book Alleges 9/11 Commissioner Philip Zelikow Minimized Scrutiny of Bush Admin Failure to Prevent al-Qaeda Attack,"

Democracy Now!, February 5, 2008.

213. Chris Strohm, "Groups Call for the Resignation of Sept. 11 Commission Director," *Government Executive,* Washington DC, March 22, 2004.

214. "Statement of the Family Steering Committee for The 9/11 Independent Commission: Staff Director Zelikow and Transition Briefings," Family Steering Committee for the Independent 9/11 Commission, March 20, 2004.

215. Breitweiser, *Wake-Up Call,* 160. (See note 2.)

216. "Statement of the Family Steering Committee for The 9/11 Independent Commission: Staff Director Zelikow and Transition Briefings," Family Steering Committee for the Independent 9/11 Commission, March 20, 2004. Lorie van Auken noted that the FSC "set up conference calls with whatever team was in charge of the upcoming hearing. Zelikow, or his assistant Chris Kojm, monitored the calls."

217. NBC, Transcript, "Guests: Former Gov. Thomas Kean (R- N.J.), Chair of 9/11 Commission; Former Rep. Lee Hamilton (D-Ind), Vice chair of 9/11 Commission; Former Bush Advisor Karen Hughes," NBC Meet The Press, April 4, 2004.

218. Joe Conason, "Widows Watch Part II ...," *Salon,* April 6, 2004.

219. Shenon, *The Commission,* 388-89. (See note 74.)

220. Ibid., 389.

221. Ibid. 9/11 Commission staff's parody was in reference to the conduct of the Warren Commission and its findings. There was a determination on the part of Warren Commission staff Arlen Specter, Gerald Ford, and others to draw conclusions that contradicted evidence they were presented with by witnesses. The Warren Commission concluded that President John F. Kennedy was first struck by a bullet which entered at the back of his neck and exited through the lower front portion of his neck. But on March 21, 1964, Dr. Robert Nelson McClelland gave testimony to Warren Commission staff, Arlen Specter, at Parkland Memorial Hospital. Dr. McClelland stated "the wound in the neck, the anterior part of the neck, was an *entrance* wound and that it

had perhaps taken a trajectory off the anterior vertebral body and again into the skull itself, exiting out the back, to produce the massive injury in the head. However, this required some straining of the imagination to imagine that this would happen, and it was much easier to explain the apparent trajectory by means of two bullets ... than by just one ..." McClelland stated this was the view of all the doctors at Parkland. Dr. McClelland's testimony posed a problem for the Warren Commission since their thesis had a bullet from Lee Harvey Oswald's gun entering the president from the rear, not the front. "Testimony of Dr. Robert Nelson McClelland," Warren Commission, March 21, 1964. *http:// jfkassassination.net/russ/testimony/mcclella.htm* . See also James W. Douglass, *JFK and the Unspeakable: Why He Died & Why It Matters*, (Orbis Books, 2008), 307-321; and Charles A. Crenshaw, M.D., *Trauma Room One: The JFK Medical Coverup Exposed*, (Paraview Press, 2001), 61-62. Doctor Crenshaw was in Trauma Room One at Parkland Hospital in Dallas. He and Dr. Malcolm Perry noticed "a small opening in the midline of his [JFK's] throat .... It was a bullet entry wound." Dr. Malcolm Perry "decided to perform a tracheostomy [a surgical incision followed by insertion of a tube] on the President's throat, where the bullet had entered his neck." Dr. Perry repeatedly said at a press conference on November 23, 1963, "The wound appeared to be an *entrance* wound in the front of the throat; yes, that is correct." (emphasis added). However, the Warren Commission dismissed the consensus of all the doctors at Parkland Hospital and chose to draw a different conclusion regarding where a bullet had entered JFK's head. This was done in order to prop up the Warren Commission's "lone gunman" assassination theory. Any bullet entering the president from the front of his neck could not have been fired from the Texas School Book Depository where Oswald was said to have been firing three shots from a sixth floor window.

222. "Thomas Kean Runs Away From 911 Cover Up," We Are Change, September 6, 2011. *https://www.youtube.com/watch?v=HkoZjvQi8ms*

223. "Commission Sensitive" Outline of 9/11 Commission Report, March 2003. *https://www.scribd.com/document/14863585/List-of-Sections-of-9-11-Commission-and-People-Who-DraftedThem?ad_group=725X104635X435dd763f1c1f937e2342f8 40a209054&campaign= SkimbitLtd&keyword=660149026&medium=affiliate&sour*

ce=hp_affiliate; Kean and Hamilton, *9/11 Commission Report*, v-vii.

224. Kean and Hamilton, *Without Precedent*, 271. (See note 102.)

225. Ernest R. May, "When Government Writes History," *The New Republic*, May 16, 2005.

6 ~ AN OPEN LETTER TO FORMER MAYOR GIULIANI FROM THE FAMILY STEERING COMMITTEE, MAY 22, 2004

226. Philip Shenon and Kevin Flynn, "Threats and Responses: The Panel; Panel Criticizes New York Action in Sept. 11 Attack," *New York Times*, May 19, 2004.

227. Ibid.

228. In May 2003 Bernard Kerick was appointed Interim Minister of Interior of Iraq and senior policy adviser to US presidential envoy to Iraq, Paul Bremer.

229. "9/11 Commissioner Apologizes for Comments At Hearing, Says Giuliani," *New York DailyNews*, May 28, 2004.

230. Transcript, "9-11 Commission Hearing May 19, 2004," National Commission On Terrorist Attacks Upon the United States, May 19, 2004.

231. Ibid. See also, Jim Dwyer, "Threats and Responses: Assessment; Contradicting Other Evidence, Giuliani Says Firefighters Heard Order to Evacuate," *New York Times*, May 20, 2004.

232. Oral History of Fire Lt. Warren Smith, WTC Task Force, December 4, 2001, pp. 11, 27. *https://static01.nyt.com/packages/pdf/nyregion/20050812_WTC_GRAPHIC/9110223. PDF*

233. Transcript, "9-11 Commission Hearing May 19, 2004," National Commission On Terrorist Attacks Upon the United States, May 19, 2004.

234. Ibid.

235. Peter Jennings, "9/11 Rudy Giuliani Interview," ABC, September 11, 2001.

236. Transcript, "9-11 Commission Hearing May 19, 2004," National Commission

On Terrorist Attacks Upon the United States, May 19, 2004.

237. Ibid.

238. Ibid.

239. Ibid.

240. 9-11 Hearings, C-SPAN, May 19, 2004.

241. Transcript, "9-11 Commission Hearing May 19, 2004," National Commission On Terrorist Attacks Upon the United States, May 19, 2004.

242. Ibid.

243. 9-11 Hearings, C-SPAN, May 19, 2004.

244. Transcript, "9-11 Commission Hearing May 19, 2004," National Commission On Terrorist Attacks Upon the United States, May 19, 2004.

245. Joel Roberts, "Venting At Rudy & 9/11 Panel," CBS, May 21, 2004

246. Stephanie Gaskell, "Kin Fury Boils Over – 'My Son Died From Your Incompetence'," *New York Post*, May 20, 2004.

247. Ibid.

248. Family Steering Committee, "An Open Letter to former Mayor Giuliani from the Family Steering Committee," New York City, May 22, 2004.

249. Ibid.

250. Ibid.

251. David Saltonstall, "Rudy Gets Earful at Stop Here: Some FDNY Survivors Rally Against Him". *Daily News*, New York, April 24, 2007.

252. "Giuliani Faces Questions About 9/11: Post-terrorist Attack Hero Status Challenged by Some Firefighters' Families," NBC, March 30, 2007.

253. Michael Wilson, "Among Firefighters in New York, Mixed Views on Giuliani," *New York Times*, June 17, 2007.

254. Ibid.

255. David Staltonstall, "FDNY Hero Sticks Up for Rudy vs. Union," *Daily News*, New York, March 10, 2007.

256. David Saltonstall, "Rudy Gets Earful at Stop Here: Some FDNY Survivors Rally Against Him". *Daily News*, New York, April 24, 2007.

257. "Board Members and Honorary Trustees," 9/11 Memorial and Museum, 2019.

7 - THE FINAL REPORT

258. "Statement of the Family Steering Committee Regarding Conflicts of Interest and the 9/11 Commission," Family Steering Committee to the 9/11 Commission, April 18, 2004.

259. Kristen Breitweiser, Mindy Kleinberg, Patty Casazza and Lorie Van Auken, "What Can A Citizen Do?" *Wall Street Journal*, May 11, 2004.

260. Team 8, "NORAD EXERCISES Hijack Summary," 9/11 Commission, undated document stamped "commission sensitive."

261. National Transportation Security Summit, Washington DC, October 30, 2001, "MTI Report S-01-02," Mineta Transportation Institute, San Jose State University, 2001. The administrative official speaking was Ellen Engelman.

262. Steven Komarow and Tom Squitieri, "NORAD Had Drills of Jets as Weapons," *USA Today*, April 19, 2004.

263. Kristen Breitweiser, Mindy Kleinberg, Patty Casazza and Lorie Van Auken, "What Can A Citizen Do?" *Wall Street Journal*, May 11, 2004.

264. Gourley, "Testimony of Lorie Van Auken," *The 9/11 Toronto Report*, 10. (See note 29.)

265. Gold, "Interview with Lorie Van Auken, September 27, 2014," *We Were Lied To About 9/11: The Interviews*, 156. (See note 111.)

266. Gourley, "Testimony of Lorie Van Auken," *The 9/11 Toronto Report*, 12. (See note 29.)

267. Ibid. See also Patty Casazza, Monica Gabrielle, Mindy Kleinberg, and Lorie Van Auken, "September 11ᵗʰ Advocates Comment On The Impending Release Of Philip Shenon's Book: The Commission: The Uncensored History of the 9/11 Investigation," February 4, 2008. "Essentially, Mr. Zelikow determined who was or was not interviewed as a witness, and which information was or was not looked at. He also influenced which documents would be requested from the various agencies."

268. "FSC Statement Regarding the Hearings on June 16th and 17ᵗʰ," Family Steering Committee, June 14, 2004.

269. Kean and Hamilton, *Without Precedent,* 267-268. (See note 102.)

270. 9/11 Commissioner, Timothy Roemer, "9/11 Panel Distrusted Pentagon Testimony: Commissioners Considered Criminal Probe of False Statements," CNN, August 2, 2006.

271. Dan Eggen, "9/11 Panel Suspected Deception by Pentagon," *Washington Post,* August 2, 2006.

272. "The Family Steering Committee for the 9/11 Independent Commission Statement Regarding the Final Report," Family Steering Committee, July 20, 2004.

273. Breitweiser, *Wake-Up Call,* 174. (See note 2.)

274. Ibid., 160.

275. "President Bush Receives 911 Commission Report," *Associated Press,* July 22, 2004.

276. Shenon, *The Commission,* 35-39. (See note 74.)

277. Kean and Hamilton, *Without Precedent,* 65. (See note 102.)

278. Ibid., 38.

279. Ibid., 15.

280. Ibid., 29-30.

281. Ibid., 323.

282. Timothy Naftali, *Blind Spot: The Secret History of American Counterterrorism*, (Basic Books, 2005), xii.

283. "Statement of the Family Steering Committee for the 9/11 Independent Commission," Family Steering Committee, July 26, 2004.

284. Kean and Hamilton, *The 9/11 Commission Report*. p. xvi.

285. Mindy Kleinberg and Lorie Van Auken. "FSC Questions To The 9/11 Commission with Ratings of its Performance in Providing Answers." *http://911truth.org/downloads/Family_Steering_Cmte_review_of_Report.pdf*

286. Evan Solomon, "Truth, Lies and Conspiracy ... – Interview with Lee Hamilton," CBC, August 21, 2006.

287. Ben Yogada, "The 9/11 Commission Report: How a Government Committee Made a Piece of Literature," *Slate*, November 8, 2004.

288. Ibid.

289. Ernest R. May, "When The Government Writes History," *New Republic*, May 22, 2005.

290. James Carney, "Briefing Paper: If You Don't Have Time to Read It," *Time*, August 2, 2004.

291. Richard A. Posner, "The 9/11 Report: A Dissent," *New York Times*, August 29, 2004.

292. Ernest R. May, "When The Government Writes History," *New Republic*, May 22, 2005.

293. David Corn, "The 9/11 Report: Bad News For Bush," *The Nation*, July 23, 2004.

294. Frank Rich, *The Greatest Story Ever Told: The Decline and Fall of Truth from 9/11 to Katrina*, (Penguin, 2006), 229-307.

295. Benjamin DeMott, "Whitewash as Public Service: How the 9/11 Commission Report Defrauds the Nation," *Harper's Magazine*, October 2004.

296. Ibid.

297. Kean and Hamilton, *Without Precedent,* 267. (See note 102.)

298. Robert Windrem and Victor Limjoco, "9/11 Commission Controversy," MSNBC, January 30, 2008.

299. Ibid.

300. Ibid.

301. Ibid.

302. Rachel Maddow, *The Rachel Maddow Show,* MSNBC, April 24, 2013.

8 ~ THE 9/11 COMMISSION'S RECOMMENDATIONS

303. "Statement of the Family Steering Committee for the 9/11 Independent Commission," Family Steering Committee, July 26, 2004.

304. "Testimony of Beverly Eckert," US House of Representatives Committee on Government Reform Hearings to Review 9/11 Commission Recommendations, Washington DC, August 3, 2004.

305. "Testimony of Robin K. Wiener," US House of Representatives Committee on Government Reform Hearings to Review 9/11 Commission Recommendations, Washington DC, August 3, 2004.

306. "Testimony of Sally Regenhard," member of the Family Steering Committee of the 9-11 Commission and Chairperson of the Skyscraper Safety Campaign," US House of Representatives Committee on Government Reform Hearings to Review 9/11 Commission Recommendations, Washington DC, August 3, 2004.

307. "Testimony of Mary Fetchet," US Senate Governmental Affairs Committee, Washington DC, August 17, 2004.

308. Kevin Johnson, "Letter Shifts Heat to FBI," *USA Today,* May 28, 2002.

309. "Testimony of Mary Fetchet," US Senate Governmental Affairs Committee, August 17, 2004.

310. Breitweiser, *Wake-Up Call,* 202-204. (See note 2.)

311. Ibid., 257-258.

312. "Testimony of Kristen Breitweiser," US Senate Governmental Affairs Committee, Washington DC, August 17, 2004.

313. Clifton Adcock, "The Sooner State's Ties to the Twin Towers are Tight, Despite the Distance," *The Oklahoma Gazette*, July 9, 2011.

314. Transcript of PBS NewsHour show, "Intelligence Investigation," September 11, 2001.

315. Daniel Golden, James Bandler, and Marcus Walker, "Bin Laden Family Could Profit from a Jump in Defense Spending Due to Ties to US Bank," *Wall Street Journal*, September 27, 2001.

316. US Department of Defense, press briefing, "Dr. Hamre's Briefing on Year 2000 Issues," January 15, 1999. See Scott Simmie, "The Scene at NORAD on Sept. 11: Playing Russian War Games. And then Someone Shouted to Look at the Monitor," *Toronto Star*, December 9, 2001.

317. Dr. Henry Kissinger, "Guiding Principles For Intelligence Reform," Congressional Record, September 21, 2004.

318. "In Response to Kissinger's Testimony," Family Steering Committee, September 23, 2004.

319. "An Open Letter to 9/11 Legislation Conferees," Family Steering Committee, October 18, 2004.

320. "Regarding the Release of CIA Inspector General's Report," Family Steering Committee, October 20, 2004.

321. "An Open Letter to the President," Family Steering Committee, October 20, 2004.

322. "Family Steering Committee Questions Partisan Stalemate in 9/11 Commission Bill Conference," Family Steering Committee, October 21, 2004.

323. "9/11 Family Steering Committee Asks, "Where is the President? The Country Needs a 9/11 Bill!" Family Steering Committee, Washington DC, October 22, 2004.

324. "Sounding The Alarm," Family Steering Committee, October 25, 2004.

325. "On the Failure to Pass 9/11 Intelligence Reform Legislation," Family Steering Committee, October 27, 2004.

326. Breitweiser, *Wake-Up Call*, 207. (See note 2.)

327. Ibid., 208.

328. Ibid., 208.

329. Ibid., 209.

330. Ibid., 213.

331. "Ever Since" Kerry-Edwards 2004 TC ad, Kerry-Edwards 2004 Inc., October 18, 2004.

332. Robert Draper, *Dead Certain: The Presidency of George W. Bush*, (Free Press, 2007), 263.

333. Transcript, "Recent Video of bin Laden Airs; Iraq Missing Explosives Still an Issue," CNN Lou Dobbs Tonight, October 29, 2004.

334. Rachel Weiner, "Tom Ridge: I Was Pressured To Raise Terror Alert To Help Bush Win," *Huffington Post*, September 20, 2009. See also Tom Ridge, *The Test of our Times: America Under Siege ... and How We Can Be Safe Again*, (Thomas Dunne Books, 2009), 226-241.

335. Ray Nowosielski, "Bob Kerrey Interview," *In Their Own Words: The Untold Stories of 9/11 Families*, Banded Artists/Standard Issue Films, 2006.

336. Nowosielski, "Mindy Kleinberg Interview," *In Their Own Words: The Untold Stories of 9/11 Families*. (See note 335.)

337. "An Open Letter to Members of the 108th Congress on the 9/11 Bill Conference Report," Family Steering Committee, December 9, 2004.

338. "Final Statement of the Family Steering Committee," January 11, 2005.

339. Family Steering Committee, "Family Steering Committee Press Conference Remarks," September 10, 2003.

9 ~ QUESTION TO NORAD: "WHY WEREN'T NORAD JETS ABLE TO INTERCEPT THE HIJACKED PLANES IF THEY WERE AIRBORNE WITHIN EIGHT MINUTES OF NOTIFICATION?"

340. Carol Ashley, "Statement on Aviation Security," 9/11 Commission Hearings, Washington DC, January 26, 2004.

341. Family Steering Committee for the 9/11 Independent Commission, "Unanswered Questions," NORAD Question #2.

342. Thomas H. Kean, Lee Hamilton and National Commission on Terrorist Attacks, *The 9/11 Commission Report: Final Report of the National Commission on Terrorist Attacks Upon the United States*, (W.W. Norton & Company, 2004), 16.

343. "Continental Air Defense: A Dedicated Force is No Longer Needed." *General Accounting Office*, Report to US Congress, May 3, 1994. In this GAO report there is a section of information about "Scramble Activity by Air Defense United and Alert Sites, 1989-92."

344. Linda Slobodian, "NORAD on Heightened Alert: Role of Air Defence Agency Rapidly Transformed in Wake of Sept. 11 Terrorist Attacks," *Calgary Herald*, October 13, 2001.

345. "Use of Military Jets Jumps Since 9/11," *Associated Press*, August 13, 2002. See also Leslie Miller, "NORAD scrambled jets 67 times from September 2000 to June 2001," *Associated Press*, August 8, 2002.

346. On August 23, 1958, the Federal Aviation Act of 1958 was signed into law by President Eisenhower. See also, Adriene LaFrance, "The Site of a 1950s Plane Crash Just Became a National Landmark," *The Atlantic*, April 24, 2014.

347. Air Traffic Control Center, "ATCC Controller's Read Binder," August 1998. *www.xavius.com/080198.htm*

348. "Point Paper on Training and Exercises," North American Aerospace Defense Command,October 13, 2001.

349. Family Steering Committee for the 9/11 Independent Commission, September 11 Inquiry: Questions to be Answered January, 2003 sub-head ~ NORAD.

350. Dean Jackson, "The NORAD Papers IV: How NORAD Radar Operators Identified Aircraft Flying Over American Airspace on 9/11 And Its Implications," *911Truth.org,* September 10, 2008.

351. Glen Johnson, "Otis Fighter Jets Scrambled Too Late to Halt the Attacks," *Boston Globe*, September 15, 2001.

352. Kelly Young, "Space Golf Shot Might Stay in Orbit for Years," *New Scientist*, November 17, 2006.

353. Nicole Martin, "Pilots 'Must Have Been Murdered' Before Jets Were Aimed at Buildings," *The Independent*, Dublin, September 12, 2001.

354. Nicole Martin and Andrew Hibberd, "Hijackers May Have Murdered the Pilots," *Telegraph*, London, UK, September 12, 2001.

355. John Farmer, *The Ground Truth: The Untold Story of America Under Attack on 9/11*, (Riverhead Books, 2009), 241-243.

356. Mindy Kleinberg, "Statement of Mindy Kleinberg," National Commission on Terrorist Attacks Upon the United States, Public Hearing, Washington DC, March 31, 2003, 2-3.*https://9-11commission.gov/hearings/hearing1/witness_kleinberg.htm*

357. Ibid.

358. Ibid.

359. Family Steering Committee for the 9/11 Independent Commission, "Unanswered Questions," sub-head ~ NORAD. The FSC also asked: Have the passenger manifests been released? If not, why not? Were there any discrepancies in the manifests? Did the names and number of passengers match? Were each of the hijackers listed on the manifest and assigned to a seat? In her testimony before the 9/11 Commission on January 26, 2004, Carol Ashley asked "Why were all four planes carrying a light load?" American Flights 77 and 11, and United Flights 93 and 175 had been averaging 220 passengers a flight. Transcontinental flights did not fly with low occupancy. However, on 9/11 these four flights from the east coast to California flew with these numbers of occupants and occupancy rates: AA Flight 77: 62 (28%); United Flight 175: 60 (27%); AA Flight

11: 87 (39%); United Flight: 93: 40 (18%).

360. Kean and Hamilton, *The 9/11 Commission Report*, 34.

361. Mindy Kleinberg, "Statement of Mindy Kleinberg," 9/11 Commission, March 31, 2003, 8-9.

362. Peter Jennings, "9/11 Interviews," ABC, September 11, 2002. In 2011 it was reported on a Boston radio station interview with Lt. Col. Tim Duffy and Lt. Col. Dan Nash that "The same minute they left, (Otis Air Force Base) the first plane struck the towers." The North Tower was hit at 8:46 a.m. Michael May, "9/11 Stories: The Fighter Pilots Who Got The Call," WBUR, Boston, September 7, 2011.

363. Mike Taibbi, "Chain of Events at NORAD on September 11," *Dateline NBC*, September 23, 2001.

364. "NORAD's Response Times," North American Aerospace Defense Command News Release, September 18, 2001.

365. Garrett M.Graff, "Behind the 9/11 White House Order to Shoot Down US Airliners: 'It Had to be Done'," *History.com*, September 9, 2019. Also, "Cheney: Order to Shoot Down Hijacked 9/11 Planes 'Necessary'," Fox News, September 4, 2011.

366. David Kohn, "The President's Story: The President Talks In Detail About His Sept. 11 Experience," CBS, September 11, 2002. Also "Cheney: Order to Shoot Down Hijacked 9/11 Planes 'Necessary'," FOX News, September 4, 2011.

367. 9/11 Commission *Report*, p. 245.

368. Mike Kelly, "Atlantic City F-16 Fighters Were Eight Minutes Away From 9/11 Hijacked Planes," *Bergen Record*, December 5, 2003.

369. Peter Lance, *Cover Up: What the Government is Still Hiding about the War on Terror*, (HarperCollins/ReganBooks, 2004), 230-231.

370. Joel Roberts, "9/11 Attack was Preventable," CBS, December 17, 2003.

371. Dan Eggen, "Pentagon's Version of 9/11 Far from Truth," Panel Found

Commission Members Wanted Justice Dept. Probe, *Denver Post*, August 2, 2006.

372. "Paul Thompson, Author, 'The Terror Timeline,' September 11 Investigation Campaign," National Press Club, C-SPAN, September 11, 2006.

373. Vigilant Guardian: An annual NORAD exercise held traditionally in October, often in conjunction with Global Guardian. "NORAD Exercises Hijack Summary, 1998-2001," a "Commission Sensitive" document.

374. 9/11 Commission interview with Merchant and Goddard, "Memorandum for the Record: NORAD Field Site Visit: Interview with Major Paul Goddard (Canadian Forces), and Ken Merchant," March 4, 2004. Amalgam Warrior took place October 15-20, 1996. It included the 101st Fighter Squadron from Otis Air Force Base. According to an article on October 27, 2000 in the *Elison News Service*, Amalgam Warrior took place on October 27, 2000. Amalgam Virgo had previously taken place in Florida on June 1-2, 2001. The planning document, SEADS Concept Proposal for Amalgam Virgo 01, featured a photo of Osama bin Laden on its cover together with five photos of military planes around the terrorist. Amalgam Virgo 02 was in the planning stages on September 11, 2001. It included a hijacking of a Delta 757 by "military personnel acting as civilian passengers." Another NORAD simulation prior to 9/11, named Fertile Rice, featured Osama bin Laden directing a drone filled with explosives targeting Washington DC.

375. 9/11 Commission interview with Merchant and Goddard. "Hijacks were included in these exercises to exercise transition in Rules of Engagement (ROE)." Vigilant Guardian, a hijack exercise, was mislabeled by the 9/11 Commission as an exercise to defend against Russian bombers. See Steven Komarow and Tom Squiteri, "NORAD Had Drills of Jets as Weapons," *USA Today*, April 18, 2004.

376. Commissioner Jamie Gorelick questions to NORAD General Richard Myers, National Commission on Terrorist Attacks Upon the United States, Twelfth Public Hearing, Washington DC, June 17, 2004.

377. FSC Statement Regarding the Hearings on June 16 and 17, June 14, 2004. SEADS Concept Proposal for Amalgam Virgo 01. *https://en.wikipedia.org/wiki/*

Amalgam Virgo#/media/File:AmalgamVirgoJun1-2-2001.jpg

378. "Ptech Questions for the FBI and US Customs," Family Steering Committee, March 22, 2004.

10: QUESTION TO THE FAA ~ "WHY WERE THESE FOUR PLANES ABLE TO EVADE ALL RADAR?"

379. Family Steering Committee for the 9/11 Commission, Unanswered Questions: FAA, question 2.

380. "Statement of Mindy Kleinberg," 9/11 Commission, (New York), March 31, 2003.

381. Kristen Breitweiser, "Statement of Kristen Breitweiser," Joint 9/11 Inquiry, September 18, 2002.

382. Raymond C. Watson, *Radar Origins Worldwide: History of Its Evolution in 13 Nations Through World War II,* (Trafford Publishing, 2009), 2ff.

383. Kean and Hamilton, *The 9/11 Commission Report,* 14.

384. Ibid.,17-18.

385. Ibid., 34.

386. 9/11 Commission, Staff report, "The Four Flights," August 26, 2004, 11.

387. Kean and Hamilton, *The 9/11 Commission Report,* 28.

388. Family Steering Committee for the 9/11 Independent Commission, Unanswered Questions ~ Federal Aviation Administration.

389. 9/11 Commission Memorandum for the Record (MFR) Interview: John Hawley, October 8, 2003. *https://catalog.archives.gov/OpaAPI/media/2610202/ content/9-11/MFR/t-0148-911MFR-00608.pdf*

390. Interview of Michael Canavan, 9/11 Commission Public Hearing, May 23, 2003, *http://www.9-11commission.gov/archive/hearing2/9-11Commission Hearing_2003-05-23.htm*

391. Family Steering Committee for the 9/11 Independent Commission,

Unanswered Questions ~ Federal Aviation Administration.

392. Kean and Hamilton, *The 9/11 Commission Report* note 228, p. 465; "Memorandum for the Record: Interview with CINCNORAD (Commanded in Chief NORAD), General Edward 'Ed' Eberhart," 9/11 Commission, 1 March 2004, 4; "Memorandum for the Record, Interview with NORAD Deputy Commander, Lieutenant General Rick Findley, Canadian Forces (CF)," 9/11 Commission March 1, 2004, 2.

393. "Memorandum for the Record, Interview with NORAD Deputy Commander, Lieutenant General Rick Findley, Canadian Forces (CF)," 9/11 Commission, March 1, 2004, 3.

394. Elizabeth Woodworth, "General Ralph Eberhart during the 9/11 Attacks," *911Truth.org*, February 15, 2015; Vigilant Guardian 01-02 Planning Document; "'Real-World or Exercise': Did the US Military Mistake the 9/11 Attacks for a Training Scenario?" Shoestring 911, March 22, 2012; 9/11 Commission, Twelfth Public Hearing, June 17, 2004; "'Let's Get Rid of This Goddamn Sim': How NORAD Radar Screens Displayed False Tracks All Through the 9/11 Attacks," Shoestring 911, August 12, 2010. *http://shoestring911.blogspot.com/2010/08/*

395. 9/11 Commission, "Memorandum for the Record," Interview with NORAD Deputy Commander, Lieutenant General Rick Findley, Canadian Forces (CF), March 1, 2004, 3.

396. 9/11 Commission, Twelfth Public Hearing, June 17, 2004.

397. William B. Scott, "Exercise Jump-Starts Response to Attacks," *Aviation Week & Space Technology*, June 3, 2002; 9/11 Commission, Twelfth Public Hearing, June 17, 2004, 70; Lynn Spencer, *Touching History: The Untold Story of the Drama That Unfolded in the Skies Over America on 9/11* (Free Press, 2008), 269.

398. 9/11 Commission, Twelfth Public Hearing, June 17, 2004, 70; Spencer, *Touching History*, (Free Press, 2008), 269.

399. 1st Fighter Wing History Excerpt, 1st Fighter Wing History Office, Langley Air Force Base, Hampton, VA, July through December 2001: 61. Source date Sept. 11, 2001.

400. Gerry J. Gilmore, "Eberhart Tabbed to Head US Northern Command," *American Forces Press Service*, May 8, 2002.

401. Family Steering Committee for the 9/11 Independent Commission, Unanswered Questions,sub-head ~ NORAD, Question #4.

402. Family Steering Committee for the 9/11 Independent Commission, September 11 Inquiry: Questions to be Answered January, 2003 ~ Federal Aviation Administration.

403. Kean and Hamilton, *The 9/11 Commission Report*, statement by deputy, Capt. Charles J. Leidig, 463, footnote 190. *www.9-11commission.gov/hearings/hearing12/leidig_statement.pdf*

404. General Myers Confirmation Hearing, Senate Armed Services Committee, Washington DC, September 13, 2001. *http://emperors-clothes.com/9-11backups/mycon.htm*

405. Kean and Hamilton, *The 9/11 Commission Report*, 465. Memorandum for the Record: Interview with CINCNORAD, 5, March 1, 2004. *https://www.archives.gov/files/declassification/iscap/pdf/2012-042-doc29.pdf*

406. Mary Fetchet, "Statement of Mary Fetchet," 9/11 Commission, March 31, 2003.

407. Mindy Kleinberg, "Statement of Mindy Kleinberg," 9/11 Commission, March 31, 2003. 3,11.

408. Paul Thompson, "Omissions and Errors in the Commission's Final Report: NORAD/FAA, P-56 Responses, Pre-9/11 Exercises," in Cynthia McKinney, *The 9/11 Commission Report One Year Later - A Citizen's Response: Did The Commission Get It Right?* (Congressional Briefing, Washington DC. July 22, 2005) 32. On the fifth anniversary of the attacks, Paul Thompson told the National Press Club: "The official story of the military response on the day of 9/11 has changed ... I've counted seven different accounts by the military itself. ... *Vanity Fair* and the *Washington Post*, and ... the 9/11 Commission ... noted these different accounts [of NORAD's response to the hijackings] and were so disturbed by the differences that they recommended some kind of investigation" into NORAD's

contradictory statements and scenarios.

409. Dr. Bob Arnot, "What Was Needed to Halt the Attacks? … Quick Response Not In Evidence Tuesday," MSNBC, September 12, 2001. "Before American Flight 11 left Boston for Los Angeles, the pilot was issued what's called a standard instrument departure, or SID. A SID requires the airplane to fly to specific "fixes," what you might call road signs in the sky. As pilots move from fix to fix, they are required to stay within 300 feet of their assigned altitude and within … a mile of [their] course. Pilots are supposed to hit each fix with pinpoint accuracy."

410. "Timeline of Disaster: From Flight Training to Building Collapsing," ABC, September 14, 2001.

411. "Prepared Statement of Monte R. Belger," Twelfth Public Hearing, 9/11 Commission, June 17, 2004. *https://govinfo.library.unt.edu/911/hearings/hearing12/belger_statement.pdf*

11 ~ QUESTION TO THE CIA: WAS THE CIA MONITORING THE FINANCIAL MARKETS IN THE WEEKS PRECEDING SEPTEMBER 11TH?

412. Michael C. Ruppert, "Suppressed Details of Criminal Insider Trading Lead Directly into The CIA'S Highest Ranks: CIA Executive Director "Buzzy" Krongard Managed Firm that Handled "Put" Options on UAL," *San Francisco Chronicle*, September 29, 2001.

413. Ibid.

414. Carl Bernstein, "The CIA and the Media," *Rolling Stone*, October 20, 1977.

415. Ibid.

416. "Statement of Kristen Breitweiser," Joint 9/11 Inquiry, September 18, 2002.

417. "FSC Recommended List of Witnesses and Questions, Part 2: Intelligence, CIA," Question 13.

418. Family Steering Committee for the 9/11 Independent Commission. See ~ "Unanswered Questions," sub-head ~ CIA: Question 11; SEC: Question 1.

419. Fran Shor, "Follow The Money: Bush, 9/11 and Deep Threat," *Counterpunch*, May 21, 2002.

420. "German Bank Probes Terrorist Insider Trading Before Sept. 11th Attacks," *Washington Post*, September 22, 2001

421. Wing-Keung Wong, Howard E. Thompson, and Kweehong Teh, "Was There Abnormal Trading in the S&P 500 Index Options Prior to the September 11 Attacks?," *Multinational Finance Journal*, Vol. 15, no. 3/4, June 25, 2015, 45-46.

422. Family Steering Committee for the 9/11 Independent Commission, Unanswered Questions, sub-head: Questions about Al Qaeda and State Sponsored Terrorism: Question 24.

423. Kean and Hamilton, *The 9/11 Commission Report*, 2004, 499.

424. Doug Greenburg, "FBI Briefing on Trading," Informal FBI Briefing to the 9/11 Commission, August 15, 2003. This classified document was declassified in a FOIA request in 2009.

425. Family Steering Committee questions to the FBI and Director Robert Mueller, March 18, 2004.

426. Rick Perera, "Computer Disk Drives from WTC Could Yield Clues," IDG News Service, Berlin, Germany, December 20, 2001.

427. Erik Kirschbaum, "German Firm Probes last-minute World Trade Center Transactions," *Reuters*, December 19, 2001.

428. Family Steering Committee for the 9/11 Independent Commission. See ~ "Unanswered Questions," sub-head ~ Part 2: Intelligence: FBI Question 12, third bullet.

429. Field McConnell, "Were Specific Companies in the World Trade Center Targeted on 9/11?," Abeldanger.com. April 4, 2010.

430. "Paul Bremer Interview," Noon Hour News, News 4, NBC, New York, September 11, 2001, 12:46 p.m. *https://www.youtube.com/watch?v=j2pW6WZhZrQ*

431. Marsh & McLennan September 11th Memorial, *http://memorial.mmc.com*

432. "Interview with Paul Bremer," NBC, September 11, 2001.*https://www. youtube.com/watch?v=wgGxmBGZwYU*

433. Ibid.

434. Matthew Goldstein, "Citigroup Facing Subpoena in IPO Probe," *TheStreet. com*, August 9, 2002.

435. Margaret Cronin Fisk, "SEC & EEOC Attack Delays Investigation," *National Law Journal*, September 17, 2001; "SEC Office Destroyed; IPO Probe in Jeopardy," *New York Post*, September 12, 2001.

436. Charlie Bagli, "Insurers Agree to Pay Billions at Ground Zero," *New York Times*, March 24, 2007; "Jury Awards $2.2 Billion in 9/11 Insurance," United Press International, December 6, 2004

437. "WTC Leased to Silverstein, Westfield," CNN, September 12, 2001.

438. Sarah Fruchnicht, "Owner of World Trade Center is trying to sue airlines for billions for 9/11 attacks even though he was already paid $5 billion in insurance," *Daily Mail*, London, UK, July 16, 2013.

439. Kean and Hamilton, *The 9/11 Commission Report*, 2004, 172.

12 ~ QUESTION TO MAYOR GIULIANI: "WHY WAS THE WORLD TRADE CENTER STEEL REMOVED SO QUICKLY, WITHOUT BEING EXAMINED, FROM THE SCENE OF A MASS MURDER?"

440. Robin Wiener, "Testimony of Robin K. Wiener," US House of Representatives Committee on Government Reform, Hearings to Review 9/11 Commission Recommendations, August 3, 2004.

441. Steve Coulter, "Jeffrey Wiener Scholarship Fund Honors 9/11 Victim, TBS Grad," *Trumbull Times*, September 4, 2015.

442. "Missing Person Material, September 11: Bearing Witness to History," September 2002, National Museum of American History, *http://amhistory.si.edu/ september11/collection/record.asp?ID=139*

443. Steven Warran, "The Remains of Jeffrey Wiener," stevenwarran.blogspot.

ca, December 15, 2009. *https://stevenwarran.blogspot.ca/2009/12/remains-of-jeffrey-wiener.html*

444. David Kohn, "Culling Through Mangled Steel; Engineer Becomes World Trade Center Detective," CBS News, March 12, 2002.

445. Family Steering Committee for the 9/11 Independent Commission, Unanswered Questions,Port Authority/WTC/City of New York, question 12; and Statement and Questions Regarding the 9/11 Commission Interview of Mayor Rudy Giuliani and Members of his Administration,question 1)

446. "Learning from 9/11: Understanding the Collapse of the World Trade Center," US House of Representatives Committee on Science, March 2, 2002.

447. Ibid.

448. Shannon McCaffrey, "Skyscrapers to Face Stricter Codes," Associated Press,March 7, 2002.

449. Family Steering Committee for the 9/11 Independent Commission, Unanswered Questions,Port Authority/WTC/City of New York, question 12 and Statement and Questions Regarding the 9/11 Commission Interview of Mayor Rudy Giuliani and Members of his Administration, question 1.

450. BPAT WRC Building Performance Study WTC Steel Data Collection, FEMA, Appendix D

451. Bill Manning, "Editorial: $elling Out the Investigation," *Fire Engineering Magazine*, January 2002. See also, Joe Calderone, "Firefighter Mag Raps 9/11 Probe," *New York Daily News*, January 4, 2002. "A respected firefighting trade magazine with ties to the city Fire Department is calling for a "full-throttle, fully resourced" investigation into the collapse of the World Trade Center." The reporter relates that Senator Chuck Schumer (D-NY) had joined a group of relatives of firefighters in asking for the blue-ribbon panel recommended in Bill Manning's editorial in *Fire Engineering Magazine*; "The Towers: Experts Urging Broader Inquiry in Towers' Fall," *New York Times*, December 25, 2001.

452. Ray McGinnis, phone interview with Fire Commissioner Chris Gioia, January 25, 2020.

453. *The 9/11 Commission Report*, 302.

454. Manning, "Editorial: $elling Out the Investigation," *Fire Engineering Magazine*, January 2002.

455. Family Steering Committee for the 9/11 Independent Commission, Unanswered Questions,Port Authority/WTC/City of New York, question 12 and Statement and Questions Regarding the 9/11 Commission Interview of Mayor Rudy Giuliani and Members of his Administration, Q 1.

456. Manning, "Editorial: $elling Out the Investigation." (See note 451.)

457. Family Steering Committee question quote from *New York Daily News*, April 16, 2002.

458. "250 Tons of Scrap Stolen From Ruins," *Telegraph*, London, UK, September 29, 2001.

459. Christopher Bollyn, "New Seismic Data Refutes Official WTC Explanation," *American Free Press*, September 2, 2002.

460. Trudy Walsh, "Handheld APP Eased Recovery Tasks," *Government Computer News*, September 11, 2002, Vol. 21 No. 27a.

461. *Johns Hopkins Public Health Magazine* (Fall 2001)

462. Interview with Ground Zero chaplain Herb Trimpe, *Times-Herald Record*, (Hudson Valley, NY), September 8, 2002.

463. "David Long 9/11 Eyewitness," Truth Action (Ottawa), May 8, 2009. *https://www.youtube.com/watch?v=DQbEuBgAKso*

464. Oral History of Thomas Vallebuona, WTC Task Force, January 2, 2002, pp. 5-6. *https://static01.nyt.com/packages/pdf/nyregion/20050812_WTC_GRAPHIC/9110418.PDF*

465. Peter Jennings, "9/11 Rudy Giuliani Interview," ABC, September 11, 2001.

466. "Kenneth Holden, Commissioner of the New York Department of Design and Construction, Testimony," 9/11 Commission Public Hearing, New York City, April 1, 2003.

467. Evan Solomon, "Truth, Lies and Conspiracy – Interview with Lee Hamilton," CBC, August 21, 2006.

468. Family Steering Committee for the 9/11 Independent Commission, Unanswered Questions, Mayor Rudy Giuliani and Members of his Administration. Question 12.

469. Family Steering Committee for the 9/11 Independent Commission, Unanswered Questions: Mayor Rudy Giuliani. Mayor Giuliani's decision to have all his records sealed for 25 years is in the tradition of Rear Admiral Leigh Noyes. On December 11, 1941, Noyes, United States Navy Director of Communications, instituted a fifty-four-year censorship policy, sealing all "pre-Pearl Harbor Japanese military and diplomatic intercepts" by US military until 1995. Noyes also ordered department staff to "destroy all notes or anything in writing." The order to destroy files concerning naval matters was an order that could only be issued under the authority of the United States Congress. And on September 17, 1945, Fleet Admiral Ernest King blocked public access to all documents related to pre-Pearl Harbor US military intercepts of the "Japanese naval fleet's radio messages during the fall of 1941." He had these classified as TOP SECRET. King also "threatened imprisonment and loss of Navy and veteran's benefits to any naval personnel who disclosed the success of the code-breaking. He warned that 'writings of irresponsible people' would test the loyalty of all concerned." See Robert Stinnett, *Day Of Deceit*, (Free Press, 2001), 255-256.

13 - QUESTION TO PRESIDENT GEORGE W. BUSH: "AS COMMANDER-IN-CHIEF ON THE MORNING OF 9/11, WHY DIDN'T YOU RETURN IMMEDIATELY TO WASHINGTON DC OR THE NATIONAL MILITARY COMMAND CENTER ONCE YOU BECAME AWARE THAT AMERICA WAS UNDER ATTACK?"

470. Mindy Kleinberg, "Statement of Mindy Kleinberg," 9/11 Commission, March 31, 2003.

471. Family Steering Committee for the 9/11 Independent Commission, Unanswered Questions, Statement and Questions Regarding the 9/11

Commission: President George W. Bush, question 1.

472. 9/11 Commission, Transcript, 9/11 Commission staff, Statement no. 17, Improvising a Homeland Defense, June 17, 2004.

473. James Bamford, *A Pretext for War*, (Doubleday, 2004), 17.

474. Tom Bayles, "The Day Before Everything Changed, President Bush Touched Locals' Lives," *Sarasota Herald-Tribune*, September 10, 2002.

475. Susan Taylor Martin, "Of Fact, Fiction: Bush on 9/11," *St. Petersburg Times*, FL, July 4, 2004.

476. Philip Melanson and Peter F. Stevens, *The Secret Service: The History of an Enigmatic Agency*, (Basic Books, 2003).

477. Family Steering Committee for the 9/11 Independent Commission. Unanswered Questions, Statement and Questions Regarding the 9/11 Commission: Questions to the Secret Service 1, 2.

478. Jennifer Barrs, "From a Whisper to a Tear," *Tampa Tribune*, Sept 1, 2002.

479. Sammon, "Suddenly, a Time to Lead," *Washington Times*, October 7, 2002. See also Joel Achenbach, "On 9/11, a Telling Seven-Minute Silence," *Washington Post*, June 19, 2004.

480. "US President Remarks, President Bush Holds Town Hall Meeting on December 4," Weekly Compilation of Presidential Documents 37, No. 49, December 10, 2001. And Scott Pelley and David Kohn, "The President's Story: The President Talks in Detail About His Sept. 11 Experience, Moment to Moment," CBS, September 11, 2002.

481. Bill Sammon, "Suddenly, a Time to Lead," *Washington Times*, October 7, 2002.

482. Stephanie Schorow, "What Did Bush See and When Did He See It?," *Boston Herald*, October 22, 2002.

483. Lorie Van Auken, "9/11 Families Report: Unanswered Questions And The Call For Accountability," Cynthia McKinney, *The 9/11 Commission Report One*

Year Later. A Citizen's Response: Did The Commission Get It Right? Congressional Briefing, Washington DC, July 22, 2005, 10. *http://911truth.org/downloads/ McKinney-911Commission-OneYearLater.pdf*

484. Allen Wood and Paul Thompson, "An Interesting Day: President Bush's Movements and Actions on 9/11," Center for Cooperative Research, May 9, 2003.

485. Marcia Kramer, "9/11 Intelligence Sources Say Eight Planes, Five Still Missing," Live Chopper 2, CBS, September 11, 2001. *https://www.youtube.com/ watch?v=V77mabYL_Bg*

486. William Safire, "Inside The Bunker," *New York Times*, September 13, 2001. See also Dan Balz and Bob Woodward, "America's Chaotic Road to War (Part 1: Sept 11)," *Washington Post*, January 27, 2002.

487. Richard Cheney, Transcript, "The Vice President Appears on Meet The Press with Tim Russert," Interview with Tim Russert, *NBC Meet The Press*, September 16, 2001.

488. Scott Pelley and David Kohn, "The President's Story: The President Talks in Detail About His Sept. 11 Experience, Moment to Moment," CBS, September 11, 2002.

489. Kevin Ryan, "Secret Service Failures on 9/11: A Call for Transparency," Washington's Blog, March 25, 2012.

490. Family Steering Committee for the 9/11 Independent Commission. Unanswered Questions, Statement and Questions Regarding the 9/11 Commission: President George W. Bush, question 8.

491. Mindy Kleinberg and Lorie Van Auken, Members of the Family Steering Committee for the 9/11 Independent Commission, FSC Questions to the 9/11 Commission with Ratings of its Performance in Providing Answers. *http://911truth.org/downloads/Family_Steering_Cmte_review_of_Report.pdf*

492. Carol Ashley, "Statement on Aviation Security," for the National Commission on Terrorist Attacks Upon the United States, (Washington DC), January 26, 2004. *https://govinfo.library.unt.edu/911/hearings/hearing7/for_the_record_ashley.pdf*

493. Patty Casazza and Bob McIlvaine, "9/11: Families, First Responders, & Experts Speak Out Symposium," West Hartford, CT, November 3, 2007.

494. Carol Ashley, "Statement on Aviation Security." The foreign intelligence agencies that alerted America about a specific terrorist attack included Turkey, Israel, Jordan, Morocco, Italy, Belgium, Spain, Egypt, Germany, United Kingdom, and Yemen.

495. Family Steering Committee for the 9/11 Independent Commission. Unanswered Questions, Statement and Questions Regarding the 9/11 Commission: President George W. Bush, question 11.

496. "Bush Knew: Prez Was Warned of Possible Hijackings before Terror Attacks," *New York Post*, May 15, 2002.

497. Jason Burke and Ed Vulliamy, "Bush Knew of Terrorist Plot to Hijack US Planes," *Guardian*, London, UK, May 19, 2002.

498. David E. Sanger, "Bush was Warned bin Laden Wanted to Hijack Planes," *New York Times*, May 16, 2002.

499. Carol Ashley, "Statement on Aviation Security…" (See note 492.)

500. Memorandum to the 9/11 Commission, The Family Steering Committee Statement and Questions Regarding the 9/11 Commission Interview with President Bush, February 16, 2004. *https://ratical.org/ratville/CAH/FSCstmtQs.pdf*

501. Family Steering Committee, Unanswered Questions, Statement and Questions Regarding the 9/11 Commission: President George W. Bush, question 31.

14 - QUESTIONS TO THE PORT AUTHORITY/WTC/CITY OF NEW YORK: "WHAT IS THE NAME OF THE INDIVIDUAL WHO MADE THE ANNOUNCEMENT IN 2 WTC WHO TOLD WORKERS TO RETURN TO THEIR OFFICES? WHY WERE THE ROOF ACCESS DOORS LOCKED? WHY WAS THERE NO ROOF-TOP EVACUATION?"

502. Family Steering Committee for the 9/11 Independent Commission, Unanswered Questions, Port Authority/WTC/City of New York. Question 6; Mayor Rudy Giuliani and Members of his Administration, question 10.

503. Mary Fetchet, "Statement of Mary Fetchet," 9/11 Commission, March 31, 2003.

504. Ibid.

505. Jim Dwyer and Kevin Flynn, *102 Minutes: The Untold Story of the Fight to Survive Inside the Twin Towers*, (Times Books, 2005), 72.

506. Katie Walmsley, "9/11 Anniversary: Survivor Reflects on Escaping Death," ABC, September 10, 2011.

507. "Jackasses With Bullhorns," *Newsday*, September 12, 2001.

508. Breitweiser, *Wake-up Call*, 38. (See note 2.)

509. WABC reporting live from World Trade Center, New York, September 11, 2001.

510. Mary Fetchet, "Statement of Mary Fetchet," 9/11 Commission, March 31, 2003.

511. Ibid.

512. Ibid.

513. Donna Marsh O'Connor, National Press Club, Washington DC, September 12, 2006. *https://www.youtube.com/watch?v=-CrlDr-IEAA*

514. Family Steering Committee for the 9/11 Independent Commission, Unanswered Questions,Mayor Rudy Giuliani and Members of his Administration, question 2.

515. "Testimony of The Honorable Rudolph W. Giuliani, Former Mayor, City of New York," 9/11 Commission, New School University, New York, May 19, 2004. *http://transcripts.cnn.com/TRANSCRIPTS/0405/19/se.01.html*

516. Michael Mink, "Chief Peter Ganci Died Leading Rescue Efforts At 9/11's Ground Zero," *Investor's Business Daily*, Los Angeles, CA, September 3, 2016.

517. "Stairwell Sign from the World Trade Center," Smithsonian National Museum of American History. *https://amhistory.si.edu/september11/collection/record.asp?ID=74*

518. Scot J. Paltrow and Queena Sook Kim, "Could Helicopters Have Saved People From the Top of the Trade Center?," *Wall Street Journal*, October 23, 2001.

519. Bill Wagstaff, "Rescue Squabble Revives NYC Police, Fire Rivalry," Aviation International News, Midland Park, NJ, May 27, 2008.

520. Scot J. Paltrow and Queena Sook Kim, "Could Helicopters Have Saved People From the Top of the Trade Center?," *Wall Street Journal*, October 23, 2001.

521. "New York City's Anti-terrorism Efforts Go High Tech," CNN, June 7, 1999.

522. Brian Michael Jenkins and Frances Edwards-Winslow, *Saving City Lifelines: Lessons Learned in the 9/11 Terrorist Attacks*, (Mineta Transportation Institute, 2003), 30. Previous exercises for responding to a terrorist attack around the WTC occurred on November 8-9, 1997, and on May 11, 2001.

523. Curtis L. Taylor and Sean Gardiner, "Heightened Security Alert Had Just Been Lifted," *Newsday*, New York, September 12, 2001.

524. "FC Section 1027.3 Unobstructed and Unimpeded Egress Required," (New York City Fire Code, 2003), 238.

525. "Statement of Sally Regenhard," 9/11 Commission, November 19, 2003.

15 ~ QUESTION TO VICE PRESIDENT DICK CHENEY: "DID YOU HAVE OPEN LINES WITH THE SECRET SERVICE, NORAD, THE FAA, AND DOD? WHO WAS IN THE SITUATION ROOM WITH YOU?"

526 "The 'Misunderestimated' President," BBC, January 7, 2009.

527. Breitweiser, *Wake-Up Call*, 23. (See note 2.)

528. Family Steering Committee, questions to Vice President Richard Cheney, question 5.

529. Mindy Kleinberg and Lorie Van Auken, FSC Questions to the 9/11 Commission with Ratings of its Performance in Providing Answers, East Brunswick, NJ, 2004.*http://911truth.org/downloads/Family_Steering_Cmte_review_of_Report.pdf*

530. US Department of Homeland Security United States Secret Service, Freedom of Information Act Appeal - File Numbers 20080330 and 20080331. Released to Aidan Monaghan on April 23, 2010.

531. Stephen F. Hayes, *Cheney: The Untold Story of America's Most Powerful and Controversial Vice President*, (HarperCollins, 2007), 329-330.

532. "Moment of Crisis Part 2: Sept. 11 Scramble: A Plane Hits the Pentagon; Bush Takes Flight; Others Give Orders From Bunkers," ABC, September 14, 2002.

533. Inspectors James Todak and Dennis Chomicki, Interviews with ATSAIC Scott Johnson and SA James Scott, US Secret Service memorandum, October 1, 2001. FOIA released to Aidan Monaghan, April 23, 2010.

534. Tim Russert, Meet the Press with Dick Cheney, NBC, September 16, 2001.

535. USSS Statement and Interview Reports, 9/11 Commission, July 28, 2003. Interview Reports with Secret Service agents Nelson Garabito, Carl Truscott, and Danny Spriggs. *http://www.scribd.com/doc/14353654/DH-B5-Secret-Service-Requests-Fdr-Entire-Contents-5-Withdrawal-Notice-Doc-Req-Notes-Garabito-Shortly-After-9am-FAA-Van-Steenbergen-Said-4-Planes*

536. Kevin Ryan, "Secret Service Failures on 9/11: A Call for Transparency," Washington's Blog, March 25, 2012.

537. Susan Taylor Martin, "Of Fact, Fiction: Bush On 9/11," *St. Petersburg Times*, Tampa Bay, FL, July 4, 2004. See also Ralph Lopez, "9/11 Report Testimony Altered to Hide Cheney Role in Pentagon Hit," *Digital Journal*, February 2, 2015.

538. United States Secret Service, Actions of TSD Related to Terrorist Incident, September 12, 2001. FOIA released to Aidan Monaghan on April 23, 2010.

539. Evan Thomas, "The Story of September 11," *Newsweek*, Dec 31, 2001.

540. "Vice President Dick Cheney," News Hour with Jim Lehrer, PBS, September 9, 2002.

541. Barton Gellman and Jo Becker, "A Different Understanding with the President," *Washington Post*, June 24, 2007.

542. Family Steering Committee, Questions to Vice President Richard Cheney, question 8.

543. Kleinberg and Van Auken, FSC Questions to the 9/11 Commission.

544. Breitweiser, *Wake-Up Call,* 121. (See note 2.)

545. Family Steering Committee, Questions to Vice President Richard Cheney, question 7.

546. J. Michael Waller, "Preparing for the Next Pearl Harbor," *Insight on the News,* June 18, 2001.

547. Mark Danner, "How Dick Cheney Became the Most Powerful Vice President," *Nation* February 11, 2014.

16: QUESTION TO SECRETARY OF DEFENSE, DONALD RUMSFELD: "HOW IS IT POSSIBLE THAT THE NATIONAL MILITARY COMMAND CENTER, LOCATED IN THE PENTAGON AND IN CONTACT WITH LAW ENFORCEMENT AND AIR TRAFFIC CONTROLLERS FROM 8:46 A.M., DID NOT COMMUNICATE TO THE SECRETARY OF DEFENSE ALSO AT THE PENTAGON ABOUT THE OTHER HIJACKED PLANES ESPECIALLY THE ONE HEADED TO WASHINGTON?"

548. Mindy Kleinberg, "Statement of Mindy Kleinberg," 9/11 Commission, March 31, 2003, 10.

549. "Air Defense Interception Protocol," Joint Chiefs of Staff, June 1, 2002.

550. Phil Donahue, "Interview with Kristen Breitweiser of Families of 9/11," NBC, August 5, 2002.

551. Matthew L. Wald, "After The Attacks: Sky Rules; Pentagon tracked Deadly Jet But Found No Way to Stop It," *New York Times,* September 15, 2001.

552. "Primary Target," CBS, September 11, 2001.

553. Jim Yardley, "A Trainee Noted for Incompetence," *New York Times,* May 4, 2002.

554. Larry King Live, "Interview with Donald Rumsfeld," CNN, December 5, 2001.

555. "The Pentagon Strike," *Fayetteville Observer*, September 16, 2001.

556. Mindy Kleinberg, "Statement of Mindy Kleinberg," 9/11 Commission, March 31, 2003, 9.

557. Jim Mitchell, "Assistant Secretary Clarke Interview," WBZ Radio 1030, Boston, MA, September 15, 2001

558. Victoria Clarke, "Assistant Secretary Clarke Interview with WBZ Boston," interview by WBZ Radio 1030, Boston, MA, September 15, 2001. Andrew Cockburn, *Rumsfeld: His Rise, Fall and Catastrophic Legacy*, (Scribner, 2007), 3.

559. David Ray Griffin, *The 9/11 Commission Report: Omissions and Distortions*, (Olive Branch Press, Northampton, MA, 2005), 217-219.

560. Department of Defense, Washington DC, September 15, 2001

561. 9/11 Commission Transcript, Testimony of Donald Rumsfeld prepared for Delivery to the National Commission on Terrorist Attacks upon the United States.

562. Richard Clarke, *Against All Enemies*, (Free Press, 2004), 22.

563. Clarke, *Against All Enemies*, 1. (See note 562.)

564. Mike Ferullo, "Rumsfeld Urges Missile Defense System During Confirmation Hearing," CNN, January 11, 2001.

565. Donald Rumsfeld, *Known and Unknown: A Memoir*, (Sentinel, 2011), 334.

566. Vince Gonzales, "The War on Waste, Eye on America," CBS, January 29, 2002.

567. Milan Simonich, "Army History Unit Piecing Together Accounts of Pentagon Attack," *Pittsburg Post-Gazette*, December 16, 2001.

568. "Results in Brief: Improvements Needed in Transparency and Accountability of US Reserve component Equipment Transfers," Pentagon Inspector General, Washington DC, September 2012.

569. Scot J. Paltrow, "Behind the Pentagon Doctored Legers, A Running Tally of Epic Waste," *Reuters*, November 18, 2013.

570. Jamie McIntyre, "America Under Attack: Bush Holds Press Briefing," CNN, September 11, 2001.

571. Ibid.

572. Peter B. Collins, "The Boiling Frogs Presents Lorie Van Auken," Boiling Frogs, Podcast Show #51, August 19, 2011. *http://www.boilingfrogspost.com/2011/08/19/podcast-show-51*

573. Carol Ashley, "Statement on Aviation Security," 9/11 Commission, January 26, 2004.

574. Ron Suskind, *The Price of Loyalty: George W. Bush, the White House, and the Education of Paul O'Neill*, (Simon & Schuster, 2004), 85.

575. Family Steering Committee, Questions about Al Qaeda and State Sponsored Terrorism, question 10.

17 ~ QUESTION TO PRESIDENT GEORGE W. BUSH: "WHO APPROVED THE FLIGHT OF THE BIN LADEN FAMILY OUT OF THE UNITED STATES WHEN ALL COMMERCIAL FLIGHTS WERE GROUNDED. . . A PRIVILEGE NOT AVAILABLE TO AMERICAN FAMILIES WHOSE LOVED ONES WERE KILLED ON 9/11?"

576. Family Steering Committee, Questions to President George W. Bush, question 19.

577. Donna Marsh O'Connor, "September 11 Investigation Campaign," C-SPAN, National Press Club, Washington DC, September 11, 2006. *http://www.c-span.org/video/?194234-1/september-11-investigation-campaign#* Donna Marsh O'Connor begins to speak at minute 15:20.

578. Donna Marsh O'Connor, "9/11 Families Call For A New Investigation," National Press Club, Washington DC, September 12, 2006.

579. Kathy Steele, "Phantom Flight from Florida," *The Tampa Tribune*, October 5, 2001.

580. Ibid.

581. Craig Unger, *House of Bush, House of Saud: The Secret Relationship Between*

the World's Two Most Powerful Dynasties, (Scribner, 2004).

582. Kathy Steele, "Phantom Flights..." (See note 579.)

583. Craig Unger, "Saving the Saudis," *Vanity Fair,* October 2003.

584. Craig Unger, "Saving the Saudis." (See note 583)

585. Family Steering Committee, Questions about Al Qaeda and State Sponsored Terrorism, question 20.

586. Craig Unger, "Saving the Saudis." (See note 583)

587. Ibid.

588. Alexander Bolton, "Clarke Claims Responsibility. Ex-counterterrorism Czar Approved post-911 Flights For bin Laden Family. *The Hill,* May 26, 2004. In an email from Jon Gold on October 20, 2020, wrote "those flights...included Khalil bin Laden, someone wanted by Brazil investigators for 'possible terrorist connections... Senator Frank Lautenberg put the flight manifests on his site years ago and his [Khalil bin Laden's] name appeared on one of them."

589. Craig Unger, "Saving the Saudis." See note 583)

590. Ibid.

591. Ibid.

592. Ibid.

593. Levi Pulkkinen, "Key Witness in Seattle Terror Plot was Sex Offender," *Seattle Post-Intelligencer,* July 26, 2012.

594. Susan Kelleher and Steve Miletich, "Suspect's Troubled Past: Rap Sheet, Hallucinations," *Seattle Times,* June 24, 2011.

595. Susan Kelleher, "Suspect's Life Marked by Mental Illness, Acquaintance Says," *Seattle Times,* June 24, 2011.

596. "FBI Sting Foils Portland Terror Plot," CBS, November 27, 2010.

597. Ben Nuckols, "Lawyer: FBI Entrapped Baltimore Bomb Plot Suspect," *Associated Press,* December 13, 2010.

598. Glen Greenwald, "The FBI Successfully Thwarts its Own Terrorist Plot," *Salon*, November 28, 2010.

599. David K. Shipler, "Terrorist Plots, Hatched by the F.B.I.," *New York Times*, April 28, 2012.

600. Trevor Aaronson, *The Terror Factory: Inside the FBI's Manufactured War on Terrorism*, (Ig Publishing, 2013), 11.

601. Ibid., 15.

602. Greg Palast, "The Bush-bin Laden Family Connections & A Hidden Agenda," BBC Newsnight, November 1, 2001.

18 ~ QUESTION TO THE CIA ~ "PLEASE EXPLAIN THE ROLE OF THE ISI, PAKISTAN'S INTELLIGENCE AGENCY, IN AIDING BIN LADEN AND/OR THE AL QAEDA FROM 1998 THROUGH THE PRESENT."

603. Presidential Directive, National Security Decision Memorandum 40, Responsibility for the Conduct, Supervision and Coordination of Covert Action Operations, Washington DC, February 17, 1970. Signed: Richard Nixon.

604. William Blum, *Killing Hope: US Military and CIA Interventions Since World War II*, (Common Courage Press, 1995). Peter Dale Scott, "Transnational Repression: Parafascism and the US," *Lobster Magazine*, No. 12, 1986, 16.

605. Robert Dreyfuss, *Devil's Game: How the United States Helped Unleash Fundamentalist Islam*, (Metropolitan Books, 2005), 279-280.

606. Mary Anne Weaver, "The Real Bin Laden," *New Yorker*, January 24, 2000.

607. Michael Moran, "Bin Laden Comes Home to Roost," MSNBC, August 24,1998.

608. Veronique Marus and Marc Rock, "The Most Dreaded Man of the United States, Controlled a Long Time by the CIA," *Le Monde*, September 14, 2001.

609. Family Steering Committee, Questions to the CIA, question 15.

610. J. Orlin Grabbe, "When Osama Bin Ladin Was 'Tim Osman': Michael

Riconosciuto & Ted Gunderson's 1986 Meeting with 'Tim Osman' (Osama bin Laden)," *Laissez Faire City Times,* San Jose, Costa Rica, November 8, 2001.

611. "The CIA's Intervention in Afghanistan," Interview with Zbigniew Brzezinski, President Jimmy Carter's National Security Adviser, *Le Nouvel Observateur*, Paris, January 15-21, 1998. Translated from French by Bill Blum, Centre for Research on Globalization, October 5, 2001.

612. Gary C. Schroen, *First In: An Insider's Account of How the CIA Spearheaded the War on Terror in Afghanistan*, (Presidio Press, 2005), 12-14.

613. Bob Woodward, *Bush at War*, (Simon & Schuster, 2004), 4. See also, Barbara Slavin and Susan Page, "Attacks Throw Harsh Spotlight On CIA Director," *USA Today*, September 24, 2001.

614. "How Not to Catch a Terrorist," *The Atlantic*, December 2004; Matthew Continetti, "Scheuer v. Clarke," *Weekly Standard*, November 22, 2004.

615. "Intelligence Investigation," News Hour, PBS, September 11, 2001. See also Kevin Ryan, "Two Oklahoma Airports: David Boren, KuwAm, and 9/11," *DigWithin.net*, October 28, 2012. Ryan cites FBI summary documents that show Wiley Post Airport in Bethany, Oklahoma, was where 9/11 accomplices Mohamed Atta, Marwan al-Shehhi, Waleed al-Shehri, Saeed al-Ghamdi, and Hani Hanjour, were seen either visiting or flying planes. Wiley Post Airport is 20 miles from Norman, Oklahoma. How did the hijackers get connected to the flight schools in Oklahoma? See also, Andrew Griffith, "The OKC-9/11 Link the Media and Authorities Willfully Ignored," *Red Dirt News*, Oklahoma City, OK, September 9, 2011. *911Pilots.org* contends that the aircraft were electronically hijacked through employment of a system called the uninterruptible autopilot that enables a remote source to take complete control of the aircraft autopilot and flight management computers and guide it to its target. *If* proven, it would add a twist to David Boren's reference to "those who took over the aircraft."

616. Andrew de Borchgrave, "The Real Culprit of 9/11," *Washington Times*, July 22, 2004.

617. Amir Mateen, "ISI Chief's Parleys Continue in Washington," *The News*,

(Pakistan), September 10, 2001.

618. "US to Pressure Pakistan on Support for Taliban," *Deutsche Presse-Agentur*, Hamburg, Germany, September 12, 2001.

619. Dan Balz, Bob Woodward, and Jeff Himmelman, "Afghan Campaign's Blueprint Emerges," *Washington Post*, January 29, 2002.

620. Manoj Joshi, "India Helped FBI Trace ISI-Terrorist Links," *Times of India*, October 9, 2001.

621. James Taranto, "Our Friends the Pakistanis," *Wall Street Journal*, October 10, 2001.

622. On May 15, 2003, September Eleventh family members Carol Ashley, Patty Casazza, Beverly Eckert, Mary Fetchet, Monica Gabrielle, Bill Harvey, Mindy Kleinberg, Steve Push, and Lorie Van Auken met with Chairman Kean, Deputy Director Chris Kojm and Family Liaisons Emily Walker and Ellie Hartz in Madison, New Jersey. Porter Goss was part of the CIA's Operation 40 assassination squad in the 1960s and retired from clandestine work in 1971. Elected seven times to Congress, he was a co-sponsor of the USA Patriot Act. Goss publicly declared his opposition to the creation of an independent 9/11 Commission. He and Bob Graham co-chaired the Joint 9/11 Intelligence Inquiry. In May 2002 Goss called the uproar over the President's Daily Brief of August 6, "Bin Ladin Determined To Strike in US," "a lot of nonsense."

19 ~ QUESTION TO MAYOR GIULIANI: "ON 9/11, NO AIRCRAFT HIT WTC 7. WHY DID THE BUILDING FALL AT 5:20 PM THAT EVENING? . . . DOES "PULL" MEAN DEMOLISHED?"

623. Family Steering Committee, Unanswered Questions, Statement and Questions Regarding the 9/11 Commission Interview of Mayor Rudy Giuliani and Members of his Administration, question 13.

624. Front Line, Des Moines, Iowa, Sunday, June 10, 2001.

625. NOVA/PBS (1997) Interview with Stacey Loizeaux, Controlled Demolition, Inc.

626. Mark and Douglas K. Loizeaux, "Demolition by Implosion," *Scientific American*, October 1995.

627. Press Release, University of Louisiana at Monroe, Monroe, LA, September 20, 2004.

628. Lee Ann McAdoo, "9/11 Firefighter Blows WTC 7 Cover-up Wide Open," InfoWars, September 11, 2014.

629. Ibid.

630. "Randy McNally Building," Wikipedia.org. *https://en.wikipedia.org/wiki/Rand_McNally_Building*

631. Kevin Barrett, "Insurer Caps WTC-Demolition Asbestos Payout at 10 Million," Veterans Today, April 10, 2012.

632. *The 9/11 Commission Report*, p. 256.

633. "Jury Awards $2.2 Billion in 9/11 Insurance," United Press International, December 6, 2004.

634. Oral History of EMS Chief John Peruggia, WTC Task Force, October 25, 2001, p. 8. *https://static01.nyt.com/packages/pdf/nyregion/20050812_WTC_GRAPHIC/9110160.PDF*

635. Associated Press, "The Scene at the Towers," *Traverse City Record-Eagle*, Traverse City, Michigan, September 11, 2001.

636. Jason Bermas and Dylan Avery interview with Barry Jennings, February 2007, featured in documentary, *Fabled Enemies*. See *www.fabledenemies.com.* EMT Nicole Ferrell recalled when she was outside WTC7 "there were people screaming out of" the building "saying they couldn't get out, and my partner took one straggler fireman ... and was trying to break the door because the door obviously had shifted or something. They couldn't get the door open." See Oral History of EMT Nicole Ferrell, WTC Task Force, December 13, 2001, p. 6. *https://static01.nyt.com/packages/pdf/nyregion/20050812_WTC_GRAPHIC/9110304.PDF*

637. Ibid.

638. Shenon, *The Commission*, 347. (See note 74.)

639. Bermas and Avery, *Fabled Enemies*. (See note 636.)

640. Oral History of Captain Ray Goldbach, WTC Task Force (October 24, 2001), p. 8. *https://static01.nyt.com/packages/pdf/nyregion/20050812_WTC_GRAPHIC/9110150.PDF*

641. Oral History of EMT DeCosta Wright, WTC Task Force, October 11, 2001, pp. 11-12. *http://graphics8.nytimes.com/packages/pdf/nyregion/20050812_WTC_GRAPHIC/91102*

642. Oral History of Chief Thomas McCarthy, WTC Task Force, October 11, 2001, pp. 10-11. *http://graphics8.nytimes.com/packages/pdf/nyregion/20050812_WTC_GRAPHIC/91102*

643. Oral History of Richard Zarillo, EMT – FDNY, October 25, 2001, 6. *https://static01.nyt.com/packages/pdf/nyregion/20050812_WTC_GRAPHIC/9110161.PDF*

644. James Glanz, "Engineers Suspect Diesel Fuel in Collapse of 7 World Trade Center," *New York Times*, November 29, 2001.

645. FEMA Building Performance Assessment Team Report (BPAT), Washington DC, May, 2002.

646. Jane Standley, "September 11 Terrorist Attacks," BBC, September 11, 2001, 10:45 a.m. (EST) *https://archive.org/details/bbc200109111039-1121*

647. Jane Standley, "Terrorism Attacks in US," BBC, September 11, 2001. 4:20 EST to 4:30 EST. During a WTC Task Force Interview with Lieutenant Michael Cahill, EMS Division 6, Cahill reports he was at WTC7 when the building fell, after reporting to his superiors who had set up a triage station. The interviewer with the FDNY, Christopher Eccleston, tells Cahill in reply "Building seven came down I believe around 4:25?" Oral History of Lieutenant Michael Cahill, EMS Division 6, WTC Task Force, October 17, 2001, 34. *https://static01.nyt.com/packages/pdf/nyregion/20050812_WTC_GRAPHIC/9110143.PDF.*

648. September Eleventh family member, Matt Campbell, email correspondence with Ray McGinnis, October 14, 2020. Campbell provided his September 23,

2014, email correspondence from *Reuters* President and Editor in Chief, Steve Adler. It confirmed that someone "phoned in the information" to *Reuters* about the WTC7 building having collapsed before it actually collapsed, which *Reuters* passed on to the BBC.

649. Allan Dodds Frank, "Breaking News: America Under Attack," CNN, September 11, 2001, 11:07 a.m. *https://archive.org/details/cnn200109111053-1134*

650. Dylan Avery, "Interview with Craig Bartmer, NYPD Officer Heard Building 7 Bombs,"February 10, 2007.

651. "America Under Attack," CNN, September 11, 2001. *https://youtu.be/cU_43SwWD9A*

652. Amy Goodman, *The Exception to the Rulers: Exposing Oily Politicians, War Profiteers, and the Media That Love Them*, (Hyperion, 2004), 15-16.

653. "City Had Been Warned of Fuel Tank at 7 World Trade Center," *New York Times*, December 20, 2001.

654. BPAT, "WTC Building Performance Study," FEMA, May 2002, Chapter 5.

655. "Burning Diesel Is Cited in Fall of 3rd Tower," *New York Times*, March 2, 2002.

656. Lorie Van Auken, "Transcript for Lorie Van Auken's Speech - NYC Ballot Initiative – 11/24/2007," 911Blogger.com, New York, February 25, 2008. *http://911blogger.com/node/14058*

657. Arianne Cohen, "World Trade Center 7 Report Puts 9/11 Conspiracy Theory to Rest," *Popular Mechanics*, August 20, 2008.

658. "Final Report on the Collapse of World Trade Center Building 7, Federal Building and Fire Safety Investigation of the World Trade Center Disaster (NIST NCSTAR 1A)," NIST, November 20, 2008.

659. "Deputy Chief Peter Hayden," *Firehouse Magazine*, April 2002.

660. Ben Swann, "Reality Check: More Americans are Rethinking 911," Information Clearing House, September 10, 2013.

661. "New York Fire Commissioners Call For New 9/11 Investigation Citing 'Overwhelming Evidence of Explosives'," *zerohedge.com*, July 31, 2019.

662. Author phone interview with Fire Commissioner Christopher Gioia, Franklin Square & Munson Fire Department, January 25, 2020.

663. *Calling Out Bravo 7*, Firefighters for 9/11 Truth, 2020; R. J. Keough and R. A. Gill, "Fire Alarm Systems. Federal Building and Fire Safety Investigation of the World Trade Center Disaster," NIST NCSTAR 1-4C, Draft September 2005, 107, PDF 141.

664. *Calling Out Bravo 7*, Firefighters for 9/11 Truth, 2020.

665. "Deputy Chief Peter Hayden," *Firehouse Magazine*, April 2002.

666. Ibid.

667. Author phone interview with Fire Commissioner Chris Gioia, January 25, 2020.

668. J. Leroy Hulsey, Zhili Quan, and Feng Xiao, *A Structural Reevaluation of the Collapse of World Trade Center 7*, (University of Alaska Fairbanks, 2020). After the University of Alaska Fairbanks issued the final report of its four-year computer modeling study on the collapse of World Trade Center Building 7, Professor Hulsey was featured in the documentary *Seven*, directed by Dylan Avery, released in December 2020.

669. Letter from 98 signatories to Catherine Fletcher, Director, NIST Management and Organization Office, "Request for Correction Under the Data Quality Act to NIST's Final Report on the Collapse of World Trade Center Building 7," April 15, 2020. *https://files.wtc7report.org/file/public-download/RFC-to-NIST-WTC7-Report-04-15-20.pdf*

20 - THE STORY OF RECORD

670. Judd Legum and David Sirota, "2004: Vote For Bush or Die: In An Election Strategy Spawned from the Events of 9/11, the Republicans Challenged John Kerry by Politicizing Terror," *Nation*, September 9, 2004.

671. "Bush Ads with 9-11 Images Stir Controversy," *Seattle Times*, March 5, 2004.

672. Ibid.

673. Ibid.

674. Adam Nagourney, "The Republicans: The Convention in New York ~ Overview: Giuliani Lauds Bush's Leadership on Terror," *New York Times*, August 31, 2004.

675. Transcript, "John McCain, Rudy Giuliani Address Republican National Convention," CNN, August 30, 2004. *http://transcripts.cnn.com/ TRANSCRIPTS/0408/30/se.01.html*

676. "Ogonowski's House Bid Gets Boost," *Boston Globe*, April 27, 2007.

677. Aaron Blake, "9/11 victims' families carry GOP banner in Mass., Fla.," *The Hill*, Washington DC, May 7, 2007.

678. Evelyn Pringle, "Bush Gang Swore Saddam was Behind 9/11 in Lawsuit," *Counterpunch*, November 16, 2005. In the article, Evelyn Pringle refers to Laurie Mylroie as a "nutcase."

679. Ibid.

680. "Authorization for Use of Military Force Against Iraq Resolution of 2002," United States Congress, Washington DC, October 16, 2002. See also *The 9/11 Commission Report*, 333. President Bush told the 9/11 Commission that shortly after the attacks he thought those responsible might be Iraq or Iran. He said the sophistication of the piloting, especially Hani Hanjour's high-speed dive into the Pentagon, made him wonder about military training.

681. "Homeland Security Committee Holds Hearing on Unfulfilled 9/11 Recommendations," US Committee on Homeland Security and Governmental Affairs, January 10, 2007. *https://www.hsgac.senate.gov/media/minority-media/ homeland-security-committee-holds-hearing-on-unfulfilled-9/11-commission- recommendations*

682. "Testimony of Carie Lemack," Senate Committee on Homeland Security

and Governmental Affairs Hearing on Ensuring Implementation of the 9/11 Commission's Recommendations, Washington DC, January 9, 2007.

683. "Bin Laden's Goal: Kill 4 Million Americans," Newsmax, July 14, 2004. See also Paul Williams, *Osama's Revenge: The Next 9/11: What the Media and the Government Haven't Told You,* (Prometheus Books, 2004).

684. Editorial, "Under-the-Rug Oversight," *New York Times,* December 29, 2006.

685. "Testimony of Carol Ashley," Senate Committee on Homeland Security and Governmental Affairs Hearing on Ensuring Implementation of the 9/11 Commission's Recommendations, Washington DC, January 9, 2007.

686. "Statement of Mary A. Fetchet ..." Senate Committee on Homeland Security and Governmental Affairs Hearing on Ensuring Implementation of the 9/11 Commission's Recommendations, Washington DC, January 9, 2007.

687. "House Passes 911 Security Bill," CNN, January 9, 2007.

688. Roll Call Vote 110th Congress – 1st Session, Vote 284, United States Senate, July 26, 2007.

689. "Building What?" NYCCAN, 2010. *https://www.youtube.com/watch?v=AfK2h07yd9k*

690. "Geraldo at Large," FOX, November 13, 2010.

691. Matt Gertz, "Sean Spicer Cited a 9/11 Truther To Accuse The British of Spying on Trump for Obama," Media Matters For America, March 16, 2017.

692. Joe Strupp, "9/11 Families Speak Out Against Potential Beck Replacement's 'Truther' Theories," *mediamatters.org,* April 7, 2011.

693. "Voices of September 11th Gala Features Former British Prime Minister Tony Blair," Voices of September 11th, New Canaan, CT, May 17, 2010.

694. Susan Dahill, "Our Debt to Ray Kelly," Voices of September 11th, New Canaan, CT, January 1, 2014.

695. Mary Fetchet, "Voices of 9/11," NBC Nightly News with Brian Williams, September 11, 2006. *https://vimeo.com/29795259*

696. 1st Annual Always Remember Gala, Voices of September 11th, May 29, 2008. See also "National September 11 Memorial Museum Opens," FOX, May 21, 2014.

697. Patricia Cohen, "Sept. 11 Memorial Museum's Fraught Task: To Tell the Truth," *New York Times*, June 2, 2012.

698. Ibid.

699. Anita Huslin, "Charles Burlingame Attack Location, Remembering the Victims," *Washington Post*, September 16, 2001.

700. Julian Coman, "Families of 9/11 are 'the Rock Stars of Grief' says Sister of Pentagon Pilot," *Telegraph*, London, UK, June 27, 2004.

701. Debra Burlingame and Tim Sumner, "CIA Saved Lives; Senate's Partisan Enhanced Interrogation Report Endangers Americans," 9/11 Families for a Safe & Strong America, December 11, 2014. Burlingame and Sumner advocated torture as a reliable way to get terrorists to confess their crimes.

702. Debra Burlingame, "Obama Will Live To Regret Sending Gitmo Detainees To Illinois," *Breitbart.com*, December 11, 2009.

703. Michael McAuliff, "9/11 Widows Hit Cheney for Fighting KSM Trial," *New York Daily News*, November 24, 2009.

704. "9/11 Families For A Secure America Statement of Opposition to Amnesty For Illegal Aliens and Any Other Form of 'Legalization'," FSA Newsletter, May 19, 2007.

705. Peter Gadiel, "Impeach Now," VDare, June 2, 2007. *http:// www.911familiesforsecureamerica.com/pdf/gadiel/Imeach%20Now%206.2.07.pdf*

706. Peter Gadiel, "Victim's Dad: Why I'm Not Celebrating bin Laden's Death," CNN, May 3, 2011.

707. Peter Gadiel, "Opinion," Editorials, *USA Today*, July 19, 2010. Peter Gadiel testified before lawmakers, including Testimony For the House Judiciary Committee Oversight Hearing on "The Reid-Kennedy Bill's Amnesty: Impacts on Taxpayers, Fundamental Fairness and the Rule of Law," Concord, NH,

August 24, 2006. A primary goal for 9/11 Families For a Secure America is to "end 'chain migration'."

708. Glenn Kessler, "Some People Did Something: Rep. Omar's Remarks in Context," *Washington Post*, April 11, 2019.

709. "Frances Haros," 9/11 Living Memorial. *https://livingmemorial. voicesofseptember11.org/frances-haros*

710. "Mourners Use Reading of 9/11 Victims' Names to Criticize Rep. Omar and Decry Gun Violence," NBC, September 11, 2019.

711. Chandelis Duster, "Rep. Ilhan Omar Responds to Criticism from 9/11 Victim's Family," CNN, September 15, 2019. Rep. Omar told CNN that she was only trying to point out that all Americans had been attacked on September 11. And now Muslim Americans were all having to deal with their neighbors suspecting them of being terrorists.

712. Jay Kernis, "Carie Lemack: We Want Our Voice to be Louder Than Those Who Advocate for Terrorism," CNN, May 2011.

713. Tovia Smith, "Daughter Channels Sept. 11 Grief into Film, Activism," NPR, September 7, 2011.

714. Betwa Sharma, "Al-Qaida Attack Survivor Wages His Own Jihad," AOL News, October 11, 2010.

715. Carie Lemack, "The Daughter of a 9/11 Victim Reacts to the Death of bin Laden,"*Washington Post*, May 6, 2011.

716. "Mission Statement," Council on Foreign Relations, *cfr.org*, 2019.

21 ~ COVER-UP?

717. Statement from Barry Zelman, brother of Kenneth Zelman, who died on assignment with Marsh & McLennan on the 99th floor of the North Tower on September 11, 2001. Zelman made his statement at proceedings convened by Rep. Cynthia McKinney (D-GA), on Sept 9, 2004, in New York City. *https://www. youtube.com/watch?v=P-sZmKecPXI*

718. "9/11 Families Report: Unanswered Questions and the Call For Accountability," in Cynthia McKinney, *The 9/11 Commission Report One Year Later. A Citizen's Response: Did The Commission Get It Right?* (Congressional Briefing, July 22, 2005), 11. *https://911truth.org/downloads/McKinney-911Commission-OneYearLater.pdf*

719. "9/11 Family Member Patty Casazza: Government Knew Exact Date and Exact Targets, 9/11: Family Members, First Responders and Experts Speak Out!," 9/11 Symposium, Saint Joseph College, West Hartford, CT, November 3, 2007. *http://911truth.org/911-family-member-patty-casazza-government-knew-exact-date-and-exact-targets/*

720. Eric Lichtblau, "Another FBI Employee Blows Whistle on Agency," *New York Times*, August 2, 2004.

721. "Coleen Rowley's Memo to FBI Director Mueller: An Edited Version of the Agent's 13-page Letter," *TIME*, May 21, 2002.

722. Paul Sperry, "FBI Informant Revealed 9/11 Plot in April 2001," *WorldNetDaily*, March 24, 2004.

723. Brian Ross and Vic Walker, "Called Off The Trail? FBI Agents Probing Terror Links Say They Were Told, 'Let Sleeping Dogs Lie'," ABC, December 19, 2002.

724. Statement by Lorie Van Auken, "9/11 Families Report: Unanswered Questions and the Call For Accountability," in Cynthia McKinney, *The 9/11 Commission Report One Year Later. A Citizen's Response: Did The Commission Get It Right?* (Congressional Briefing, July 22, 2005), 11. *https://911truth.org/downloads/McKinney-911Commission-OneYearLater.pdf*

725. Ibid., 18.

726. Ibid.

727. Kean and Hamilton, *Without Precedent*, 81. (See note 102.)

728. Peter B. Collins, "Boiling Frogs: 'Jersey Girl' Lorie Van Auken Still Looking for Truth About 9/11," Boiling Frogs, August 26, 2011. *https://www.*

peterbcollins.com/2011/08/26/boiling-frogs-jersey-girl-lorie-van-auken-still-looking-for-truth-about-911/

729. Philip Shenon, "9/11 Commission Could Subpoena Oval Office Files," *New York Times*, October 26, 2003. Lee Hamilton expressed shock that 9/11 Commissioner Slade Gorton was having problems getting a security clearance. The *Seattle Times* reported Hamilton found it "astounding that someone like Senator Gorton can't get immediate clearance." Chairman Kean complained about the stonewalling from the White House, saying: "Any document that has to do with this investigation cannot be beyond our reach. I will not stand for it." Senator Joe Lieberman (D-CT) wondered what the White House was hiding. "After claiming they wanted to find the truth about September 11, the Bush administration has resorted to secrecy, stonewalling and foot-dragging. They have resisted this inquiry at every turn."

730. Monica Gabrielle, "The Personal Is Political," in Cynthia McKinney, *The 9/11 Commission Report One Year Later. A Citizen's Response: Did The Commission Get It Right?* (Congressional Briefing, July 22, 2005), 110. *https://911truth.org/downloads/McKinney-911Commission-OneYearLater.pdf*

731. Ibid. John Judge, Staff Member, Office of Rep. Cynthia McKinney, Staff Statement, Congressional Briefing, July 22, 2005, 110.

732. Jacob Goodwin, "Inside Able Danger-The Secret Birth, Extraordinary Life and Untimely Death of a US Military Intelligence Program," *Government Security News*, September 2005.

733. Dan Eggen, "No Evidence Pentagon Knew of Atta, Panel Says," *Washington Post*, August 13, 2005.

734. "Agent Defends Military Unit's Data on 9/11 Hijackers," FOX news, August 17, 2005.

735. Jarrett Murphy, "9-11 Probers Leave Questions Behind," *Village Voice*, New York, November 22, 2005.

736. Voices of 911, "Testimony of Janette MacKinlay," Here Is New York Voices of 911. *http://hereisnewyorkv911.org/2011/janette-mackinlay/*

737. Carol Brouillet, "Celebrating Life's Blessings – Janette MacKinlay," *911truth. org*, February 27, 2011. Janette MacKinlay, "Art to Activism," Grand Lake Theater, Oakland, CA, February 23, 2006. *http://www.communitycurrency.org/janettestalk. html*

738. Janette MacKinlay, Presentation at UC Davis, Davis 911 Truth, May 1, 2009.*http://911blogger.com/news/2011-11-27/janette-mackinlay-speaks-uc-davis-may-1-2009 ;* Brouillet, "Celebrating Life's Blessings ..." (See note 737.)

739. *The 9/11 Commission Report*, p. xvi.

740. Janette MacKinlay, Presentation at UC Davis.

741. Brouillet, "Celebrating Life's Blessings..." (See note 737.)

742. Nowosielski, *9/11 Press for Truth*, (See note 11.)

743. Ibid., "Mindy Kleinberg Interview."

744. "Interview with Rebecca Abrahams," *9/11 Press for Truth*. President Clinton told the nation on January 26, 1998, "I did not have sexual relations with that woman, Miss Lewinsky." See Steve Nelson, "Bill Clinton 15 Years Ago: 'I Did Not Have Sexual Relations With That Woman'," *US News & World Report*, January 25, 2013.

745. Joseph Nagle, "9/11 Press For Truth on Channel 12 Draws Huge Support from Colorado Public Television Viewers," KBDI (PBS), Denver, CO, June 4, 2009.

746. Jesse McKinley, "9/11 Miniseries Is Criticized as Inaccurate and Biased," *New York Times*, September 6, 2006.

747. Jesse McKinley, "FBI Agents Question Accuracy of 9/11 Series," *New York Times*, September 8, 2006.

748. Breitweiser. *Wake-Up Call*, 285. (See note 2.)

749. "Eye-opening Memoir by the Spouse of a 9/11 Victim," *Kirkus Reviews*, New York, NY, July 1, 2006.

750. Dr. Helen Stein, "Book Review: Wake-Up Call: The Political Education

of a 9/11 Widow," *Psychiatry Online*, Vol. 58, Issue 5, May, 2007, 722-723.

751. Ruth Mormon, "Wake-Up Call: The Political Education of a 9/11 Widow," RoadTrip America, September 10, 2006.

752. Randy Dotinga, "9/11: Is there Anything More to Say," *Christian Science Monitor*, September 7, 2006.

753. "Gordon and Kathleen Haberman: Parents of Andrea Lyn Haberman," *http://patriotsquestion911.com/survivors.html* Gordon and Kathleen Haberman

754. Mike Nichols, "Andrea Haberman had a Fiancé, a Job, and a Business Trip Sept. 11," *Journal Sentinel*, Milwaukee, Wisconsin, September 3, 2011.

755. "Gordon and Kathleen Haberman: Parents of Andrea Lyn Haberman," *http://patriotsquestion911.com/survivors.html* Gordon and Kathleen Haberman

756. "Gordon and Kathleen Haberman," *http://patriotsquestion911.com/survivors. html*

757. Richard Greene, "Interview with Senator Bob Kerrey: Former 9/11 Commission Member," Air America, March 2, 2008.

758. "Paul Jay interview with Sen. Bob Graham: FBI Covered Up Role of Bandar and Saudis in 9/11 Attacks (Pt.1/2)," The Real News Network, September 11, 2016.

759. "Fahad Althumairy (Non-Usper) IT – Other (UBL/Al-Qaeda) – Secret," FBI, September 4, 2002.

760. Kristen Breitweiser, "29 Pages Revealed: Corruption, Crime and Cover-up Of 9/11," *Huffington Post*, July 17, 2017.

761. Evan Solomon, "Truth, Lies and Conspiracy." CBC, August 30, 2006.

762. "9/11 Icon Bill Doyle Openly Condemns US Government Complicity and Cover-up," *911Truth.org*, July 8, 2006. See also "Bill Doyle, Father of Joseph Doyle, Endorses a New Investigation in NYC," *911Truth.org*, July 16, 2009.

763. Brian J. Tumulty, "The New Jersey Woman Who Beat Obama On the 9/11 Bill," *USA Today*, September 30, 2016. Bill Doyle told ABC there were "concrete

facts" demonstrating that most of the hijackers' funds came from Saudi Arabia. Doyle believed the suppression of documents linking Saudi Arabia to the 9/11 attacks was part of a cover-up.

764. Chris Baynes, "US Court Allows 9/11 Victims' Lawsuits Claiming Saudi Arabia Helped Plan Terror Attack," *Independent*, London, UK, March 29, 2018.

765. Tim Golden and Sebastian Rotella, "Attorney General Barr Refuses to Release 9/11 Documents to Victims' Families," ProPublica, April 18, 2020. Attorney General Barr's attitude echoed the stance of key officials regarding documents sealed after the attack on Pearl Harbor. According to the chief historian of the NSA, David W. Gaddy, it was "in the public interest" to censor the release of information involving American cryptographic success with Japan's naval systems. Gaddy stated: "The subject cannot be debated publicly; The government cannot disclose the basis for its position if the basis is itself part of the secret it must protect as part of its obligation to secure the public interest." Cited in Robert Stinnett, *Day of Deceit: The Truth About FDR and Pearl Harbor*, (Free Press, 2001), 82.

22 - THE MISSINGS ACCOUNTS: FDNY

766. Family Steering Committee for the 9/11 Independent Commission, Unanswered Questions,Port Authority/WTC/City of New York, question 9. "Why won't the Port Authority in concert with the City of NY release the 9/11 tapes?"

767. "9/11 Family Member Patty Casazza: Government Knew Exact Date and Exact Targets, 9/11: Family Members, First Responders and Experts Speak Out!," University of Hartford, CT, November 5, 2006. *http://www.911truth.org/ tag/patty-casazza/*

768. *The 9/11 Commission Report*, 306.

769. Oral History of Fire Marshall John Coyle, World Trade Center Task Force, December 28, 2001, 7-8, 10, 12, 15-16. *https://static01.nyt.com/packages/ pdf/nyregion/20050812_WTC_GRAPHIC/9110406.PDF*

770. Oral History of Captain Karin DeShore, November 7, 2001, 10-11, 15, 16, 17-18.*https://static01.nyt.com/packages/pdf/nyregion/20050812_WTC_GRAPHIC/9110192.PDF*

771. Oral History of Firefighter Keith Murphy, December 5, 2001, 19-20.*https://static01.nyt.com/packages/pdf/nyregion/20050812_WTC_GRAPHIC/9110238.PDF*

772. Ibid.

773. Oral history of Assistant Commissioner Stephen Gregory, October 3, 2001, 14-16.*https://static01.nyt.com/packages/pdf/nyregion/20050812_WTC_GRAPHIC/9110008.PDF*

774. Oral history of EMT Michael Ober, October 16, 2001, 4.

https://static01.nyt.com/packages/pdf/nyregion/20050812_WTC_GRAPHIC/9110093.PDF

775. Oral history of Firefighter William Reynolds, December 11, 2001, 3.*https://static01.nyt.com/packages/pdf/nyregion/20050812_WTC_GRAPHIC/9110288.PDF*

776. Oral history of Firefighter Christopher Fenyo, December 11, 2001, 6-7. *https://static01.nyt.com/packages/pdf/nyregion/20050812_WTC_GRAPHIC/9110295.PDF*

777. Ted Walter and Graeme MacQueen, "How 36 Reporters Brought Us the Twin Towers' Explosive Demolition on 9/11," *ae911truth.org*, July 8, 2020.

778. Pat Dawson, "Third Explosion Shatters World Trade Center," NBC: Breaking News, from Ground Zero, September 11, 2001.

779. Ann Thompson, MSNBC LIVE, September 11, 2001.

780. "On the Phone: John Bussey: The Wall Street Journal," CNBC, September 11, 2001.

781. Rick Sanchez, "Both World Trade Center Towers Have Collapsed," MSNBC, September 11, 2001.

782. Walter Perez, "9:59 AM, Eyewitness Reporting: Live Chopper 4," WNBC, September 11, 2001.

783. Cynthia McFadden, "News Live Coverage: Lower Manhattan," ABC, September 11, 2001.

784. Mika Brzezinski, "World Trade Center," CBS, September 11, 2001.

785. Marcia Kramer, "Ground Level Explosion Caused WTC to Collapse," CBS2, New York, NY, September 11, 2001.

786. Rose Arce, "Breaking News: Both Towers at WTC Collapses," CNN, September 11, 2001.

787. Steve Evans, Live from New York, BBC, September 11, 2001.

788. "BBC Reporter at Centre of Attack," *Guardian*, London, UK, September 11, 2001.

789 "Live News Coverage: Don Dahler Reporting," ABC, September 11, 2001.

790. Peter Jennings, "Interview with Marlene Cruz, WTC Survivor," ABC, September 12, 2001. The basement levels where Marlene Cruz lay for 40 minutes were 1,100 feet below the airplane's point of impact at floors 93 to 98.

791. Address by Anthony Saltalamacchia, World Trade Centers Dispatcher and Maintenance Supervisor, Freedom Law School, Justice, Peace & Freedom Conference, Dallas, TX, November 2007.

792. "United in Courage," *People,* September 12, 2001.

793. "We Will Not Forget: First-Hand Accounts of Underground Explosions in the North Tower," *The Chief Engineer*, October 29, 2001.

794. Ibid.

795. "It Was Either Be Burnt Alive or Jump," *Sydney Morning Herald*, Sydney, Australia, September 12, 2001.

796. Angela Wintle, "Interview: The Untold Story of September 11," *The Argus*, (Brighton, UK), February 26, 2007.

797. Don Harkins, Editor. "Foundational Witness Testimony, Taken Secretly by 9/11 Commission, Omitted from Final Report," Citizens 9/11 Commission Report, *Idaho Observer*, 2004.

798. "United In Courage," *People*, September 12, 2001. In addition to Kim White, other workers above the ground floor reported explosions. On the 38th floor, Joe Shearin exited the elevator and started to walk down the hallway to a meeting. A few seconds later he heard a deafening explosion and he was hurled into the air. Shearin told a reporter: "I can't even tell you how far I traveled." As he landed back on the hallway floor office workers flooded into the hallway screaming and asking him what they should do. "We Will Not Forget: A Day of Terror," *The Chief Engineer*, July, 2002.

799. Andrew Steele, "9/11 Victim's Family Member and Others Insulted by Maddow's 9/11 Truth Attack," *911Blogger.com*, May 3, 2013.

800. Shenon, *The Commission,* 118. (See note 74.)

801. Evan Solomon, "Truth, Lies and Conspiracy." (See note 286.)

802. Evan Thomas, "Interview of Eric Edelman," *Newsweek*, October 25, 2001

803. Steven Jones, "Why Indeed Did the WTC Buildings Completely Collapse," *Journal of 9/11 Studies*, Vol. 3, 2006, 1-47, 28.

804. Liz Else, "Baltimore Blasters," *New Scientist*, July 24, 2004.

805. For its part NIST chose to avoid addressing the behavior of the South Tower once it began to collapse by stating that the Final NIST 9-11 Report "does not actually include the structural behavior of the tower after the conditions for collapse initiation were reached." NIST Final 9-11 Report, p. 80, footnote 12.

806. "Live Mayor Rudolph Giuliani," *ABC*, September 11, 2001.

807. Richard Gary Shinn USAF (Ret.), *Let Me Know When You See Fire*, *AE911Truth.org*, 2010.

808. Transcript of 9/11 radio transmissions of North Brunswick Volunteer Fire/Ladder Company #3," *Newsday*, (Long Island), November 26, 2002.

809. "Press Conference of the President," Rose Garden, White House, September 15, 2006.

810. "9/11 Rescuer Saw Explosions Inside WTC 6 Lobby," Killtown, February

10, 2006. *http://killtown.blogspot.com/2006/02/911-rescuer-saw-explosions-inside-wtc.html*

811. Oral history of Lt. Rene Davilla, October 12, 2001, 25-26, 31-32, 34, 38-39. 42-50.*https://static01.nyt.com/packages/pdf/nyregion/20050812_WTC_GRAPHIC/9110075.PDF*

812. "Monica Gabrielle interview," *9/11 Press For Truth*, 2006.

813. H.S. Lew, Richard W. Bukowski, and Nicholas J. Carino, *Federal Building and Fire Safety Investigation of the World Trade Center: Design, Construction, and Maintenance of Structure and Safety Systems*, (National Institute of Standards and Technology, 2005) pp. 70-71.

814. CNN Morning News, "Transcript," September 24, 2001.

815. S. Shyam Sunder and Richard G. Gann, NCSTAR1, Final Report on the Collapse of the World Trade Center Towers, NIST, 2005, p. 183.

816. Franco Fracassi and Francesco Trento, directors, "Brian Clark, South Tower Survivor Interview," *ZERO: An Investigation Into 9/11*, TPF Telemaco, Italy, 2007.

817. "Stanley Praimnath: Survivor, World Trade Center South Tower, 81st Floor," *Time*, September 11, 2011.

818. Robin Nieto, "Fire Practically Destroys Venezuela's Tallest Building," *venezuelanaalysis.com*, October 18, 2004.

819. "Live Coverage: World Trade Center," FOX 5 News, New York City, September 11, 2001

820. Anne Karpf, "Uncle Sam's Lucky Finds," *Guardian*, London, UK, March 19, 2002.

821. NIST Report, 2005, 80. (See note 815)

822. NIST Report, 2005, xliii, 171. (See note 815)

823. Jim Dwyer, "Unit Plans Closed Hearings on Collapse of Towers," *New York Times*, November 12, 2004.

824. "New York Fire Commissioners Call For New 9/11 Investigation Citing

'Overwhelming Evidence of Explosives'," *zerohedge.com*, July 31, 2019.

825. Ted Walter, "New York Area Fire Commissioners Make History, Call for New 9/11 Investigation," Architects and Engineers for 9/11 Truth, Berkeley, CA, July 27, 2019.

826. "New York Fire Commissioners Call For New 9/11 Investigation Citing 'Overwhelming Evidence of Explosives'," *zerohedge.com*, July 31, 2019.

23 - CAMPAIGNS FOR A NEW INDEPENDENT INVESTIGATION

827. *http://peacefultomorrows.org/members/colleen-kelly/*

828. "Ailing bin Laden 'Treated for Kidney Disease'," *Times*, London, UK, November 1, 2001. Paul Thompson, "July 4-14, 2001" and "July 12, 2001," *The Terror Timeline*, 2004.

829. David Ray Griffin, *The New Pearl Harbor*, (Olive Branch Press, 2004), 71-87.

830. Griffin, *The New Pearl Harbor*, i. (See note 829.)

831. David Ray Griffin, *The New Pearl Harbor Revisited: 9/11, the Cover-up, and the Expose*, (Interlink, 2008), i. One year prior to her endorsement of Griffin's book, Monica Gabrielle spoke to the *Hartford Courant* about the lack of government accountability and the official story. She said: "I am disgruntled, disgusted and dismayed …. I am more baffled today than I was six years ago. I am more suspicious and I am less inclined to believe." Rick Green, "A 9/11 Widow: Disgust, Dismay," *Hartford Courant*, September 11, 2007.

832. "Respected Leaders and Families Launch 9/11 Truth Statement Demanding Deeper Investigation into the Events of 9/11," *911Truth.org*, October 26, 2004.

833. Ibid.

834. Evelyn Leopold, "Engine 49-Ladder 35 – Where a 9/11 'Family' Gathers Near Lincoln Center," *Huffington Post*, September 12, 2011.

835. Tina Kelley, "KEVIN SHEA; A Firefighter Asks Why He, Alone, Survived … and Why He Remembers So Little," *New York Times*, September 11, 2002.

836. "9/11 Truth Statement Demands Deeper Investigation," *911Truth.org*, October 26, 2004.

837. Ibid.

838. Donna Marsh O'Connor, September 11 Investigation Campaign, C-SPAN, National Press Club, Washington DC, September 11, 2006. *http://www.c-span.org/ video/?194234-1/september-11-investigation-campaign#* Donna Marsh O'Connor begins to speak at minute 15:20 of the CSPAN coverage. See also Remembering September 11, 2001, Vanessa Langer, *New York Times*, October 1, 2001. *http:// www.legacy.com/sept11/story.aspx?personid=116443*

839. September 11 Investigation Campaign, C-SPAN, National Press Club, September 11, 2006. *http://www.c-span.org/video/?194234-1/september-11- investigation-campaign#* Michelle Little speaks at 24:40, and Christina Kminek speaks at 30:20.

840. Ginna Hustings and Martin Orr, "Dangerous Machinery: 'Conspiracy Theorist' as a Transpersonal Strategy of Exclusion," *Symbolic Interaction*, Vol. 30, Issue 2, 127.

841. Dorothy Lorig interview, *The Demolition of Truth – Psychologists Examine 9/11*, Colorado Public Television, August 25, 2016, (1:13:51ff) *http://www.cpt12. org/9-11/*

842. Dorothy Lorig interview, *9/11: Explosive Evidence — Experts Speak Out* (ESO), Architects & Engineers for 9/11 (1:12:29ff) *https://www.ae911truth.org/continuing- ed/ae911-eso-90*

843. Jonathan Kay, *Among the Truthers: A Journey Through America's Conspiracist Underground* (Harpers, 2011), XVII. Kay states "women are not intelligent enough to wrestle with these deep puzzles of conspiracy." He also contends men who question the official account by the 9/11 Commission are suffering from a "midlife crisis." Kay was 43 when *Among the Truthers* was published.

844. Ginamaria Capogreco, "Ann Coulter Attacks 9/11 Widows," CBS, June 7, 2006.

845. "Philadelphia Defense Attorney for Federal Conspiracy Charges,"

hopelefeber.com, 2019. The website features a whole section on Conspiracy Law.

846. Lance deHaven-Smith, *Conspiracy Theory in America* (University of Texas Press, 2013, 7.

847. "Key Indicators in Media and News," Pew Research Journalism Project, March 26, 2014.

848. Lance deHaven-Smith, *Conspiracy Theory in America*, 7. (See note 846.)

849. Ibid.

850. Ibid.

851. Ibid., 9-10. DeHaven Smith points to CIA operations to introduce the term 'conspiracy theory' into everyday language on April 1, 1967, as a way to discredit assassination theories described in numerous books concerning the killing of President John F. Kennedy. See "Cable Sought to Discredit Critics of Warren Report," *New York Times*, December 25, 1977.

852. Evan Solomon, "Interview with Bob McIlvaine," CBC, August 30, 2006.

853. Author phone interview with September Eleventh family member Bob McIlvaine, March 5, 2020.

854. Patty Casazza, Monica Gabrielle, Mindy Kleinberg, Lorie Van Auken, "Open Letter to Senator Patrick Leahy," *Scoop Independent News*, Wellington, NZ, March 3, 2009.

855. Casazza, Gabrielle, Kleinberg and Van Auken, "Open Letter to Senator Patrick Leahy."

856. Alex Kingsbury, "Why Sen. Patrick Leahy Wants a 'Truth Commission'," *US News*, March 4, 2009.

857. Ibid.

858. "NYC Ballot Initiative for New 9/11 Investigation," *Reuters*, September 11, 2009. Among those endorsing the ballot initiative was Senator Lincoln Chafee (R-RI). After his retirement, Chafee was publicly endorsed and touted as a possible Commissioner of a new investigation into September 11 as described in the

New York City Ballot Initiative. It was called the Petition to Create a NYC Independent Commission with Subpoena Power to Conduct a Comprehensive and Fact-Driven Investigation of All Relevant Aspects of the Tragic Events of September 11, 2001, and Issue a Report. The petition's signers agreed "there remain many unanswered questions critical to establishing the truth about all relevant events leading up to, during and subsequent to the tragic attacks occurring on September 11, 2001." They asked that a temporary New York City commission be established "to conduct a comprehensive, fact-driven investigation into the events that took place on 9/11, as well as to thoroughly examine related events before and after the attacks, including any activities attempting to hide, cover up, impede or obstruct any investigation into these 9/11 events, following wherever the facts may lead. The Commission shall publish one or more reports of their findings." See "City of New York Concedes 9/11 Coalition Has 30,000 Valid Signatures to Put Referendum for 9/11 Investigation on November Ballot," PRNewswire, New York, September 10, 2009.

859. "Jane Pollicino Interview: NYC CAN Update 911 Family Member Speaks Out," NYC CAN, September 23, 2009. *https://www.youtube.com/ watch?v=O6H3ZQudZG0* Jane Pollicino later died of a stroke at age 59 on February 21, 2013.

860. "Statement by Jean Carnavan," sister-in-law of Sean Carnavan, age 39, who died on September Eleventh. *https://www.youtube.com/watch?v=TzC3QI8Jen U&eurl=http%3A%2F%2Fwww.911blogger.com%2Fblog&feature=player_embedded* See also bio on Sean Caravan, Remember September 11, 2001. *www.legacy.com/ Sept11/Story.aspx?PersonID=104522&location=1*

861. Dan Eggen, "9/11 Panel Suspected Deception by Pentagon," *Washington Post*, August 2, 2006.

862. "Statement by Janette MacKinlay," NYC CAN, May 2009. *https://www. youtube.com/watch?v=ZQN1wXDlt5I*

863. November 2008 New York City Ballot Initiative: "Petition to Create a NYC Independent Commission with Subpoena Power to Conduct a Comprehensive and Fact-Driven Investigation of All Relevant Aspects of the Tragic Events of

September 11, 2001 and Issue a Report; Will Glovinsky, "Clerk Shuts Down 9/11 Initiative," *The Villager*, New York, August 12-18, 2009.

864. "Remembering September 11, 2001: Thomas Joseph Sgroi, Obituary," *New York Times*, December 20, 2001. *http://www.legacy.com/sept11/story.aspx?personid=137740* Manny Badillo, nephew of Thomas Joseph Sgroi, at the 9/11/2010 Memorial Ceremony in NYC. *https://www.youtube.com/watch?v=U8mdoYOqaIc*

865. Patty Casazza, Monica Gabrielle, Mindy Kleinberg and Lorie Van Auken, "'Jersey Girls' Applaud The Efforts of Architects & Engineers for 9/11 Truth," *AE911Truth.org*, February 25, 2010.

866. Ibid.

867. See Highrise Safety Initiative Facebook timeline, February 20, 2014. *https://www.facebook.com/highrisesafetynyc/timeline?ref=page_internal*

868. Andrew J. Hawkins, "9/11 Conspiracy Group Could Force its way Onto Ballot: Long Marginalized by the Public, a Small Band of Activists Suspicious of the Government's Explanations of 7 World Trade Center's Collapse Have Hired Top Political Consultants to Put a Referendum in Front of Voters this November," *Crain's New York Business*, June 25, 2014.

869. "De Blasio Blasts 9/11 Investigation Ballot Proposal," NBC4, New York, July 11, 2014.

870. Andrew J. Hawkins, "De Blasio Blasts 9/11 Truther Ballot Initiative," *Crain's New York Business*, July 10, 2014.

871. "Coverage of the High-rise Safety Initiative," Spectrum News NY1, New York, NY, July 13, 2014. *http://911blogger.com/news/2014-07-13/ny1-coverage-high-rise-safety-initiative* Valerie Lucznikowska's nephew, Adam Arias, was a vice president for Euro Brokers and worked on the 84th floor of the South Tower. "Adam Arias – World Trade Center: A Lover and A Fighter," *New York Times*, October 24, 2001. *http://www.legacy.com/sept11/story.aspx?personid=96005*

872. Gabrielle Sierra, "9/11 Conspiracy Theory May Finally Be Settled on November Ballot," *Gothamist*, July 10, 2014.

873. "Bid to Solve 9/11 Mystery Via NYC Ballot Ends After Court Ruling," *whowhatwhy.org*, October 9, 2014.

874. "Bobby McIlvaine World Trade Center Investigation Act: A Call for Justice," 911Truth Action Project (9/11 TAP!), *911tap.org*, January 12, 2018.

875. Author phone conversation with September Eleventh family member, Bob McIlvaine, March 5, 2020.

876. Ibid.

877. Ibid.

878. "Firefighter Thomas Spinard Interview," World Trade Center Task Force, January 11, 2002, p. 5.

879. "Firefighter Fernando Camacho Interview," World Trade Center Task Force, December 12, 2001.

880. Robert G. McIlvaine, "Only One Dream Short," *New York Times*, September 19, 2001.

881. Craig McKee, "Bob McIlvaine On How His Son's Death Points to Controlled Demolition," *truthandshadows.wordpress.com*, September 10, 2016.

882. Author phone conversation with September Eleventh family member Bob McIlvaine, March 5, 2020.

883. David Ray Griffin and Elizabeth Woodworth, *9/11 Unmasked: An International Review Panel Investigation,* (Olive Branch Press, 2018), ix, 227.

884. Ibid., 227.

885. David Ray Griffin and Elizabeth Woodworth, *9/11 Unmasked.* (See note 883.) Lorie Van Auken's endorsement is on the back cover.

886. Kevin Ryan, *Another Nineteen: Investigating Legitimate 9/11 Suspects,* (CreateSpace, 2013). In her endorsement, Lorie Van Auken adds "Kevin has laid out the historical framework in a way that has never been done before. The importance of this cannot be overstated."

24 ~ SEPTEMBER ELEVENTH NARRATIVES

887. "Sept. 11 Museum Evokes Strong Emotions," *Stamford Advocate*, Stamford, CT, May 16, 2014.

888. 9/11 Memorial and Museum *https://www.911memorial.org*

889. Manny Fernandez, "Museum To Address Role Of The Hijackers," *New York Times*, September 11, 2009.

890. Doug Hanchett and Robin Washington, "Logan Lacks Video Cameras," *Boston Herald*, September 29, 2001.

891. David Harrison, "Revealed: The Men With Stolen Identities," *Telegraph*, London, UK, September 23, 2001; "Hijack Suspects Alive And Well," BBC, September 23, 2001; Lisa Getter, Elizabeth Mehren, and Eric Slater, "FBI Chief Raises New Doubts Over Hijackers' Identities," *Los Angeles Times*, September 21, 2001; Dan Eggen, George Lardner Jr., and Susan Schmidt, "Some Hijackers' Identities Uncertain," *Washington Post*, September 20, 2001; "Dead Saudi Hijack Suspect Resurfaces, Denies Involvement," *Daily Trust*, Abuja, Nigeria, September 24, 2001. In another news story, the father of Mohammed Atta said he spoke to his son by phone on September 12, 2001. According to his father, Mohammed Atta was alive the day after the attacks. (See Neil MacFarquhar, "Egyptian Man Denies Son's Involvement in Hijackings, Calls Accusations 'Nonsense'," *New York Times*, September 19, 2001). At a press conference in March 2003, Commissioner Richard Ben-Veniste was asked "If Atta belonged to the fundamentalist Muslim group, why was he snorting cocaine and frequenting strip bars?" Ben-Veniste responded by saying "You know that's a heck of a question." But the question was never dealt with by the 9/11 Commission. (See Sander Hicks, "No Easy Answer: Heroin, Al Qaeda and the Florida Flight School," *Long Island Press*, February 26, 2004). Atta was variously described in the press as 5' 10" (Elaine Allen-Emrich and Jann Baty, "Hunt For Terrorists Reaches North Port," *Charlotte Sun*, Charlotte, NC, September 14, 2001) and as short as 5'3" ("Professor Dittmar Machule," Interview by Liz Jackson, A Mission to Die For, Four Corners, October 18, 2001). He was described as "reserved," an "introvert," "polite," "very nice," not a "bodyguard type" but "more a girl type," having "a bad attitude," being

"aggressive, rude," "unpleasant, arrogant and obnoxious." He was someone who never touched liquor or women, who "was drunk [and whose] voice was slurred," and "spent $200 to $300 … on lap dances in the Pink Pony strip club." (See David Wedge, "Terrorists Partied with Hooker at Hub-Area Hotel," *Boston Herald*, October 10, 2001).

892. "9/11 Widow Dies in NY Plane Crash," BBC, February 13, 2009.

893. David W. Dunlap, "A Memorial Inscription's Grim Origins," *New York Times*, April 2, 2014.

894. Madeline Miller, "Myth Of The Week: Nisus and Euryalus," *madelinemiller. com*, March 26, 2012.

895. Dunlap, "A Memorial Inscription's Grim Origins." (See note 893.)

896. Ibid.

897. Ibid.

898. Dustin Slaughter, "Review: 'This Is Not About 9/11'," *The Declaration*, Philadelphia, PA, June 22, 2014.

899. Sarah Van Auken Interview, News 12, New York City, September 11, 2014.

900. Margaret Eby, "The Daughter of a 9/11 Victim Makes a Powerful Statement," *hellogiggles.com*, Los Angeles, CA, September 11, 2014.

901. Ibid.

902. Ibid.

903. Richard Hopkins Squires, *A Blanket Of Dust*, 2016. Jo-Anne Rowney, "Remembering 9/11: Heartbreaking final words and calls of those who died inside the Twin Towers," Mirror, UK, September 11, 2018. On Sept. 11 Kevin Cosgrove was on the 105th floor of the South Tower. He was on a landline call to emergency services from 9:45 a.m. until 9:59 a.m., as the South Tower began to collapse.

904. "Mark Crispin Miller, Bob McIlvaine, Playwright Richard Squires Discuss 'A Blanket of Dust' following Next Wednesday's Show at the Flea," *AE911Truth.*

org, June 21, 2018.

905. R. E. Griffin, "The Truth is in the Ruins," 911 Truth Action Project, June 17, 2018. *https://www.911tap.org/557-news-releases/744-world-premiere-of-a-blanket-of-dust*

906. Author phone interview with September Eleventh family member Bob McIlvaine, March 5, 2020.

907. Frederic Riskin, *9/11 The Collapse of Conscience, September 11 – October 13, 2018*, Feldman Gallery, New York, August 15, 2018. *https://feldmangallery.com/assets/pdfs/artistCV/Riskin_PressRelease_180912_204426.pdf*

908. *Everything Is Connected: Art And Conspiracy*, Met Breuer Museum, New York, September 18, 2018 to January 6, 2019. *https://www.metmuseum.org/exhibitions/listings/2018/everything-is-connected-art-and-conspiracy*

909. Zachary Small, "Conspiracy Theories Are Not Entertainment," *The Nation*, October 31, 2018.

910. *Everything Is Connected: Art And Conspiracy* (See note 908.)

CONCLUSION

911. Patty Casazza, Monica Gabrielle, Mindy Kleinberg, and Lorie Van Auken, "September 11th Advocates Comment On The Impending Release Of Philip Shenon's Book," Press Release, February 4, 2008.

912. Philip Shenon, "Ex-Senator Will Soon Quit 9/11 Panel, Leaving Gap for Victims' Advocates," *New York Times*, December 5, 2003.

913. Richard Greene, "Interview with Senator Bob Kerrey: Former 9/11 Commission Member," Air America, March 2, 2008.

914. Daniele Ganser, "All of the Theories About 9/11 are Conspiracy Theories," *911Blogger.com*, April 21, 2008.

915. "Carie Lemack Speaks to Al Jazeera," Al Jazeera, May 2, 2011.

916. Daniel Schorn, "Jersey Girls," CBS, September 6, 2006.

917. 9/11 Commission Team 8, "North American Aerospace Command Field Site Visit, Interview with CINC NORAD General Edward "Ed" Eberhart," Peterson Air Force Base, Colorado Springs (CO), March 1, 2004.

918. "Statement of Mindy Kleinberg," 9/11 Commission, March 31, 2003.

919. "Interview of Patty Casazza," *9/11 Press For Truth,* 2006.

920. Patty Casazza, "9/11 Family Member Patty Casazza: Government Knew Exact Date ..." Casazza flagged that "these people who supposedly hijacked these planes ... many of these people, like Osama bin Laden himself, were once our own patsies." The September Eleventh families are not unique in American history regarding decades-long quests to correct the story of record. In 1995 the families of Admiral Husband Kimmel and Lieutenant General Walter Short urged the Congress and Senate to reopen an investigation into "the circumstances leading to Japan's attack." The families complained that "crucial Japanese intercept records had been denied to the Hawaiian commanders in 1941," though these were made available to over thirty key civilian and military leaders, including President Roosevelt. (See Robert Stinnett, *Day Of Deceit,* (Free Press, 2001), 255-257, 317ff). Commander Arthur McCollum, head of Far East Section, Office of Naval Intelligence, had ordered – as part of an eight-part plan to provoke Japan into committing "an overt act of war" – a directive to "Keep the main strength of the US fleet now in the Pacific ... in the vicinity of the Hawaiian Islands." FDR had moved the Pacific Fleet from San Pedro, Long Beach and San Diego to the more vulnerable Pearl Harbor. On November 25, 1941, knowing a Japanese fleet had left Japan bound for Hawaii, "the US Navy issued an order forbidding US and Allied shipping to travel via the North Pacific." When Admiral Kimmel "sent 46 warships safely into the North Pacific in late November 1941 .... the White House ... countermanded his orders and ordered all ships returned to" Pearl Harbor. During the week prior to December 7th, Naval intelligence advised Hawaiian commanders to search for a Japanese Fleet southwest of Hawaii. (See James Perloff, "Hawaii Was Surprised; FDR Was Not," *New American,* December 7, 2019; Also, John Toland, *Infamy: Pearl Harbor And Its Aftermath,* (Berkley Books, 1982). On May 25, 1999, the United States Senate, by a vote of 52–47, passed a non-binding

resolution to exonerate Admiral Kimmel and Lt. General Short and requested that President Clinton posthumously restore both men to full rank. However, Clinton did not act on the resolution.

921. Hannah Arendt, *The Origins of Totalitarianism*, (Schocken, 1951), 439.

922. James Madison, "Letter to Thomas Jefferson," May 13, 1798.

923. René Girard and Malcolm B. DeBevoise (translator), *The One by Whom Scandal Comes: Studies in Violence, Mimesis, & Culture*, (Michigan State University Press, East Lansing, MI, 2014), 30.

924. Bob Braun, "Sept. 11 'Jersey Girls' Mostly Leave High-Profile Activism to Others These Days," *Star-Ledger*, Newark, NJ, September 9, 2012.

925. Author interview with Fire Commissioner Christopher Gioia, Franklin Square & Munson Fire Department, January 25, 2020.

926. Nowosielski, "Patty Casazza Interview," *In Their Own Words: The Untold Stories of the 9/11 Families*. (See note 335.)

927. Kristen Breitweiser, "Iran and 9/11: Down the Rabbit Hole of Blame," *Huffington Post*, October 25, 2017.

928. Donna Marsh O'Connor, "Remarks," 9/11 Symposium, Saint Joseph College, West Hartford, CT, November 3, 2007.

929. Thomas Merton, *Raids on the Unspeakable* (New Directions Publishing, 1966), 4.

930. Nowosielski, "Monica Gabrielle Interview," *In Their Own Words: The Untold Stories of the 9/11 Families*. (See note 335.)

931. Nowosielski, "Paul Thompson Interview," *9/11 Press For Truth*. (See note 11.)

Index of Names

A Note On The Type

This book was set in Palatino, a typeface designed by Hermann Zapf in 1949 at the Stempel Type Foundry in Frankfurt, Germany, and later by the Mergenthaler Linotype Company in New York City. It was named after the 16th century Italian master of calligraphy Giambattista Palatino. Based on the humanist types of the Italian Renaissance, Palatino mirrors the letters formed by a broad nib pen reflecting Zapf's expertise as a calligrapher.